YUI 3 Cookbook®

Evan Goer

O'REILLY®

Beijing · Cambridge · Farnham · Köln · Sebastopol · Tokyo

YUI 3 Cookbook

by Evan Goer

Published by O'Reilly Media, Inc., 1005 Gravenstein Highway North, Sebastopol, CA 95472.

O'Reilly books may be purchased for educational, business, or sales promotional use. Online editions are also available for most titles (*http://my.safaribooksonline.com*). For more information, contact our corporate/institutional sales department: 800-998-9938 or *corporate@oreilly.com*.

Editor:	Mary Treseler	**Indexer:**	BIM Indexing
Production Editor:	Kristen Borg	**Cover Designer:**	Karen Montgomery
Copyeditor:	Rachel Monaghan	**Interior Designer:**	David Futato
Proofreader:	Kiel Van Horn	**Illustrator:**	Robert Romano

June 2012:   First Edition.

Revision History for the First Edition:

   2012-05-22   First release

See *http://oreilly.com/catalog/errata.csp?isbn=9781449304195* for release details.

ISBN: 978-1-449-30419-5

[LSI]

1337699974

Table of Contents

Preface

Welcome to the *YUI 3 Cookbook*. If you're already invested in the Yahoo! User Interface library (YUI), that's excellent! This book is full of useful recipes and insights. Go forth and use it to build something great!

If you're *not* already invested in YUI, that's fine too. Perhaps you picked up this book because you like to stay informed. Or perhaps you picked up this book because you've been assigned to a project that uses YUI, you're deathly afraid of this alien technology, and even now you're idly wondering whether to rewrite the entire project from scratch.

Either way, you're probably thinking to yourself, "What exactly is YUI good for?" Or perhaps even more accurately, "What can I build with YUI that I can't just do with jQuery?"

The *short* answer is that with the help of auxiliary libraries such as Underscore and Backbone, there's little you can't build with jQuery. jQuery is an excellent document object model (DOM), events, and Ajax abstraction library, and people use it to build beautiful pages every day.

The *longer* answer is that every library is designed to address a particular set of problems. YUI focuses on keeping the complexity of web applications from spiraling out of control. Its key strengths are modularity and structure.

- "Modularity" means that YUI is not a monolithic library, but a toolkit for assembling highly tailored libraries. If you need `AutoComplete` and `Calendar`, you can load just those widgets and leave out all the others. If you need DOM manipulation but not XHR requests, you can load just the core DOM APIs without Ajax. Modularity is not tacked on as an afterthought, but baked deep into YUI's design.

- "Structure" means that YUI's APIs guide you toward building applications as a set of orderly components. Because of this, YUI components all have very similar behaviors. If you know how to work with a YUI `ScrollView`, you already know a lot about how to work with a `Slider`, a `DataTable`, or any other YUI widget.

The *most realistic* answer is that the best way to determine whether a framework or library works for you is to try it out yourself. YUI is a powerful open source JavaScript and CSS toolkit for building web applications, but there are many other fine choices out there. This book aims to demystify YUI and help you make an informed decision.

YUI 2 Versus YUI 3

To begin the demystification process, let's start with the difference between YUI 2 and YUI 3.

YUI 2 burst on the scene at a critical moment, when the field of frontend engineering was starting to coalesce as a discipline. Even years after YUI 3's release, many people still think of YUI as YUI 2.

YUI 2 code looks like this:

```
var nodes = YAHOO.util.Dom.getElementsByClassName('demo');
```

Although this looks uncomfortably like Java, bear in mind that back in early 2006, carefully namespacing your API under objects was a cutting-edge technique. The status quo was throwing your code into the global namespace and hoping for the best. Because of this focus on safety, YUI 2 gained a reputation as an industrial strength but verbose API.

YUI 3 launched in 2009 as a major revamp. The revamp not only baked modules and module loading into the core, but also cleaned up the API and eliminated most of the verbose method names.

YUI 3 code looks like this:

```
var nodes = Y.all('.demo');
```

which should look familiar if you are used to calling `dojo.query('.demo')`, `$$('.demo')`, or `$('.demo')`.

However, thanks to ancient tutorials, rotting code examples, questionable "webmaster" forums, and other sources of bad advice, people who are vaguely aware of YUI often think it means long Java-esque method names. That's unfortunate, because in YUI 3, the simple things are actually pretty simple. You can use YUI to manipulate the DOM and invoke page effects with very small amounts of code.

That by itself is not a reason to use YUI, as many libraries also provide powerful APIs for DOM manipulation and effects. Still, if you're creating a quick prototype or a temporary marketing page with a couple of fades, rest assured that you can knock that page out with YUI just about as easily as with anything else.

Why Use YUI?

While YUI is succinct enough for "light" JavaScript work, where it really shines is in providing a solid foundation for more maintainable code.

As an example, say your boss asks you to design a form with a JavaScript date picker. You find a prepackaged widget that looks nice and seems to work well, so you copy and paste it into your code. Everyone is happy.

Then your boss tells you that the requirements have changed, and what the form actually needs is a double-pane calendar. So you hack that functionality into the widget. You manage to get it to work, but the code isn't pretty, and worse, now you're locked in.

To avoid lockin, *every* component in YUI is designed for extension. Every YUI widget shares the same solid API core and offers the same extension points, including a common rendering lifecycle with standard hooks to intercept or override. YUI lets you extend components in a classlike hierarchy, mix in new methods and properties, plug new behaviors into instances, and even inject arbitrary behavior before and after methods. In short, there is always a clean way to extend a YUI component instead of creating an unmaintainable mess.

While YUI is a very comprehensive toolkit, its overall "size" is as small or as large as you like. Nobody loads "all of YUI." Instead, you load what you need: DOM manipulation, custom events, animations and page effects, Ajax, widgets, function and array utilities, templating, vector graphics, MVC—you name it, YUI probably has it.

And if YUI doesn't have it, that's no problem either. YUI is designed from the ground up to run safely alongside third-party code. You can even use the YUI Loader to wrap and load other libraries into the page as if they were ordinary YUI modules.

With this comprehensive toolkit comes comprehensive documentation and tools. YUI includes detailed user guides, tutorials, API reference documentation, hundreds of examples, and YUI Theater, an incredible video resource that documents the evolution of the frontend engineering profession. YUI also includes an entire suite of tools for professional code development: a builder, a documentation generator, a test framework and test runner, a minification and compression tool, and more.

As an open source project, YUI has accumulated a vibrant developer community. Most active YUI community members are experienced engineers who have a broad background with other frameworks and libraries. If you have technical questions about how to use YUI effectively, the community is a wealth of information.

Finally, YUI adheres to the bizarre, unfashionable philosophy that library code should, as much as possible, run as-is in a wide array of environments. This is actually a bit confusing to developers, who tend to assume that since there is no "YUI Mobile" fork of the library, that must mean YUI doesn't work on mobile devices. In fact, the YUI team tests all library code on a wide selection of mobile devices, and adds methods and synthetic events to help you abstract away differences between platforms. Likewise, YUI runs in a Node.js server environment as-is. There is no YUI Mobile Edition or YUI Tablet Edition or YUI Server Edition. There is just YUI.

Library or Framework?

Web developers tend to call larger projects "frameworks," and medium-size and smaller projects "libraries." The line between the two is fuzzy, and tends to lead to religious disagreements. For a large but also highly modular project such as YUI or Dojo, the most accurate term might actually be "toolkit." This book cheerfully refers to YUI as all three.

There is also a mini-trend of calling small JavaScript libraries "micro-frameworks." However, this book will follow the last fifty years of software engineering practice and continue to refer to them as "libraries."

Who This Book Is For

There are two main audiences who will benefit most from this book:

- JavaScript developers who are new to YUI. These developers will most likely benefit from reading the simpler recipes (which tend to cluster at the beginning of each chapter) and from focusing on the "Problem" and "Solution" sections of each recipe.
- JavaScript developers who have light to moderate YUI experience and are looking to deepen their knowledge. These developers will most likely be interested in the more advanced recipes and in reading the in-depth "Discussion" sections.

This book will not teach you JavaScript. It assumes that you are familiar with the basic mechanics of the language, up through and including prototypes, anonymous functions, and at least some standard ECMAScript and DOM methods. If you are an experienced engineer who picks up new languages in weeks, reading this book *might* help you learn some JavaScript through osmosis, but it isn't the best place to start. A much better place to start is *Eloquent JavaScript* by Marijn Haverbeke (No Starch Press), followed by *JavaScript: The Good Parts* by Douglas Crockford (O'Reilly).

The reason this book assumes you already know JavaScript is that all libraries fail. There will be bugs. There will be situations where the library's abstractions fall apart. Getting yourself unstuck means being able to understand what is going on both in the library code and beyond. Or as former Yahoo! architect Nicholas Zakas puts it, "Library knowledge is not frontend knowledge any more than knowing how to use a hammer makes you a carpenter."

If you are already a YUI expert, this book probably covers a lot of familiar ground. Still, it might help you with corners of the library that you know less well, or provide some extra insight into why some aspect of YUI works the way it does.

This book is not a comprehensive reference manual for the entire YUI library. Some components are explored in detail. Some get short shrift. Many don't get mentioned at all. Each recipe solves a specific problem, but very few cover every available method, parameter, and configuration option. For that, please consult the API reference documentation.

Resources and Community

YUI is released under a liberal BSD license and offers a wide variety of free resources. Its source code, documentation, ticketing system, and roadmaps are all out in the open. Some of the most useful resources include:

YUI library (http://yuilibrary.com)
> The central hub for all things YUI 3, including downloads, examples, user guides, and reference documentation.

YUI on GitHub (https://github.com/yui/)
> The master source code repository for all projects under the YUI umbrella, available for forking and contribution.

#yui IRC on freenode.net
> YUI's official IRC channel, with many core YUI team members and prolific YUI community members available to answer questions. Alternatively, try the YUI library forums (*http://yuilibrary.com/forum/*). The forums are often more useful for YUI 2 questions.

@yuilibrary and @yuirelay
> @yuilibrary is YUI's official Twitter account. @yuirelay is a Twitter bot that attempts to retweet items about YUI, the JavaScript library, without including items about Yui, the Japanese pop singer.

YUI Configurator (http://yuilibrary.com/yui/configurator/)
> An online tool for calculating YUI module dependencies.

YUI Theater (http://yuilibrary.com/theater/)
> An archive of video training and presentations curated over the last half decade. Some presentations cover general frontend topics rather than YUI-specific topics. The older videos are a fascinating record of the development of frontend engineering as a discipline. Also available as a YouTube channel (*http://www.youtube.com/yuilibrary*).

YUI blog (http://yuiblog.com)
> Provides articles about new YUI releases, YUIConf, YUI Open Hours (a semiregular conference call to answer questions and solicit feedback), and even general frontend topics unrelated to YUI.

Online YUI Compressor (http://refresh-sf.com/yui/)
> An online tool for safely minifying JavaScript and CSS with YUI Compressor. The online version is handy if you just want to try out YUI Compressor, but in a production setup, you should download and run YUI Compressor locally as part of your build system.

YSlow (http://developer.yahoo.com/yslow/)
> A tool for analyzing general performance problems with web applications.

JS Rosetta Stone (http://jsrosettastone.com/)
> A reference for switching back and forth between common tasks in jQuery and YUI 3. Maintained by Paul Irish and the YUI Team.

You can file bug reports and enhancement requests for YUI directly on the yuilibrary.com website. Follow the instructions under "Report a Bug" (*http://yuilibrary .com/yui/docs/tutorials/report-bugs/*).

YUI accepts code contributions through GitHub's fork/pull request model. To contribute a bug fix or feature enhancement to YUI, follow the instructions under "Contribute Code to YUI" (*http://yuilibrary.com/yui/docs/tutorials/contribute/*). If you are new to Git, follow the instructions under "Set Up Your Git Environment" (*http://yuili brary.com/yui/docs/tutorials/git/*).

Conventions Used in This Book

About the Examples

The code examples in this book are deliberately very short. Each example focuses on solving a single problem or introducing a tiny number of new concepts, and most are short enough to take in at a glance. There are some longer examples, particularly in Chapter 7, but the vast majority are 15 lines of JavaScript or fewer.

All client-side JavaScript examples run in a very lean but valid HTML5 document that is some variation of Example P-1:

Example P-1. YUI 3 Cookbook boilerplate

```
<!DOCTYPE html>
<title>YUI 3 Cookbook boilerplate</title>

<div id="demo"></div>

<script src="http://yui.yahooapis.com/3.5.0/build/yui/yui-min.js"></script>
<script>
YUI().use('node-base', function (Y) {
    Y.one('#demo').setHTML('This is the YUI 3 Cookbook Boilerplate.');
});
</script>
```

The boilerplate is terse in order to keep focus on the JavaScript, while still providing a fully self-contained, runnable code example. Most examples will work from your local filesystem, but a handful must be run from a real web server. These are flagged accordingly.

Some recipes contain secondary examples that omit the HTML boilerplate and just show the JavaScript. In these cases, you can assume that the JavaScript is running in the same HTML document as the primary example.

All code in *YUI 3 Cookbook* is built to run against YUI 3.5.0. Keep in mind that YUI modules marked as "beta" can behave differently across minor versions of YUI 3.

All examples and related files in this book may be freely forked or downloaded from GitHub (*https://github.com/yahoo/yui3-cookbook*).

Typesetting Conventions

The following typographical conventions are used in this book:

Italic
> Indicates new terms, URLs, email addresses, filenames, and file extensions.

`Constant width`
> Used for program listings, as well as within paragraphs to refer to program elements such as variable or function names, databases, data types, environment variables, statements, and keywords. Also used for API, widget, and module names.

`Constant width bold`
> Shows commands or other text that should be typed literally by the user.

`Constant width italic`
> Shows text that should be replaced with user-supplied values or by values determined by context.

> This icon signifies a tip, suggestion, or general note.

> This icon indicates a warning or caution.

Using Code Examples

This book is here to help you get your job done. In general, you may use the code in this book in your programs and documentation. You do not need to contact us for permission unless you're reproducing a significant portion of the code. For example, writing a program that uses several chunks of code from this book does not require permission. Selling or distributing a CD-ROM of examples from O'Reilly books does require permission. Answering a question by citing this book and quoting example code does not require permission. Incorporating a significant amount of example code from this book into your product's documentation does require permission.

We appreciate, but do not require, attribution. An attribution usually includes the title, author, publisher, and ISBN. For example: "*YUI 3 Cookbook* by Evan Goer (O'Reilly). Copyright 2012 Yahoo! Inc., 978-1-449-30419-5."

If you feel your use of code examples falls outside fair use or the permission given above, feel free to contact us at *permissions@oreilly.com*.

Safari® Books Online

Safari Books Online (*www.safaribooksonline.com*) is an on-demand digital library that delivers expert content in both book and video form from the world's leading authors in technology and business.

Technology professionals, software developers, web designers, and business and creative professionals use Safari Books Online as their primary resource for research, problem solving, learning, and certification training.

Safari Books Online offers a range of product mixes and pricing programs for organizations, government agencies, and individuals. Subscribers have access to thousands of books, training videos, and prepublication manuscripts in one fully searchable database from publishers like O'Reilly Media, Prentice Hall Professional, Addison-Wesley Professional, Microsoft Press, Sams, Que, Peachpit Press, Focal Press, Cisco Press, John Wiley & Sons, Syngress, Morgan Kaufmann, IBM Redbooks, Packt, Adobe Press, FT Press, Apress, Manning, New Riders, McGraw-Hill, Jones & Bartlett, Course Technology, and dozens more. For more information about Safari Books Online, please visit us online.

How to Contact Us

Please address comments and questions concerning this book to the publisher:

O'Reilly Media, Inc.
1005 Gravenstein Highway North
Sebastopol, CA 95472
800-998-9938 (in the United States or Canada)
707-829-0515 (international or local)
707-829-0104 (fax)

We have a web page for this book, where we list errata, examples, and any additional information. You can access this page at:

http://oreil.ly/yui3cookbook

To comment or ask technical questions about this book, send email to:

bookquestions@oreilly.com

For more information about our books, courses, conferences, and news, see our website at *http://www.oreilly.com.*

Find us on Facebook: *http://facebook.com/oreilly*

Follow us on Twitter: *http://twitter.com/oreillymedia*

Watch us on YouTube: *http://www.youtube.com/oreillymedia*

Acknowledgments

This book would not have been possible without the hundreds of people responsible for the YUI project—the people who participated in the discussions, filed the bugs, issued the pull requests, and wrote the code that makes YUI what it is today. It is a great honor to have had the opportunity to write the first formal book for YUI 3. I only hope this book meets their expectations.

Thanks to all the wonderful people out in the greater YUI community who provided early review feedback: Pat Cavit, Jeff Craig, Chris George, John Iannicello, Todd Kloots, Subramanyan Murali, Anthony Pipkin, Kim Rowan, Robert Roy, Rich Tretola, Alberto Santini, Victor Tsaran, and Nicholas Zakas. Special thanks to Daniel Barreiro, one of the sharpest and most thorough technical reviewers it's ever been my pleasure to work with.

I owe a great debt to the entire YUI team past and present for creating YUI, for shepherding it over the years, and for taking time out to provide me with deeper insights about how YUI works. Thanks to Thomas Sha, Eric Miraglia, Dwight "Tripp" Bridges, Adam Moore, Matt Sweeney, Derek Gathright, Allen Rabinovich, Satyen Desai, Jeff Conniff, Georgiann Puckett, Dav Glass, and Reid Burke. Much thanks to Jenny Donnelly for instigating this book and giving me the opportunity to write it; Luke Smith, my inside man in the YUI team; Ryan Grove and Eric Ferraiuolo for all their guidance; and Irene Lai, without whose generosity this project would have finished sometime in 2014.

Finally, a huge thank you to my editor, Mary Treseler, my parents, friends, and coworkers who offered so much support, and above all, my wife and best friend, Sarah. When I was trying to decide whether to take on this project, she was the one who said without hesitation, "Well, *of course* you should say yes." Without her good humor, unwavering support, and willingness to patiently listen to her husband rambling on about JavaScript, this book would never have happened.

CHAPTER 1

Loading Modules

Consider the humble `<script>` element. Introduced in 1995, it is still the gateway for injecting JavaScript into the browser. Unfortunately, if you want to build sophisticated applications, `<script>` shows its age:

- `<script>` conflates the concepts of loading code and executing code. Programmers need fine-grained control over both phases.

- `<script>` is synchronous, blocking the browser's flow/paint cycle until the entire script downloads. This is why performance guides currently recommend moving `<script>` to the bottom of the page. The good news is that HTML now provides the `async` and `defer` attributes, so this issue might improve over time.

- `<script>` has a shared global context with no formal namespacing or security built in. This is bad enough when you're simply trying to protect your own code from your own mistakes, but becomes disastrous when your code must run alongside an unknown number of third-party scripts.

- `<script>` has no information about its relationships with other `<script>` elements. A script might require another script as a dependency, but there is no way to express this. If `<script>` elements are on the page in the wrong order, the application fails.

The root of the problem is that unlike nearly every programming environment on the planet, JavaScript in the browser has no built-in concept of modules (defined in Recipe 1.1). For small scripts, this is not necessarily a big deal. But small scripts have a way of growing into full-fledged applications.

To protect code from interference, many JavaScript libraries use a global object to contain all the library's methods. For example, the hypothetical "Code Ninja" library might instantiate a global object named `NINJA` that supplies methods such as `NINJA.throwShuriken()`. Here, `NINJA` serves as a kind of namespace. This is a reasonable first line of defense.

YUI 3 takes things one step further. There is a global YUI object, but you work with this object "inside out." Instead of using YUI just as a namespace, you call YUI().use() and then write all of your code *inside a callback function nested inside use() itself.* Within this scope is a private instance of the library named Y, which provides access to YUI methods such as Y.one() and objects such as Y.AutoComplete.

The disadvantage of YUI 3's approach is that at first glance, it looks profoundly weird.

The advantages of YUI 3's approach are:

- YUI can decouple loading into registration and execution phases. YUI.add() registers code as modules with the YUI global object, to be loaded on demand. YUI().use() provides access to those modules in a safe sandbox.

- YUI can load modules synchronously or asynchronously, since registration is now a separate phase from execution.

- Other than a few static methods, YUI avoids using the shared global context. The Y instance that carries the API is private, impossible to overwrite from outside the sandbox.

- YUI supports real dependency logic. When you register modules with YUI.add(), you can include metadata about other modules, CSS resources, and more. YUI().use() uses this information to build a dependency tree, fetching modules that are needed to complete the tree and skipping modules that are already present. YUI can even load modules conditionally based on browser capabilities. This frees you up to write code optimized for different environments, enabling you to support older, less capable browsers without serving unnecessary code to modern browsers.

Work on YUI's module and loader system began in the middle of 2007, and the system was revamped for the release of YUI 3 in 2009. In the years since, JavaScript modules have quite rightfully become a hot topic. Server-side JavaScript environments now provide native support for the CommonJS module format. The Dojo toolkit has adopted AMD modules as its native format. Future versions of the ECMAScript standard are likely to bake support for modules into JavaScript's core.

As mentioned in the Preface, there are many great JavaScript libraries available, each bringing its own philosophy and strengths. If you are looking for a single feature that captures YUI's design goals, the module system is an excellent place to start. The module system prioritizes code safety and encapsulation. It has intelligent defaults, but it also grants you a tremendous amount of fine-grained control. It works well for small page effects, but it really shines when you're assembling larger applications. You will see these principles expressed time and time again throughout the library.

Because the module and loader system is one of YUI's signature features, this chapter is extensive. If you are just starting out with YUI, you can get away with reading just the first or second recipe, but be sure to return later to learn how to load modules optimally and how to package your own code into modules for later reuse.

Most of the examples in this chapter make some visible change to the page in order to prove that the code works. The typical example uses `Y.one("#demo")` to grab the `<div>` with an `id` of `demo`, followed by `setHTML()` to change the `<div>`'s contents. If you haven't seen YUI's DOM manipulation API in action yet, please peek ahead at Recipes 2.1 and 2.3.

Recipe 1.1 defines the canonical way to load YUI onto the page. This is the most important recipe in the entire book.

Recipe 1.2 describes SimpleYUI, a convenient bundle of DOM manipulation, event façades, UI effects, and Ajax. Using SimpleYUI makes loading YUI more like loading other, more monolithic JavaScript libraries. This is a good alternative place to start if Recipe 1.1 is making your head spin.

Recipe 1.3 explains the concept of loading individual YUI modules, rather than larger rollups. For production-quality code, you can improve performance by identifying and loading only the modules you really need.

Recipe 1.4 introduces the YUI configuration object, which is important for defining your own modules and for gaining fine-grained control over the YUI Loader.

Recipes 1.5 and 1.6 describe loading different categories of modules. Recipe 1.5 explains how to load third-party modules from the YUI gallery, and Recipe 1.6 explains how to incorporate legacy YUI 2 widgets as YUI 3 modules.

Recipe 1.7 explains how to load the YUI core modules from your own servers rather than Yahoo! edge servers. You should strongly consider doing this if you are dealing with private user data over SSL, as loading third-party JavaScript from servers outside your control breaks the SSL security model.

Recipes 1.8, 1.9, 1.10, and 1.11 take you step-by-step through the process of creating your own modules. After Recipe 1.1, these four recipes are the ones that every serious YUI developer should know by heart. Understanding how to create modules is vital for being able to reuse your code effectively.

Recipe 1.12 introduces the `YUI_config` object, which makes it easier to share complex YUI configurations between pages and sites.

Recipe 1.13 demonstrates how to create your own custom rollups, similar to core rollups such as `node` and `io`.

Recipe 1.14 explains how to load jQuery and other third-party libraries into the YUI sandbox as if they were YUI modules. The YUI Loader and module system are flexible enough to wrap and asynchronously load just about anything you might want to use alongside YUI.

The next six recipes discuss more advanced loading scenarios. Recipe 1.15 covers the concept of conditional loading, where YUI fetches a module only if a browser capability test passes. The YUI core libraries use this powerful technique to patch up old browsers without penalizing modern ones. Recipe 1.16 is a variation of Recipe 1.15 where instead of using conditional loading to patch old browsers, you use it to patch YUI itself.

Recipes 1.17 and 1.18 explain how to load modules in response to user actions, or even in anticipation of user actions. The ability to fetch additional modules after the initial page load provides you with great control over the perceived performance of your application.

Recipe 1.19 explains how to load YUI into an iframe while still maintaining control via the YUI instance in the parent document.

Finally, Recipe 1.20 discusses static loading. By default, YUI modules load asynchronously. Static loading is an advanced technique that trades flexibility and developer convenience for extra performance.

1.1 Loading Rollups and Modules

Problem

You want to load YUI on the page and run some code.

Solution

Load the YUI seed file, *yui-min.js*. Then call `YUI().use()`, passing in the name of a module or rollup you want to load, followed by an anonymous callback function that contains some code that exercises those modules.

Within the callback function, the `Y` object provides the tailored YUI API you just requested. Technically, you can name this object anything you like, but you should stick with the `Y` convention except for rare circumstances, such as Recipe 1.19.

Example 1-1 loads the YUI `Node` API, then uses that API to get a reference to the `<div>` with an `id` of `demo` and set its content. For more information about how to select and modify node instances, refer to Chapter 2.

Example 1-1. Loading the YUI Node API

```
<!DOCTYPE html>
<title>Loading the YUI Node API</title>

<div id="demo"></div>

<script src="http://yui.yahooapis.com/3.5.0/build/yui/yui-min.js"></script>
<script>
YUI().use('node', function (Y) {
    Y.one('#demo').setHTML('Whoa.');
});
</script>
```

In YUI, you do not need to litter your pages with dozens of `<script>` elements. The Loader is specifically designed to kill this antipattern. As a corollary, you should *never* fetch the YUI seed file more than once.

Discussion

`YUI().use()` supports loading both modules and rollups.

A *module* in YUI is a named collection of reusable code. To learn how to create your own modules, start with Recipe 1.8 and related recipes.

A *rollup* is a kind of "supermodule" that represents multiple smaller modules. For example, `node` is a rollup that pulls in `node-base`, `node-style`, and several other modules for manipulating the DOM. Rollups exist for convenience, although sometimes it pays to be more selective and load individual modules, as described in Recipe 1.3.

But how does this even work? The line:

```
YUI().use('foo', function (Y) {...});
```

is pretty mystifying. To break this down step-by-step:

The first `<script>` element in Example 1-1 loads the YUI seed file, which defines the `YUI` global object. `YUI` is not just a namespace object; it is a module registry system. It contains just enough code to bootstrap your way to the rest of the library: some critical YUI utility functions, the Loader code that loads scripts onto the page, and Loader metadata that describes the core YUI modules and their dependencies.

The second `<script>` element calls `YUI().use()`. This call has two stages:

1. Calling `YUI()` creates a new YUI instance. A YUI instance is a host object for assembling a customized YUI API. The instance starts out fairly bare bones—it does not yet provide APIs for doing things like DOM manipulation or Ajax calls.

2. Calling `use()` then augments that instance with additional methods. `use()` takes one or more string parameters representing the names of modules and rollups to load, followed by a callback function (more on that a little later). Somewhat simplified, the `use()` method works in the following manner:

    a. The `use()` method determines which modules it actually needs to fetch. It calculates dependencies and builds a list of modules to load, excluding any modules already loaded and registered with the global `YUI` object.

    b. After resolving dependencies, `use()` constructs a "combo load" URL, and the Loader retrieves all the missing modules from Yahoo's fast edge servers with a single HTTP request. This happens asynchronously so as not to block the UI thread of the browser.

    c. When `use()` finishes loading modules, it decorates the YUI instance with the complete API you requested.

d. Finally, use() executes the callback function, passing in the YUI instance as the Y argument. Within the callback function, the Y object is a private handle to your own customized instance of the YUI library.

In other words, a YUI instance starts out small and relies on use() to carefully build up the API you requested. YUI().use() automatically handles dependencies and tailors its downloads for the browser you're running in. This is already a huge advantage over downloading libraries as giant monolithic blocks of code.

The use() callback function is referred to as the "YUI sandbox." It encapsulates all your code into a private scope, making it impossible for other scripts on the page to accidentally clobber one of your variables or functions. In fact, if you want to run multiple applications on the same page, you can even create multiple independent sandboxes. Once any sandbox loads a module, other sandboxes can use that module without interference and without having to fetch the code again.

Keep in mind that any code you write directly in a use() callback function is not actually a module itself, and is therefore not reusable. A use() callback should contain only the code required to wire modules into that particular page. Any code that might be reusable, you should bundle into a custom module using YUI.add(). For more information, refer to Recipe 1.8.

To improve performance, by default YUI loads the *minified* version of each module. The minified version has been run through YUI Compressor, a utility that shrinks the file size of each module by stripping out whitespace and comments, shortening variable names, and performing various other optimizations described in Recipe 12.12.

As shown in the next section, Recipe 1.2, it is possible to load YUI with the simpler pattern that other libraries use. SimpleYUI is great for learning purposes, but less appropriate for production code.

 In addition to the Y instance, YUI passes an obscure second parameter to your use() callback. This object represents the response from the Loader, and includes a Boolean success field, a string msg field that holds a success or error message, and a data array that lists all modules that successfully loaded. Unfortunately, this reporting mechanism is not 100% reliable in all browsers.

1.2 Loading SimpleYUI

Problem

You want to load YUI onto the page like people loaded JavaScript libraries in the good old days, without all this newfangled module loading and sandboxing nonsense.

Solution

Instead of pointing `<script>` to *yui-min.js*, point it to *simpleyui-min.js*. SimpleYUI includes all modules in YUI's `node`, `event`, `io`, and `transition` rollups, flattened out into a single JavaScript file. These modules are more than enough to create interesting page effects and simple applications.

As shown in Example 1-2, loading SimpleYUI on the page automatically instantiates a global Y instance that provides access to the YUI API.

Example 1-2. Loading SimpleYUI

```
<!DOCTYPE html>
<title>Loading SimpleYUI</title>

<div id="demo"></div>

<script src="http://yui.yahooapis.com/3.5.0/build/simpleyui/simpleyui-min.js"></script>
<script>
Y.one('#demo').setHTML('This message brought to you by SimpleYUI.');
</script>
```

Discussion

SimpleYUI provides the same functionality you would have received by loading these modules individually, as described in Recipe 1.1. So why use SimpleYUI at all? If you are new to YUI, SimpleYUI acts like jQuery and other popular JavaScript libraries: you simply load a script onto the page and start calling methods from a global object. SimpleYUI is a great way to try out YUI, particularly for people who are still getting used to YUI's idioms.

SimpleYUI is a starter kit that contains DOM, event, and Ajax functionality. However, SimpleYUI is in no way crippled or limited to just these modules; it also includes the Loader, so you are free to call Y.use() at any time to pull in additional modules such as `autocomplete` or `model`. For an example of calling Y.use() from within YUI().use(), refer to Example 1-22.

The disadvantages of using SimpleYUI are that it pulls in code that you might not need, and that it lacks a sandbox. You can address the latter issue by wrapping your code in an anonymous function and then immediately executing that function, as shown in Example 1-3.

Example 1-3. Loading SimpleYUI in a generic sandbox

```
<!DOCTYPE html>
<title>Loading SimpleYUI in a generic sandbox</title>

<div id="demo"></div>

<script src="http://yui.yahooapis.com/3.5.0/build/simpleyui/simpleyui-min.js"></script>
```

```
<script>
var message = 'BOGUS MESSAGE';

(function () {
    var message = 'This message brought to you by sandboxed SimpleYUI.';
    Y.one('#demo').setHTML(message);
}());
</script>
```

JavaScript's scoping rules ensure that variables outside the function can be referenced from within the function. However, any variables redeclared inside the function will trump any values declared outside. Or, looking at this the other way around, code outside the sandbox cannot overwrite private variables inside the sandbox.

Experienced JavaScript developers often use this kind of generic sandbox with other libraries. It is a fine defensive pattern in general, but less common in YUI simply because the standard loading pattern shown in Example 1-1 provides a sandbox already.

 If you search the Web, you'll find a popular alternative pattern that works just as well, but is a little less aesthetically pleasing:

```
(function(){})()
```

JavaScript guru Douglas Crockford refers to this as the "dogballs" pattern.

Strictly speaking, you don't need to resort to SimpleYUI to get a global Y object. YUI().use() returns a Y instance, so you can always do:

```
var Y = YUI().use(...);
```

In any case, these caveats about performance and sandboxing might not be important to you, depending on your situation. Some engineering groups use SimpleYUI as a way to segment different projects: critical pages and core pieces of infrastructure use the YUI sandbox, while prototypes and temporary marketing pages use SimpleYUI to make life easier for designers and prototypers. SimpleYUI is also a good tool for developers who are starting to transition code into the YUI "inside-out" sandbox pattern. Projects in transition can load SimpleYUI and leverage those APIs in existing legacy code, rather than having to immediately migrate large amounts of legacy JavaScript into YUI modules.

1.3 Identifying and Loading Individual Modules

Problem

You want to load the smallest possible amount of code necessary to accomplish a given task.

Solution

The YUI API documentation indicates which modules supply which individual methods and properties. As you write your code, consult the documentation and include only the specific modules you need in your `YUI().use()` call, in order to avoid loading code that contains unnecessary functionality.

Example 1-4 illustrates loading smaller, focused modules instead of larger rollups. As mentioned in Recipe 1.1, YUI passes a second parameter to the `use()` callback that represents the response from the Loader. Example 1-4 converts this object into a string with `Y.JSON.stringify()`, using `stringify()`'s extended signature to pretty-print the output, and then displays the string by inserting it into a `<pre>` element. You could do all of this by loading the `node` and `json` rollups, but it turns out that the script only really requires the smaller modules `node-base` and `json-stringify`.

Example 1-4. Using individual modules

```
<!DOCTYPE html>
<title>Using individual modules</title>

<pre id="demo"></pre>

<script src="http://yui.yahooapis.com/3.5.0/build/yui/yui-min.js"></script>
<script>
YUI().use('json-stringify', 'node-base', function (Y, loaderResponse) {
    var pre = Y.one('#demo');
    pre.set('text', Y.JSON.stringify(loaderResponse, null, 4));
});
</script>
```

 The example uses `set('text')` rather than `setHTML()`. Methods like `setHTML()` and `set('innerHTML')` are insecure when used for non-HTML strings or strings whose actual content or origin is unknown.

Discussion

YUI is broken into small modules that enable you to define very tight sets of dependencies. For convenience, YUI users often load rollups, which represent a group of related modules. For example, the `node` rollup is an alias for loading a list of modules that includes `node-base`, `node-style`, `node-event-delegate`, and `nodelist`.

Likewise, the `json` rollup includes `json-parse` and `json-stringify`, on the assumption that most applications that work with JSON need to convert JSON in both directions. However, if your application only needs to convert objects into strings, you can load `json-stringify` and avoid loading deadweight code from `json-parse`.

If you understand exactly which modules your implementation needs, you can save bytes by loading just those modules instead of loading rollups. However, this does require checking the YUI API documentation carefully for which methods and properties come from which modules, so that you're not caught off-guard by "missing" features.

One option is to use rollups when prototyping and developing, then replace them with a narrower list of modules when you are getting ready to release to production. The YUI Configurator is a handy tool for determining an exact list of dependencies. If you take this approach, be sure to have a test suite in place to verify that your application still works after narrowing down your requirements. For more information about testing YUI, refer to Chapter 12.

See Also

Recipe 1.13; the YUI Configurator (*http://yuilibrary.com/yui/configurator/*); the YUI JSON User Guide (*http://yuilibrary.com/yui/docs/json/*).

1.4 Loading a Different Default Skin

Problem

You want the Loader to load the "night" skin for all YUI widgets—a darker CSS skin that is designed to match themes that are popular on mobile devices.

Solution

Pass in a YUI configuration object that includes a skin property with an alternative defaultSkin name. Some modules provide one or more named CSS skins. By default, when the Loader loads a module with a skin, the Loader attempts to fetch the module's "sam" skin file. However, if you are loading modules that happen to have multiple skins, you can instruct the Loader to fetch a different skin across the board.

Example 1-5 loads and instantiates a Calendar widget with its alternative, darker "night" skin. By convention, all YUI skin styles are scoped within a class name of yui3-skin-*skinname*. This means that to actually *apply* the night skin once it has loaded on the page, you must add the class yui3-skin-night to the <body> or to a containing <div>.

Example 1-5. Changing YUI's default skin

```
<!DOCTYPE html>
<title>Changing YUI's default skin</title>

<div id="demo" class="yui3-skin-night"></div>

<script src="http://yui.yahooapis.com/3.5.0/build/yui/yui-min.js"></script>
<script>
YUI({
    skin: { defaultSkin: 'night' }
```

```
}).use('calendar', function (Y) {
    new Y.Calendar({ width: 300 }).render('#demo');
});
</script>
```

Discussion

YUI offers a great variety of configuration options that control the behavior of the Loader and certain properties of the YUI sandbox. For example, to prevent the Loader from dynamically loading any CSS, you can pass in a fetchCSS: false. This setting is useful if you plan to manually add all YUI CSS resources as static <link> elements, and you don't want the Loader to fetch the same CSS resources twice.

One of the most important use cases is configuring metadata for custom modules. The Loader already has metadata for core YUI modules included in the seed file, but to properly load any modules you have created, you must provide the Loader with your module names, dependencies, and more. For recipes that demonstrate how to do this, refer to Recipes 1.10 and 1.11.

See Also

More information about skins and loading CSS in Recipes 7.9 and 7.10; a variety of Slider skins shown side by side (*http://yuilibrary.com/yui/docs/slider/slider-skin.html*); the YUI Global Object User Guide (*http://yuilibrary.com/yui/docs/yui/*); YUI config API documentation (*http://yuilibrary.com/yui/docs/api/classes/config.html*); YUI Loader API documentation (*http://yuilibrary.com/yui/docs/api/classes/Loader.html*).

1.5 Loading Gallery Modules

Problem

You want to load a useful third-party module from the YUI gallery and use it alongside core YUI modules.

Solution

Load the gallery module from the Yahoo! content delivery network (CDN) with YUI().use() as you would with any other YUI module. Gallery module names all start with the prefix gallery-. Once loaded, gallery modules attach to the Y just like core YUI modules.

Example 1-6 loads the To Relative Time gallery module, which adds a toRelative Time() method. This method converts Date objects to English strings that express a relative time value, such as "3 hours ago".

To ensure that the example loads a specific snapshot of the gallery, the YUI configuration specifies a gallery build tag. For more information, refer to the Discussion.

Example 1-6. Using the To Relative Time gallery module with YUI Node

```
<!DOCTYPE html>
<title>Using the "To Relative Time" gallery module with YUI Node</title>

<div id="demo"></div>

<script src="http://yui.yahooapis.com/3.5.0/build/yui/yui-min.js"></script>
<script>
YUI({
    gallery: 'gallery-2010.08.25-19-45'
}).use('gallery-torelativetime', 'node', function (Y) {
    var entryTime = new Date(2011,10,1);
    Y.one('#demo').setHTML(Y.toRelativeTime(entryTime));
});
</script>
```

Discussion

The YUI gallery is a repository for sharing third-party modules. Modules in the gallery range from tiny standalone utilities to large families of related components.

YUI contributors can choose to serve their gallery modules from the Yahoo! CDN. Developers who want to take advantage of this feature must:

- Sign and submit a YUI Contributor License Agreement (CLA)
- Release their code under the open source BSD license, the same license YUI uses
- Host their source code on GitHub, the same repository where YUI is hosted

Some gallery modules have not gone through these steps and so are not served from the Yahoo! CDN. You can use non-CDN gallery modules by downloading and installing them on your own server. For more information about hosting modules locally, refer to Recipe 1.7.

The main difference between gallery modules and the core modules is that for the core modules, the YUI engineering team is fully responsible for fixing bugs, reviewing code, and testing changes. Gallery modules have whatever level of support the module's owner is willing to provide.

Updates to gallery modules get picked up on the CDN when the YUI team pushes out the gallery build, which occurs roughly every week. Each gallery build has a build tag, such as gallery-2011.05.04-20-03. If you omit the gallery configuration option, YUI falls back to loading a default gallery build tag associated with the particular version of core YUI you are using. Thus, the following code works:

```
YUI().use('gallery-torelativetime', 'node', function (Y) {
    var entryTime = new Date(2011,10,1);
    Y.one('#demo').setHTML(Y.toRelativeTime(entryTime));
});
```

However, it is better to declare an explicit, tested gallery build tag. Otherwise, upgrading your YUI version later on will silently change the gallery tag, which might not be what you want.

For gallery modules served from the Yahoo! CDN, the YUI engineering team lightly examines code changes for serious security issues (such as blatant malware) and glaring bugs. Beyond that, there is no guarantee of code quality. Non-CDN gallery modules are completely unreviewed. Before using any gallery module, be sure to carefully evaluate the module's functionality, source code, and license for yourself.

See Also

The YUI gallery (*http://yuilibrary.com/gallery/*); Luke Smith's To Relative Time gallery module (*http://yuilibrary.com/gallery/show/torelativetime*); the tutorial "Contribute Code to the YUI Gallery" (*http://yuilibrary.com/yui/docs/tutorials/gallery/*).

1.6 Loading a YUI 2 Widget

Problem

You want to use one of your favorite widgets from YUI 2, but it hasn't been ported over to YUI 3 yet.

Solution

Load the widget as a YUI 3 module using its YUI 2in3 wrappers, as shown in Example 1-7.

Example 1-7. Loading a YUI 2 TreeView in YUI 3

```
<!DOCTYPE html>
<title>Loading a YUI 2 TreeView in YUI 3</title>

<div id="demo"></div>

<script src="http://yui.yahooapis.com/3.5.0/build/yui/yui-min.js"></script>
<script>
YUI().use('yui2-treeview', function (Y) {
    var YAHOO = Y.YUI2,
        tree = new YAHOO.widget.TreeView('demo', [
            {
                label: 'hats',
                children: [
                    { label: 'bowler' },
                    { label: 'fedora' }
                ]
            },
            {
                label: 'gloves'
            }
```

```
        ]);
    tree.render();
});
</script>
```

Discussion

With YUI 2in3, core YUI 2 widgets such as `ImageCropper`, `ColorPicker`, and `Progress Bar` are represented as first-class YUI 3 modules. Any YUI 2 widget you load this way attaches to the Y object as `Y.YUI2`. To make this look more like classic YUI 2–style code, you can rename `Y.YUI2` to `YAHOO`, as shown in Example 1-7.

Although you may freely intermix YUI 3 code with YUI 2 wrapped modules, keep in mind that just because it loads like YUI 3 doesn't mean it behaves like YUI 3. For example, new YUI 2 widgets take their container `<div>`'s `id` as a string, as in `'demo'`. For YUI 3 widgets, you pass in the *CSS selector* for the `<div>`, as in `'#demo'`.

By default, the version of YUI 2 you get is version 2.8.2. However, you can retrieve any previous version by setting the `yui2` field in the YUI object config:

```
YUI({ yui2: '2.7.0' }).use('yui2-treeview', function (Y) {
    ...
});
```

To load the absolute latest and greatest (and final!) version of YUI 2, use:

```
YUI({
    'yui2': '2.9.0',
    '2in3': '4'
}).use('yui2-treeview', function (Y) {
    ...
});
```

The `2in3` property configures the version of the YUI 2in3 wrapper to use, which must be at version 4 to load version 2.9.0.

See Also

YUI 2in3 project source (*https://github.com/yui/2in3/tree/master/dist/2.9.0/build*); YUI 2 `TreeView` documentation (*http://developer.yahoo.com/yui/treeview/*).

1.7 Loading Locally Hosted Builds

Problem

You want to load YUI from your own servers instead of from Yahoo! servers.

Solution

By default, the `YUI` object is configured to fetch from Yahoo! servers. You can change this by:

1. Downloading the latest stable YUI SDK zip file from *http://yuilibrary.com*.
2. Unzipping the zip file in some directory under your web server's web root.
3. Creating a `<script>` element that points to the *yui-min.js* file.

For example, if you unzipped the SDK under the top level directory */js* and pointed the first `<script>` element's `src` at the local seed file (as shown in Example 1-8), this automatically configures YUI to load all YUI core modules locally. This also disables combo loading (discussed shortly).

Example 1-8. Loading a local copy of YUI

```
<!DOCTYPE html>
<title>Loading a local copy of YUI</title>

<div id="demo"></div>

<script src="/js/yui/build/yui/yui-min.js"></script>
<script>
YUI().use('node', function (Y) {
    Y.one('#demo').setHTML('All politics is local.');
});
</script>
```

To verify that YUI is loading from your own site rather than `yui.yahooapis.com`, use your browser's component inspector   (such as Firefox's Web Inspector pane or Chrome's Developer Tools pane).

Discussion

Yahoo! maintains a distributed collection of servers known as a *content delivery network* (CDN). A CDN is designed to serve files from systems that are physically close to the user who made the request. By default, YUI uses the Yahoo! CDN, which grants all YUI users free access to the same network that runs Yahoo's own high-traffic sites. This saves your own bandwidth, reduces your own server load, and greatly improves performance thanks to browser caching and improved geographical distribution.

However, there are plenty of reasons to go it alone. Perhaps your organization forbids loading resources from remote servers as a matter of policy. Or perhaps your pages use SSL, in which case loading remote resources is a bad idea, as it exposes your users' secure information to the remote site. In these cases, you can serve YUI from your own server.

Each release of YUI provides a full developer kit for download under *http://yuilibrary .com/downloads/*. The zip file contains the library, API documentation, and example files.

 If you want the latest-and-greatest version of YUI's source, you can check it out by running:

```
git clone https://github.com/yui/yui3.git
```

For more information about how to send code to the upstream YUI project, refer to the tutorial "Contribute Code to YUI" (*http://yuilibrary .com/yui/docs/tutorials/contribute/*).

Download the zip file, unzip it into your preferred location under your web server's root, and then reference the local YUI seed file in your web page:

```
<script src="path/yui/yui-min.js"></script>
```

where *path* is the path under the web root in which the YUI module directories reside, such as */js/yui/build*. In addition to the core YUI 3 SDK, you can also download and serve up the latest build of the YUI gallery and the YUI 2in3 project from your own server.

Loading a local YUI seed file automatically reconfigures the Loader to work with local files. Under the covers, this is like instantiating a sandbox with a configuration of:

```
YUI({
    base: '/js/yui/build/',
    combine: false
}).use('node', function (Y) {
    Y.one('#demo').setHTML('All politics is local.');
});
```

The `base` field defines the server name and base filepath on the server for finding YUI modules. By default, this is `http://yui.yahooapis.com/version/build`. For alternative seed files, YUI inspects your seed file URL and resets `base` appropriately. This means you rarely have to set `base` yourself, at least at the top level. Sometimes you might need to override `base` within a module group, as described in Recipe 1.11.

The `combine` field selects whether YUI attempts to fetch all modules in one "combo load" HTTP request. A *combo loader* is a server-side script designed to accept a single HTTP request that represents a list of modules, decompose the request, and concatenate all the requested JavaScript into a single response.

Loading a seed file from `yui.yahooapis.com` sets the `combine` field to true. For seed files loaded from unknown domains, YUI changes `combine` to `false`, on the assumption that a random server does not have a combo loader installed. Setting `combine` to `false` is a safety measure that ensures that local installations of YUI "just work," at the cost of generating lots of HTTP requests. To set up a production-quality local YUI installation, you should install your own local combo loader and set combine back to true. Implementations are available for a variety of server environments:

- PHP Combo Loader (*http://yuilibrary.com/projects/phploader/*), the reference implementation, written by the YUI team. Old and stable, but not under active development.
- Node.js Combo Loader (*https://github.com/rgrove/combohandler*), written and maintained by Ryan Grove.
- Perl Combo Loader (*https://github.com/brianjmiller/cgi-combo*), written and maintained by Brian Miller.
- ASP.NET Combo Loader (*https://github.com/gmoothart/NCombo*), written and maintained by Gabe Moothart.
- Python/WSGI Combo Loader (*https://github.com/chrisgeo/comboloader*), written and maintained by Chris George.
- Ruby on Rails Combo Loader (*https://github.com/sjungling/rails-yui_loader/*), written and maintained by Scott Jungling.

To install and operate a particular combo loader, refer to that combo loader's documentation.

See Also

YUI 3 SDK downloads (*http://yuilibrary.com/downloads/#yui3*); Brian Miller's article on locally served YUI3 (*http://blog.endpoint.com/2011/02/locally-served-yui3.html*), which includes a configuration for serving up local copies of the gallery and YUI 2in3.

1.8 Creating Your Own Modules

Problem

You want to bundle and reuse your own code as a YUI module.

Solution

Use YUI.add() to register your code as a module with the YUI global object. At minimum, YUI.add() takes:

- A name for your module. By convention, YUI module names are lowercase and use hyphens to separate words.
- A callback function that defines your actual module code. To expose a property or function in the module's public interface, you attach the component to the Y object.

Once YUI.add() executes, you can use your code like any other YUI module. In Example 1-9, YUI().use() immediately follows the module definition, loading the modules it needs and then executing module methods in a callback function.

Example 1-9. Creating and using a Hello World module

```
<!DOCTYPE html>
<title>Creating and using a Hello World module</title>

<div id="demo"></div>

<script src="http://yui.yahooapis.com/3.5.0/build/yui/yui-min.js"></script>
<script>
YUI.add('hello', function (Y) {
    Y.namespace('Hello');

    Y.Hello.sayHello = function () {
        return 'GREETINGS PROGRAMS';
    };
});

YUI().use('node-base', 'hello', function (Y) {
    Y.one('#demo').setHTML(Y.Hello.sayHello());
});
</script>
```

To help avoid naming collisions, you can use `Y.namespace()` to manufacture a `Hello` namespace for the `sayHello()` method. `Y.namespace()` is a handy utility, though in this simple example, the call is essentially equivalent to:

```
Y.Hello = {};
```

 Example 1-9 represents only the most basic building block for creating modules. This example is not enough to create truly reusable code. Real-world modules declare dependencies and other metadata, and are defined in a separate file from where they are used. For more information, refer to Recipes 1.9 and 1.10.

Discussion

As mentioned in the introduction and in Recipe 1.1, YUI separates module *registration* from module *execution*. `YUI.add()` registers modules with the `YUI` global object, while `YUI().use()` attaches modules to a `Y` instance so that you can execute the module's functions. `YUI.add()` and `YUI().use()` are designed to work together; first you register some code, and then later you retrieve and execute it.

When designing your applications, always think about how to move as much code as possible out of `use()` and into `add()`. Code in an `add()` callback is reusable, while code in the `use()` callback is unreusable "glue" code designed to wire an application into a particular page.

If you compare `YUI().use()` and `YUI.add()` closely, you might notice the lack of parentheses on the `YUI` for `YUI.add()`. This is a key distinction:

- `YUI.add()` is a static method that registers module code with the `YUI` global object.
- `YUI().use()` is a factory method that creates YUI instances with the given configuration.

The `YUI` global object stores a common pool of available code. The `Y` object holds the particular subset of code that you want to actually register in a `YUI.add()` or use in a `YUI().use()`. Again, the name `Y` is just a strong convention. Within a sandbox, you can name the instance anything you like, but you should do this only if you are creating nested `use()` sandboxes, or if you need to inform other developers that this instance is "weird" in some way. For an example, refer to Recipe 1.19.

The heart of `YUI.add()` is the callback function that defines your module code. Any functions or objects that you attach to the `Y` in the `add()` callback function become available later on in the `use()` callback function. Anything you do not attach to the `Y` remains private. For an example of a private function in a module, refer to Example 1-10.

When attaching functions and objects, consider using a namespace rather than attaching directly to the `Y`, as this space is reserved for a small number of core YUI methods. You can either add namespaces manually by creating empty objects, or call the `Y.name space()` utility method. `Y.namespace()` takes one or more strings and creates corresponding namespaces on the `Y` object. Any namespaces that already exist do not get overwritten. `Y.namespace()` is convenient for creating multiple namespaces at once and for creating nested namespaces such as `Y.Example.Hello`. `Y.namespace()` also returns the last namespace specified, so you can use it inline:

```
Y.namespace('Hello').sayHello = function () { ...
```

You might be wondering about the YUI core modules—do they use `YUI.add()`? In fact, YUI core modules all get wrapped in a `YUI.add()` at build time, thanks to the YUI Builder tool. If you download and unzip the YUI SDK, you will find the raw, unwrapped source files under the */src* directory, and the wrapped module files under the */build* directory. In other words, there's no magic here—the core YUI modules all register themselves with the same interface as your own modules.

See Also

Instructions for using YUI Builder (*http://yuilibrary.com/projects/builder*).

1.9 Creating a Module with Dependencies

Problem

You want to create a custom YUI module and ensure that it pulls in another YUI module as a dependency.

Solution

Use YUI.add() to register your code as a module with the YUI global object, and pass in a configuration object that includes your module's dependencies. After the module name and definition, YUI.add() takes two optional parameters:

- A string version number for your module. This is the version of your module, not the version of YUI your module is compatible with.
- A configuration object containing metadata about the module. By far the most common field in this configuration object is the requires array, which lists your module's dependencies. For each module name in the requires array, YUI pulls in the requirement wherever it is needed, loading it remotely if necessary.

Example 1-10 is a variation on Example 1-9. Instead of returning a string value, Y.Hello.sayHello() now changes the contents of a single Y.Node. The hello module now declares a dependency on node-base to ensure that node.setHTML() is always available wherever hello runs.

To make things a little more interesting, sayHello() uses a private helper function named setNodeMessage(). Users cannot call setNodeMessage() directly because it is not attached to Y. setNodeMessage() uses Y.one() to normalize the input to a YUI node, then sets the message text.

Example 1-10. Creating a module that depends on a YUI node

```
<!DOCTYPE html>
<title>Creating a module that depends on a YUI node</title>

<div id="demo"></div>

<script src="http://yui.yahooapis.com/3.5.0/build/yui/yui-min.js"></script>
<script>
YUI.add('hello', function (Y) {

    function setNodeMessage(node, html) {
        node = Y.one(node);
        if (node) {
            node.setHTML(html);
        }
    }

    Y.namespace('Hello').sayHello = function (node) {
        setNodeMessage(node, 'GREETINGS PROGRAMS');
    };

}, '0.0.1', {requires: ['node-base']});

YUI().use('hello', function (Y) {
    Y.Hello.sayHello(Y.one('#demo'));
});
</script>
```

Unlike Example 1-9, the use() call in Example 1-10 does not need to explicitly request node-base. The new, improved hello module now pulls in this requirement automatically.

Discussion

Example 1-10 lists the module node-base in the requires array for the hello module. This guarantees that YUI().use() loads and attaches hello to the Y *after* attaching node-base (or any other modules you add to that array).

When providing requirements, take care to avoid circular dependencies. For example, if hello declares that the goodbye module must be loaded before hello, but the good bye module declares that hello must be loaded before goodbye, you have a problem. The Loader does have some logic to defend against metadata with circular dependencies, but you shouldn't count on your code running correctly.

For performance reasons, you should also provide your module's requirements in the Loader metadata, as described in Recipe 1.10.

As mentioned earlier, requires is the most important field. Some of the other fields for YUI.add() include:

optional

An array of module names to automatically include with your module, but only if the YUI configuration value loadOptional is set to true. For example, autocom plete-base declares an optional dependency on autocomplete-sources, which contains extra functionality for populating an AutoComplete widget from YQL and other remote sources. loadOptional is false by default.

Even if loadOptional is false, an optional dependency still causes a module to activate if the module's code happens to already be loaded on the page. Modules can be present on the page due to an earlier YUI().use() call, or by loading module code statically, as shown in Recipe 1.20.

skinnable

A Boolean indicating whether your module has a CSS skin. If this field is true, YUI automatically creates a <link> element in the document and attempts to load a CSS file using a URL of:

> base/module-name/assets/skins/skin-name/module-name.css

where *base* is the value of the base field (discussed in Recipe 1.11) and skin-name is the name of the skin, which defaults to the value sam. For more information about creating skins, refer to Recipe 7.10.

use

Deprecated. An array of module names used to define "physical rollups," an older deprecated type of rollup. To create modern rollups, refer to Recipe 1.13.

In addition to module dependencies, Example 1-10 also illustrates a private function within a module. Since JavaScript lacks an explicit private keyword, many JavaScript developers signify private data with an underscore prefix, which warns other developers that the function or variable "should" be private. In many cases, this form of privacy is good enough.

However, the setNodeMessage() function in the example is truly private. Once YUI executes the add() callback, module users can call sayHello(), but they can never call setNodeMessage() directly, even though sayHello() maintains its internal reference to setNodeMessage(). In JavaScript, an inner function continues to have access to all the members of its outer function, even after the outer function executes. This important property of the language is called *closure*.

See Also

Recipe 7.10; Douglas Crockford on "Private Members in JavaScript" (*http://www.crock ford.com/javascript/private.html*).

1.10 Creating Truly Reusable Modules

Problem

You want to create a custom YUI module by defining the module's code in a separate file, then reuse the module in multiple HTML pages.

Solution

Examples 1-9 and 1-10 each define a custom module, but then proceed to use() the module in the same <script> block on the same HTML page. Truly reusable modules are defined in a file separate from where they are used.

This creates a problem. For modules not yet on the page, Loader needs metadata about a module *before* attempting to load that module, such as where the module resides and what its dependencies are. Fortunately, you can provide this information by configuring the YUI object, as shown in Example 1-11.

Example 1-11. Creating a reusable module

add_reusable.html: Creates a YUI instance and passes in a configuration object that defines the hello module's full path and dependencies.

```
<!DOCTYPE html>
<title>Creating a reusable module</title>

<div id="demo"></div>

<script src="http://yui.yahooapis.com/3.5.0/build/yui/yui-min.js"></script>
<script>
YUI({
```

```
    modules: {
        'hello': {
            fullpath: 'hello.js',
            requires: ['node-base']
        }
    }
}).use('hello', function (Y) {
    Y.Hello.sayHello(Y.one('#demo'));
});
</script>
```

With this metadata, you do not need to manually add an extra `<script>` element to load the *hello.js* file. The `fullpath`, which can point to a local file or remote URL, is enough information for the YUI Loader to fetch the code. Declaring `node-base` as a dependency instructs the Loader to fetch `node-base` before fetching `hello` .

Since YUI module names often contain dashes, it is a YUI convention to always quote module names in configuration metadata, even if those quotes are not strictly necessary.

hello.js: Contains only the JavaScript for the `hello` module, identical to the version in Example 1-10. This file resides in the same directory as *add_reusable.html*.

```
YUI.add('hello', function (Y) {

    function setNodeMessage(node, html) {
        node = Y.one(node);
        if (node) {
            node.setHTML(html);
        }
    }

    Y.namespace('Hello').sayHello = function (node) {
        setNodeMessage(node, 'GREETINGS PROGRAMS');
    };

}, '0.0.1', {requires: ['node-base']});
```

Discussion

Example 1-11 is a minimal example of a single, simple module. The configuration object gets more complex as you add more modules and more dependencies, as shown shortly in Example 1-12.

So why doesn't YUI need a giant configuration object to load the core YUI modules? The answer is that YUI cheats—this information is included in the YUI seed. The default seed file includes both the Loader code and metadata for all the core YUI modules, but you can load more minimal seeds if need be. For more information about alternate seed files, refer to "YUI and Loader changes for 3.4.0" (*http://www.yuiblog.com/blog/2011/07/01/yui-and-loader-changes-for-3-4-0/*).

You might have noticed that the metadata `requires: ['node-base']` is provided twice: once in the YUI configuration that gets passed to the Loader, and again in the

`YUI.add()` that defines the module. If the Loader has this metadata, why bother repeating this information in `YUI.add()`?

The answer has to do with certain advanced use cases where the Loader is not present. For example, if you build your own combo load URL, load a minimal seed that lacks the Loader code, and then call `YUI().use('*')` as described in Recipe 1.20, the metadata in `YUI.add()` serves as a fallback for determining dependencies.

1.11 Defining Groups of Custom Modules

Problem

You want to define a group of related modules that all reside under the same path on the server.

Solution

In your YUI configuration, use the `groups` field to create a group of related modules that share the same `base` path and other characteristics.

 Example 1-12 is configured to run from a real web server. If you prefer to open *add_group.html* as a local file, change the `base` configuration field to be a relative filepath such as *./js/local-modules/*.

Example 1-12. Defining a module group

add_group.html: Defines the `local-modules` module group, which contains four modules that reside under */js/local-modules*, plus a CSS skin file. The main module, `reptiles-core`, pulls in the `node` rollup for DOM manipulation and two more local modules for additional giant reptile-related functionality.

```
<!DOCTYPE html>
<title>Defining a module group</title>

<div id="demo"></div>

<script src="http://yui.yahooapis.com/3.5.0/build/yui/yui-min.js"></script>
<script>
YUI({
    groups: {
        'local-modules': {
            base: '/js/local-modules/',
            modules: {
                'reptiles-core': {
                    path: 'reptiles-core/reptiles-core.js',
                    requires: ['node', 'reptiles-stomp', 'reptiles-fiery-breath'],
                    skinnable: true
                },
```

```
            'reptiles-stomp': {
                path: 'reptiles-stomp/reptiles-stomp.js'
            },
            'reptiles-fiery-breath': {
                path: 'reptiles-fiery-breath/reptiles-fiery-breath.js'
            },
            'samurai': {
                path: 'samurai/samurai.js'
            }
        }
    }
}).use('reptiles-core', function (Y) {
    Y.Reptiles.info(Y.one('#demo'));
});
</script>
```

/js/reptiles/giant-reptiles.js: Defines the `reptiles-core` module, which pulls in three other modules and provides an `info()` method that appends a `<ul>` into the DOM.

```
YUI.add('reptiles-core', function (Y) {
    var reptiles = Y.namespace('Reptiles');

    reptiles.traits = [
        'dark eyes',
        'shiny teeth'
    ];

    reptiles.info = function (node) {
        var out = '', i;
        for (i = 0; i < reptiles.traits.length; i += 1) {
            out += '<li>' + reptiles.traits[i] + '</li>';
        };
        out += '<li>' + reptiles.breathe() + '</li>';
        out += '<li>' + reptiles.stomp() + '</li>';
        node.append('<ul class="reptile">' + out + '</ul>');
    };
}, '0.0.1', {requires: ['node', 'reptiles-stomp', 'reptiles-fiery-breath']});
```

/js/reptiles/stomp.js: Defines the `Y.Reptiles.stomp()` method.

```
YUI.add('reptiles-stomp', function (Y) {
    Y.namespace('Reptiles').stomp = function () {
        return 'STOMP!!';
    };
}, '0.0.1');
```

/js/reptiles/fiery-breath.js: Defines the `Y.Reptiles.breathe()` method.

```
YUI.add('reptiles-fiery-breath', function (Y) {
    Y.namespace('Reptiles').breathe = function () {
        return 'WHOOOSH!';
    };
}, '0.0.1');
```

/js/local-modules/reptiles-core/assets/skins/sam/reptiles-core.css: Defines the CSS skin for the `reptiles-core` module. YUI attempts to load this file because the `skinnable` field for `reptiles-core` is set to `true`. For more information about how this works, refer to the Discussion.

```
.reptile li { color: #060; }
```

The `samurai` module definition is empty. Feel free to make up your own definition.

Discussion

For multiple custom modules, consider using this convention for your module structure:

```
base/
  module-foo/
    module-foo.js
    assets/
      skins/
        sam/
          module-foo.css
          sprite.png
  module-bar/
    ...
```

that is, a base path with one directory per module. Each module directory contains at least one JavaScript file, possibly more if you include the *-min.js* or *-debug.js* versions of your modules. If the module has a skin, it should also contain an *assets/* directory, as shown in Recipe 7.10. If it has localized language resources, it should contain a *lang/* directory, as shown in Recipe 11.6.

Module groups create a configuration context where you can load modules from somewhere other than the Yahoo! CDN. You do not need to use module groups for logical groupings of your own modules ("all my widgets," "all my utility objects," and so on). For those kinds of logical groupings, it is more appropriate to create custom rollups, as described in Recipe 1.13. Module groups are for providing the Loader with a different set of metadata for loading modules from a *particular server and set of paths*: your own custom modules, third-party modules on some remote server, your own local copy of the core YUI library or YUI gallery, and so on.

In many cases, a module group is a necessity. Consider loading a local CSS skin. As described in Recipe 1.9, setting `skinnable` to `true` causes YUI to attempt to fetch a skin from:

```
base/module-name/assets/skins/skin-name/module-name.css
```

`base` defaults to the same prefix that you loaded the YUI seed file from, typically something like *http://yui.yahooapis.com/3.5.0/build*. So what happens if you try to load skin CSS from your own local server without using a module group?

```
<script src="http://yui.yahooapis.com/3.5.0/build/yui/yui-min.js"></script>
<script>
YUI({
    modules: {
        'reptiles-core': {
            fullpath: '/js/local-modules/reptiles-core/reptiles-core.js',
            skinnable: true
        },
        ...
    }
}).use('reptiles-core', ...);
```

This configuration fails because YUI attempts to load your skin from *http://yui.ya-hooapis.com/3.5.0/build/reptiles-core/assets/skins/sam/reptiles-core.css*, instead of your local server.

What if you set base to act locally? For example:

```
YUI({
    base: '/js/local-modules/',
    modules: {
        'reptiles-core': {
            path: 'reptiles-core/reptiles-core.js',
            skinnable: true
        },
        ...
    }
}).use('reptiles-core', ...);
```

This is also undesirable because now YUI is configured to fetch *all* modules, including the YUI core and gallery modules, from this local path. Using a module group enables you to set the base path for all of your local modules without messing up the loader configuration for the core modules.

See Also

Recipe 1.13; Recipe 7.9; Recipe 7.10; Recipe 11.6; the YUI Loader section of the YUI Global Object User Guide (*http://yuilibrary.com/yui/docs/yui/#loader*).

1.12 Reusing a YUI Configuration

Problem

You want to reuse a complex configuration across multiple pages.

Solution

Before creating any YUI instances, load a separate script file containing a YUI_config object that stores all custom module configuration and other metadata you need. If the page contains a YUI_config object, YUI automatically applies this configuration to any YUI instances on the page.

Example 1-13 is a variation of Example 1-12, but with the module metadata broken out into its own reusable file.

 Example 1-13 is configured to run from a real web server. If you prefer to open *add_yui_config.html* as a local file, change all */js* filepaths to relative filepaths such as *./js/*.

Example 1-13. Reusing a YUI configuration

add_yui_config.html: Loads and exercises the `reptiles-core` module using an implicit YUI configuration supplied by */js/yui_config.js*. The key word is "implicit"—you do not need to explicitly pass `YUI_config` into the `YUI()` constructor.

```
<!DOCTYPE html>
<title>Reusing a YUI configuration</title>

<div id="demo"></div>

<script src="http://yui.yahooapis.com/3.5.0/build/yui/yui-min.js"></script>
<script src="/js/yui_config.js"></script>
<script>
YUI().use('reptiles-core', function (Y) {
    Y.Reptiles.info(Y.one('#demo'));
});
</script>
```

/js/yui_config.js: Provides the configuration data for loading a set of custom modules.

```
var YUI_config = {
    groups: {
        'local-modules': {
            base: '/js/local-modules/',
            modules: {
                'reptiles-core': {
                    path: 'reptiles-core/reptiles-core.js',
                    requires: ['node', 'reptiles-stomp', 'reptiles-fiery-breath'],
                    skinnable: true
                },
                'reptiles-stomp': {
                    path: 'reptiles-stomp/reptiles-stomp.js'
                },
                'reptiles-fiery-breath': {
                    path: 'reptiles-fiery-breath/reptiles-fiery-breath.js'
                },
                'samurai': {
                    path: 'samurai/samurai.js'
                }
            }
        }
    }
};
```

The other JavaScript files in this example are identical to the ones in Example 1-12.

Discussion

At construction time, each YUI instance attempts to merge the common `YUI_config` object into the configuration object you passed into the `YUI()` constructor. Thus, something like:

```
<script src="/js/yui_config.js"></script>
<script>
YUI({ lang: 'jp' }).use('reptiles-core', function (Y) {
    Y.Reptiles.info(Y.one('#demo'));
});
</script>
```

would safely add the `lang` property without clobbering the module metadata. Properties you supply to the constructor override properties in `YUI_config`.

If you're careful about how you merge configuration data, you can add new module groups or even new modules within an existing module group, as shown in Example 1-14.

Example 1-14. Merging common and page-specific YUI configuration

add_yui_config_merged.html: Loads and exercises the `reptiles-core` module using an implicit YUI configuration supplied by */js/yui_config_incomplete.js*, and merges some extra configuration information into the `YUI()` constructor.

```
<!DOCTYPE html>
<title>Merging common and page-specific YUI configuration</title>

<div id="demo"></div>

<script src="http://yui.yahooapis.com/3.5.0/build/yui/yui-min.js"></script>
<script src="/js/yui_config_incomplete.js"></script>
<script>
YUI({
    groups: {
        'local-modules': {
            base: '/js/local-modules/',
            modules: {
                'reptiles-stomp': {
                    path: 'reptiles-stomp/reptiles-stomp.js'
                }
            }
        }
    }
}).use('reptiles-core', function (Y) {
    Y.Reptiles.info(Y.one('#demo'));
});
</script>
```

/js/yui_config.js: Provides some (intentionally incomplete) configuration data for loading a set of custom modules. The configuration is broken in two places: first, the `reptiles-stomp` module definition is missing, and second, the `base` path is incorrect. However, the configuration object provided in the HTML file fixes both problems.

```
// WARNING: Config intentionally incomplete/broken
var YUI_config = {
    groups: {
        'local-modules': {
            base: '/js/BOGUS_PATH',
            modules: {
                'reptiles-core': {
                    path: 'reptiles-core/reptiles-core.js',
                    requires: ['node', 'reptiles-stomp', 'reptiles-fiery-breath'],
                    skinnable: true
                },
                'reptiles-fiery-breath': {
                    path: 'reptiles-fiery-breath/reptiles-fiery-breath.js'
                },
                'samurai': {
                    path: 'samurai/samurai.js'
                }
            }
        }
    }
};
```

Example 1-14 supplies an incomplete `YUI_config` object in order to demonstrate that the merging actually works. More generally, you would use `YUI_config` to provide a complete, working configuration for everything that is common across your site, and then supply additional page-specific information either in the YUI instance constructor, or by modifying `YUI_config` (which would affect all instances on the page).

Once you're within a YUI instance, you can call `Y.applyConfig()` at any time to merge in additional configuration. You can even call `Y.applyConfig()` to load more module metadata, perhaps along with on-demand loading techniques such as those shown in Recipes 1.17 and 1.18.

1.13 Defining Your Own Rollups

Problem

You would like to define a particular stack of modules under a friendly alias for convenient reuse.

Solution

Define an empty module and provide it with a `use` field containing an array of other module or rollup names. Then load and use it as you would any other module.

Example 1-15 represents a simple rollup that serves as an alias for `node-base` and `json` (which is itself a rollup of `json-parse` and `json-stringify`). The custom `my-stack` rollup behaves like any of the other popular core YUI rollups, such as `node`, `io`, `json`, or `transition`.

Example 1-15. Defining your own rollups

```
<!DOCTYPE html>
<title>Defining your own rollups</title>

<div id="demo"></div>

<script src="http://yui.yahooapis.com/3.5.0/build/yui/yui-min.js"></script>
<script>
YUI({
    modules: {
        'my-stack': {
            use: ['node-base', 'json']
        }
    }
}).use('my-stack', function (Y) {
    var dataStr = '{ "rollups": "are neat" }',
        data    = Y.JSON.parse(dataStr);

    Y.one('#demo').setHTML(data.rollups);
});
</script>
```

Discussion

As Example 1-15 demonstrates, a rollup is just an alias for a list of other rollups and modules. The example uses core YUI modules, but you can also include gallery modules, your own custom modules, or anything else.

Rollups are great for logically grouping modules that represent major components of your application stack, or for grouping modules that are closely related, but don't strictly depend on each other. For example, `json-parse` and `json-stringify` are completely independent modules, but applications often end up using both anyway.

Another benefit of rollups is that they free you up to encapsulate your code into even smaller chunks than you otherwise might have. You can use rollups to bundle very tiny modules into larger units, making it easier for others to use your code without having to worry about the fiddly details of what to include.

See Also

Recipe 1.1; Recipe 1.10.

1.14 Loading jQuery as a YUI Module

Problem

You want to load jQuery and some jQuery plugins into the sandbox alongside YUI, just like any YUI module.

Solution

Create a module group that defines module metadata for the main jQuery library and any other jQuery-related code that you want to load as well. Use `base` and `path` (or `fullpath`) to point to the remote files.

If you need to load multiple jQuery files in a particular order, use `requires` to specify the dependency tree, and set `async: false` for the overall module group. Setting `async: false` is necessary for loading any code that is *not* wrapped in a `YUI.add()`—it ensures that third-party code loads synchronously, in the correct file order.

After defining jQuery files as YUI modules, you can then `use()` them alongside any ordinary YUI modules you like. Example 1-16 pulls in the YUI `calendar` module along with jQuery and jQuery UI, which includes the jQuery Datepicker plugin. Unlike YUI core widgets, the jQuery Datepicker's CSS does not get loaded automatically, so you must load it as a separate CSS module. For more information about loading arbitrary CSS as a YUI module, refer to Recipe 7.9.

> Experienced jQuery developers might have noticed that the example simply renders the Datepicker without bothering to wrap it in a `$(docu ment).ready()`. The standard YUI loading pattern with JavaScript at the bottom of the page usually makes DOM readiness a nonissue. However, if you modify elements that occur after your `<script>` element or load YUI in an unusual way, you might need to wait for DOM readiness. For YUI's equivalent of jQuery's `ready()`, refer to Recipe 4.2.

Example 1-16. Loading jQuery as a YUI module

```
<!DOCTYPE html>
<title>Loading jQuery as a YUI module</title>
<style>
h4 { margin: 25px 0px 10px 0px; }
div.container { width: 300px; }
</style>

<body class="yui3-skin-sam">

<h4>YUI 3 Calendar Widget</h4>
<div class="container" id="ycalendar"></div>

<h4>jQuery UI Calendar Plugin</h4>
<div class="container" id="datepicker"></div>

<script src="http://yui.yahooapis.com/3.5.0/build/yui/yui-min.js"></script>
<script>
YUI({
    groups: {
        'jquery': {
            base: 'http://ajax.googleapis.com/ajax/libs/',
            async: false,
```

```
            modules: {
                'jquery': {
                    path: 'jquery/1.7/jquery.min.js'
                },
                'jquery-ui': {
                    path: 'jqueryui/1.8/jquery-ui.min.js',
                    requires: ['jquery', 'jquery-ui-css']
                },
                'jquery-ui-css': {
                    path: 'jqueryui/1.8/themes/base/jquery-ui.css',
                    type: 'css'
                }
            }
        }
    }
}).use('calendar', 'jquery-ui', function (Y) {
    new Y.Calendar().render('#ycalendar');
    $('#datepicker').datepicker();
    Y.one('body').append('<p>YUI and jQuery, living together, mass hysteria!</p>');
});
</script>
</body>
```

As with any module, it's critical to define your dependencies correctly. Here, the jquery-ui module declares a dependency on jquery and jquery-ui-css, which ensures that YUI adds jQuery's code to the page *above* jQuery UI's code. If you somehow got the dependencies backward and declared that jquery depended on jquery-ui, then YUI would add jQuery *below* jQuery UI, which would break the Datepicker plugin.

Of course, you're not restricted to just core jQuery and jQuery UI. As long as you declare your paths and dependencies correctly, you can load any third-party jQuery plugin (or any other library code, for that matter).

Discussion

Loading jQuery, Dojo, Scriptaculous, or any other major framework into a YUI sandbox is not exactly a recipe for great efficiency. If you've loaded the code necessary to do both Y.one('#demo') and $('#demo') in the same page, you've loaded an awful lot of duplicate code for rummaging around the DOM.

That said, the YUI Loader is an excellent standalone script and CSS loader. It can load any third-party JS or CSS file you like, in any order you like, as long as you provide the correct metadata. Some reasons you might want to do this include:

Easy code reuse
> You have found some critical feature or component that is available only in some other library.

Better collaboration
> You are working primarily in YUI, but you have teammates or contractors who have written non-YUI code that you need to quickly integrate, or vice versa.

Improving perceived performance

Your non-YUI pages are currently littered with blocking `<script>` and `<link>` elements at the top of the document. You're looking for a quick way to migrate over to a more advanced loading pattern, and perhaps even take advantage of some advanced YUI Loader tricks such as those covered in Recipes 1.15 and 1.17.

In fact, if you want to use the Loader to load non-YUI scripts only, and you are *sure* that you don't need to load any core YUI modules, consider loading the `yui-base-min.js` seed rather than the `yui-min.js` seed:

```
<script src="http://yui.yahooapis.com/3.5.0/build/yui-base/yui-base-min.js"></script>
```

The `yui-base-min.js` seed includes the YUI module registry and the YUI Loader, but leaves out all the metadata for the core YUI modules. This makes it a little more efficient to load the YUI seed solely for loading and managing third-party scripts.

YUI is designed to be compatible with most major libraries, although you might run into strange conflicts here and there. The most common reason for bugs is when the other library modifies the prototype of a native JavaScript or native DOM object. YUI provides solid abstraction layers around native objects, but these abstractions can break if the other library changes object behavior at a deep level.

The other thing to watch out for is forgetting that different libraries use different abstractions. For example, you can't pass a YUI `Node` instance directly into some other library for further DOM manipulation. If you are building some kind of Frankenstein's Monster application that does some DOM manipulation with YUI and some in Dojo, keep a close eye on each point where the two libraries communicate.

See Also

jQuery (*http://docs.jquery.com*); jQuery UI.Datepicker (*http://docs.jquery.com/UI/Date picker*); jCarousel (*http://sorgalla.com/projects/jcarousel/*); the jQuery–YUI 3 Rosetta Stone (*http://www.jsrosettastone.com/*); an explanation of the different seed files in YUI and Loader changes for 3.4.0 (*http://www.yuiblog.com/blog/2011/07/01/yui-and-loader -changes-for-3-4-0/*).

1.15 Loading Modules Based on Browser Capabilities

Problem

You want YUI to supply additional fallback code to support users who have legacy browsers, but without penalizing users who have modern browsers. (This is called *capability-based loading.*)

Solution

In your YUI configuration, use the `condition` field to flag a module as conditional. A conditional module loads only if some other module specified by `trigger` is present, and then only if the `test` function returns `true`.

Example 1-17 demonstrates a simple `suitcase` module that can store data on the client. By default, the module tries to use `localStorage`, but if the browser is too old to support this feature natively, YUI loads an extra module that stores data using cookies instead.

Example 1-17. Loading modules based on browser capabilities

add_capability.html: Creates a YUI instance and passes in a configuration object that defines metadata for the `suitcase` module and for the `suitcase-legacy` conditional module.

```
<!DOCTYPE html>
<title>Loading modules based on browser capabilities</title>

<div id="demo"></div>

<script src="http://yui.yahooapis.com/3.5.0/build/yui/yui-min.js"></script>
<script>
YUI({
    modules: {
        'suitcase': {
            fullpath: 'suitcase.js'
        },
        'suitcase-legacy': {
            fullpath: 'suitcase-legacy.js',
            condition: {
                trigger: 'suitcase',
                test: function () {
                    try {
                        return window.localStorage ? false : true;
                    } catch(ex) {
                        return true;
                    }
                }
            },
            requires: ['suitcase', 'cookie']
        }
    }
}).use('node', 'suitcase', function (Y) {
    var type = Y.Cookie ? 'battered, legacy' : 'sleek, ultra-modern';
    Y.Suitcase.set('foo', 'bar');
    Y.one('#demo').setHTML('In your ' + type + ' suitcase: ' + Y.Suitcase.get('foo'));
});
</script>
```

The suitcase-legacy module has a trigger condition. If the suitcase module is passed into use(), YUI executes suitcase-legacy's test function. If the browser does *not* support localStorage, the function returns true, which causes YUI to also fetch suitcase-legacy and all its dependencies. If the function does support localStorage, YUI skips fetching suitcase-legacy.

Within the use() callback, the presence of Y.Cookie is a quick way to check whether suitcase-legacy was successfully triggered.

suitcase.js: Defines a simple get/set API for storing data on the client using local Storage. Note that the suitcase module is written without any "knowledge" of the suitcase-legacy API. Capability-based loading is designed to help you avoid having to include extra conditionals or other unnecessary code in your main modules.

```
YUI.add('suitcase', function (Y) {
    Y.Suitcase = {
        get: function (name) {
            return localStorage.getItem(name);
        },
        set: function (name, value) {
            localStorage.setItem(name, value);
        }
    };
}, '0.0.1');
```

suitcase-legacy.js: Defines the legacy cookie-based get/set API. Because of dependency ordering, YUI must load suitcase-legacy after suitcase, which means that the get() and set() methods from suitcase-legacy always overwrite the get() and set() methods from suitcase. In other words, if both modules are loaded on the page, calling Y.Suitcase.get() will use cookies, not localStorage.

```
YUI.add('suitcase-legacy', function (Y) {
    Y.Suitcase = {
        get: function (name) {
            return Y.Cookie.get(name);
        },
        set: function (name, value) {
            Y.Cookie.set(name, value);
        }
    };
}, '0.0.1', { requires: ['suitcase', 'cookie'] });
```

Fortunately for users (but unfortunately for demonstration purposes), localStorage is widely available in most browsers. If you don't have a really old browser available that can show the legacy module in action, feel free to hack the example and change the test function to just return true.

 The Suitcase object is a toy example. YUI already provides more professional storage APIs called Cache and CacheOffline. Like Suitcase, CacheOffline is able to use localStorage when that feature is available.

Discussion

Supporting older, less capable browsers often requires supplying extra JavaScript to correct for bugs and to emulate more advanced native features. After writing and testing code to correct older browsers, the last thing you want to do is penalize cutting-edge users by forcing them to download extra code.

YUI's capability-based loading solves this problem by enabling you to break legacy code out into separate modules. Older browsers can load and execute the extra code they need, while newer browsers suffer only the small performance hit of evaluating a few conditionals.

The core YUI library uses capability-based loading to do things like:

- Avoid loading support for physical keyboard events on iPhones
- Make DOM-ready events safer on old versions of Internet Explorer, without penalizing other browsers
- Seamlessly use the best graphics feature available for the given browser: SVG, Canvas, or VML

While capability-based loading was originally designed for patching up legacy browsers, you can also flip this idea around and serve up extra code that unlocks features in a *more* capable browser. For example, let's say your application must perform an expensive calculation. Older browsers run the calculation directly and suffer an annoying UI freeze. However, if the browser supports the Web Worker API, YUI could trigger a conditional module that uses workers to run the calculation in the background. Usually you want to avoid "penalizing" newer browsers with an extra download, but if the benefits are high enough, it might be worth doing.

Most conditional modules should be abstracted behind another API. In Example 1-17, the modules are designed so that developers can call `Y.Suitcase.get()` and `Y.Suitcase.set()` without knowing whether the legacy implementation was in effect. Of course, this abstraction can be slower than the native implementation, or break down at the edges in some other way. For example, anyone who tries to store a 3 MB object in `Y.Suitcase` using a legacy browser will be sorely disappointed.

For obvious reasons, capability test functions should execute quickly. A typical capability test either checks for the existence of an object property, or creates a new DOM element and runs some subsequent operation on that element. Unfortunately, touching the DOM is expensive, and even more unfortunately, sometimes capability tests need to do substantial work, since just because a browser exposes a certain property or method doesn't mean that the feature works properly. As an example, the test function in Example 1-17 needs a try/catch statement in order to work around an edge-case bug in older versions of   Firefox.

Capability testing can be a surprisingly deep rabbit hole. In extreme cases where capability testing has become hopelessly complex or slow, you might consider using the

`Y.UA` object. `Y.UA` performs user-agent sniffing, which many web developers regard as evil. Still, `Y.UA` is there, just in case you really do need to use the Dark Side of the Force. `Y.UA` can also be useful when capability testing isn't helpful for answering the question, such as when you need to detect certain CSS or rendering quirks.

See Also

The W3C standard for web storage (*http://www.w3.org/TR/webstorage/*); the YUI Cookie API (*http://yuilibrary.com/yui/docs/cookie/*).

1.16 Monkeypatching YUI

Problem

You want to conditionally load extra code at runtime to patch a YUI bug or hack new behavior into YUI.

Solution

In your YUI configuration, define one or more patch modules, using the `condition` field to flag those modules as conditional. Set the `trigger` field to the name of the module to patch, and create a test function that simply returns `true`.

Example 1-18 loads a module that patches `node-base`, changing the behavior of `setHTML()`. Ordinarily, `setHTML()` is a safer version of setting `innerHTML`; before blowing away the node's internal contents, `setHTML()` walks the DOM and cleanly detaches any event listeners. For whatever reason, you've decided this safer behavior is undesirable. The "patch" clobbers `setHTML()`, turning it into a simple alias for setting `innerHTML`.

 Example 1-18 is configured to run from a real web server. If you prefer to open *add_monkeypatching.html* as a local file, change the `base` configuration field to be a relative filepath such as *./js/patches/*.

Example 1-18. Monkeypatching YUI

add_monkeypatching.html: Creates a YUI instance and passes in a configuration object that defines metadata for the `node-patches` conditional module.

```
<!DOCTYPE html>
<title>Monkeypatching YUI</title>

<div id="demo"></div>

<script src="http://yui.yahooapis.com/3.5.0/build/yui/yui-min.js"></script>
<script>
YUI({
    groups: {
```

```
        patches: {
            base: '/js/patches/',
            modules: {
                'node-patches' : {
                    path: 'node-patches/node-patches.js',
                    condition: {
                        name: 'node-patches',
                        trigger : 'node-base',
                        test : function () { return true; }
                    }
                }
            }
        }
    }
}).use('node-base', function (Y) {
    Y.one('#demo').setHTML("Hmmm, setHTML() is unusually fast these days.");
});
</script>
```

/js/patches/node-patches/node-patches.js: Provides additional code that overrides Node's
setHTML() method. The patch module loads only if node-base is loaded.

```
YUI.add('node-patches', function (Y) {
    Y.Node.prototype.setHTML = function (content) {
        this.set('innerHTML', content);
    }
});
```

Discussion

Monkeypatching refers to modifying the behavior of a program at runtime without
altering the upstream source. Monkeypatching can be useful for implementing quick
fixes, but as the name implies, it isn't necessarily the best approach for long-term
stability.

Example 1-18 represents a somewhat contrived behavior change. More generally, you
could use monkeypatching to temporarily address a serious bug in the YUI library, or
to inject behavior that you need in a development or staging environment, but not in
production.

 When patching someone else's code, you can use Y.Do.before() and
Y.Do.after() to cleanly inject behavior into a program without clobbering an existing method. For more information, refer to Recipe 4.12.

See Also

Recipe 1.15; YUI Tutorial: "Report a Bug" (*http://yuilibrary.com/yui/docs/tutorials/re
port-bugs/*).

1.17 Loading Modules on Demand

Problem

You have a feature that your application needs only some of the time. You want to load this code only for users who need it, without affecting the initial page load.

Solution

Instead of loading the optional code up front, call Y.use() *within* the top-level YUI().use() sandbox to load the optional code on demand.

For example, suppose you need to display a confirmation pane when the user clicks a button. The straightforward approach is to load the overlay module with YUI().use(), create a new Overlay instance, and then bind a click event to the button that will show() the overlay. For examples of using overlays, refer to Recipe 8.2.

Although there's nothing wrong with that approach, users still have to load the over lay module and its dependencies even if they never click the button. You can improve the performance of the initial page view by deferring loading and executing code until the moment the user needs it, as shown in Example 1-19:

1. Create a top-level showOverlay() function.
2. Within showOverlay(), call Y.use() to load the overlay module.
3. Within the Y.use() callback function:
   a. Create a new Overlay instance, initially set to be invisible.
   b. Redefine the showOverlay() function to do something else. The next time show Overlay() is called, it will simply show the hidden overlay instance.
   c. Call the newly redefined showOverlay() from within showOverlay() to make the overlay instance visible.
4. Bind "hide" and "show" callback functions as click events for the two respective buttons:
   - The "hide" callback first checks whether the overlay has been created.
   - The "show" callback calls showOverlay(). The first button click invokes the "heavy" version of showOverlay(), the version that loads the overlay module, instantiates an overlay, and then redefines itself. Subsequent clicks invoke the "light" version of showOverlay(), which flips the overlay into the visible state.

Example 1-19. Loading the overlay module on demand

```
<!DOCTYPE html>
<title>Loading the overlay module on demand</title>
<style>
.yui3-overlay-content {
    padding: 2px;
    border: 1px solid #000;
```

```
        border-radius: 6px;
        background-color: #afa;
    }
</style>

<button id="show">Show Overlay</button>
<button id="hide">Hide Overlay</button>

<script src="http://yui.yahooapis.com/3.5.0/build/yui/yui-min.js"></script>
<script>
YUI().use('node-base', function (Y) {
    var overlay;

    var showOverlay = function () {
        Y.use('overlay', function () {
            overlay = new Y.Overlay({
                bodyContent: 'Hello!',
                centered: true,
                height: 100,
                render: true,
                visible: false,
                width: 200,
                zIndex: 2
            });

            showOverlay = function () {
                overlay.show();
            };

            showOverlay();
        });
    };

    Y.one('#hide').on('click', function () {
        if (overlay) {
            overlay.hide();
        }
    });

    Y.one('#show').on('click', function () {
        showOverlay();
    });
});
</script>
```

Discussion

Example 1-19 illustrates two concepts. The first is the ability of functions in JavaScript to redefine themselves. A function calling itself (*recursion*) is common enough, but a function that redefines and then calls itself is less common. This pattern is useful if you have a function that needs to do one thing the first time it is called, and something else on subsequent calls. Use this technique sparingly, as there's a good chance you'll confuse people who read your code later on—including, possibly, yourself.

The second concept is the difference between the exterior `YUI().use()`, which creates a new YUI sandbox, and the interior `Y.use()`, which loads modules into the existing sandbox that's referenced by the `Y` variable. `Y.use()` enables you to load and attach additional modules at any time, for any reason. This is sometimes called *lazy loading*.

Lazy-loading modules can greatly improve your application's perceived performance. Native applications have a great advantage in that they start out with most or all of their code preloaded, while web applications have to bootstrap themselves over the network.

To compensate for this, you can divide your application into two pieces: a minimal *interactivity core* that provides just enough functionality to render the application, and additional components that you can lazy-load in the background as the user starts poking around. Example 1-19 attempts to be "smart" by loading extra code only if it is needed, but your application doesn't have to be this fancy. You could wait for your interactivity core to finish loading and then start loading all secondary components in the background, in order of priority.

Loading modules in response to user actions can cause a delay at the moment when the user triggers the loading. If this becomes a problem, you can just lazy-load all modules in the background regardless of whether they are needed, or alternatively, you can try to improve performance with *predictive loading*, as described in Recipe 1.18.

See Also

Eric Ferraiuolo's `gallery-base-componentmgr` module (*http://yuilibrary.com/gallery/show/base-componentmgr*), which makes it easy to lazy-load `Y.Base`-derived objects and their dependencies.

1.18 Enabling Predictive Module Loading on User Interaction

Problem

You have a feature that your application needs only some of the time, but that requires a lot of extra code to run. You want to load this code only for users who need it, without impacting the initial page load. You want to minimize any delay that occurs if a user does invoke the feature.

Solution

Use predictive loading to load the necessary code after the initial page load, but just before the user tries to invoke the feature.

In Example 1-19, the application defers loading the `overlay` module until the user clicks the button, which improves the initial page load time. However, this could cause an annoying delay when the user makes the first click.

Example 1-20 adds a refinement to the previous example. It calls Y.use() to load the overlay module in the background, but only if the user's mouse hovers over the Show Overlay button or if the button acquires focus. If the user then clicks on the button and the module has not yet loaded, the click event gets queued up until the Overlay widget is ready. To do this, the example separates loading from execution by creating a load Overlay() function and a showOverlay() function.

1. The loadOverlay() function has different behavior depending on whether the overlay has already been instantiated, the overlay module is currently loading, or the overlay module needs to start loading.

   a. loadOverlay() takes a callback function, which turns out to be showOver lay(). If the overlay has already been instantiated, loadOverlay() executes the callback and returns immediately.

   b. If the overlay module is currently loading, this means the overlay is not yet ready to show. loadOverlay() queues the callback up in the callbacks array and returns immediately.

   c. If both of these conditions fail, this means the loadOverlay() function has been invoked for the first time. It is therefore time to start loading the overlay module. loadOverlay() calls Y.use() to load the overlay module on the fly.

   d. The Y.use() callback instantiates the overlay, sets overlayLoading to false (indicating that it is permissible to show the overlay), and finally executes any showOverlay() callbacks that have queued up while the code was loading.

2. The showOverlay() function is considerably simpler. If the overlay is already instantiated, the function shows the overlay. Otherwise, showOverlay() calls load Overlay() with itself as the callback, which guarantees that loadOverlay() has at least one instance of showOverlay() queued up and ready to fire as soon as the overlay is instantiated.

3. The hideOverlay() function is simpler still. If the overlay is already instantiated, the function shows the overlay.

4. Finally, the script attaches event handlers to the Show Button and Hide Button. The on() method attaches an event handler, while the once() method attaches an event listener that automatically detaches itself the first time it is called.

Example 1-20. Loading the overlay module predictively

```
<!DOCTYPE html>
<title>Loading the overlay module predictively</title>
<style>
.yui3-overlay-content {
    padding: 2px;
    border: 1px solid #000;
    border-radius: 6px;
    background-color: #afa;
}
</style>
```

```
<button id="show">Show Overlay</button>
<button id="hide">Hide Overlay</button>

<script src="http://yui.yahooapis.com/3.5.0/build/yui/yui-min.js"></script>
<script>
YUI().use('node-base', function (Y) {
    var callbacks = [],
        overlay,
        overlayLoading,
        showButton = Y.one('#show'),
        hideButton = Y.one('#hide');

    var loadOverlay = function (callback) {
        if (overlay) {
            if (callback) {
                callback();
            }
            return;
        }

        if (callback) {
            callbacks.push(callback);
        }

        if (overlayLoading) {
            return;
        }

        overlayLoading = true;

        Y.use('overlay', function () {
            var callback;

            overlay = new Y.Overlay({
                bodyContent: 'Hello!',
                centered: true,
                visible: false,
                height: 100,
                width: 200,
                zIndex: 2
            }).render();

            overlayLoading = false;

            while (callback = callbacks.shift()) {
                if (Y.Lang.isFunction(callback)) {
                    callback();
                }
            }
        });
    };
```

```
    var showOverlay = function () {
        if (overlay) {
            overlay.show();
        } else {
            loadOverlay(showOverlay);
        }
    };

    var hideOverlay = function () {
        if (overlay) {
            overlay.hide();
            callbacks = [];
        }
    };

    showButton.once('focus', loadOverlay);
    showButton.once('mouseover', loadOverlay);
    showButton.on('click', showOverlay);
    hideButton.on('click', hideOverlay);
});
</script>
```

For more information about the Overlay widget, refer to Recipe 8.2.

Discussion

While on-demand loading modules can help reduce initial load times, it can cause a delay when the user triggers the main event that requires the extra code. The goal of predictive loading is to start the loading a little earlier by using some other, related browser event that signals the user's possible intent to use the feature.

A reasonable way to predict that the user is likely to click a button is to listen for mouseover or focus events on the button or its container. You must listen for both events, since some users may use the mouse while others may use the keyboard. To get an even earlier indication of the user's intent, you could attach the focus and mouseover listeners to the button's container. For more information about using on() and once() to attach event handlers, refer to Chapter 4.

Thanks to these event handlers, the loadOverlay() function is called when the user is about to click the Show Overlay button. Since dynamic script loading is an asynchronous operation, loadOverlay() accepts an optional callback function as an argument, and calls that function once the overlay is ready to use.

To ensure that user clicks don't get lost while the overlay module is loading, multiple calls to loadOverlay() just add more callbacks to the queue, and all queued callbacks will be executed in order as soon as the overlay is ready. By the time the user actually clicks, the overlay should be ready to go, but if the user does manage to click while the code is loading, the overlay still appears as expected.

1.19 Binding a YUI Instance to an iframe

Problem

You want to manipulate an iframe using JavaScript in the parent document, without actually having to directly load YUI into the iframe.

Solution

Create a child YUI instance within your main YUI instance and bind the child instance to the iframe, as shown in Example 1-21. Every YUI instance has a win and a doc configuration value. By default, these values point to the native DOM window and document that are hosting YUI, but you can change them to point to the window and document of a different frame.

To set win and doc, use document.getElementById() to get a DOM reference to the iframe, then set win to the frame's contentWindow and doc to the frame's content Window.document. Note that win and doc are core configuration values and cannot be set to be YUI Node objects, as this would presuppose that every YUI instance has the node rollup loaded and available.

Example 1-21. Binding a YUI instance to an iframe

```
<!DOCTYPE html>
<title>Binding a YUI instance to an iframe</title>

<iframe src="iframe.html" id="frame"></iframe>

<script src="http://yui.yahooapis.com/3.5.0/build/yui/yui-min.js"></script>
<script>
YUI().use('node', function (Y) {
    var frame = document.getElementById('frame'),
        win = frame.contentWindow,
        doc = frame.contentWindow.document;

    YUI({ win: win, doc: doc }).use('node', function (innerY) {
        var innerBody = innerY.one('body');
        innerBody.addClass('foo');
        innerBody.append('<p>YUI3 was loaded!</p>');
    });
});
</script>
```

Nested instances are one of the few reasons to name the callback something other than Y. innerY is a fully functional YUI instance bound to the iframe's window and document. It has all the capabilities of a conventional Y instance, but scoped to the iframe. For example, calling innerY.one('body') gets the iframe's body, not the parent's body.

For security reasons, modern browsers prevent a parent document from manipulating a framed document with JavaScript unless the URLs of both documents have the same domain, protocol, and port. For this reason, be sure to host your iframes on the same server as the parent document.

If you try out Example 1-21 on your local filesystem using   Chrome, the example fails due to Chrome's strict security policies around local files and JavaScript. In this case, just copy the example files to a real web server.

Discussion

If `win` and `doc` are not configured properly, iframes can be tricky to work with. For instance, the following code fails:

```
var frame = Y.one('#foo');
var h1 = frame.one('h1');
```

The first line is just fine: it retrieves a `Y.Node` instance for the iframe with an `id` of `foo`. But a naive call to `frame.one()` or `frame.all()` fails because YUI is scoped to work on the parent document.

One approach would be to add `<script>` markup and JavaScript code directly in the iframe, but this is clunky. The better strategy is to bind the iframe's window and document objects to a nested YUI instance. Within that instance, the YUI `Node` API works as expected on the iframe's content. Driving the iframe from the parent keeps all your code in one place and avoids having to fetch all your JavaScript code a second time from within the iframe. The iframe also has access to the `Y` instance for easy communication with the parent document.

If the iframe needs additional modules, you can first load them into the parent instance with a `Y.use()`, and then in the `Y.use()` callback, call `innerY.use()` to attach the module to the inner YUI instance. Example 1-22 is identical to Example 1-21, except that it also pulls in the `event` rollup in order to set a `click` event on the body of the iframe.

Example 1-22. Loading additional modules into an iframe

```
<!DOCTYPE html>
<title>Loading additional modules into an iframe</title>

<iframe src="iframe.html" id="frame"></iframe>

<script src="http://yui.yahooapis.com/3.5.0/build/yui/yui-min.js"></script>
<script>
YUI().use('node', function (Y) {
    var frame = document.getElementById('frame'),
        win = frame.contentWindow,
        doc = frame.contentWindow.document;

    YUI({ win: win, doc: doc }).use('node', function (innerY) {
```

```
            var innerBody = innerY.one('body');
            innerBody.addClass('foo');
            innerBody.append('<p>YUI3 was loaded!</p>');

            Y.use('event', function () {
                innerY.use('event', function () {
                    innerBody.on('click', function () {
                        innerBody.replaceClass('foo', 'bar');
                    });
                });
            });
        });
    });
</script>
```

If your application makes heavy use of iframes, consider using `Y.Frame`, a utility included in the YUI Rich Text Editor widget.

See Also

"Security in Depth: Local Web Pages" (*http://blog.chromium.org/2008/12/security-in -depth-local-web-pages.html*) and Chromium Issue 47416 (*http://code.google.com/p/ chromium/issues/detail?id=47416*), which describe the Chrome team's security concerns around local files, JavaScript, and frames; Andrew Wooldridge's "Hidden YUI Gem—Frame" (*http://andrewwooldridge.com/blog/2011/04/14/hidden-yui-gem-frame/*), which discusses a handy utility for working with iframes.

1.20 Implementing Static Loading

Problem

You want to improve YUI's initial load time by first loading all the modules you need in a single HTTP request, then attaching all modules to the Y instance at once.

Solution

Use the YUI Configurator (*http://yuilibrary.com/yui/configurator/*) to handcraft a combo load URL for the YUI seed file and the exact list of modules you need. Then use this URL to fetch all YUI code in a single HTTP request. Once the code has downloaded, call `use('*')` to attach all YUI modules in the registry.

Ordinarily, the callback function passed into `use()` executes asynchronously after YUI calculates dependencies and fetches any missing resources. However, if you know that you have already loaded all modules you need onto the page, you can provide the special value `'*'` to `use()`, as shown in Example 1-23. This special value means that all necessary modules have already been loaded statically, and instructs YUI to simply attach every module in the registry to the Y. Even conditional modules, described in Recipe 1.15, get attached right away—regardless of the results of their `test` function.

Example 1-23. Loading node-base and dependencies statically

```
<!DOCTYPE html>
<title>Loading node-base and dependencies statically</title>

<div id="demo"></div>

<script type="text/javascript" src="http://yui.yahooapis.com/combo?
3.5.0/build/yui-base/yui-base-min.js&3.5.0/build/oop/oop-min.js&
3.5.0/build/event-custom-base/event-custom-base-min.js&
3.5.0/build/features/features-min.js&3.5.0/build/dom-core/dom-core-min.js&
3.5.0/build/dom-base/dom-base-min.js&3.5.0/build/selector-native/selector-native-min.js&
3.5.0/build/selector/selector-min.js&3.5.0/build/node-core/node-core-min.js&
3.5.0/build/node-base/node-base-min.js&3.5.0/build/event-base/event-base-min.js"></script>
<script>
YUI({
    bootstrap: false,
}).use('*', function (Y) {
    Y.one('#demo').setHTML('Real Programmers manage their dependencies manually.');
});
</script>
```

For good measure, the example sets `bootstrap` to `false`, which prevents the Loader from filling in any missing dependencies.

> This technique can improve performance, but not without tradeoffs. For more information, refer to this recipe's Discussion.

Discussion

Static loading is yet another tool in your toolbox for managing application performance.

The YUI module system is designed to break large frameworks into tiny, digestible chunks that can be loaded asynchronously. This flexibility provides a huge performance advantage over monolithic libraries that force you to download the entire API whether you need it or not.

However, while dynamically constructing a custom library improves performance tremendously, it brings its own performance cost. First, calculating dependencies does not come for free. It is reasonably fast when done on the client side and very fast when done on the server side, but the cost is not zero. Second, loading YUI requires a minimum of two HTTP requests: one call to load the YUI seed file and one call to fetch the combo-loaded YUI modules.

If you are willing to throw the flexibility of the module system away, it is possible to squeeze a little extra performance from YUI. By listing all modules in the combo load URL, you can fetch everything in a single HTTP request and eliminate the need to calculate dependencies.

The disadvantage of this technique is that you are now responsible for managing your own dependencies across your entire application. If you want to upgrade to a new YUI minor version, add a YUI module to support a new feature, or remove a module that is no longer needed, you must recalculate your dependencies and update all your combo URLs yourself. If different pages might have different module requirements, you will have to maintain multiple distinct combo URLs. Static loading also makes it harder to take advantage of capability-based loading and other advanced techniques. If you are considering static loading, be sure to measure the real-world performance difference and weigh it against these increased maintenance costs.

CHAPTER 2

DOM Manipulation

The *document object model* (DOM) is not a particularly pleasant API to program against.

The main reason for this is that historically, browser DOM implementations have been incredibly buggy and inconsistent. Although JavaScript itself has its share of design flaws, many common complaints about JavaScript are actually complaints about the DOM.

A perhaps less appreciated reason is that the DOM is a low-level API that exposes only basic capabilities. By design, low-level APIs avoid making too many assumptions about how developers might want to use the underlying objects. Certain popular DOM extensions such as `innerHTML` and `querySelector` could be considered more mid-level, as they evolved based on what developers were actually doing.

JavaScript libraries have the advantage of being free to provide higher-level APIs that are more intuitive and terse than the lower-level DOM. However, each library comes with a strong mental model for how to work with the DOM. It would be a mistake to bake those models deeply into the DOM itself. (Imagine how unhappy jQuery developers would be if the only way to work with the DOM was the YUI way, or vice versa.)

In any case, the rise of JavaScript libraries has made it far easier to manipulate the DOM. A good DOM abstraction layer can:

- Correct for bugs and implementation differences in specific browsers. YUI accomplishes this using *feature detection* (testing for the existence of a feature) and *capability detection* (verifying whether the feature works properly). If a behavior is missing or incorrect, YUI corrects the problem. YUI's sophisticated Loader can fetch extra code to correct bugs, if and only if that code is needed.

- Enable you to use advanced features from newer specifications, even if the browser doesn't implement those features natively. If the feature is present, YUI uses the fast native implementation. If not, YUI implements the feature in JavaScript, providing you with a uniform interface.

- Provide a much more pleasant and capable API. Although stock DOM methods can get the job done, YUI and other frameworks offer friendly façades and helper methods that provide powerful capabilities with only a small amount of code.

Before JavaScript libraries, most web developers would learn about browser bugs the hard way, slowly building up their own personal bag of tricks. Individual browser bugs are not always difficult to work around, but some bugs are nastier than others, and it takes a special kind of thick-headedness to want to spend your time solving the cross-browser problem in general. Fortunately, YUI and its cousins all bake in years of hard-won experience around writing portable code, freeing up your time for the fun stuff—actually writing your application.

Recipe 2.1 describes how to retrieve a single element reference using CSS selector syntax. This recipe introduces the Node object, a façade that provides a consistent, easy-to-use API for working with the DOM. Whenever this book refers to a Node object, it is referring to a YUI node as opposed to a native DOM node (unless explicitly stated otherwise).

Recipe 2.2 explains how to manipulate CSS classes. For this common operation, YUI supplies sugar methods that properly handle elements with multiple classes.

Recipe 2.3 demonstrates how to exercise the Node API to get and set element attributes.

Recipe 2.4 explains how to use the browser's internal HTML parser to serialize and deserialize string content in and out of the DOM.

Recipe 2.5 covers CSS selectors that return multiple nodes as a NodeList object. You can iterate through a NodeList and operate on individual Node objects, or you can use the NodeList to perform bulk operations on every member.

Recipe 2.6 describes how to create new elements in the DOM. This is one of the fundamental operations that enable you to construct and display complex widgets and views.

Finally, Recipes 2.7 and 2.8 describe how to augment the Node API itself. This is something of a power-user feature, but it is straightforward enough to consider using in your own applications.

2.1 Getting Element References

Problem

You want to retrieve a reference to an element so that you can manipulate the element further.

Solution

Use a CSS selector with the Y.one() method to retrieve a single Node reference.

Loading Example 2-1 in a browser displays an unimpressive blank page. The code retrieves a `Node` reference to the demo `<div>` element, but doesn't actually do any work with that reference. Don't worry—in Recipe 2.2, the example actually starts calling `Node` methods, and things will get a little more interesting.

Example 2-1. Getting an element by ID

```
<!DOCTYPE html>
<title>Getting an element by ID</title>

<div id="demo"></div>

<script src="http://yui.yahooapis.com/3.5.0/build/yui/yui-min.js"></script>
<script>
YUI().use('node', function (Y) {
    var demo = Y.one('#demo');
});
</script>
```

Discussion

`Y.one()` is your standard entry point for manipulating the DOM with YUI. Example 2-1 illustrates one of the most common patterns, retrieving a single node by its unique ID. This is like the workhorse DOM method `document.getElementById()`, with two key differences:

- `Y.one()` is shorter.
- `Y.one()` returns a YUI `Node` façade object that wraps the underlying native DOM `Element` object.

However, `Y.one()` doesn't just mimic `document.getElementsById()`. As shown in Example 2-2, `Y.one()` takes any CSS selector, returning the first node that matches. If the selector fails to match any elements, `Y.one()` returns `null`. This enables you to sift through the DOM using familiar CSS selector syntax. This technique wasn't conceived of when the DOM was originally designed, but it has proven to be so useful that most browsers now offer native support.

There is a counterpart to `Y.one()` named `Y.all()`, which returns all nodes that match the selector. For more information, refer to Recipe 2.5.

Example 2-2. Getting an element with various selectors

```
<!DOCTYPE html>
<title>Getting an element with various selectors</title>

<div id="demo" dir="rtl"></div>

<script src="http://yui.yahooapis.com/3.5.0/build/yui/yui-min.js"></script>
<script>
YUI().use('node', function (Y) {
    var aDiv1 = Y.one('#demo');        // the demo <div>
    var aDiv2 = Y.one('div');          // the demo <div> (the first and only <div>)
```

```
    var aDiv3 = Y.one('body div.bar');  // null; there's no <div class="bar">
    var aScript = Y.one('body script'); // the first <script> in the <body>
    var aDiv4 = Y.one('html > div');    // null; there's no <div> direct child of <html>
    var aDiv5 = Y.one('body > div');    // the demo <div> again
    var aDiv6 = Y.one('div[dir=rtl]');  // the demo <div> one last time
});
</script>
```

If you pass in a CSS selector that matches multiple elements, Y.one() returns the first match. By default, YUI keeps its selector engine light by using CSS 2.1 as its baseline. If you need the extra power of CSS3 selectors, load the optional selector-css3 module.

Y.one() returns a YUI Node instance, which smooths over browser inconsistencies and offers a more capable interface than the native DOM Node and DOM Element. Once you have a YUI Node reference, you can:

- Add classes to the node by calling addClass(), as described in Recipe 2.2
- Hide the node by calling hide(), as described in Recipe 3.1
- Remove the node from its parent entirely by calling remove()
- Destroy the node, all its children, and remove all its plugins and event listeners by calling destroy(true)
- Change the node's properties by calling set(), as described in Recipe 2.3
- Move the node on the page by calling setXY(), which normalizes element positions to use YUI's unified, cross-browser coordinate system

and perform *many* other operations, as described in the Node API.

You can often chain methods when working with Node. For example, instead of doing:

```
var demo = Y.one('#demo');
demo.remove();
```

to retrieve the Node reference and then remove the node from the document, you can chain these operations:

```
Y.one('#demo').remove();
```

From any given node, you can walk down the DOM tree by calling one() or all() on the node itself. This returns the first child node (or a list of multiple child nodes) that matches the selector. To walk up the tree, call ancestor() or ancestors() on the node; this returns the first ancestor node (or a list of multiple ancestor nodes) that matches the selector. To walk sideways, call next() or previous(). The next() and previous() methods are like native DOM nextSibling() and previousSibling(), but they always return a sibling element as a YUI node, and they ignore adjacent text nodes in all browsers.

Alternatively, you can walk the DOM by successively calling get("parentNode") or get("children"). For more information about get(), refer to Recipe 2.3.

The input for `Y.one()` can take a CSS selector string or a native `HTMLElement`. You can use this to create methods that accept flexible input by filtering arguments through `Y.one()`:

```
function foo(node, bar) {
    node = Y.one(node);
    if (node) { ...
```

In addition to the `Node` API methods, a `Node` is also a YUI `EventTarget`. Among other things, this means you can attach event listeners to the element by calling the `on()` method. Chapters 3 and 4 discuss events in detail.

Every YUI node wraps a native DOM object, which you can retrieve by calling `getDOMNode()`, as shown in Recipe 3.6. YUI uses this pattern of wrapping native objects in façade objects throughout the library, in Recipe 2.5, in Chapter 4, and elsewhere.

 Use caution when mixing the YUI `Node` API with native DOM operations, particularly destructive native DOM operations. For example, if an event handler holds a YUI `Node` reference, and you destroy the underlying native DOM node with a native `innerHTML` assignment or similar operation, this can lead to memory leaks.

See Also

The `Node` User Guide (*http://yuilibrary.com/yui/docs/node/*).

2.2 Manipulating CSS Classes

Problem

You want to dynamically change one or more classes on an element.

Solution

Call `Node`'s `addClass()` and `removeClass()` methods to add and remove classes without affecting other classes on the element.

Example 2-3 correctly adds and removes classes without clobbering the original `garish` class. Note that you do not need to wrap `addClass()` or `removeClass()` in a `hasClass()` check, as these methods perform this check for you internally.

Example 2-3. Manipulating CSS classes

```
<!DOCTYPE html>
<title>Manipulating CSS classes</title>
<style>
.garish { color: #f00; }
.moregarish { background: #0f0; }
```

```
.ohpleasegodno { text-decoration: blink; overflow-x: -webkit-marquee; }
</style>

<div id="demo" class="garish ohpleasegodno">Things could always be worse...</div>

<script src="http://yui.yahooapis.com/3.5.0/build/yui/yui-min.js"></script>
<script>
YUI().use('node', function (Y) {
    var div = Y.one('#demo');

    div.addClass('moregarish');
    if (div.hasClass('moregarish')) {
        Y.log('Lime green FTW!');
    }
    div.removeClass('ohpleasegodno');
});
</script>
```

Discussion

The native DOM attribute `className` enables you to easily set an element's class to whatever value you like. However, since elements may have multiple classes in any order, blindly getting and setting `className` is usually a bad idea. `hasClass()`, `addClass()`, and `removeClass()` all correctly handle multiple class names on an element.

In addition to those methods, `Node` provides `replaceClass()` for swapping one class for another, and `toggleClass()` for alternately adding and removing a class. All five methods are also available on the `NodeList` API, enabling you to manipulate classes in bulk. For more information, refer to Recipe 2.5.

Alternatively, you can change an element's appearance by calling `setStyle()` to set an individual CSS declaration, or do a mass string assignment of all CSS declarations by calling `setStyles()`. However, `addClass()` is a more powerful technique because it avoids hardcoding presentation information in JavaScript. `setStyle()` is arguably useful as a quick way to toggle an element between `display:block` and `display:none`, but YUI provides sugar methods for hiding elements, as described in Recipe 3.1.

For most widgets and views, you will want to make a distinction between "core" styles and "skin" styles. For example, in a floating overlay or lightbox, `position:absolute` is a core style, and `background-color:silver` is a skin style. Both types of styles should be encapsulated in classes. `setStyle()` is not ideal for manipulating skin styles. In some cases you can use `setStyle()` with core styles, but often it is better to use higher-level methods such as `hide()`, `show()`, and `setXY()`.

When it comes to controlling presentation, you can get even more abstract than calling `addClass()`. For example, all YUI widgets have a `visible` attribute that, when set to `false`, adds the class yui3-*widget name*-hidden to the bounding box. However, this class doesn't include any CSS rules by default; it simply flags the widget as "hidden" and enables you, the designer of the widget, to choose what that means. It could mean `display:none`, an animated fade, minimizing the widget into an icon, or anything else. For more information about widgets, refer to Chapter 8.

2.3 Getting and Setting DOM Properties

Problem

You want to change a link on the fly to point to a new location.

Solution

Use `Node`'s `set()` method to set the link's `href` property, as shown in Example 2-4.

Example 2-4. Setting DOM properties

```
<!DOCTYPE html>
<title>Setting DOM properties</title>

<a id="demo">Quo vadimus?</a>

<script src="http://yui.yahooapis.com/3.5.0/build/yui/yui-min.js"></script>
<script>
YUI().use('node', function (Y) {
    Y.one('#demo').set('href', 'http://yuilibrary.com');
});
</script>
```

`Node` has an equivalent `get()` method that retrieves the value of a DOM property as a string.

Discussion

The `get()` and `set()` methods are generic YUI methods for viewing and modifying DOM properties. A DOM property is a JavaScript concept that is related to, but not quite the same thing as, an HTML attribute. For example, the native DOM property `src`:

```
someImg.src = 'http://example.com/foo.gif';
```

is related to the HTML attribute `src`:

```
<img src="http://example.com/foo.gif">
```

However, in general the relationship is not one-to-one. An image's DOM properties include (but are *definitely* not limited to): align, alt, border, className, height, hspace, id, innerHTML, isMap, parentNode, src, tagName, useMap, vspace, and width. From this list, you can see that:

- Many properties, such as src and border, correspond directly to an HTML attribute name

- Some properties, such as className, map to an HTML attribute but under a different name

- Other properties, such as parentNode and innerHTML, have no corresponding HTML attribute

- Some HTML attributes, such data-* attributes, currently have no corresponding DOM property

 To make matters more confusing, although most JavaScript developers refer to img.src and img.innerHTML as DOM "properties," the official W3C terminology for img.src and img.innerHTML is in fact DOM "attributes" (*http://www.w3.org/TR/DOM-Level-2-HTML/html.html#ID -642250288*) . This book refers to them as "properties."

If a property represents a Node or a NodeList, get() retrieves the YUI wrapper object (Node or NodeList) rather than a native DOM object. Unless you explicitly call getDOM Node() to get the underlying native object, YUI always maintains the Node façade.

Unfortunately, the exact property list varies from element to element and from browser to browser. Most browsers support a large set of properties defined by the W3C, plus a few useful nonstandard ones. Recent W3C specifications have folded in some popular extensions, such as innerHTML.

In addition to get() and set() for manipulating DOM properties, Node also provides getAttribute(), setAttribute(), and removeAttribute() for manipulating HTML attributes. These YUI methods are thin wrappers around the native methods of the same name, but have slightly different semantics:

- Calling get() on a DOM property that does not exist returns undefined. Calling set() on a made-up property has no effect. get() and set() also support several useful properties that cannot be accessed via getAttribute() and setAttribute(), such as text, children, and options.

- Calling getAttribute() on an HTML attribute that does not exist returns an empty string. This adheres to the W3C DOM specification, correcting for the fact that native browser implementations of getAttribute() actually return null in this case. Calling setAttribute() on a made-up attribute works just fine. This means you can use getAttribute() and setAttribute() to store string metadata on nodes. However, a better approach would be to use getData() and setData(), which stores data on the YUI façade object and avoids disturbing the DOM. You can also use getAttribute() and setAttribute() (but *not* get() and set()) to access the new data-* HTML5 attributes.

See Also

Recipes 8.7 and 8.8 for working with data-* attributes; Recipe 11.4 to see the setAttrs() sugar method and the removeAttribute() method setting up and tearing down multiple attributes at once; Marko Dugonjić's blog post, "The Difference Between *href* and *getAttribute('href')* in JavaScript" (*http://www.maratz.com/blog/archives/2005/08/29/the-difference-between-href-and-getattributehref-in-javascript/*).

2.4 Changing an Element's Inner Content

Problem

You want to retrieve an element's content and conditionally replace that content with something else.

Solution

Use Y.one() to get a node reference. Then call the getHTML() method to inspect the element's inner content as a string, followed by setHTML() to change the element's contents. If the demo <div> is empty, the script immediately replaces the contents with a different string. See Example 2-5.

Example 2-5. Changing an element's inner content

```
<!DOCTYPE html>
<title>Changing an element's inner content</title>

<div id="demo"></div>

<script src="http://yui.yahooapis.com/3.5.0/build/yui/yui-min.js"></script>
<script>
YUI().use('node', function (Y) {
    var demo = Y.one('#demo'),
        hi = '<em>HELLO</em> from the ' + demo.get('tagName')
            + ' with id=' + demo.get('id');

    if (demo.getHTML() === '') {
        demo.setHTML(hi);
    }
});
</script>
```

The <em> and </em> tags in the string get parsed and written into the DOM as an <em> element. As an alternative to calling setHTML(), you can get and set the innerHTML DOM property:

```
if (demo.get('innerHTML') === '') {
    demo.set('innerHTML', hi);
}
```

 Methods like setHTML() and set('innerHTML') are insecure when used for non-HTML strings or strings whose actual content or origin is unknown. When you need to guard against unknown content, you can use set('text'). See also Y.Escape, discussed in Recipe 9.13.

Discussion

First introduced by Internet Explorer, innerHTML has long been standard equipment in browsers, and has recently been codified as a standard. innerHTML is a powerful feature that grants you direct access to the browser's fast HTML parser, serializing and de-serializing strings in and out of the DOM.

Some browsers have buggy implementations of innerHTML that behave strangely in cases where HTML has implicit "wrapper" elements. For example, some browsers might fail if you use innerHTML to insert a <tr> string directly into a <table> without a <tbody> wrapper. YUI uses feature detection to make innerHTML safer to use, adding wrapper elements for browsers that require it.

The setHTML() method is a YUI sugar method. It has the same semantics as innerHTML, but it first walks old child nodes and cleanly detaches them from the parent. The more aggressive innerHTML simply destroys and replaces the old elements. Using setHTML() is a bit slower, but it avoids breaking references to the old nodes and prevents memory leaks in old versions of Internet Explorer.

An alternative approach for creating elements is to use Y.Node.create() to create individual Node objects. For a comparison of setHTML(), Y.Node.create(), and other methods for modifying the DOM, refer to Recipe 2.6.

2.5 Working with Element Collections

Problem

You want to add the class highlight to all list elements within the demo <div>.

Solution

Use Y.all() to retrieve a NodeList containing all list elements that match the criteria. Then call addClass() on the NodeList to add the class to each member Node, as shown in Example 2-6.

Example 2-6. Operating on a collection of elements

```
<!DOCTYPE html>
<title>Operating on a collection of elements</title>
```

```
<style>
.highlight { background: #c66; }
</style>

<div id="demo">
    <ul>
        <li>Apples</li>
        <li>Bananas</li>
        <li>Cherries</li>
    </ul>
    <ol>
        <li>Strawberries</li>
        <li>Tomatoes</li>
    </ol>
</div>

<script src="http://yui.yahooapis.com/3.5.0/build/yui/yui-min.js"></script>
<script>
YUI().use('node', function (Y) {
    var listItems = Y.all('#demo li');
    listItems.addClass('highlight');
});
</script>
```

If you didn't need to reuse the reference to the NodeList later on, an even more compact solution would be to replace the two lines of JavaScript with simply:

```
Y.all('#demo li').addClass('highlight');
```

Discussion

In Example 2-1, Y.one() retrieved a Node instance representing the *one* element matched by the "#demo" CSS selector:

```
var demo = Y.one('#demo');
```

Similarly, Example 2-6 uses Y.all() to retrieve a NodeList instance representing *all* the elements matched by the "#demo li" CSS selector:

```
var listItems = Y.all('#demo li');
```

If the selector fails to match any elements, Y.all() returns an empty NodeList. This enables you to safely do things like Y.all('script').remove() to remove all <script> elements—if there are no <script> elements on the page, nothing happens.

This is deliberately different behavior from Y.one(), which returns null if no match is found. Y.one() is designed to make it easy to perform node existence tests, while Y.all() is designed to make it easy to do bulk operations. YUI is interesting in that it has two abstractions for fetching DOM nodes. Some libraries rely on a single abstraction (reaching into the DOM always returns a collection), but the choice of Y.one() and Y.all() enables you to write cleaner code—you know ahead of time whether you will receive a single node or a collection.

As the suffix "List" implies, NodeList is an arraylike collection, providing methods such as pop(), shift(), push(), indexOf(), and slice(). NodeList also includes a subset of the more popular Node methods, such as addClass(), on(), and remove(). This enables you to perform bulk operations on every member node in only a few lines of code, without having to manually loop over the NodeList's contents. For example:

- Y.all(*selector*).on(*type, fn*) attaches an event listener to every element matched by the selector. However, it is often better to use event delegation, described in Recipe 4.5.
- Y.all(*selector*).transition(*config*) runs a CSS Transitions-based animation on every element matched by the selector. For more information about the YUI Transition API, refer to Chapter 3.
- Y.all(*selector*).each(*fn*) executes an arbitrary function on each element matched by the selector.

The one() and all() methods are also available on each Node object. The difference is that calling Y.all(*selector*) queries the entire document for matches, while calling *node*.all(*selector*) restricts the query to search only through that node's descendants. For an example of this in action, refer to Example 2-8.

See Also

Recipe 9.2, which describes some useful static Y.Array methods that also work with NodeLists.

2.6 Creating New Elements

Problem

You want to create a new element and add it to the document.

Solution

Retrieve a Node instance and call append(*child*) to add the new node to the document as a child of the selected node, as shown in Example 2-7.

Example 2-7. Creating a new element and adding it to the DOM

```
<!DOCTYPE html>
<title>Creating a new element and adding it to the DOM</title>

<div id="demo"></div>

<script src="http://yui.yahooapis.com/3.5.0/build/yui/yui-min.js"></script>
<script>
YUI().use('node', function (Y) {
    Y.one('#demo').append("<h1>Don't Forget the Heading!</h1>");
```

```
});
</script>
```

Alternatively, create the node and then call appendTo(*selector*) on the new node:

```
var heading = Y.Node.create("<h1>Don't Forget the Heading!</h1>");
heading.appendTo('#demo');
```

Discussion

Creating new elements is a key operation in any web application. For example, if you inject a visible widget onto a page, the widget is responsible for bootstrapping itself into existence by creating, modifying, and appending elements into the document as needed.

Many developers use a design strategy called *progressive enhancement* to ensure that their pages provide at least basic functionality when JavaScript is turned off or broken. The idea is to first provide a working skeleton of static markup and only *then* enhance the page's behavior with JavaScript. Certain types of projects such as games, bookmarklets, or internal business applications might not need progressive enhancement, but in general, failing to follow this strategy can lead to costly errors. YUI includes several patterns that directly or indirectly support progressive enhancement, such as feature detection and Widget's HTML_PARSER attribute, described in Recipe 7.5.

Even today, many older tutorials and scripts rely on the document.write() method, which compiles strings into elements and writes those elements into the DOM as the document is loading. Calling document.write() after the document has loaded wipes out and replaces the entire page content, which can lead to surprising bugs. Calling document.write() before the document has loaded makes it difficult for the browser to optimize how it fetches resources and renders the page.

YUI's Node API provides much better approaches than document.write() for creating new elements. These approaches fall into several families:

- The static Y.Node.create() method, which creates a new node disconnected from the document. This is the workhorse method for creating Y.Node objects in YUI.
- cloneNode(), which can create a shallow copy of a Y.Node (only copy the open and close tags) or a deep copy (copy all attributes and internal contents). Cloning is a useful optimization when you need to create several similar nodes: use Y.Node.create() to create a template node, and then clone the template. Like Y.Node.create(), cloned nodes are created outside the document.
- setHTML() and the innerHTML DOM property, discussed in Recipe 2.4. These methods use the browser's HTML parser to compile a string into elements and insert those elements into the DOM all in one step, completely replacing the element's inner contents.

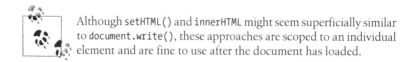 Although setHTML() and innerHTML might seem superficially similar to document.write(), these approaches are scoped to an individual element and are fine to use after the document has loaded.

- appendChild(), insertBefore(), and replaceChild(). These are YUI DOM façade methods. They act like the similarly named native DOM methods, but return YUI Node objects. Use these methods if you feel more comfortable working with an API that looks more like the DOM.

- append(), prepend(), insert(), and replace(). These are YUI sugar methods. In addition to having shorter names, they are also chainable. These methods can either attach existing Node objects, or compile strings into objects and then attach the results.

Y.Node.create() and cloneNode() involve a two-step process: first you create the Node objects you want, and then you assemble them into a tree and add them to the document with append() or a similar method. Appending a tree of Node objects into the document makes them visible, but requires the browser to run an expensive reflow and repaint operation. It is therefore best to use append() "off document" to completely assemble a Node structure, then perform a final append() to add the entire structure into the document in one operation.

The other approach is to pass raw strings of HTML into innerHTML, setHTML(), or append() and its cousins. It can be very efficient to serialize strings directly into the DOM without needing to mess with intermediate Node objects. However, if you want to manipulate the nodes later, you must then incur the overhead of flagging the markup to be locatable (by adding classes and IDs) and calling Y.one() or Y.all() to get node references. The more methodical Y.Node.create() ensures that you already have references to everything you need. Often, the choice between compiling and parsing HTML strings versus assembling nodes as objects boils down to which approach yields the cleanest code.

See Also

Mike Davies on the costs of ignoring progressive enhancement (*http://isolani.co.uk/blog/javascript/BreakingTheWebWithHashBangs*).

2.7 Adding Custom Methods to Nodes

Problem

You want to be able to determine whether an individual node contains one of the new elements that were added in the HTML5 specification.

Solution

Use `Y.Node.addMethod()` to add a `hasHTML5()` method to all `Node` objects, as shown in Example 2-8. `addMethod()` takes three arguments: the string name of the method to bind to `Node`, a function that actually becomes the method, and an optional context with which to call the method.

To determine whether an element is new in HTML5:

1. Define a string that lists all HTML5 element names. This string serves as a CSS selector.
2. Use `Node.all()` to return a `NodeList` of all child elements that match this selector. Within `addMethod()`, the `this` object refers to the YUI node where the method is operating, and the `domNode` parameter represents the native DOM object that underlies the YUI node.
3. Return `true` if any HTML5 elements were found; `false` otherwise.

Example 2-8. Adding the hasHTML5() method

```
<!DOCTYPE html>
<title>Adding the hasHTML5() method</title>

<article id="demo"><p>Hello</p></article>

<script src="http://yui.yahooapis.com/3.5.0/build/yui/yui-min.js"></script>
<script>
YUI().use('node', function (Y) {
    Y.Node.addMethod('hasHTML5', function(node) {
        var html5elements = 'article, aside, audio, bdi, canvas, command, ' +
            'datalist, details, figcaption, figure, footer, header, ' +
            'hgroup, keygen, mark, meter, nav, output, progress, rp, rt, ' +
            'ruby, section, source, summary, time, video, wbr';

        return (this.one(html5elements) !== null);
    });

    Y.log(Y.one('#demo').hasHTML5());
    Y.log(Y.one('body').hasHTML5());
});
</script>
```

 `Y.log()` logs debug messages to the browser console. For more information, refer to Recipe 12.1.

Strictly speaking, most HTML 4.01 elements are also HTML5 elements, so perhaps this method should have been named `hasNewInHTML5()` or the even more horrible `hasElementNewInHTML5()`.

Discussion

Having a Node façade makes it straightforward to augment the DOM. The YUI team uses Node to make it easy to fix browser bugs, normalize browser behaviors, and add features. There is no reason why you can't also use this abstraction layer for your own purposes.

When you use addMethod(), any values you return from your function automatically get normalized to maintain the façade:

- If you return a native DOM node, addMethod() wraps it as a YUI node.
- If you return a native DOM collection or array, addMethod() wraps it as a YUI NodeList.
- If you return some other value (other than undefined), the value passes through unaltered.
- If you declare no return value, addMethod() returns the underlying Node instance, which enables your method to be chained.

There is also an equivalent Y.NodeList.addMethod() for augmenting NodeLists. Any method you add in this manner will automatically get iterated over the NodeList's members when that method is called.

Augmenting Node with new methods is probably the kind of thing you should bundle into a module for reuse. For more information, refer to Recipe 1.8.

2.8 Adding Custom Properties to Nodes

Problem

To celebrate International Talk Like a Pirate Day (September 19), you want to create a custom property that provides the pirate-speak version of the element's text.

Solution

Add the property to Y.Node.ATTRS. A custom property is an object that contains a getter function, and optionally a setter function if the property is writable.

In Example 2-9, the getter function uses a simple object as a map for replacing English words with pirate-speak. It acts by:

1. Getting the Node's text property, which represents the plain-text content. The text property is a YUI abstraction over browser native properties such as inner Text and textContent. (Within Y.Node.ATTRS, the this object refers to the node in question.)

2. Creating an object to serve as a mapping between English words and pirate words. The mapping in Example 2-9 is pretty short; you should feel free to expand it.

3. Performing a `String.replace()` on the normal text. The regular expression matches all words in the string. For each word matched, `replace()` calls a function that replaces the word with a pirate word or leaves the word alone, depending on the contents of the map.

4. Returning the pirate text, with a bonus "Arrrr!" thrown in.

To prove that the property works, the example sets the demo `<div>`'s content to an English sentence, then immediately turns around and uses the `pirate` property to change the `<div>` to the pirate-speak equivalent.

Example 2-9. Adding a read-only pirate property

```
<!DOCTYPE html>
<title>Adding a read-only pirate property</title>

<div id="demo"></div>

<script src="http://yui.yahooapis.com/3.5.0/build/yui/yui-min.js"></script>
<script>
YUI().use('node', function (Y) {
    var demo = Y.one('#demo');

    Y.Node.ATTRS.pirate = {
        getter: function() {
            var normalText = this.get('text'),
                pirateMap = {'hello':'ahoy', 'my':'me', 'the':"th'",
                    'you':'ye', 'to':"t'", 'is':'be', 'talk':"be talkin'"},
                pirateText = normalText.replace(/\b\w*\b/g, function (word) {
                    return pirateMap[word] || word;
                });

            return pirateText + ' Arrrr!';
        }
    };

    demo.setHTML('It is fun to talk like a pirate!');
    demo.setHTML(demo.get('pirate'));
});
</script>
```

Discussion

Although converting an element's text to pirate-speak is an admittedly silly example, there are all sorts of other simple text transformations that you might want to implement as custom properties. For example, the ROT13 transformation replaces each letter with the letter 13 places further in the alphabet: *a* (letter 1) becomes *n* (letter 14), *u* (letter 21) wraps around to *h* (letter 8), and so on. ROT13 is useful for obscuring joke punchlines, plot spoilers, and answers to puzzles. Other possibly interesting transformations on node text include disemvowelling, reversing text, pretty-printing code in `<pre>` elements, and more.

Custom properties also don't necessarily have to revolve around the element's text content. For example, you could have designed the hasHTML5() method from Recipe 2.7 as a custom property with a getter function.

As with the hasHTML5() method described in Recipe 2.7, you should probably register the pirate property in a custom YUI module using YUI.add(). For more information, refer to Recipe 1.8.

Keep in mind that custom YUI node properties do not end up as custom properties in the DOM, so you can access them only by calling get() and set() on the YUI node. You cannot retrieve custom properties by accessing myNode.myProperty, either on the YUI node or the underlying native DOM node.

UI Effects and Interactions

Originally, JavaScript provided only small niceties like the occasional animation, fade, or rollover. Today's browsers have advanced to the point where it is possible to build and maintain sophisticated applications. But sometimes, the small niceties are all you need.

Many YUI developers are frontend engineers who tend to take an application-centric view of the code they are writing. The amount of work that goes into JavaScript dominates all else, and the HTML and CSS is something to tweak later or (hopefully) hand off to a designer.

But if you're a designer who codes, or you're working on a very content-heavy page, it might be the HTML and CSS that dominates. In this more page-centric view, the HTML page needs only some snippets of JavaScript to sprinkle in some user interface effects.

To support this kind of use case, YUI enables you to add interesting UI effects with little overhead. You can make an element draggable in one line of code. You can fade an element in response to a click in just three lines of code. You can perform an interesting sequence of animations in only a few lines of code.

In some ways, YUI is actually better suited for the page-centric world than you might expect. If the JavaScript is meant to be a light cosmetic addition to the page, then the worst thing you can do is load a huge monolithic library just to do a fade. YUI's flexible module system enables you to be far more selective about which components you load to create a particular effect.

Recipe 3.1 demonstrates how to hide and show an element immediately.

Recipe 3.2 introduces a slightly fancier approach to hiding and showing, by explaining how to gracefully fade an element in and out of visibility.

Recipe 3.3 builds on these concepts by introducing the YUI `Transition` API, which makes it easy to do basic DOM animations.

Recipe 3.4 demonstrates a more complicated transition that animates multiple properties on independent timers, and chains a second transition after the first.

Recipe 3.5 describes how to register slide effects and other custom transitions with YUI under a string name.

Recipe 3.6 uses the handy `Y.DOM.inViewportRegion()` to create a simple "infinite scroll" interaction.

Recipe 3.7 explains how to make an element draggable and several variations on this behavior. It also covers the concept of plugins, which are discussed in more detail in Chapter 8.

Recipe 3.8 introduces the `resize` module, an extension of the Drag and Drop (DD) API that makes elements and widgets resizable.

Recipe 3.9 provides a complete working example of a table with rows that you can reorder by dragging. In addition to showing how to use drop targets, this example introduces some new event-related concepts, such as inspecting the event object and using a central event manager for event handlers.

3.1 Hiding an Element

Problem

When the user clicks a button, you want to hide an element from view.

Solution

Use `Y.one()` to get the `<button>` and the `<div>` as a YUI node. Then add a `click` event listener to the button using `Node`'s `on()` method. When the user clicks the button, the callback function executes and calls `hide()` on the demo `<div>`. See Example 3-1.

Example 3-1. Hiding an element in response to a click

```
<!DOCTYPE html>
<title>Hiding an element in response to a click</title>
<style>
#demo { width: 100px; height: 100px; border: 1px #000 solid; background: #d72; }
</style>

<button id="hide">Hide</button>
<div id="demo"></div>

<script src="http://yui.yahooapis.com/3.5.0/build/yui/yui-min.js"></script>
<script>
YUI().use('node', function (Y) {
    var hideButton = Y.one('#hide'),
        demo = Y.one('#demo');

    hideButton.on('click', function () {
        demo.hide();
    });
```

```
});
</script>
```

If you use `Y.one()` inline, the code is even more compact:

```
YUI().use('node', function (Y) {
    Y.one('#hide').on('click', function () {
        Y.one('#demo').hide();
    });
});
```

Discussion

Not surprisingly, YUI offers a `show()` method as a counterpart to `hide()`. If you need to hide *and* show the `<div>`, add a second HTML `<button>` with an `id` of `show`. Then add another event listener:

```
YUI().use('node', function (Y) {
    Y.one('#hide').on('click', function () {
        Y.one('#demo').hide();
    });

    Y.one('#show').on('click', function () {
        Y.one('#demo').show();
    });
});
```

Technically speaking, you can always set `display: none` yourself by setting the style, as described in Chapter 2. Calling `hide()` is more elegant than setting the style manually, and it also offers some extra functionality as described in Recipe 3.2.

Nearly all page effects are triggered by some sort of *event*—a button click, a mouseover, or some other action by the user or the system. Most of the examples in this chapter use the `on()` method for setting an event listener on that node. This method takes a string representing the type of the event (such as `'click'` or `'mouseover'`) and a function to execute when the event occurs.

The `node` rollup exposes a small amount of event functionality via `on()`, but to get the full power of the YUI `Event` API, you must use `event-base` and related modules, or pull in the `event` rollup. For much more information about how the YUI event system works in general, refer to Chapter 4.

3.2 Fading an Element

Problem

You want to make an element disappear a little more gracefully, as having it disappear immediately is kind of jarring.

Solution

Use the hide() method as before, but load the transition module as well. Among other features, the transition module augments hide() and show() with additional functionality, enabling you to fade the element in and out by passing true to hide() and show(). See Example 3-2.

Example 3-2. Fading an element in response to a click

```
<!DOCTYPE html>
<title>Fading an element in response to a click</title>
<style>
#demo { width: 100px; height: 100px; border: 1px #000 solid; background: #d72; }
</style>

<button id="hide">Hide</button> <button id="show">Show</button>
<div id="demo"></div>

<script src="http://yui.yahooapis.com/3.5.0/build/yui/yui-min.js"></script>
<script>
YUI().use('node', 'transition', function (Y) {
    Y.one('#hide').on('click', function () {
        Y.one('#demo').hide(true);
    });

    Y.one('#show').on('click', function () {
        Y.one('#demo').show(true);
    });
});
</script>
```

Passing true to hide() and show() without loading the transition module has no effect.

Discussion

The transition module enables you to perform simple animations. It relies on the API defined by the CSS3 Transitions specification, which describes how to change CSS values over time. The YUI transition module presents you with the same API regardless of whether the browser supports CSS3 Transitions natively.

With the transition module enabled, hide() and show() support three optional arguments. You can invoke a fade by passing in true as the first argument to hide(). This activates a default transition that fades the element over a period of 0.5 seconds.

You can also change the behavior of the default fade. For example, you can change the duration by passing in a configuration object instead of true:

```
YUI().use('node', 'transition', function (Y) {
    Y.one('#hide').on('click', function () {
        Y.one('#demo').hide({ duration: 2.0 });
    });
```

```
        Y.one('#show').on('click', function () {
            Y.one('#demo').show({ duration: 1.5 });
        });
    });
```

This stretches the duration to 2.0 seconds for the hide(), and 1.5 seconds for the show(). In general, you can pass in:

- true, as in hide(true). This triggers hide()'s default transition. It is sugar for hide('fadeOut').

- A string name for a predefined transition, as in hide('fadeOut'). In addition to fadeIn and fadeOut, YUI also ships with a sizeIn and sizeOut transition, which means you can call hide('sizeOut') to shrink an element to oblivion. For more information about how to register your own custom transitions, refer to Recipe 3.5.

- An arbitrary transition object. For examples, refer to Recipes 3.3 and 3.4.

You can also provide a callback function to execute when the transition completes, as shown in Example 3-3. For example, when the hide() completes, you can remove the element from the DOM entirely by calling remove() on the node. As long as you save the node reference, you can still reverse the hide() operation by inserting the node back into the DOM and then calling show().

Example 3-3. Fading and removing an element in response to a click

```
YUI().use('node', 'transition', function (Y) {
    var demo = Y.one('#demo');

    Y.one('#hide').on('click', function () {
        demo.hide({ duration: 2.0 }, function () {
            demo.remove();
        });
    });

    Y.one('#show').on('click', function () {
        Y.one('#show').insert(demo, 'after');
        demo.show({ duration: 1.5 });
    });
});
```

The code is not symmetric—the node gets removed in a callback for demo.hide(), but it gets reinserted just before calling demo.show(). If you tried to make the show() code mirror the hide() code, then the <div> would appear to pop into existence after 1.5 seconds, which is not the desired effect.

See Also

Recipe 3.5; the CSS3 Transitions specification (*http://www.w3.org/TR/css3-transitions/*).

3.3 Moving an Element

Problem

You want to animate an element and move it across the page.

Solution

Set the element's CSS `position` property to `absolute`. Then load the `transition` module and call the node's `transition()` method, passing in a configuration object. As you can see in Example 3-4, the configuration object includes these properties:

`delay`
> An optional delay in seconds before starting the transition.

`duration`
> The time in seconds to run the transition.

`easing`
> The optional name of a predefined mathematical function for controlling the element's acceleration.

`left`
> The final state of the element's `left` CSS property. You can animate a large number of CSS properties, including the size, position, text color, and more.

Example 3-4. Moving an element across the screen

```
<!DOCTYPE html>
<title>Moving an element across the screen</title>
<style>
#demo {
    width: 100px; height: 100px; border: 1px #000 solid; background: #d72;
    position: absolute;
}
</style>

<div id="demo"></div>

<script src="http://yui.yahooapis.com/3.5.0/build/yui/yui-min.js"></script>
<script>
YUI().use('node', 'transition', function (Y) {
    Y.one('#demo').transition({
        delay: 1.0,
        duration: 2.0,
        easing: 'ease-in',
        left: '500px'
    });
});
</script>
```

Discussion

Calling hide(true) is convenient for simply fading an element. For more general access to CSS3 Transitions, use the transition() method.

JavaScript has always had timers and DOM manipulation, so it's easy to think about creating basic animations by changing an element in many small steps over a certain timeframe. But the devil is in the details. JavaScript timers are unreliable over short time slices. Constant DOM repaints are expensive and compete with myriad other tasks the browser might be trying to do. In short, creating robust, nonjittery animations in older browsers is not easy. CSS3 Transitions greatly simplifies DOM animations by natively handling many of these fiddly details for you.

Naturally, the YUI Transition API has you covered either way. For all browsers, YUI presents a consistent, friendly interface for configuring transitions. If the browser does not support transitions natively, YUI loads additional fallback code that implements the API in pure JavaScript.

The basic concept of CSS transitions is that over a certain duration, using a certain *easing function*, the transition() method transitions an element from one CSS state to another. The easing function, also known as a *transition timing function*, controls how the element accelerates from one CSS state to another over the specified time period. Here, the concept of "acceleration" doesn't just apply to the element's position. An element transitioning from red to green could stay red for most of the transition, then quickly accelerate into green—or vice versa. For a complete list of available timing functions and CSS properties you can animate, refer to the CSS3 Transitions specification.

Example 3-4 starts the animation one second after the page loads. You can, of course, trigger this from an event instead:

```
YUI().use('node', 'transition', function (Y) {
    var demo = Y.one('#demo');

    demo.on('mouseover', function () {
        demo.transition({
            duration: 2.0,
            easing: 'ease-in',
            left: '500px'
        });
    });
});
```

The transition() method can also animate different CSS properties independently. It is even possible to chain transitions together, as shown in Recipe 3.4.

 To simply jump an element to a new location without any animation, use the setXY() method. setXY() works on elements regardless of whether you remembered to set the CSS position.

See Also

The CSS3 Transitions specification's sections on transition timing functions (*http://www.w3.org/TR/css3-transitions/#transition-timing-function_tag*) and animatable properties (*http://www.w3.org/TR/css3-transitions/#animatable-properties-*).

3.4 Creating a Series of Transitions

Problem

You want to perform a series of transitions that work together to create an effect.

Solution

Use durations and delays to animate CSS properties independently. In the configuration object, you can specify CSS properties as simple values. But if you specify a CSS property as an object, each CSS property can have its own delay, duration, and easing function that overrides the default.

In addition to playing tricks with durations and delays, Example 3-5 chains a second transition after the first one by creating an on object with an end function. YUI calls this event handler function after all animations in the first transition finish.

Example 3-5. A series of transitions

```
<!DOCTYPE html>
<title>A series of transitions</title>
<style>
#demo {
    width: 200px; height: 200px; border: 1px #000 solid; background: #d72;
    position: absolute;
    text-align: center;
    opacity: 0.3;
}
</style>

<div id="demo"></div>

<script src="http://yui.yahooapis.com/3.5.0/build/yui/yui-min.js"></script>
<script>
YUI().use('node', 'transition', function (Y) {
    var demo = Y.one('#demo');

    demo.transition({
        duration: 2.5,
        width: '100px',
        height: '100px',
        left: {
            easing: 'ease-in',
            value: '500px'
        },
```

```
        opacity: {
            delay: 1.0,
            duration: 1.75,
            value: 1.0
        },
        on: {
            start: function () {
                demo.setHTML("It's just a jump to the left...");
            },
            end: function () {
                demo.setHTML('And then a step to the riiight!');
                demo.transition({
                    duration: 2.0,
                    left: '0px',
                    easing: 'linear'
                });
            }
        }
    });
});
</script>
```

Discussion

Moving the <div> back and forth across the screen requires changing the left CSS property twice. Since you can't define the same property twice in the same configuration object, this requires calling another transition() function.

Naively, you might try chaining the second transition() immediately after the first, as in: node.transition({...}).transition({...}). Here the second transition() function gets called almost immediately after the first, so the two animations clobber each other. Instead, set the second transition() in an end callback, as shown in the example. This ensures that the second transition() picks up properly where the first one leaves off.

You can also use start and end to set and remove extra CSS properties that you need for the transition, such as overflow or position. For an example of this, refer to Recipe 3.5.

Use caution when trying out complex transitions in older browsers. The fallback code handles simple transitions smoothly, but more complex series of transitions can cause jumps and jitters. As mentioned in Recipe 3.3, emulating CSS transitions in pure Java-Script is inherently less precise than the real thing.

3.5 Defining Your Own Canned Transitions

Problem

You have a standard animation configuration that you want to use over and over, but passing the full config to transition() each time is cumbersome.

Solution

Append your named transition to the `Y.Transition.fx` object. Example 3-6 adds two named transitions: a `slideFadeIn` for hiding elements, and a `slideFadeOut` for reversing the operation. This registers the transition and enables you to refer to it by name, like `fadeIn` and `fadeOut`.

For this particular slide effect, the element must have its CSS `position` set to `relative`. The example uses the `start` callback to just clobber the element's `position` property, whatever it might be. A more sophisticated transition could be more careful about applying and removing this property.

Example 3-6. Defining a named slideFadeOut transition

```
<!DOCTYPE html>
<title>Defining a named slideFadeOut transition</title>
<style>
#demo { width: 100px; height: 100px; border: 1px #000 solid; background: #d72; }
</style>

<button id="hide">Hide</button>
<button id="show">Show</button>
<div id="demo"></div>

<script src='http://yui.yahooapis.com/3.5.0/build/yui/yui-min.js'></script>
<script>
YUI().use('node', 'transition', function (Y) {
    function setRelativePosition() {
        this.setStyle('position', 'relative');
    }

    Y.Transition.fx.slideFadeOut = {
        opacity: 0,
        right: '-100px',
        easing: 'ease-out',
        on: { start: setRelativePosition }
    };

    Y.Transition.fx.slideFadeIn = {
        opacity: 1.0,
        right: '0px',
        easing: 'ease-in',
        on: { start: setRelativePosition }
    };

    Y.one('#hide').on('click', function () {
        Y.one('#demo').hide('slideFadeOut');
    });

    Y.one('#show').on('click', function () {
        Y.one('#demo').show('slideFadeIn');
    });
});
</script>
```

Discussion

Registering a named transition makes it easy to reuse that code, particularly for people with less JavaScript expertise than you have. If you are a frontend engineer or lead prototyper, `Y.Transition.fx` makes it easy to register a whole host of canned transitions for other designers and prototypers on your team to use.

Example 3-6 demonstrates using named transitions in `hide()` and `show()`, but you can always use named transitions in a general `transition()` call as well.

To simplify things even further, you can redefine the default transition behavior of `hide()` and `show()`, as Example 3-7 illustrates. This enables your team to simply call `hide(true)` without having to care whether this causes a fade, resize, slide, or something more complex.

Example 3-7. Redefining the default hide and show transition

```
YUI().use('node', 'transition', function (Y) {
    function setRelativePosition() {
        this.setStyle('position', 'relative');
    }

    Y.Transition.fx.slideFadeOut = {
        opacity: 0,
        right: '-100px',
        easing: 'ease-out',
        on: { start: setRelativePosition }
    };

    Y.Transition.fx.slideFadeIn = {
        opacity: 1.0,
        right: '0px',
        easing: 'ease-in',
        on: { start: setRelativePosition }
    };

    Y.Transition.HIDE_TRANSITION = 'slideFadeOut';
    Y.Transition.SHOW_TRANSITION = 'slideFadeIn';

    Y.one('#hide').on('click', function () {
        Y.one('#demo').hide(true);
    });

    Y.one('#show').on('click', function () {
        Y.one('#demo').show(true);
    });
});
```

3.6 Creating an Infinite Scroll Effect

Problem

You want to create an "infinite scroll" interaction that appends new results as the user scrolls down the page.

Solution

Load the dom module, which provides the Y.DOM.inViewportRegion() method. Then define two functions: addContent(), which is responsible for adding new content to the page, and fillToBelowViewport(), which is responsible for calling addContent() until the last paragraph is no longer in the viewport.

Then add a scroll event listener that calls fillToBelowViewport() as the user scrolls. Finally, call addContent() to initially populate the page, followed by fillToBelow Viewport() to guarantee that the viewport starts out overfilled. The initial fillToBelow Viewport() might do nothing, depending on the size of the user's screen.

One slightly tricky aspect to inViewportRegion() is that Y.DOM is designed to work independently of YUI Node, which means its methods all operate on native HTMLElement objects. For convenience, Example 3-8 loads the Node API anyway. The scroll listener uses Y.one() to fetch a Node instance, and then calls getDOMNode() to get the underlying native HTMLElement object, to be passed into Y.DOM.inViewportRegion().

The YUI Node API also has a handy generateID() method, which the example uses to generate a unique ID on the last paragraph. Every time new content gets added, a new ID gets saved as a handle for use in the scroll listener.

Example 3-8. Creating an infinite scroll effect

```
<!DOCTYPE html>
<title>Creating an infinite scroll effect</title>
<style>
p { font-family: courier; color: #333; }
</style>

<div id="demo"></div>

<script src="http://yui.yahooapis.com/3.5.0/build/yui/yui-min.js"></script>
<script>
YUI().use('dom-core', 'node', function (Y) {
    var lastParaId;

    function addContent(numParas) {
        var i, content = '',
            para = '<p>All work and no play makes Jack a dull boy.</p>';

        for (i = 0; i < numParas; i += 1) {
            content += para;
        }
```

```
        Y.one('#demo').append(content);
        return Y.one('#demo p:last-child').generateID();
    }

    function fillToBelowViewport() {
        var lastPara = Y.one('#' + lastParaId).getDOMNode();
        if (Y.DOM.inViewportRegion(lastPara)) {
            lastParaId = addContent(10);
        }
    }

    Y.on('scroll', fillToBelowViewport);

    lastParaId = addContent(20);
    fillToBelowViewport();
});
</script>
```

Discussion

Example 3-8 is the skeleton of an infinite scroll interaction. Most real-world infinite scrolls use Ajax to fetch new content. Since Ajax requests can take a noticeable amount of time, you could add a spinner or some other animation to indicate that the page is fetching more data. You could also improve perceived performance by fetching Ajax data a bit earlier, perhaps by triggering off of an element a few positions *above* the last paragraph or by tracking scroll velocity.

Y.DOM contains a few methods for creating elements and manipulating classes, which means that in a pinch, you can use it as a lightweight substitute for the full YUI Node API. However, it is really more useful for doing things like checking whether an element is in a certain region or whether two elements intersect.

See Also

The ImageLoader User Guide (*http://yuilibrary.com/yui/docs/imageloader/*); YUI DOM API documentation (*http://yuilibrary.com/yui/docs/api/classes/DOM.html*).

3.7 Dragging an Element

Problem

You want to enable users to drag an element around the screen.

Solution

The easiest way to make an element draggable is to load the dd-drag module, create a new Y.DD.Drag instance, and configure that instance to work on a particular node, as shown in Example 3-9.

Example 3-9. Creating a draggable node

```
<!DOCTYPE html>
<title>Creating a draggable node</title>
<style>
#demo { width: 100px; height: 100px; border: 1px #000 solid; background: #d72; }
</style>

<div id="demo"></div>

<script src="http://yui.yahooapis.com/3.5.0/build/yui/yui-min.js"></script>
<script>
YUI().use('dd-drag', function (Y) {
    var dd = new Y.DD.Drag({ node: '#demo' });
});
</script>
```

Alternatively, you can load the `dd-plugin` module and plug the `Y.Plugin.Drag` plugin into the `Node` instance, as shown in Example 3-10. Every node exposes a method named `plug()` that can augment that node with additional behavior. Plugins enable you to add behavior to a YUI object in a reversible, nondestructive way.

Example 3-10. Creating a draggable node using a plugin

```
YUI().use('dd-plugin', function(Y) {
    Y.one('#demo').plug(Y.Plugin.Drag);
});
```

In YUI, a *plugin* is a specialized object designed to augment or change the behavior of another object. YUI has a specific interface for consuming plugins (the `plug()` and `unplug()` methods), and a dedicated API for writing plugins. For more information, refer to Recipes 7.7 and 7.8.

Discussion

When you create a `DD.Drag` instance, you can configure the drag behavior by passing a configuration object into the constructor. For example, if you want the element to be draggable only by a `<p>` handle within the `<div>`, you can configure that by setting the `handles` attribute, as Example 3-11 shows.

Example 3-11. Creating a draggable node with a handle

```
<!DOCTYPE html>
<title>Creating a draggable node with a handle</title>
<style>
#demo { width: 100px; height: 100px; border: 1px #000 solid; background: #d72; }
#demo p { margin: 0px; padding 3px; border-bottom: 1px #000 solid; background: #e9e; }
</style>

<div id="demo"><p>handle</p></div>

<script src="http://yui.yahooapis.com/3.5.0/build/yui/yui-min.js"></script>
```

```
<script>
YUI().use('dd-drag', function (Y) {
    var dd = new Y.DD.Drag({
        node: '#demo',
        handles: ['p']
    });
});
</script>
```

In addition to drag functionality, a DD.Drag instance gains new methods such as add
Handle() and stopDrag(). For example, an equivalent to Example 3-11 would be to
create the DD.Drag instance, then call the dd.addHandle() method:

```
YUI().use('dd-drag', function (Y) {
    var dd = new Y.DD.Drag({ node: '#demo' });
    dd.addHandle('p');
});
```

While DD.Drag defines a particular set of dragging functionality, you can change its
behavior by loading yet more modules and plugging plugins into the drag instance.

For example, by default the dragged element follows your mouse or finger around the
screen. To change the behavior so that the element stays in place and a "ghost" proxy
element follows the pointer around instead, load the dd-proxy module and plug the
drag instance with Plugin.DDProxy, as shown in Example 3-12.

Example 3-12. Creating a draggable-by-proxy node

```
<!DOCTYPE html>
<title>Creating a draggable-by-proxy node</title>
<style>
#demo { width: 100px; height: 100px; border: 1px #000 solid; background: #d72; }
</style>

<div id="demo"></div>

<script src="http://yui.yahooapis.com/3.5.0/build/yui/yui-min.js"></script>
<script>
YUI().use('dd-drag', 'dd-proxy', function (Y) {
    var dd = new Y.DD.Drag({ node: '#demo' });
    dd.plug(Y.Plugin.DDProxy);
});
</script>
```

You can also use a plugin to constrain the draggable area, as shown in Example 3-13.
(By default, the user can drag the element anywhere on the screen.) To constrain a
draggable element inside a container element, load the dd-constrain module, plug the
instance with the Plugin.DDConstrained plugin, and configure Plugin.DDConstrained to
use the box <div> as the container.

Example 3-13. Creating a constrained draggable node

```
<!DOCTYPE html>
<title>Creating a constrained draggable node</title>
<style>
#demo { width: 100px; height: 100px; border: 1px #000 solid; background: #d72; }
#box  { width: 400px; height: 300px; border: 1px #000 dashed; background: #ccc; }
</style>

<div id="box"><div id="demo"></div></div>

<script src="http://yui.yahooapis.com/3.5.0/build/yui/yui-min.js"></script>
<script>
YUI().use('dd-drag', 'dd-constrain', function (Y) {
    var dd = new Y.DD.Drag({ node: '#demo' });
    dd.plug(Y.Plugin.DDConstrained, { constrain2node: '#box' });
});
</script>
```

Plugins are powerful because you can mix and match them for different situations. Example 3-14 combines the functionality of Examples 3-12 and 3-13 to create a constrained draggable-by-proxy node.

Example 3-14. Creating a constrained draggable-by-proxy node

```
<!DOCTYPE html>
<title>Creating a constrained draggable-by-proxy node</title>
<style>
#demo { width: 100px; height: 100px; border: 1px #000 solid; background: #d72; }
#box  { width: 400px; height: 300px; border: 1px #000 dashed; background: #ccc; }
</style>

<div id="box"><div id="demo"></div></div>

<script src="http://yui.yahooapis.com/3.5.0/build/yui/yui-min.js"></script>
<script>
YUI().use('dd-drag', 'dd-proxy', 'dd-constrain', function (Y) {
    var dd = new Y.DD.Drag({ node: '#demo' });
    dd.plug(Y.Plugin.DDProxy);
    dd.plug(Y.Plugin.DDConstrained, { constrain2node: '#box' });
});
</script>
```

3.8 Creating a Resizable Node

Problem

You want to enable users to resize a node by dragging its edges and corners.

Solution

Make sure the node has a CSS position of relative, then plug it with Y.Plugin
.Resize, as shown in Example 3-15.

Example 3-15. Making an element resizable

```
<!DOCTYPE html>
<title>Making an element resizable</title>
<style>
#demo {
    width: 100px; height: 100px; border: 1px #000 solid; background: #d72;
    position: relative;
}
</style>

<div id="demo"></div>

<script src='http://yui.yahooapis.com/3.5.0/build/yui/yui-min.js'></script>
<script>
YUI().use('resize', function (Y) {
    var resize = new Y.Resize({ node: '#demo' });
});
</script>
```

Similar to Drag and Drop, an alternative to using the plugin approach is to create a new
Resize instance and configure it to work on a particular node:

```
YUI().use('resize-plugin', function (Y) {
    Y.one('#demo').plug(Y.Plugin.Resize);
});
```

Discussion

The Resize API uses the Drag and Drop API under the hood and has similar semantics.
You can use Resize as a plugin to a node or widget, or use it as a standalone instance.
Also like Drag and Drop, Resize supports resize constraints and resizing by proxy. For
instance, Example 3-16 uses a "plug the plugin" approach to constrain the resize to a
width between 50 and 200 pixels. The height is unconstrained. (That's right—plugins
are themselves pluggable.)

Example 3-16. Creating a constrained resizable node

```
YUI().use('resize-plugin', 'resize-constrain', function (Y) {
    var demo = Y.one('#demo');
    demo.plug(Y.Plugin.Resize);
    demo.resize.plug(Y.Plugin.ResizeConstrained, {
        minWidth: 50,
        maxWidth: 200
    });
});
```

When a user resizes an element, you can also listen for resize events that bubble up to the `Resize` instance (not the node the resize is acting on). Here, it's a little more convenient to create an explicit `Resize` instance rather than plugging the node. Example 3-17 illustrates how to toggle the node's appearance when the user starts and stops the resize.

Example 3-17. Responding to resize events

```
<!DOCTYPE html>
<title>Responding to resize events</title>
<style>
#demo {
    width: 100px; height: 100px; border: 1px #000 solid; background: #d72;
    position: relative;
}
#demo.resizing { background: #27d; }
</style>

<div id="demo"></div>

<script src='http://yui.yahooapis.com/3.5.0/build/yui/yui-min.js'></script>
<script>
YUI().use('resize', function (Y) {
    var resize = new Y.Resize({ node: '#demo' });
    resize.on('resize:start', function () {
        this.get('node').addClass('resizing');
    });
    resize.on('resize:end', function () {
        this.get('node').removeClass('resizing');
    });
});
</script>
```

Conveniently, the `Resize` instance stores a handle to the node it is acting on, which you can retrieve by calling `get('node')`. This handle is actually a YUI attribute, not to be confused with an HTML attribute. For more information about the `Attribute` API, refer to Recipe 7.1.

See Also

The `Resize` User Guide (*http://yuilibrary.com/yui/docs/resize/*); `Resize` API documentation (*http://yuilibrary.com/yui/docs/api/modules/resize.html*).

3.9 Implementing a Reorderable Drag-and-Drop Table

Problem

You want to enable the user to reorganize a table's rows using Drag and Drop.

Solution

Use `Y.all()` and `each()` to configure each row in the table body as a draggable node and as a drop target, as shown in Example 3-18. Constrain each row to the interior of the table, and set each row not only to be draggable by proxy, but to stay in place when the user drops the proxy on the target.

This means that there are three main elements of concern:

The dragged element
   The row the user is trying to drag, which stays in place

The proxy element
   A "ghost" row that follows the user's mouse or finger

The drop target
   The row that the proxy is hovering over, or that has been dropped on

After configuring drag and drop targets, use the Drag and Drop Manager, `Y.DD.DDM`, to handle events that bubble up from dragged elements and drop targets. The most important event is the `drop:hit` event, which fires when the user drops the element over a drop target. Here the handler function checks whether the proxy's midpoint was above or below the drop target's midpoint. Based on this check, it inserts the dragged element either before or after the drop target. The proxy automatically disappears, and the DOM change causes the browser to slide the dragged row into its new position. Other events such as `drag:start` and `drag:end` need listeners only for cosmetic reasons.

Example 3-18. Reorderable drag-and-drop table

```
<!DOCTYPE html>
<title>Reorderable drag-and-drop table</title>
<style>
table.dd {
    border: 1px #000 solid; border-spacing: 1px;
    background: #844; width: 25em;
}
table.dd th { background: #999; padding: 0.2em; }
table.dd td { background: #ddd; padding: 0.2em; }
table.dd td.over { background: #9c9; }
table.dd tr.being-dragged { opacity: 0.5; }
</style>

<table class="dd">
<thead>
    <tr><th>Type</th><th>From</th><th>Weaknesses</th></tr>
</thead>
<tbody>
    <tr><td>Vampires</td><td>Transylvania</td><td>Crosses, Garlic</td></tr>
    <tr><td>Werewolves</td><td>The Forest</td><td>Silver, Teen Angst</td></tr>
    <tr><td>Zombies</td><td>Unwise Experiments</td><td>Headshots</td></tr>
    <tr><td>Robots</td><td>The Distant Future</td><td>Illogic</td></tr>
    <tr><td>Ninjas</td><td>Feudal Japan</td><td>Dishonor</td></tr>
```

```
        <tr><td>Pirates</td><td>The High Seas</td><td>Rum</td></tr>
        <tr><td>Bob</td><td>Human Resources</td><td>None Known</td></tr>
    </tbody>
    </table>

    <script src="http://yui.yahooapis.com/3.5.0/build/yui/yui-min.js"></script>
    <script>
    YUI().use('dd-drag', 'dd-drop', 'dd-proxy', 'dd-constrain', function (Y) {
        var rows = Y.all('table.dd tbody tr');
        rows.each(function (row) {
            var rowDrop = new Y.DD.Drop({ node: row }),
                rowDrag = new Y.DD.Drag({ node: row });

            rowDrag.plug(Y.Plugin.DDConstrained, { constrain2node: 'table.dd' });
            rowDrag.plug(Y.Plugin.DDProxy, { moveOnEnd: false });
        });

        function midpoint(node) {
            return node.getY() + (node.get('offsetHeight') / 2);
        }

        Y.DD.DDM.on('drop:hit', function (ev) {
            var drop = ev.drop.get('node'),
                drag = ev.drag.get('node'),
                proxy = ev.drag.get('dragNode');

            if (midpoint(proxy) >= midpoint(drop)) {
                drop.insert(drag, 'after');
            }
            else {
                drop.insert(drag, 'before');
            }
            drop.all('td').removeClass('over');
        });

        Y.DD.DDM.on('drag:start', function (ev) {
            ev.target.get('node').addClass('being-dragged');
        });

        Y.DD.DDM.on('drag:end', function (ev) {
            ev.target.get('node').removeClass('being-dragged');
        });

        Y.DD.DDM.on('drop:over', function (ev) {
            ev.drop.get('node').all('td').addClass('over');
        });

        Y.DD.DDM.on('drop:exit', function (ev) {
            ev.target.get('node').all('td').removeClass('over');
        });
    });
    </script>
```

Discussion

If you've read Recipe 2.5, you should be familiar with using `Y.all()` and `NodeList` to work with a collection of nodes. The `each()` method applies a function to each node in the `NodeList`. Conveniently, the `<table>` markup supplies an explicit `<thead>` and `<tbody>`, making it easy to exclude the header rows in the `Y.all()`.

Chapter 4 discusses events in much more detail, but the key concept in Example 3-18 is `Y.DD.DDM`, which listens for all Drag and Drop custom events, signified with the prefix `drag:`. The Drag and Drop Manager provides a central point of control for handling Drag and Drop events. For more information about how to configure custom events to bubble up to a particular event target, refer to Recipe 4.7.

Each event handler function receives an event object representing the drag event. The event object provides a `target` object representing the node that is being acted upon, and the Drag and Drop API may further decorate the event object with a `drag` object, a `drop` object, and even a `dragNode` object (which can represent the proxy). This enables you to modify the relevant nodes as Drag and Drop events occur.

As mentioned in the solution, `drop:hit` is the core event handler that is actually responsible for inserting the row into a new location in the DOM. Keep in mind that if you want to implement a reorderable table, list, or anything else with YUI, you must use a Drag and Drop proxy and set `moveOnEnd` to `false`. When Drag and Drop moves a dragged node, it changes the node's `position` to be absolute and animates its *xy* coordinates appropriately. In a reorderable list or table, this is undesirable for two reasons.

First, as soon as the drag begins, the table will try to close on the missing row. You can solve this by using a proxy, preventing the table from closing on the row.

Second, when the user drops the row, the row continues to float at its current *xy* coordinates and will *look* incorrect, even if your code inserts the row into the correct DOM location. You can solve this by setting `moveOnEnd` to `false`, which prevents Drag and Drop from artificially changing the row's `position` and *xy* coordinates, and by listening for `drop:hit` as the signal to change the structure of the table. When the row drops, the browser simply reflows and displays all table rows in their natural, correct position.

The other event handlers are there to improve aesthetics and usability. For example, the `drag:start` handler clarifies which row is being dragged, while the `drop:over` handler highlights the current target to help the user see where the row will be dropped.

Some variations you could make to this recipe include:

- Instead of inserting the row into the DOM on a `drop:hit`, insert it into the DOM on every `drop:over` event. In this implementation, the dragged row appears to slide its way through its neighbors as the user drags the row around.
- The current implementation is a bit touchy when the user is trying to drag and insert an element at the top or bottom. You can make this action a little easier by expanding the possible drop targets beyond just the rows containing table data.

Events

Browser applications operate inside an *event loop*. The event loop is a browser thread that collects events such as mouse actions and keypresses and passes these events back to the JavaScript engine. To handle events, applications must register callback functions that *listen* or *subscribe to* different event types. Since events are the only way for applications to respond to user actions, they are a fundamental component in almost any client-side JavaScript program.

Event handling has evolved over the years, with browsers accreting different behaviors and quirks around working with events. Despite well-meaning attempts to clean things up, many of these inconsistencies persist to the present day. In fact, the `Event` API is arguably even more volatile between different browsers than the `Node` API. Any application that relies on events needs to protect itself against this volatility.

YUI addresses the problem using the same strategy described in Chapter 2: by wrapping event objects in a consistent façade that replicates the W3C DOM Level 2 `Event` object, with the exception that all native `HTMLElement` references are replaced with YUI `Node` references. The YUI event façade normalizes all sorts of browser inconsistencies around event propagation and event object properties.

Beyond offering normalization and more pleasant APIs, the YUI event façade opens up the possibility of defining entirely new event types. YUI supports four basic categories of events:

- DOM events, which enable your application to respond to user interactions
- Special DOM events, which enable you to subscribe to interesting moments as a page loads and renders
- Synthetic events, which enable you to define brand-new DOM events, expanding how users can communicate with your application
- Custom events, which enable components to communicate with each other by firing and subscribing to application-specific messages

Both synthetic events and custom events behave like ordinary DOM events, with the same API for attaching, detaching, delegating, and so on.

The ability to define new synthetic events and publish new custom events is one of the more powerful facets of YUI, right up there with the Loader (Chapter 1) and the Base object (Chapter 7). Custom events enable you to design your applications so that they harmonize with the browser's natural event-driven architecture. You can use custom events to implement the Observer pattern and other popular strategies for controlling message flow.

Recipe 4.1 explains how to subscribe to basic DOM events, such as clicks and mouseovers.

Recipe 4.2 describes how to subscribe to interesting moments in the lifecycle of an element or page, such as the moment when an element becomes available in the DOM.

DOM events propagate through the DOM in a certain prescribed manner, and often include some sort of default behavior, such as adding a character to a text field, or navigating the user away from the page. Recipes 4.3 and 4.4 explain how to interfere with these processes, either by stopping an event from bubbling up through the DOM or by preventing the event's default action.

Recipe 4.5 discusses *delegation*, a technique for efficiently managing large numbers of event subscriptions by delegating control to a parent container element.

Recipe 4.6 introduces custom events, which pass information around your application without involving the DOM. Recipe 4.7 demonstrates how to create more complex custom events and use them in a custom bubbling tree.

It is easy to use ordinary named functions or anonymous functions as event handlers, but object methods are tricky because assigning them as a handler causes them to lose their object context. Recipe 4.8 explains how to fix this problem by binding the method to the correct context.

Recipe 4.9 lists the many ways you can detach event subscriptions.

Recipe 4.10 describes the order in which event handlers execute, and introduces the after() method, an alternative event subscriber method that is useful when you are working with custom events.

Recipe 4.11 introduces synthetic events. Synthetic events behave like DOM events externally, but are internally a wrapper for other DOM events plus some custom logic.

Recipe 4.12 explains how to use YUI's aspect-oriented programming (AOP) API. This API is not strictly event-related, but it does enable you to apply behavior in response to some other behavior...which is *kind of* like responding to an event. But not really.

4.1 Responding to Mouseovers, Clicks, and Other User Actions

Problem

When the user hovers over a `<div>`, you want to change the element's background color.

Solution

Load the node rollup, then use `Y.one()` to select the node, followed by `Y.Node`'s `on()` method to set an event handler. The first argument of `on()` specifies the event to listen for—in this case, a `mouseover` event. The second argument provides an event handler function for YUI to execute when the event occurs.

Within the event handler function, the argument `ev` represents the event, and `ev.target` refers to the node where the event originally occurred. The `target` enables you to manipulate the target node—in this case, by adding and removing a class. See Example 4-1.

Example 4-1. Changing the background color on mouseover

```
<!DOCTYPE html>
<title>Changing the background color on mouseover</title>
<style>
div { border: 1px #000 solid; background: #a22; height: 100px; width: 100px; }
.over { background: #2a2; }
</style>

<div id="demo"></div>

<script src="http://yui.yahooapis.com/3.5.0/build/yui/yui-min.js"></script>
<script>
YUI().use('node-base', function (Y) {
    Y.one('#demo').on('mouseover', function (ev) {
        ev.target.addClass('over');
    });
    Y.one('#demo').on('mouseout', function (ev) {
        ev.target.removeClass('over');
    });
});
</script>
```

Although `node` and `node-base` perform DOM manipulation, they also pull in basic event handling support. For the most part, you need to load `event-*` modules only if you need specialized event features, such as synthetic events.

 Within the event handler function, by default YUI sets the `this` object to be the same node as `ev.currentTarget`, discussed next. You could therefore rewrite Example 4-1 to call `this.addClass()` instead. To override the value of `this` in the event handler, refer to Recipe 4.8.

Discussion

The event object ev contains a variety of useful properties, depending on the type of event.

For example, charCode represents a character generated during a keyboard event, while keyCode represents a key pressed during a keyboard event. Browsers can be wildly inconsistent about the values they report for keyCode and charCode in response to key down, keypress, and keyup events. The YUI event façade harmonizes these differences away.

Events may also include pageX and pageY, which represent the coordinates of the user's mouse. Example 4-2 uses pageX and pageY to create a <div> that jumps to wherever the user clicks on the page. The setXY() method moves the node on YUI's normalized coordinate system, which avoids cross-browser confusion over left, scrollLeft, offsetLeft, clientLeft, and different box models.

Example 4-2. Following the user's click

```
YUI().use('node', function (Y) {
    Y.one('document').on('click', function (ev) {
        Y.one('#demo').setXY([ev.pageX, ev.pageY]);
    });
});
```

As described in Recipe 4.3, events start at their originating element and bubble upward through the DOM. All event objects carry two (and sometimes three) properties that track which nodes were involved:

ev.target
> Refers to the node where the event *originated*. When using native methods, browsers disagree on whether to return ev.target as a text node or an element node under certain circumstances. YUI always normalizes ev.target to refer to a YUI element Node, never a text node.

ev.currentTarget
> Refers to the node where the event handler function was *listening*. Alternatively, you can think of ev.currentTarget as the element where the event has bubbled to. See also Recipe 4.5, which resets ev.currentTarget in an interesting way.

ev.relatedTarget
> Refers to a secondary target, if any. This property is relevant only for events that involve motion across the screen, such as a mouse move, drag, or swipe. For example, in a mouseover, this property represents the node where the mouse exited, while in a mouseout, it represents the node where the mouse entered.

In Example 4-2, ev.target is either the <div> or the <body> depending on where you click, while ev.currentTarget is always the document node, since that's where the listener was set. For more information about how events propagate through the DOM, refer to Recipe 4.3.

While you can count on most browsers supporting a core set of popular DOM events, use caution when listening for unusual or proprietary DOM events. YUI maintains a whitelist of supported DOM events in the static property `Y.Node.DOM_EVENTS`. If a native DOM event does not appear in `Y.Node.DOM_EVENTS`, or if the browser does not natively support that DOM event, the YUI event simply won't trigger when that event is fired. If necessary, you can always mix additional native DOM event names into the whitelist.

You can also invent your own DOM events, as described in Recipe 4.11. YUI provides a number of highly useful premade synthetic events, including `valueChange`, `mouseenter`, `mouseleave`, `hover`, and `touch`. YUI automatically registers synthetic events in the `Y.Node.DOM_EVENTS` whitelist.

Beyond DOM events, YUI also has a powerful custom event infrastructure that enables you to handle events that don't necessarily have anything to do with the DOM. For more information, refer to Recipes 4.6 and 4.7.

See Also

The YUI DOM event whitelist (*http://yuilibrary.com/yui/docs/event/#event-whitelist*); Peter Paul Koch's event compatibility tables (*http://www.quirksmode.org/dom/events/index.html*), which attempts to catalog which DOM events are available in which browsers.

4.2 Responding to Element and Page Lifecycle Events

Problem

Rather than waiting for the entire page to load, you want to run some JavaScript on an element as soon as that element is available.

Solution

Set an event handler for the `available` event. The `available` event triggers as soon as the element is present in the DOM.

In the previous recipe, Example 4-1 fetched a node with `Y.one()` and then called the resulting YUI Node's `on()` method. But if the document hasn't loaded yet, this approach fails—the first call to `Y.one()` will fail to find the node, and just return `null`.

Example 4-3 solves this problem by listening for the `available` event on the top-level Y object, using `Y.on()`. To specify where it should listen, `Y.on()` takes a third argument that can be a CSS selector, similar to `Y.one()`.

Example 4-3. Changing an element immediately on availability

```
<!DOCTYPE html>
<title>Changing an element immediately on availability</title>
```

```
<script src="http://yui.yahooapis.com/combo?3.5.0/build/yui-base/yui-base-min.js
&3.5.0/build/oop/oop-min.js&3.5.0/build/event-custom-base/event-custom-base-min.js
&3.5.0/build/features/features-min.js&3.5.0/build/dom-core/dom-core-min.js
&3.5.0/build/dom-base/dom-base-min.js&3.5.0/build/selector-native/selector-native-min.js
&3.5.0/build/selector/selector-min.js&3.5.0/build/node-core/node-core-min.js
&3.5.0/build/node-base/node-base-min.js&3.5.0/build/event-base/event-base-min.js"></script>
<script>
YUI().use('*', function (Y) {
    if (Y.one('#demo') === null) {
        Y.log("We're sorry, the #demo node is currently not available.");
        Y.log('Your function() call is very important to us. Please try again later.');
    }

    Y.on('available', function () {
        Y.one('#demo').setHTML('Sorry, I changed the div as fast as I could!');
    }, '#demo');
});
</script>

<div id="demo"></div>
```

Example 4-3 is constructed specifically so that JavaScript loads and executes before the browser has a chance to parse the demo `<div>`. First, the JavaScript appears near the top of the page, rather than the bottom as is the norm for YUI. Second, rather than using the Loader to dynamically construct a combo load URL, the example explicitly includes the combo URL in the static HTML. Calling use('*') then statically attaches whatever modules are already on the page, namely node-base and its dependencies. This is the same pattern shown in Recipe 1.20.

If the example had used the standard pattern of "load the small YUI seed, then use() the node-base module," node-base would have loaded asynchronously, most likely giving the browser enough time to parse the rest of the document, which would make waiting for the available event unnecessary.

Discussion

Browsers already provide a load event, but sometimes you might want to begin interacting before that event fires. For example:

- The page contains a great deal of complex markup that takes a long time to render, but you want to interact with an element very early.
- The page loads some large image files, and you want to interact with the page before all these resources finish loading.
- Your site serves its markup in stages: first sending over the heading and navigation markup, then sending over the content. This improves perceived performance, as the user now has something to look at while the backend is busy retrieving data. However, you also want to modify certain elements on the page as soon as they become available.

To help you interact with the page earlier, YUI provides three additional lifecycle events:

- `available` fires as soon as YUI can detect its presence in the DOM. This is the earliest moment when you can interact with an element in the DOM.
- `contentready` fires as soon as YUI can detect an element and its `nextSibling` in the DOM. This ensures that the element's children are in the DOM tree as well.
- `domready` fires as soon as the entire DOM has loaded and is ready to modify. This event fires before image files and other resources have loaded, while the native `load` event waits until all page resources are finally available.

  If you use the standard YUI sandbox pattern with scripts at the bottom, there is a good chance that the `domready` moment will occur after it is time to attach event handlers, and possibly even after the `load` event. `domready` is more likely to be useful in situations where you choose to load blocking scripts at the top of the page.

 Internet Explorer 7 and below can crash if you modify content before the DOM is complete. In these situations, YUI ensures that `available` and `contentready` fire after `domready`.

`Y.on()` provides a unified interface for assigning event handlers in YUI, while the `on()` method for `Y.Node` and `Y.NodeList` is a useful shortcut for assigning event handlers to nodes.

`Y.on()` is particularly useful for events that are not related to specific nodes, such as the `domready` lifecycle event, and custom events that are configured to bubble or broadcast to `Y`. For more information about controlling how custom events bubble and broadcast, refer to Recipe 4.7.

`Y.on()` can also assign event handlers to nodes that do not yet exist. For example, if you call `Y.on('click', callback, '#myelement')` in the `<head>` of the document, `Y.on()` polls for the existence of `myelement` in the DOM for several seconds before finally giving up. Note that calling `Y.one('#myelement').on( ... )` before `myelement` exists would fail, since `Y.one('#myelement')` would just return `null`. Take care to avoid assigning many listeners for nonexistent elements, as excessive polling can affect performance.

4.3 Controlling Event Propagation and Bubbling

Problem

You would like to stop an event from bubbling up to a certain element in the DOM.

Solution

At some lower level in the DOM tree, assign an event handler to catch the event and call `ev.stopPropagation()` to prevent the event from bubbling up any further (see Example 4-4).

Example 4-4. Controlling event propagation and bubbling

```
<!DOCTYPE html>
<title>Controlling event propagation and bubbling</title>

<div id="i-want-candy">
    <ul id="candy-filter">
        <li class="veggie">Broccoli</li>
        <li class="candy">Chocolate Bar</li>
        <li class="veggie">Eggplant</li>
        <li class="candy">Lollipops</li>
    </ul>
</div>

<script src="http://yui.yahooapis.com/3.5.0/build/yui/yui-min.js"></script>
<script>
YUI().use('node-base', function (Y) {
    Y.one('#candy-filter').on('click', function (ev) {
        if (! ev.target.hasClass('candy')) {
            ev.stopPropagation();
        }
    });
    Y.one('#i-want-candy').on('click', function (ev) {
        Y.one('body').append('<b>Yum! </b>');
    });
});
</script>
```

Ordinarily, any click event that happens within the `<div>` would bubble up to the top of the DOM tree, causing the `<div>` to respond with a "Yum!" as the event passes through.

However, the `<ul>`'s click event handler interferes with the bubbling. If the original target node does not have a class of `"candy"`, the `<ul>`'s event handler calls `ev.stop Propagation()`, which prevents the parent `<div>` from ever receiving the click event.

Discussion

When a user clicks on an element, the element's container also receives a click, as does that element's container, and so on out to the document. All of these should receive a click event, but in what order should the browser report these events? Early on, Internet Explorer chose to report events inside-to-out, which we now call *bubbling*. Netscape initially reported events outside-to-in, which we now call *capturing*, but shortly thereafter adopted IE's bubbling model as well.

The benefit of bubbling is that it enables you to efficiently handle events by placing event handlers on containers. Consider a table with 100 draggable rows. You could assign 100 event handlers to each individual row, or you could set a single event handler on the common container. Asking the question, "which of my children is of interest?" is more efficient than assigning many individual event handler functions, and takes advantage of commonality between instances. Bubbling also means that the contents of the container can change without forcing you to add and remove more event listeners. YUI events support an advanced version of this concept called *delegation*. For more information, refer to Recipe 4.5.

Child elements can use `stopPropagation()` to prevent their parents from discovering events that occurred lower down in the tree. However, any other event handlers on the current target still execute for that event. To stop bubbling upward *and* prevent other event handlers at the same level from executing, call `stopImmediatePropagation()`.

While `stopPropagation()` and `stopImmediatePropagation()` affect how the event bubbles through the DOM, they do not prevent any default behaviors associated with the event. For more information, refer to Recipe 4.4.

See Also

More information about bubbling, capturing, and `stopPropagation()` in Ilya Kantor's tutorial, "Bubbling and capturing" (*http://javascript.info/tutorial/bubbling-and-captur ing*).

4.4 Preventing Default Behavior

Problem

When a user clicks a link, you want to handle the `click` event in your own application and prevent the user from navigating away.

Solution

Use `ev.preventDefault()` to prevent the default behavior of the link from taking effect, as shown in Example 4-5.

Example 4-5. Preventing default behavior

```
<!DOCTYPE html>
<title>Preventing default behavior</title>

<a href="http://www.endoftheinternet.com/">The End of the Internet</a>

<script src="http://yui.yahooapis.com/3.5.0/build/yui/yui-min.js"></script>
<script>
YUI().use('node-base', function (Y) {
```

```
    Y.one('a').on('click', function (ev) {
        ev.preventDefault();
        Y.one('body').append('<p>Now why would you ever go there?</p>');
    });
});
</script>
```

Discussion

Once an event finishes bubbling, the browser might also carry out some default be-havior associated with the originating element. For example:

- Clicking a form submit button submits the form data to the server.
- Clicking a form reset button resets all form fields to their default values.
- Pushing a key when focused on a textarea adds that character to the textarea.

JavaScript enables you to trap these behaviors and do something different. For example, if the default browser behavior would be to submit a form, you can call `ev.prevent Default()` to keep the user on the page and perhaps do some other work instead.

The key thing to remember is that bubbling and default behaviors occur in separate phases and can be canceled separately. To completely stop an event, call the conve-nience method `ev.halt()`, which is the equivalent of calling both `ev.stopPropaga tion()` and `ev.preventDefault()`.

4.5 Delegating Events

Problem

You have a region on the page whose content changes frequently, but which contains elements that need to respond to user interaction. You want to avoid manually de-taching old subscriptions and attaching new event subscriptions as the content changes.

Solution

Use the node's `delegate()` method to assign the event handler. `delegate()`'s first two parameters are the same as `on()`'s, specifying the name of the event and the handler function to call. The third parameter is a filter that specifies which child elements the handler should be listening for.

Example 4-6 implements Recipe 4.3 with fewer lines of code. It also adds two buttons that enable the user to dynamically add more candy or veggies to the list. Thanks to event delegation, there is no need to attach new event subscriptions to newly created list items—all "candy" list items automatically gain the correct click behavior for free.

Example 4-6. Delegating with a CSS selector

```
<!DOCTYPE html>
<title>Delegating with a CSS selector</title>

<div id="i-want-candy">
    <ul>
        <li class="veggie">Broccoli</li>
        <li class="candy">Chocolate Bar</li>
        <li class="veggie">Eggplant</li>
        <li class="candy">Lollipops</li>
    </ul>
</div>

<p><button name="candy">+ candy</button> <button name="veggie">+ veggie</button></p>

<script src="http://yui.yahooapis.com/3.5.0/build/yui/yui-min.js"></script>
<script>
YUI().use('node-event-delegate', function (Y) {
    Y.one('#i-want-candy').delegate('click', function () {
        Y.one('body').append('<b>Yum! </b>');
    }, 'li.candy');

    Y.all('button').on('click', function (ev) {
        var name = ev.target.get('name'),
            item = '<li class="' + name + '">' + name + '</li>';
        Y.one('#i-want-candy ul').append(item);
    });
});
</script>
```

As with on(), the event handler triggers for click events that have bubbled up to the
<div>. However, the CSS selector 'li.candy' causes the event handler to trigger only
for events from an <li> element with a class of candy. In the handler function, YUI also
automatically sets the this object and ev.currentTarget to be the element matched by
the filter. The overall effect is that delegate() makes the handler function behave *as
if* it were subscribed on the list item, even though in reality, there is only one subscription on the parent element.

> Even though Examples 4-4 and 4-6 appear to behave the same way to
> the user, there is a key difference in that the former actually calls
> ev.stopPropagation() to stop the event from bubbling.

Discussion

Delegation in YUI is a kind of advanced treatment of bubbling that offers extra convenience and performance over assigning individual listeners.

As described earlier, bubbling enables you to handle many child events with a single
event subscription on a parent container. Delegation takes this concept one step further

by providing a handy filtering mechanism for designating the child elements of interest, and by setting ev.currentTarget to be the matched child element. The latter helps create the illusion that the event handler is subscribed directly on the child element instead of the container. If you end up needing a reference to the container anyway, dele gate() stores that in the event property ev.container.

Internally, delegate() assigns a single event handler to the container element. When an event bubbles up to the container, YUI invokes a test function on the event, only calling the event handler function if the test passes. The default test function compares the child element against the CSS selector you provided. If you provide a custom test function instead of a CSS selector string, YUI executes that test function instead, as shown in Example 4-7.

Example 4-7. Delegating with a function

```
YUI().use('node-event-delegate', function (Y) {
    function isCandy(node, ev) {
        return node.hasClass('candy');
    }

    Y.one('#i_want_candy').delegate('click', function (ev) {
        Y.one('body').append('<b>Yum! </b>');
    }, isCandy);
});
```

For each node that the event bubbles through on its way to the parent, the test function receives the currentTarget node and the event as parameters. Of course, there's no need to create a custom test function if a CSS selector will do the trick.

Besides being much more efficient than assigning lots of individual event handlers, delegate() is ideal for dynamic content. As Example 4-6 illustrates, when you add another child element to the container, it gets a "subscription" for free, since the element will pass the test just like its siblings. Likewise, if you remove a child element, you don't need to worry about cleaning up its event handler.

4.6 Firing and Capturing Custom Events

Problem

When something interesting in your application occurs, you want to send a message to some other component in your application.

Solution

Use Y.on() to listen for a particular custom event. Then use Y.fire() to generate and fire a custom event.

`Y.fire()`'s first argument is the name of the event. YUI custom event names may include a prefix with a colon to help identify the origin of the event, although this is not strictly necessary.

All subsequent arguments to `Y.fire()` are optional and get passed into the event handler function as additional arguments. Example 4-8 passes custom data as fields on a single object in order to look more like a familiar DOM event, but you may pass data (or not) any way you like.

For obvious reasons, take care to declare all your event handlers before actually firing the event.

Example 4-8. Firing and capturing a custom event

```
<!DOCTYPE html>
<title>Firing and capturing a custom event</title>

<div id="demo"></div>

<script src="http://yui.yahooapis.com/3.5.0/build/yui/yui-min.js"></script>
<script>
YUI().use('node', 'event-custom', function (Y) {
    function theEagleHasLanded() {
        return true;
    }

    Y.on('moon:landing', function (ev) {
        var msg = Y.Lang.sub("{first} {last}: That's one small step for [a] man...", ev);
        Y.one('#demo').setHTML(msg);
    });

    if (theEagleHasLanded()) {
        Y.fire('moon:landing', {first: 'Neil', last: 'Armstrong'});
    }
});
</script>
```

The example uses `Y.Lang.sub()` to substitute the values of `ev.first` and `ev.last` into the message string. This is equivalent to:

```
var msg = ev.first + " " + ev.last + ": That's one small step for [a] man...";
```

For more information about `Y.Lang.sub()` templating, refer to Recipe 9.7.

Discussion

YUI's custom event system is designed for creating event-driven applications. After all, the DOM itself is an event-driven architecture; custom events just extend this idea to be more general, enabling you to program "with the grain" of the system.

A custom event can represent any interesting moment you like. At their simplest, they are easy to generate; `Y.fire('foo:bar')` is often all you need. However, in general, custom events have all the behaviors and flexibility of DOM events. You can change how custom events bubble and propagate, as shown in Example 4-9. You can set default behaviors for custom events, and users of your event can then choose to suppress those default behaviors.

As with DOM events, if you have multiple event handlers listening for an event, YUI executes the event handlers in the order in which they were subscribed. In addition to `on()`, custom events also provide an `after()` subscriber that can execute handlers *after* the event's default behavior executes. For more information, refer to Recipe 4.10.

A common pattern in YUI is to use custom events with `Base`, as shown in Recipe 4.7. When you extend `Base`, you must provide a `NAME` static property, which then becomes the prefix for any custom events that the object fires. For more information about the `Base` family of objects, refer to Chapter 7.

Take care not to confuse custom event prefixes with event categories, discussed in Recipe 4.9.

4.7 Driving Applications with Custom Events

Problem

You want to create relationships between objects in your system that allow events to bubble from child to parent like DOM events.

Solution

Create your application components by extending `Y.Base` using the `Y.Base.create()` method (discussed in Recipe 7.3). Objects that extend `Base` gain the `EventTarget` interface, which adds methods for firing events and hosting event subscriptions. These methods include:

- `on()` for defining listeners and `detach()` for removing listeners
- `fire()` for firing custom events
- `publish()` for defining custom events that can bubble and have other behaviors
- `addTarget()` and `removeTarget()` for controlling which objects events will bubble to

Example 4-9 illustrates how to use these methods to create a system of objects that pass messages using custom events.

 Example 4-9 shows off only a subset of the `Base` object's functionality relating to events. For more information about this very important object, refer to Chapter 7.

Example 4-9. Driving applications with custom events

```
<!DOCTYPE html>
<title>Driving applications with custom events</title>

<script src="http://yui.yahooapis.com/3.5.0/build/yui/yui-min.js"></script>
<script>
YUI.add('apollo', function (Y) {
    var Apollo = Y.namespace('Apollo');

    Apollo.LunarModule = Y.Base.create('eagle', Y.Base, [], {
        initializer: function () {
            this.publish('landing', {
                broadcast: 2,
                defaultFn: function () {
                    Y.log("ARMSTRONG -- That's one small step for [a] man...");
                }
            });
        },
        reportLanding: function (status) {
            this.fire('landing', { ok: status });
        },
        tellJoke: function () {
            this.fire('joke');
        }
    });

    Apollo.CommandModule = Y.Base.create('columbia', Y.Base, [], {
        initializer: function () {
            this.on('eagle:joke', function (ev) {
                ev.stopPropagation();
                Y.log('COLLINS -- Haha Buzz, you crack me up!');
            });
        }
    });

    Apollo.MissionControl = Y.Base.create('houston', Y.Base, [], {
        initializer: function () {
            this.on('eagle:landing', function (ev) {
                if (ev.ok) {
                    Y.log('HOUSTON -- We copy you down, Eagle.');
                }
                else {
                    ev.halt();
                }
            });
            this.on('eagle:joke', function () {
                Y.log('HOUSTON -- Stop goofing around and get back to work.');
            });
        }
    });
}, '11', {requires: ['base-build']});

YUI().use('event-custom', function (Y){
    Y.Global.on('eagle:landing', function () {
        Y.log('WORLD -- Yay!');
```

```
        });
    });

    YUI().use('apollo', function (Y) {
        var lunarModule = new Y.Apollo.LunarModule(),
            commandModule = new Y.Apollo.CommandModule(),
            missionControl = new Y.Apollo.MissionControl();

        lunarModule.addTarget(commandModule);
        commandModule.addTarget(missionControl);

        lunarModule.tellJoke();          // => COLLINS -- Haha Buzz, you crack me up!

        lunarModule.reportLanding(true); // => HOUSTON -- We copy you down, Eagle.
                                         // => ARMSTRONG -- That's one small step for [a] man.
                                         // => WORLD -- Yay!
    });
    </script>
```

Y.Base.create() is covered in Recipe 7.3. For now, the most important things to know are that Y.Base.create():

- Creates a new class derived from Base, which includes the EventTarget API
- Provides a prefix for events fired from that class, such as eagle
- Enables you to define extra methods and add them to the class's prototype

The module code defined inside YUI.add() uses Y.Base.create() to create a LunarMod ule object that can fire two events: eagle:landing and eagle:joke. When a Base-derived object fires an event, the custom event name automatically includes the NAME property as a prefix, which identifies the source of the event.

eagle:joke is a vanilla custom event. To define an event with any specialized behavior, you must call the publish() method. When LunarModule initializes itself, it publishes an eagle:landing custom event with:

- A broadcast of 2, indicating that event:landing should be broadcast globally. If broadcast is 0, the event is received only by objects in the event's bubble tree. A value of 1 means that YUI also broadcasts the event to the top-level Y object, which means Y.on() can handle the custom event. A value of 2 means that the event is *also* broadcast to the Y.Global object, which means any YUI instance on the page can respond to the event. Events fired from an EventTarget have a default broadcast of 0.
- A defaultFn to trigger for the event. A default function is analogous to the default actions that browsers take in response to DOM events, such as link clicks and form submits. As with DOM events, you can suppress the default function for custom events.

The `YUI.add()` callback also defines objects for the `CommandModule` and `MissionCon trol`. These objects don't publish or fire any events of their own, but they do define some event listeners for `eagle:joke` and `eagle:landing`.

The page then creates two YUI sandboxes with `YUI().use()`. The first sandbox defines a listener using `Y.Global`, so it receives any events with a `broadcast` of `2`.

The second sandbox creates an instance for each of these three objects and then uses `addTarget()` to wire up a chain of event targets. The `LunarModule` instance sends its events to the `CommandModule` instance, and the `CommandModule` instance sends its events onward to the `MissionControl` instance. This works *exactly* like event bubbling in the DOM; an event fired by an `<a>` bubbles up to its parent `<p>`, which in turn bubbles up to its parent `<div>`. `addTarget()` is how you set up the default flow of information within an event-driven application.

Finally, the second YUI sandbox fires both events in turn. The browser console displays how the objects respond:

1. The `eagle:joke` event bubbles to the `CommandModule` instance...and then stops. As with DOM events, you can control the bubbling behavior of custom events using `ev.halt()` and `ev.stopPropagation()`. If you comment out the call to `stopPropaga tion()`, `eagle:joke` continues on up to `MissionControl`, which responds with disapproval.

2. The `eagle:landing` event bubbles up to `CommandModule`, which has no particular response, and then up to `MissionControl`. As with DOM events, custom events can carry payloads of additional information. In this case, the event façade passed to `eagle:landing` subscribers will also have a Boolean `ok` property indicating success or failure:

    • If the landing succeeds, `MissionControl` acknowledges the landing, the default function fires, and the event also gets broadcast to `Y.Global`. Because the first YUI sandbox set a listener using `Y.Global.on()`, it responds as well.

    • If the landing fails, `MissionControl` calls `ev.halt()`, which is the equivalent of calling `ev.stopPropagation()` and `ev.preventDefault()`. The `eagle:landing` default function does not fire and `Y.Global` never receives the event at all. (Let the conspiracy theories begin.)

Discussion

As shown in Recipe 4.6, with only a few lines of code, you can pass messages around an application by firing off simple "throwaway" custom events and catching them with `Y.on()`.

However, `EventTarget`'s `publish()` and `addTarget()` methods enable you to take the event-driven concept much further. If you have worked with the DOM, it is natural to think of applications in the same way: components wired together in a tree, firing off events with various payloads and default behaviors, catching these events as they bubble through the tree, and so on. Components in the core YUI library such as Cache, DataSource, and Y.log() make heavy use of custom events and default functions. For that matter, Node instances are also EventTargets—the event façade is the same whether you are working with DOM events or custom events.

Exposing custom events decouples component code from its use in implementation code. Component *designers* should call publish() and fire(), but component *users* should rarely fire() events themselves. Instead, component users should call component methods that internally call fire(). Likewise, component designers are encouraged to publish custom events with default functions, but should rarely need to prevent those functions. Calling preventDefault() on a custom event is a hook meant for component users.

Unlike elements in the DOM, it is not immediately obvious where a custom object should bubble its events to. This is why addTarget() exists—to help you define your own bubbling hierarchy. Alternatively, you can use broadcast and rely on Y.on() or Y.Global.on() to handle events. Y.on() is useful if you want to use Y as a "master switch" for handling custom events, while Y.Global.on() is useful for passing messages between sandboxes. For example, if you have a "dashboard" page that runs multiple applications, setting broadcast to 2 would enable you to pass information to a master control component that uses Y.Global. Using addTarget() gives you more fine-grained control, while using broadcast is a bit simpler.

As mentioned in Recipe 4.3, bubbling is a mechanism for the order in which you report events that affect all objects in a tree. One way to think about addTarget() is as a way to help represent that one object is a part of another. Thus, if you store objectChild as a property of objectParent or in a collection that belongs to objectParent, you might set up a bubble chain by calling objectChild.addTarget(objectParent).

The publish() method provides a great deal of flexibility for defining custom events. Example 4-9 demonstrates broadcast and defaultFn, but many other configuration options exist. For example:

- The emitFacade field controls whether the custom event sets emitFacade to true, which in turn means that the event can have more complex behaviors that allow it to bubble, execute default functions, and so on. In a simple Y.fire(), event Facade is false. However, if you publish and fire events from an object derived from Base, eventFacade defaults to true.

- The bubbles field controls whether the event is permitted to bubble. By default, bubbles is true. If bubbles is false, the event ignores the chain created by add Target(). In that case, the only way to allow the event to be caught by another object is to set broadcast to 1 or 2.

- The preventedFn field specifies a function to fire if and only if ev.preventDe fault() is called. This provides a fallback action in case the default action is prevented.

You can also configure custom objects to have a different prefix, to be unpreventable, to execute a function when something stops their propagation, and more. To learn more about defining custom events, refer to the `EventTarget` API documentation.

So why does Example 4-9 show off using `Base` instead of just extending `EventTarget` directly? The main reason is that in the real world, experienced YUI developers tend to prefer using `Base` and its children over using `EventTarget` by itself. In addition to `EventTarget`, `Base` also includes the important `Attribute` API and other methods that work together to create a stable foundation for constructing application components. However, if you are sure you only need `EventTarget`, feel free to use `Y.augment()` or `Y.extend()` to add just that functionality. For more information about how the core YUI objects all work together, refer to Chapter 7.

One subtle point to think about is whether to define event behavior for an entire class, or only for particular instances. In the example, `CommandModule` and `MissionControl` set their event listeners in their own `initializer()` function, which ensures that all instances of `CommandModule` listen for `eagle:joke`. To define an event listener only for a particular instance of `CommandModule`, you could call `commandModule.on()` in the `YUI().use()`.

4.8 Using Object Methods as Event Handlers

Problem

You want to use an object method as an event handler. The method works fine when you call it directly, but fails mysteriously when called as an event handler.

Solution

The method fails because when used as an event handler, the method is bound to the wrong context.

Ordinarily within a method, the `this` object contains a reference to the method's parent object. This enables the method to use other properties and methods on the object.

However, assigning an object method as an event handler changes the value of `this`. In a native DOM `addEventListener()`, `this` gets set to be the DOM node where the event occurred, while in   Internet Explorer's `attachEvent()` method, `this` gets set to the global `window` object. In a YUI `on()` subscriber, YUI sets `this` to be the `Y.Node` instance where the event occurred. In all these cases, the method will now fail if it makes any internal reference to `this`.

Fortunately, the `on()` method provides a simple fix. After you specify the handler function, the next parameter to `on()` overrides the value of `this` within the handler function. See Example 4-10.

Example 4-10. Using object methods as event handlers

```
<!DOCTYPE html>
<title>Using object methods as event handlers</title>
<style>
.notice  { color: #00c; }
.warning { color: #e80; }
.caution { color: #f00; }
</style>

<p>"Though this be madness, there is method in it."</p>

<script src="http://yui.yahooapis.com/3.5.0/build/yui/yui-min.js"></script>
<script>
YUI().use('node', function (Y) {
    var notifier = {
        msgType: 'caution',
        mark: function (ev) {
            ev.target.addClass(this.msgType);
        }
    };
    Y.one('p').on('click', notifier.mark, notifier);
});
</script>
```

Example 4-10 uses the third parameter in on() to bind the handler function to the correct context—in this case, the method's parent object.

To see the example fail, remove the last parameter. this.type falls back to looking for a type property on the Node instance, rather than on the notifier object.

Discussion

The reason this changes inside event handlers is a fundamental behavior of JavaScript. When you pass a reference to a method like notifier.mark to some other function, the JavaScript engine:

1. Finds an object named notifier.

2. Finds an object property on that object named mark.

3. Extracts the *value* of that property. In this case, function(ev) { ev.target.add Class(this.msgType); }

4. Passes that value in to the function.

In other words, JavaScript rips the method free of its initial context and passes it in as a simple function. It is as if the code were:

```
Y.one('p').on('click', function (ev) {
    ev.target.addClass(this.msgType);
});
```

which is bad, because this.msgType is undefined for the paragraph node.

After the context override parameter, any extra parameters provided to on() get passed in as arguments to the event handler function. Example 4-11 is a variation of the previous example where notifier now maintains an array of message types, and the mark() method now takes an integer level to pick out the right type.

Example 4-11. Passing arguments to an object method in an event handler

```
YUI().use('node', function (Y) {
    var notifier = {
        msgType: ['notice', 'warning', 'caution'],
        mark: function (ev, level) {
            ev.target.addClass(this.msgType[level]);
        }
    };
    Y.one('p').on('click', notifier.mark, notifier, 2);
});
```

Since correcting the context is a problem that goes beyond just event handlers, YUI provides a general solution. The Y.bind() method takes a function and a context object, and returns a wrapped function, with the wrapper now properly bound to the new context. Example 4-12 demonstrates an equivalent solution to Example 4-10.

Example 4-12. Fixing the context with Y.bind()

```
YUI().use('node', function (Y) {
    var notifier = {
        msgType: 'caution',
        mark: function (ev, level) {
            ev.target.addClass(this.msgType);
        }
    };
    var fn = Y.bind(notifier.mark, notifier);
    Y.one('p').on('click', fn);
});
```

Like the extended syntax for on(), Y.bind() also supports passing in additional arguments:

```
    var fn = Y.bind(notifier.mark, notifier, 2);
```

However, these arguments get passed into the callback *before* the event argument, ev. To pass in extra arguments *after* the ev argument, use Y.rbind().

For event handlers, you can use on()'s extended signature or Y.bind(), depending on which syntax you prefer.

Also note that the ECMAScript 5 standard defines a native Function.prototype .bind() method. Y.bind() enables you to cover your bases in both older and newer browsers.

4.9 Detaching Event Subscriptions

Problem

You want to remove an event handler from an event target.

Solution

Calling on() returns the subscription's handle object. Saving this object enables you to call detach() on the handle later to remove the subscription. See Example 4-13.

Example 4-13. Detaching event subscriptions

```
<!DOCTYPE html>
<title>Detaching event subscriptions</title>

<button id="annoying_patron">Boy Howdy!</button>
<button id="librarian">Sssh!</button>

<script src="http://yui.yahooapis.com/3.5.0/build/yui/yui-min.js"></script>
<script>
YUI().use('node-base', function (Y) {
    var handle = Y.on('click', function () {
        Y.one('body').append('<p>Boy howdy, this sure is a nice library!</p>');
    }, '#annoying_patron');

    Y.on('click', function () {
        Y.one('body').append('<p>Sssh!</p>');
        handle.detach();
    }, '#librarian');
});
</script>
```

YUI also provides once(), a sugar method for creating single-use event subscriptions. As written, Example 4-13 allows the librarian to say "Sssh!" multiple times. You could use once() as an easy way to configure the librarian event handler to fire once, then detach itself.

Discussion

YUI provides a great variety of ways to detach events—possibly more than it should.

In old browsers, it was important to detach event subscriptions in order to avoid memory leaks. This is a mostly solved problem today, but it is still possible to create pages that consume lots of memory because they fail to clean up node references and other objects.

One common reason to detach event subscriptions is when you are implementing an object destructor, such as the destroy() method of a Widget or Plugin. To make mass detachments easier, YUI allows you to add an arbitrary prefix to the event type when

---

subscribing to events. For example, ordinarily you might subscribe to a click event by calling:

```
someNode.on('click', ...)
```

but you are also free to add a prefix foo, separated by a vertical bar:

```
someNode.on('foo|click', ...)
```

This prefix is called an *event category*. If you assign many event listeners under the same category, you can detach them in one step by supplying a wildcard:

```
someNode.detach('foo|*');
```

Other YUI detaching techniques include, but are by no means limited to:

node.remove(true)
: Removes that node from the DOM. Passing in true destroys that node as well, nulling out internal node references and removing all plugins and event listeners.

node.empty()
: Destroys all of a node's child nodes.

node.detach(type)
: Removes any event handlers on the node that match the specified type.

node.detach(type, function)
: Removes any event handlers that match the specified type and handler function. This requires duplicating the signature of the original subscription, so it is usually easier to just save the subscription handle in the first place.

Y.detach(type, function, selector)
: Removes any DOM event handlers in the sandbox that match the specified type and handler function, and that reside on a node that matches the CSS selector.

See Also

Tony Gentilcore's blog post "Finding memory leaks" (*http://gent.ilcore.com/2011/08/finding-memory-leaks.html*).

4.10 Controlling the Order of Event Handler Execution

Problem

You have multiple event handlers listening for an event on the same event target, and you want to make sure the handlers all execute in a particular order.

Solution

Specify your on() event listeners in the order in which you would like the handlers to execute, as shown in Example 4-14.

Example 4-14. Controlling event handler execution order (DOM events)

```
<!DOCTYPE html>
<title>Controlling event handler execution order (DOM events)</title>

<p>Click me, then check your browser error console for exciting log action!</p>

<script src="http://yui.yahooapis.com/3.5.0/build/yui/yui-min.js"></script>
<script>
YUI().use('node-base', function (Y) {
    var p = Y.one('p');
    p.on('click', function () { Y.log('I will execute first.') });
    p.on('click', function () { Y.log('I will execute second.') });
    p.on('click', function () { Y.log('I will execute third.') });
});
</script>
```

For custom events, you can also use the `after()` method to execute handlers in a separate sequence that runs after the ordinary sequence of `on()` handlers. In Example 4-15, the two `on()` handlers execute in the order they were assigned, and then the `after()` handler executes. `after()` handlers also have special behavior around `prevent Default()`, as described in the upcoming Discussion.

Example 4-15. Controlling event handler execution order (custom events)

```
<!DOCTYPE html>
<title>Controlling event handler execution order (custom events)</title>

<p>Check your browser error console for exciting log action!</p>

<script src="http://yui.yahooapis.com/3.5.0/build/yui/yui-min.js"></script>
<script>
YUI().use('event-base', function(Y) {
    Y.on('my:example', function () { Y.log('I will execute first.') });
    Y.after('my:example', function () { Y.log('I will execute third.') });
    Y.on('my:example', function () { Y.log('I will execute second.') });

    Y.fire('my:example');
});
</script>
```

Unlike custom events, for DOM events `after()` is just a synonym for `on()` with no special behavior. To avoid confusion, do not use `after()` with DOM events.

Discussion

For custom events, and custom events *only*, `after()` has two key features. First, if your `on()` handlers are scattered around your code, `after()` can help create order out of chaos. Second, if you call `preventDefault()` from an `on()` subscriber to prevent a custom event's default function, no `after()` handlers are notified about the event.

In general, for custom events (not DOM events!), you can think of the relationship as:

1. on() handlers act before a state change.
2. The default function carries out a state change.
3. after() handlers view and respond to a state change, if that state change occurs.

This is a fundamental pattern when you are using Base-derived objects. Calling set() to change an attribute fires a change event, but calling preventDefault() cancels the requested value change. This means that if you need to respond to the attribute's value actually changing (as opposed to a change *attempt*), you should set an after() listener rather than an on() listener.

 If you need a single-use after() listener, use the onceAfter() sugar method. This is the equivalent of the once() method, which creates a single-use on() listener.

For DOM events, the overall execution sequence is:

1. All on() and after() event handlers on the target execute in order of specification, unless an event handler calls stopImmediatePropagation().
2. If there is another event target to bubble to *and* no event handler has called stopPropagation() or stopImmediatePropagation() yet, the event bubbles upward. Return to the previous step.
3. The default behavior for that DOM event executes, unless an event handler calls preventDefault().

For custom events, the overall execution sequence is:

1. All on() event handlers on the target execute in order of specification, unless an event handler calls stopImmediatePropagation().
2. If there is another event target to bubble to *and* no event handler has called stopPropagation() or stopImmediatePropagation() yet, the event bubbles upward. Return to the previous step.
3. The default function for that custom event executes, unless an event handler calls preventDefault().
4. If preventDefault() was *not* called, bubbling starts again for all the after() handlers:
    a. All after() event handlers on the target execute in order of specification, unless an event handler calls stopImmediatePropagation() or preventDefault() had been called earlier.
    b. If there is another event target to bubble to *and* no event handler has called stopPropagation() or stopImmediatePropagation() yet, the event bubbles upward. Return to the previous step.

There is also a `before()` method, but it is just a synonym for `on()` for both DOM events and custom events. `Y.before()` should not be confused with `Y.Do.before()`. For more information about `Y.Do`, refer to Recipe 4.12.

4.11 Creating Synthetic DOM Events

Problem

You want to handle a DOM event that the browser does not support directly.

Solution

Use `Y.Event.define()` to define a *synthetic event*, an event composed of ordinary DOM events (or other synthetic events) and custom logic to determine when to actually fire the event. A YUI synthetic event behaves like an ordinary DOM event and can be handled with the same API. A synthetic event must define its own `on()` method to define how to listen for the event, its own `detach()` method to define how to remove its event handlers, and so on.

Example 4-16 defines a `middleclick` event. The synthetic event is built using `mouseup` rather than `click` because, in many browsers, `click` events do not report accurate information in `event.button`. To demonstrate that ordinary subscription and delegation both work, the example sets an `on()` listener and a `delegate()` listener.

If your mouse does not have a middle button, you can convert this example to a `rightclick` synthetic event by changing the conditional to `ev.button === 3`. Suppressing the browser context menu is left as an exercise for the reader.

Example 4-16. Defining a middleclick synthetic event

```
<!DOCTYPE html>
<title>Defining a middleclick synthetic event</title>

<div id="container">
<p id="demo">Middle-click this paragraph.</p>
<p>Or this paragraph.</p>
<p>Or perhaps even this one.</p>
</div>

<script src="http://yui.yahooapis.com/3.5.0/build/yui/yui-min.js"></script>
<script>
YUI().use('node', 'event-synthetic', function (Y) {
    Y.Event.define('middleclick', {
        _handler: function (ev, notifier) {
            if (ev.button === 2) {
                notifier.fire(ev);
```

```
        }
    },
    on: function (node, sub, notifier) {
        sub.handle = node.on('mouseup', this._handler, this, notifier);
    },
    delegate: function (node, sub, notifier, filter) {
        sub.delegateHandle = node.delegate('mouseup', this._handler,
            filter, this, notifier);
    },
    detach: function (node, sub, notifier) {
        sub.handle.detach();
    },
    detachDelegate: function (node, sub, notifier) {
        sub.delegateHandle.detach();
    }
});

Y.one('#demo').on('middleclick', function () {
    Y.one('body').append('<b>Awesome! </b>');
});
Y.one('#container').delegate('middleclick', function () {
    Y.one('body').append('<b>Thanks! </b>');
}, 'p');
});
</script>
```

The on() method receives three parameters:

node

> The node where the caller subscribed to the event. Often (but not always!) you will attach ordinary event listeners to this node. The middleclick example assigns a mouseup event to the target node. Some synthetic events need to assign multiple listeners to a node, or assign listeners to the node's children, parents, or even the document object.

sub

> An object that represents the subscription to the synthetic event. Since synthetic events often involve multiple DOM events interacting with each other, the sub object is a handy place for sharing information between events and for storing event handles, so that the event is easy to detach later on.

notifier

> The object from which to fire the synthetic event. For any synthetic event, there is some set of conditions that indicate the synthetic event has occurred. In Example 4-16, the conditions are very simple—a single DOM event and a single conditional. Once the conditions are satisfied, on() must call notifier.fire() to indicate that the synthetic event has occurred.

The detach() method receives the same three parameters—including sub, which should ideally contain all the handles required to detach the event. In this case, there is only a single mouseup event to detach, but in general, a synthetic event may have event handlers scattered all over the document.

The middleclick event also supports event delegation. Since middleclick is so simple, its delegate() is almost identical to on(), with common logic factored out into a "protected" _handler() method. However, some synthetic events require different logic for delegation versus basic subscription. If a synthetic event does not implement a dele gate() method, Y.delegate() and node.delegate() will not work for that event. The same is true for detach() and other methods in the interface.

Discussion

At first glance, synthetic events might seem esoteric. Shouldn't click, mouseover, and submit be good enough for anybody? Synthetic events turn out to have an enormous range of use cases, such as:

- Correctly implementing tricky edge behavior that browsers handle poorly. For example, YUI provides a synthetic valueChange event that handles atomic changes to input fields and textareas. Unlike the standard DOM change event, valueChange fires when the field value changes, not when the field loses focus. Unlike the input event and the various key events, valueChange reliably handles multikeystroke inputs, copy-and-paste operations, mouse operations, and a variety of input method editors. valueChange was invented for the AutoComplete widget, but is a useful component in its own right.

- Harmonizing between touch events and mouse events. Rather than creating a specialized "YUI Mobile" library to program against, YUI's philosophy around mobile device support is to present a single unified API. To that end, YUI provides an assortment of synthetic events such as gesturemovestart and gesturemoveend that encapsulate touch events and mouse events in a single interface.

- Bringing newly standardized DOM events to older browsers. For example, HTML now defines an invalid event for form elements. A synthetic invalid event would enable you to use a consistent scheme for client-side error checking.

- Handling complex combinations of clicks, drags, swipes, and keyboard combinations for power users.

4.12 Responding to a Method Call with Another Method

Problem

Each time your application creates a node with Y.Node.create(), you want to log this information to the browser console using Y.log().

Solution

Use `Y.Do.after()` to configure YUI to automatically call a function after each call to `Y.Node.create()`. Automatically inserting a method before or after another method is a technique borrowed from a software methodology named *aspect-oriented programming* (AOP). As Example 4-17 shows, the first parameter of `Y.Do.after()` specifies the *advice function* to call, and the second and third parameters specify the object and the method name where the advice function should be inserted, known in AOP as the *joinpoint*.

Example 4-17. Using AOP to log node creation

```
<!DOCTYPE html>
<title>Using AOP to log node creation</title>

<script src='http://yui.yahooapis.com/3.5.0/build/yui/yui-min.js'></script>
<script>
YUI().use('node', function (Y) {
    var logCreate = function (fragment) {
        Y.log('CREATED: ' + fragment);
    };
    var logHandle = Y.Do.after(logCreate, Y.Node, 'create');

    var musketeers = Y.Node.create('<ul></ul>');
    Y.Node.create('<li>Athos</li>').appendTo(musketeers);
    Y.Node.create('<li>Porthos</li>').appendTo(musketeers);
    Y.Node.create('<li>Aramis</li>').appendTo(musketeers);

    logHandle.detach();
    Y.Node.create("<li>d'Artagnan</li>").appendTo(musketeers);

    musketeers.appendTo(Y.one('body'));
});
</script>
```

Like assigning an event handler with `on()`, calling `Y.Do.after()` returns a handle that you can use to tear down the configuration. Example 4-17 adds "d'Artagnan" after detaching the handle, so the browser console displays only four entries: one for the empty `<ul>` and one each for Athos, Porthos, and Aramis, but nothing for d'Artagnan.

As the example illustrates, `logCreate()` (the advice function) receives the same arguments as `Y.Node.create()` (the method called at the joinpoint). As with the `on()` method, you can provide the advice function a different execution context with the fourth parameter, or pass in extra arguments with the fifth and subsequent parameters. For more information about binding functions to a new context, refer to Recipe 4.8.

There is also a `Y.Do.before()` method with the same signature as `Y.Do.after()`.

Discussion

Although good developers try to neatly encapsulate the separate concerns of their code, programs often have *crosscutting concerns* that foil these efforts, such as data persistence or logging. AOP is a strategy for dealing with crosscutting concerns by altering the program's behavior. In AOP, you apply *advice* (typically a method) at certain points of interest called *joinpoints* (typically some other method), as mentioned earlier.

For example, you have a variety of objects designed to hold data. Each time one of these objects calls a set() method to change an internal value, you want to save off the old value so that it is possible to undo the change. You could try manually hacking this extra "save" behavior into each object's set() method, but the AOP approach would be to inject the save() behavior as an advice function, right before the set() joinpoint.

Y.Do.before() and Y.Do.after() are useful for situations where you want to add behavior around some method that, by its nature, might be scattered through your application. You can also use them just to add behavior around a method when you can't or don't want to change the method's internals (either by pasting new behavior directly in the method, or by altering the method to fire off a custom event).

For example, you are using a DataSource to fetch some remote data. If the fetch succeeds, you need to call another function in response. You could fire a custom event on success and listen for that, but AOP provides a clean, concise way to call your reactTo Success() function immediately afterward:

```
myDataSource.on('request', function (ev) {
    Y.Do.after(reactToSuccess, ev.callback, 'success');
});
```

You can also use Y.Do.before() to modify the arguments the intercepted method will receive or prevent an event from executing, and you can use Y.Do.after() to read and possibly modify the return value. This can be a simpler way to modify an object—rather than creating an extension, you can use AOP to just modify a few of the object's instances. This technique is particularly useful in plugins that change the behavior of their host object. For an example, refer to Recipe 7.8.

Ajax

Originally, browsers could not easily fetch more data without triggering a full page refresh. Perhaps the most important early approach for solving the I/O problem came from Internet Explorer 5, which introduced a scriptable ActiveX control for performing asynchronous HTTP requests. This feature evolved into a common cross-browser object called `XmlHttpRequest` (XHR).

Injecting XHR data into the DOM became more and more popular, and in 2005, designer Jesse James Garrett dubbed the technique "Ajax," for "Asynchronous JavaScript + XML." Today, "Ajax" more loosely means any technique that makes asynchronous remote calls, ranging from classic XHR to other techniques such as JSONP ("JSON with Padding") and iframe injection. The response can be HTML partials, data in JSON or XML, or any number of other formats.

Fetching more data with JavaScript is a powerful technique, but opens up the possibility of injecting harmful content into the page. To foil script injection attacks, XHR is subject to the *same origin policy*. By default, an XHR call to a server with a different domain will fail. However, it is possible to coerce XHR to make cross-domain calls, and there are other non-XHR techniques that bypass this restriction entirely. This chapter explores various techniques for making same-domain and cross-domain calls with YUI.

Recipe 5.1 introduces `Y.io()`, YUI's wrapper for the classic XHR object.

Recipe 5.2 runs through the various events in the XHR lifecycle. Listening for these events provides more fine-grained control over what is happening during the transaction.

Recipe 5.3 explains how to use Node's `load()` method as an easy way to populate an element with HTML content from another page.

One of the primary motivators for XHR is asynchronous form submissions. Recipe 5.4 describes how to submit general form data using XHR, while Recipe 5.5 explains how to upload a file.

Recipe 5.6 introduces JSONP, an alternative method for fetching remote data. JSONP doesn't work with all web services, but when available, it is an elegant way to make cross-domain requests.

YQL is a proxy service that enables easy cross-domain requests for nearly any source of data on the Web you can think of. Recipes 5.7 and 5.8 explain how to use YQL to access web services and scrape HTML.

Finally, Recipes 5.9 and 5.10 introduce DataSource and DataSchema. DataSource is a universal adapter for fetching and processing data from nearly any remote or local source, while DataSchema helps normalize data within DataSource objects and elsewhere.

5.1 Fetching and Displaying XHR Data

Problem

You want to fetch and display data from a web service that resides on your own domain.

Solution

First, you need a web service to access. Example 5-2 relies on the script in Example 5-1, which you can drop into any server that runs PHP.

Example 5-1. Example PHP web service

```php
<?php
header('Content-type: application/json');

$response = array();
if (isset($_GET['suspect']) && $_GET['suspect'] === 'butler') {
    $response['guilty']  = 'YES';
    $response['comment'] = 'We are as shocked as you are.';
}
else {
    $response['guilty']  = 'NO';
    $response['comment'] = 'Perhaps this murder will never be solved.';
}
echo json_encode($response);
?>
```

Alternatively, you can rewrite this trivial web service in JavaScript or whatever server-side language suits your fancy.

Once this web service is working, create an HTML page that loads the io-base module along with node-base and json-parse. Then call Y.io(), passing in:

- A URI (uniform resource identifier) or path to a web service running on the same domain
- A configuration object with a `data` property specifying the name/value parameters to pass in, and an `on` property containing one or more callback functions to execute in response to different events in the XHR lifecycle.

Example 5-2 is a simple example that sets a callback function for the `complete` event and makes a request to the local `io.php` web service, passing in a single `GET` parameter named `suspect`. The callback receives two arguments:

id
> A unique transaction ID object from which you can call `isInProgress()` to check whether the transaction is still running, or `abort()` to stop the transaction.

response
> An object containing the response status, headers, and content. The string content is stored in the `responseText` property.

In this example, the `complete` handler is responsible for dealing with success and failure. However, you can also divide up your logic more cleanly by setting callbacks for `suc cess`, `failure`, and other events, as shown shortly in Recipe 5.2.

Example 5-2. Fetching and displaying data with XHR

```
<!DOCTYPE html>
<title>Fetching and displaying data with XHR</title>
<style>
h1   { font: bold 300px tahoma, sans-serif; text-align: center; margin: 0px; }
p    { font: 13px tahoma, sans-serif; text-align: center; color: #444; }
.NO  { color: red; }
.YES { color: green; }
</style>

<h1 id="guilty"></h1>
<p id="comment"></p>

<script src="http://yui.yahooapis.com/3.5.0/build/yui/yui-min.js"></script>
<script>
YUI().use('io-base', 'node-base', 'json-parse', function (Y) {
    function showAnswer(answer) {
        Y.one('#guilty').setHTML(answer.guilty).addClass(answer.guilty);
        Y.one('#comment').setHTML(answer.comment);
    }

    Y.io('io.php', {
        data: 'suspect=butler',
        on: {
            complete: function (id, response) {
                if (response.status >= 200 && response.status < 300) {
                    showAnswer(Y.JSON.parse(response.responseText));
                }
```

```
            else {
                showAnswer({
                    guilty: 'NO',
                    comment: 'Something terrible has happened.'
                });
            }
        }
    }
    });
});
</script>
```

 You must run this example from a real web server, not the local filesystem.

A common pitfall when you are working with Ajax is handling only the success case. At a minimum, your code should at least attempt to handle failure in some way. Example 5-2 listens for the complete event and reacts to success or failure within a single event handler. Alternatively, YUI also fires separate success and failure events, which you can use to divide your success and failure logic into separate handlers. For more information, refer to Recipe 5.2.

Discussion

Y.io() is YUI's wrapper for "classic Ajax," the XmlHttpRequest object (XHR). Of all the different APIs YUI provides for fetching remote data, Y.io() grants you the most fine-grained control.

The key to this fine-grained control is the Y.io() configuration object. Example 5-2 represents a simple configuration, but more generally, the configuration can include:

method
> A string that specifies the HTTP method. The default is GET. For an example that uses POST, refer to Example 5-9.

data
> A string of data to send to the web service. The string should be serialized according to the Content-Type in the header (the default serialization is url-encoded). For a POST or PUT request, the data can be JSON, XML, or any other format the web service accepts.

form
> An object that identifies an HTML form to submit via XHR. For more information, refer to Examples 5-7 and 5-9.

on

An object that assigns event subscriptions for the XHR transaction. For an example of listening to multiple `Y.io()` lifecycle events, refer to Recipe 5.2.

context

An object that specifies the `this` object in the event callbacks, which is important if your callbacks are object methods. For more information about object methods, callbacks, and context, refer to Recipe 4.8.

sync

A Boolean that selects whether the transaction should be done synchronously, blocking all JavaScript execution until the call returns.

headers

An object containing HTTP header name/value pairs to send with the transaction. Some web services require a particular set of HTTP headers to function properly. By default, YUI sends an `X-Requested-With: XMLHttpRequest` header, a convention used by nearly all Ajax libraries.

timeout

A number that specifies the threshold in milliseconds before the transaction should time out.

arguments

A value that `Y.io()` will pass as the second argument to the `io:start` and `io:end` callbacks, and the third argument to the `io:complete`, `io:success`, and `io:fail` `ure` callbacks. You must quote `"arguments"` in the configuration object, as `argu ments` is a reserved word in JavaScript.

`Y.io()` is excellent for communicating with web services that you own. Its main drawback is that historically, XHR cannot easily do cross-domain requests. If you need to fetch data from another domain, subdomain, or port, you can try JSONP or YQL, introduced in Recipes 5.6 and 5.7, respectively.

Another way to work around the XHR cross-domain restriction is to provide `Y.io()` with a *transport* that makes HTTP requests on the browser's behalf. For many years, YUI has provided a premade transport in the form of a Flash component named `io.swf`. Unfortunately, Flash doesn't work on iOS devices and many Android devices. Unless you are building apps for a very locked-down, well-known browser environment, don't use `io.swf`.

Instead, use JSONP where possible, or use YQL as a proxy, or build yourself a custom server-side transport for `Y.io()`. One promising development in newer browsers is native support for cross-domain XHR, via a W3C standard called *cross-origin resource sharing* (CORS). YUI's `io-xdr` module wraps CORS support for a variety of browsers, although IE 6, IE 7, and WebKit on iOS 3 are unsupported.

See Also

The IO User Guide (*http://yuilibrary.com/yui/docs/io/*); IO API documentation (*http://yuilibrary.com/yui/docs/api/classes/IO.html*); "Example: Request JSON using Yahoo! Pipes" (*http://yuilibrary.com/yui/docs/io/xdr.html*); Nicholas Zakas's article, "Cross-domain Ajax with Cross-Origin Resource Sharing" (*http://www.nczonline.net/blog/2010/05/25/cross-domain-ajax-with-cross-origin-resource-sharing/*); MSDN's article on the XDomainRequest object (*http://msdn.microsoft.com/en-us/library/ie/dd573303%28v=vs.85%29.aspx*).

5.2 Handling Errors During Data Transport

Problem

You want to respond to failures and other events that can occur over the XHR lifecycle.

Solution

Load the io-base module and set listeners for the success and failure events. One of these two events fires shortly after complete. If the HTTP status is 2XX, success fires; otherwise, failure fires. While there is nothing wrong with simply listening for complete, success and failure can help you separate your success and failure logic more cleanly.

Example 5-3 listens for the five main events in the YUI XHR lifecycle, appending messages into the DOM as the events occur. The most significant callback function in this function is the one for failure, which customizes its message depending on the HTTP error state.

Unlike the toy io.php web service in Recipe 5.1, this book does not provide a candy_store.php web service. Unless you decide to write your own, no file is found on the server, which causes the request to fail with a 404 status.

Example 5-3. Handling errors during data transport

```
<!DOCTYPE html>
<title>Handling errors during data transport</title>

<ol id="candy_report"></ol>

<script src="http://yui.yahooapis.com/3.5.0/build/yui/yui-min.js"></script>
<script>
YUI().use('io-base', 'node-base', function (Y) {
    var ol = Y.one("#candy_report");

    Y.io('candy_store.php', {
        data: 'candy=licorice',
        on: {
```

```
        start: function (id) {
            ol.append('<li>Off to the candy store... </li>');
        },
        complete: function (id, response) {
            ol.append('<li>Back from the candy store!</li>');
        },
        success: function (id, response) {
            ol.append('<li>Yum!</li>');
        },
        failure: function (id, response) {
            var msg;
            switch(response.status) {
                case 402:
                    msg = 'Turns out, we have no candy money.';
                    break;
                case 403:
                    msg = 'Mom said no candy. Oh, well.';
                    break;
                case 404:
                    msg = 'Cannot find the store. Are you sure there is one?';
                    break;
                default:
                    msg = 'Could not obtain candy. ' + response.statusText;
            }
            ol.append('<li style="color: red">Oh no! ' + msg + ' :( </li>');
        },
        end: function (id) {
            ol.append('<li>Well, that was an adventure!</li>');
        }
    }
  });
});
</script>
```

 You must run this example from a real web server, not the local filesystem.

Discussion

Y.io() breaks the XHR transaction into four main phases, represented by five events. (For cross-domain requests, there is a sixth event named xdrReady.) As Example 5-3 demonstrates, they fire in this order:

1. start fires at the start of the transaction. The callback receives a transaction id, but not a response object (for obvious reasons). This event is a good place to either do any common setup work to receive the request, or update the user interface with some indication that the page is fetching data.

2. `complete` fires when `Y.io()` receives a response from the remote resource. The callback receives a transaction `id` and a `response` object that provides:

   - A `responseText` property, representing the response data as a string
   - A `responseXML` property, representing any XML response as an XML document
   - `status` and `statusText` properties, representing the HTTP numeric status and string status message, respectively
   - A `getResponseHeader(`*header*`)` method, which returns an individual HTTP header by name
   - A `getAllResponseHeaders()` method, which returns an `'\n'`-delimited string of all header names and values

   You can either deal with the entire response here (including error handling), or you can do any common UI updates here, and defer most of the response handling code to `success` and `failure`.

3. `success` or `failure` fires right after `complete`, depending on the HTTP status code. Like `complete`, the callback receives a transaction `id` and a `response` object. If the HTTP status is `2XX` or `304` (Not Modified) `Y.io()` fires `success`; otherwise, it fires `failure`. You can use `success` and `failure` as an alternative to `complete`, or even together with `complete`.

    Internet Explorer erroneously reports a `204` status as a (nonstandard) `1223` status. YUI therefore treats a `1223` status as success.

4. `end` fires after either `success` or `failure` has fired. The callback receives only a transaction `id`. This event is a good place to either do any common teardown work once the transaction is over, or make any final updates to the user interface that have to happen regardless of success or failure.

The `Y.io()` event lifecycle enables you to structure your transaction-handling code in a variety of ways. The simplest thing to do is to ignore this structure and just handle everything in `complete`, as shown in Example 5-2. But for more complex applications, YUI provides additional event hooks for you to use.

The bottom line is: if you use `complete` only, check for status there as well. If you use `success`, don't forget to use `failure`.

When you are handling errors, the response body is often a messy soup of HTML or other junk, but the HTTP status and headers can be useful. For example, some responses with a `3XX` status might provide a URL to redirect to, so your `failure` code could attempt a retry to the new URL if for some reason the browser wasn't able to handle the redirect transparently. A `4XX` HTTP status probably indicates something wrong with your code, so there is usually nothing to do but fail immediately. A `5XX` code indicates a problem with the remote service—this error might be transient, so it might be worth retrying a couple of times and then failing. Whatever you do, you should avoid exposing low-level error codes and headers to end users.

 As Y.io() transactions fire their lifecycle events, YUI also broadcasts io:* events to the Y instance. This means that it is possible to call Y.io() *without* specifying listeners in the transaction configuration, and instead listen with Y.on():

```
Y.io('candy_store.php', { data: 'candy=licorice' });

    Y.on('io:success', function (id, response) {
        ...
});
```

Do not use this pattern. The problem is that if you execute multiple XHR transactions, Y.on() will receive multiple io lifecycle events in an unpredictable order, which can lead to disastrous race conditions. By contrast, in Examples 5-2 and 5-3, each listener is safely scoped to a single XHR transaction and handles only a single event.

See Also

RFC 2616 Section 10, Status Code Definitions (*http://www.w3.org/Protocols/rfc2616/rfc2616-sec10.html*).

5.3 Loading Content Directly into a Node

Problem

You want an easy way to load HTML content into a node from some other HTML page on your server.

Solution

Load the node-load module, get a Node instance, and call the load() method, passing in the URL to the target HTML source along with an optional CSS selector to an element within the DOM.

Example 5-4 is a master page for an Ajax-powered documentation site. Clicking a navigation link loads a new content pane without refreshing the entire page. The example uses Y.all().on() to assign multiple event handlers. For large numbers of links, event delegation would be more efficient.

Example 5-4. Loading HTML content into a node

```
<!DOCTYPE html>
<title>Loading HTML content into a node</title>
```

```
<h1>My Awesome Documentation</h1>

<ul id="nav">
    <li><a href="install.html">Installation</a></li>
    <li><a href="examples.html">Examples</a></li>
    <li><a href="api.html">API Reference</a></li>
</ul>
<div id="main">
    <p>Some great documentation is about to appear here!</p>
    <p>Boy howdy!</p>
</div>
<p id="footer">This is a footer. Copyright 2012, by ME.</p>

<script src="http://yui.yahooapis.com/3.5.0/build/yui/yui-min.js"></script>
<script>
YUI().use('node-load', function (Y) {
    var main = Y.one('#main');

    Y.all('#nav a').on('click', function (ev) {
        ev.preventDefault();
        main.load(ev.target.get('href'), '#content');
        Y.one('h1').setHTML(ev.target.getHTML());
    });
});
</script>
```

 You must run this example from a real web server, not the local filesystem.

This example relies on loading content from static HTML files that resemble Example 5-5. Strictly speaking, these static files only need to contain the markup for the content. However, providing the header and footer markup means that if the user has JavaScript turned off, the site continues to work with almost the same fidelity.

Example 5-5. Example static HTML page (install.html)

```
<!DOCTYPE html>
<title>My Awesome Documentation</title>

<h1>Installation</h1>
<ul id="nav">
    <li><a href="install.html">Installation</a></li>
    <li><a href="examples.html">Examples</a></li>
    <li><a href="api.html">API Reference</a></li>
</ul>
<div id="main">
    <div id="content">
        <p>Here is <b>how to install</b> my awesome project.</p>
        <p>Blah blah blah...</p>
    </div>
```

```
</div>
<p id="footer">This is a footer. Copyright 2012, by ME.</p>
```

Discussion

The `node-load` module is a high-level utility that uses `Y.io()` under the hood to fetch local HTML pages. It might be a little odd to think of a static HTML page as a "web service," but that's essentially what the `load()` method is doing.

You can use `load()` and its handy CSS selector feature to slice and dice HTML from all over your server, any way you please. For example, `load()` could help you upgrade the user experience of an old site where rearchitecting or regenerating existing pages would be difficult and expensive. You could also use `load()` to access a web service designed to return HTML partials.

Example 5-4 uses `load()` as a simple form of *progressive enhancement*, where JavaScript provides a better user experience but is not essential for using the site. The basic mechanism for loading content is sound, but there are some important missing features—in particular, the document title and the URL in the location bar don't change. To fix that, you would need to write a little more code and get some help from the YUI `History` or YUI `Router` utilities.

The `load()` method's optional third argument is a callback function to execute when loading is complete. Example 5-6 uses this feature to provide a `fadeOut`/`fadeIn` transition when loading content. The click handler starts a `fadeOut` transition. When the transition completes, it executes a callback that loads content into the node. When `load()` completes, it executes a final callback that starts a `fadeIn` transition.

Example 5-6. Loading HTML content into a node with a fade

```
YUI().use('node-load', 'transition', function (Y) {
    var main = Y.one('#main');

    Y.all('#nav a').on('click', function (ev) {
        ev.preventDefault();
        main.transition('fadeOut', function () {
            main.load(ev.target.get('href'), '#content', function () {
                Y.one('h1').setHTML(ev.target.getHTML());
                main.transition('fadeIn');
            });
        });
    });
});
```

 For an alternative to using `load()` directly, YUI also has a dedicated component named `Pjax`, which uses progressive enhancement to load page content with Ajax. `Pjax` was designed to support the YUI App Framework, but it is easy to use standalone.

See Also

Recipe 3.2; Recipe 7.17; Recipe 9.12; API documentation for `node.load()` (*http://yuili brary.com/yui/docs/api/classes/Node.html#method_load*); the Pjax User Guide (*http://yuilibrary.com/yui/docs/pjax/*).

5.4 Submitting Form Data with XHR

Problem

You want to submit a form without reloading the page.

Solution

Load the `io-form` module and add a `submit` listener that stops the form submission with `preventDefault()` and invokes `Y.io()` instead. In the `Y.io()` configuration, replace the `data` object with a `form` object that has its `id` set to a YUI `Node` instance for the `<form>` element. When the user submits the form, `Y.io()` uses the `name` attribute on each field to automatically serialize all form field values for you, submitting the data to the server using the HTTP method you specify.

Example 5-7 submits data to Example 5-1, the same toy web service first shown in Recipe 5.1. The example explicitly sets a `method` of `GET`, even though this is the default. On the server side, the script receives a single `GET` parameter with a name of `"suspect"` and a value of `"butler"`, `"lord"`, or `"lady"`.

Example 5-7. Submitting form data with XHR

```html
<!DOCTYPE html>
<title>Submitting form data with XHR</title>
<style>
.YES { color: green; }
.NO  { color: red; }
</style>

<form id="form" action="io.php">
<fieldset>
    <legend>Murder Most Foul</legend>
    <label><input type="radio" name="suspect" value="butler" checked> Jeeves</label>
    <label><input type="radio" name="suspect" value="lord"> Mr. Blackstone</label>
    <label><input type="radio" name="suspect" value="lady"> Lady Haversham</label>
</fieldset>
<input type="submit" value="Who dunnit?">
</form>
<p id="answer">Scotland Yard says...</p>

<script src="http://yui.yahooapis.com/3.5.0/build/yui/yui-min.js"></script>
<script>
YUI().use('io-form', 'json-parse', function (Y) {
    function submitForm(ev) {
```

```
        ev.preventDefault();
        Y.io('io.php', {
            method: 'GET',
            form: { id: Y.one('#form') },
            on: {
                complete: function(id, response) {
                    var answer = Y.JSON.parse(response.responseText);
                    Y.one('#answer').setHTML(answer.guilty + '. ' + answer.comment)
                        .set('className', answer.guilty);
                }
            }
        });
    }

    Y.on('submit', submitForm, '#form');
});
</script>
```

 You must run this example from a real web server, not the local
filesystem.

Discussion

To keep Y.io() lean and modular, io-base provides the core wrapper for the XmlHttp
Request object, on the assumption that you want to make asynchronous requests
without using the Node API. The io-form module augments Y.io() with the ability to
serialize HTML form data, and to that end, also pulls in some of YUI's core node
modules.

Along with id, form can include two optional properties. The useDisabled property, if
set to true, includes key-value pairs of disabled form fields. By default, disabled fields
are excluded. If you load the io-upload-iframe module instead of the io-form module,
there is also an upload property that enables Ajax file uploads from <input
type="file"> form elements. For more information, refer to Recipe 5.5.

One feature of Y.io() is that its URI overrides the form's action attribute. This provides
an easy way to segment Ajax and non-Ajax requests: plain HTML form submissions
use the action attribute's URI, which could return HTML representing a confirmation
screen, while XHR form submissions use Y.io()'s URI, which could return raw JSON
data to be handled by JavaScript.

Alternatively, you could use the same URI for both kinds of requests, and have the web
service return JSON or HTML depending on whether the X-Requested-With: XMLHttp
Request request header is present. Or, if you don't want your company's web services
architect to yell at you, the less lazy and more technically correct option would be to
have Y.io() add an Accept: application/json request header and have the web service
switch off of that.

5.5 Uploading a File with XHR

Problem

You want to submit a form that uploads a file without reloading the page.

Solution

First, you need a web service to access that can handle file uploads. Example 5-9 relies on the script in Example 5-8, which you can drop into any server that runs PHP.

Example 5-8. Example PHP web service that accepts file uploads

```php
<?php
header('Content-type: application/json');

$response = array();
if (isset($_FILES['ode'])) {
    $response['name']  = filter_var($_FILES['ode']['name'], FILTER_SANITIZE_STRING);
    $response['size'] = $_FILES['ode']['size'];
}
echo json_encode($response);
?>
```

Alternatively, you can rewrite this trivial web service in JavaScript or whatever server-side language suits your fancy.

Once this web service is working, create an HTML page that loads the `io-upload-iframe` module and any extra modules you need to parse and display the data, such as `json-parse`. Add a `submit` listener that calls `preventDefault()` to stop the form submission and invoke `Y.io()` instead.

In the `Y.io()` configuration, set the `method` to `POST` and provide a `form` object with an `id` that references the `<form>` element, and an `upload` set to `true`. When the user submits the form, `Y.io()` seamlessly uses an `<iframe>` to upload the file to the server.

Example 5-9. Uploading a file with XHR

```html
<!DOCTYPE html>
<title>Uploading a file with XHR</title>

<p>Please upload a poem, essay, or image expressing your
thoughts about your favorite JavaScript library.</p>
<form id="form" enctype="multipart/form-data" action="io_fileupload.php" method="POST">
    <input type="hidden" name="MAX_FILE_SIZE" value="30000">
    File: <input name="ode" type="file">
    <input type="submit" value="Upload File">
</form>
<p id="uploaded">File not yet uploaded...</p>

<script src="http://yui.yahooapis.com/3.5.0/build/yui/yui-min.js"></script>
<script>
```

```
YUI().use('io-upload-iframe', 'json-parse', function (Y) {
    function submitForm(ev) {
        ev.preventDefault();
        Y.io('io_fileupload.php', {
            method: 'POST',
            form: {
                id: Y.one('#form'),
                upload: true
            },
            on: {
                complete: function(id, response) {
                    var file = Y.JSON.parse(response.responseText),
                        msg = 'Uploaded: ' + file.name + ' (' + file.size + ' bytes)';
                    Y.one('#uploaded').setHTML(msg);
                }
            }
        });
    }

    Y.on('submit', submitForm, '#form');
});
</script>
```

 You must run this example from a real web server, not the local filesystem.

Discussion

While the `io-form` module handles most `<form>` elements, the glaring exception is `<input type="file">`. Historically, browser JavaScript could not access local files, which means browsers could not directly POST this data using an ordinary XHR request. Newer browsers that support the File API can in fact read files into memory and post them using Ajax.

For browsers that do not support the File API, there is a well-known workaround that involves creating a hidden `<iframe>` and using that as a transport for the file data. The `io-upload-iframe` module encapsulates this workaround for you. Because most forms don't require file uploads, this extra code is broken out into its own module in order to save page weight.

5.6 Getting JSON Data Using Script Nodes (JSONP)

Problem

You want to request JSON data from a remote web service. The web service resides on a different domain, but it happens to support the JSONP protocol for supporting cross-domain calls.

The solution assumes you understand what JSONP is and how the mechanism works. For more background, refer to the Discussion.

Solution

First, construct a JSONP web service URL, but *don't* provide an explicit callback function name. Instead, provide a placeholder string, "{callback}". For example, if the JSONP call to fetch info about the user "brad" is supposed to look like:

```
http://vimeo.com/api/v2/brad/info.json?callback=myExampleCallback
```

you should instead specify the URL as:

```
http://vimeo.com/api/v2/brad/info.json?callback={callback}
```

Once you have determined the URL, load the jsonp module and call Y.jsonp(), passing in the URL and a function to handle the response. Any JSON that the web service returns will reside as direct properties of the response object.

Example 5-10 fetches and displays user info from the Vimeo video hosting service. Clicking the button causes the example to extract the current value of the username input box, construct a JSONP URL, fetch information about the user, and use Y.Lang.sub() templating to display some of the returned data in the page. As with the previous examples, you must call preventDefault() to avoid a page refresh. For example usernames, try brad, joanna, jason, or barbie.

Example 5-10. Fetching and displaying data with JSONP

```
<!DOCTYPE html>
<title>Fetching and displaying data with JSONP</title>
<style>
.user { width: 20em; background: #eee; border: 1px solid #888; min-height: 75px;}
.user img { float: right; }
.user h2 { font: normal 14px verdana; margin: 0.2em; }
.user p { font: 12px verdana; color: #333; margin: 0.2em; }
</style>

<form>
<input id='username' value='brad'> <button>Get Vimeo User</button>
</form>
<div id="demo"></div>

<script src="http://yui.yahooapis.com/3.5.0/build/yui/yui-min.js"></script>
<script>
YUI().use('jsonp', 'node-base', function (Y) {

    Y.one('button').on('click', function (ev) {
        var user = Y.one('#username').get('value'),
            url = 'http://vimeo.com/api/v2/' + user + '/info.json?callback={callback}';
```

```
        Y.jsonp(url, function (response) {
            var template = '<div class="user"><img src="{portrait_medium}">'
                + '<h2><a href="{profile_url}">{display_name}</a> ({location})</h2>'
                + '<p>{bio}</p>'
                + '<p>Videos Uploaded: {total_videos_uploaded}</p></div>'

            Y.one('#demo').setHTML(Y.Lang.sub(template, response));
        });
        ev.preventDefault();
    });
});
</script>
```

Discussion

If you're used to the cross-domain restrictions around XHR, JSONP might seem like magic. In fact, it is a little like magic, although it does require some special assistance from the server.

The basic JSONP mechanism works not through XHR, but through a different technique called *script loading*, the same technique that powers the YUI Loader. In script loading, YUI dynamically inserts a `<script>` element into the DOM to fetch a remote script. For example, YUI could insert the element:

```
<script src="http://vimeo.com/api/v2/brad/info.json">
```

Once the remote script from Vimeo finishes loading, this is the equivalent of:

```
<script>{ "id": 101193, "display_name": "Brad Dougherty", ... }</script>
```

The `<script>` element has just inserted bare JSON into the environment, which unless assigned to a variable or wrapped somehow, can cause a JavaScript error.

Fortunately, script loading is only half of the solution. Over on the server side, a web service that supports JSONP takes an extra parameter, typically named something like `callback`, `cb`, or `cbFunc`. Providing this parameter instructs the web service to wrap the response in the specified function. In other words:

```
<script src="http://vimeo.com/api/v2/brad/info.json?callback=foo">
```

instructs Vimeo to return the "JSON padded" version of the response:

```
<script>foo({ "id": 101193, "display_name": "Brad Dougherty", ... })</script>
```

This means that as long as your page defines a `foo()` function further up on the page, the cross-domain JSON data is wrapped in a function call—and through `foo()`, you can do anything you like with that data. Magic!

 Be wary of black magic, though. Making a cross-domain JSONP call means that if the remote site is malicious (or gets hacked by malicious people), attackers can easily inject arbitrary JavaScript onto your page.

YUI's jsonp module adds a little more magic. The reason you need to provide a {call
back} placeholder in the URL is that Y.jsonp() sends its own callback to the remote
web service. The Y.jsonp callback takes care of some housekeeping around the YUI
use() sandbox, then passes the JSON data on to your callback to process the
response object.

Example 5-10 shows the simplest approach, passing in a single callback function to
handle all possible responses. If you want more control, you can pass in a configuration
object instead, much like Y.io(). The configuration object enables you to assign different functions to handle success, failure, and timeout:

```
Y.jsonp(url, {
    on: {
        success: jsonpSuccess,
        failure: jsonpFailure,
        timeout: jsonpTimeout
    },
    timeout: 3000
});
```

For an example of a widget that puts this into practice, refer to Recipe 7.6.

Y.jsonp() offers a number of additional configuration options beyond these, as discussed in the API documentation. Keep in mind that Y.jsonp() has fewer options for
fine-grained control than Y.io(), since dynamic script insertion provides less low-level
control than XHR. For example, you cannot abort a JSONP request in progress or
reliably control the execution order of multiple JSONP calls.

See Also

Recipe 5.7; Recipe 7.6; Recipe 9.7; the Get User Guide (*http://yuilibrary.com/yui/docs/
get/*); the JSONP User Guide (*http://yuilibrary.com/yui/docs/jsonp/*); JSONP API documentation (*http://yuilibrary.com/yui/docs/api/modules/jsonp.html*).

5.7 Fetching and Displaying Data with YQL

Problem

You want to interact with several web services, but it's a pain to have to remember their
respective URLs, parameters, and other conditions. You are looking for a normalized
way to fetch cross-domain data.

Solution

Load the yql module and call Y.YQL(), passing in a YQL query string and callback
function to handle the response.

Example 5-11 queries Yahoo! Local for address information about pizza restaurants in Palo Alto. For any YQL query, the actual JSON payload you care about will be nested under `response.query.results.`*someobject*, where the name of *someobject* depends on the particular YQL data table you are using. Other `response` object properties provide metadata about the request.

Example 5-11. Fetching and displaying data with YQL

```
<!DOCTYPE html>
<title>Fetching and displaying data with YQL</title>

<script src="http://yui.yahooapis.com/3.5.0/build/yui/yui-min.js"></script>
<script>
YUI().use('yql', 'node-base', function (Y) {
    var query = 'select * from local.search where zip="94301" and query="pizza"';

    Y.YQL(query, function (response) {
        var ol = Y.Node.create('<ol/>');
            results = response.query.results.Result;

        Y.each(results, function (r) {
            ol.append('<li>' + r.Title + ' &mdash; ' + r.Phone + '</li>');
        });
        Y.one('body').append(ol);
    });
});
</script>
```

It is easy to register new web services with YQL, and many services are already available. To explore these services, use the YQL Console (*http://developer.yahoo.com/yql/con sole/*).

Discussion

If JSONP is a little like magic, YQL is wizardry of the highest order. YQL has been referred to as "the Swiss Army Knife of the Web," and "crack for developers."

To be a bit more prosaic, YQL is an important piece of plumbing used by many production Yahoo! services, exposed for external use. At its core, YQL is:

- A collection of Yahoo! servers that can make requests on your behalf, perform server-side transformations on the data for you, and cache the results.
- A common SQL-like query language for making REST calls.

Supporting a particular web service requires defining a *YQL data table* that specifies how to map REST web service URLs to YQL query strings. YQL provides over a hundred data tables for Yahoo! web services, and over a thousand data tables for non-Yahoo! services, written by members of the YQL developer community.

As an example, the `local.search` data table defines how to take a string query like:

```
'select * from local.search where zip="94301" and query="pizza"'
```

and construct the native REST URL for the Yahoo! Local Search API, passing in the `zip` and `query` parameters correctly. In addition to defining the basic transformation between the YQL query and the REST URL, data tables can do further transformations such as renaming parameters or even restructuring the data by executing your own JavaScript on the YQL servers. For more information, consult the YQL User Guide.

YQL is a useful service with any language, but it especially shines with client-side JavaScript:

- XHR has tight restrictions around cross-domain requests, and JSONP works only if the owner of the web service decides to help you out. YQL blows right past these restrictions. Because YQL serves as your proxy for making cross-domain calls, it always supports JSONP, regardless of whether the original web service does.

- When called through `Y.YQL()`, the YQL servers always return results as JSON, regardless of what the original web service returned.

- Fetching and transforming large amounts of data is expensive to do on the client side, particularly if the client has a weak network connection or a low-powered browser. YQL uses Yahoo!'s fast backbone and edge network to fetch and relay data, and it can run computations for you before sending the data to the client.

`Y.YQL()` is built on top of `Y.jsonp()`. You could actually make YQL calls using `Y.jsonp()` directly, but `Y.YQL()` does some extra housekeeping for you and provides some YQL-specific configuration options.

 YQL does have usage limits per requesting client. These limits might not be important for end users, since requests would be distributed among many clients. However, it is possible to run into these limits during development and testing, and they are definitely important with YUI under Node.js (discussed in more detail in Chapter 10), assuming all requests come from the same server.

See Also

Recipe 5.8; Recipe 10.4; the YQL User Guide (*http://yuilibrary.com/yui/docs/yql/*); "Example: Reusing a YQL query" (*http://yuilibrary.com/yui/docs/yql/yql-requery.html*); general YQL documentation in the YQL Guide (*http://developer.yahoo.com/yql/guide/*); test your YQL queries in the YQL Console (*http://developer.yahoo.com/yql/console/*).

5.8 Scraping HTML with YQL

Problem

You want to retrieve data from a site that hasn't even *heard* of REST web services.

Solution

Load the yql module and call Y.YQL(), passing in a YQL query string that uses the html YQL table. You can include an optional XPath expression to isolate a subsection of the page. The response includes a JSON representation of all HTML content that matches the XPath.

Example 5-12 extracts and displays product information about handmade Klein bottles from KleinBottle.com (*http://kleinbottle.com/*). The XPath grabs the first `<table>` element on the page (XPath is 1-based, not 0-based) and returns the child `<tr>`s as a JSON array. Most of the code is involved in reformatting the raw data, picking out individual cells in a vertical `<td>` column and reassembling that data into horizontal `<li>`s. The example uses Y.Lang.sub() templates to construct the YQL query and to construct the HTML to display.

Example 5-12. Scraping HTML with YQL

```
<!DOCTYPE html>
<title>Scraping HTML with YQL</title>

<script src="http://yui.yahooapis.com/3.5.0/build/yui/yui-min.js"></script>
<script>
YUI().use('yql', 'node-base', function (Y) {
    var query  = 'select * from html where url="{url}" and xpath="{xpath}"',
        params = {};

    params.url   = 'http://kleinbottle.com/specs_for_nice_klein_bottles.htm';
    params.xpath = '//table[1]/tr';
    query = Y.Lang.sub(query, params);

    Y.YQL(query, function (response) {
        var ol = Y.Node.create('<ol/>'),
            rows = response.query.results.tr,
            template = '<li><a href="{href}">{product}</a>:'
                + ' {height} x {diameter}, just <b>{price}</b>!</li>',
            data, col, colMax = 8;

        for (col = 1; col <= colMax; col += 1) {
            data = {};
            data.href     = 'http://kleinbottle.com/' + rows[0].td[col].p.a.href;
            data.product  = rows[0].td[col].p.a.content;
            data.height   = rows[1].td[col].p;
            data.diameter = rows[2].td[col].p;
            data.price    = rows[8].td[col].p;
            ol.append(Y.Lang.sub(template, data));
        }
        Y.one('body').append(ol);
    });
});
</script>
```

Readers with a background in mathematics or physics are encouraged to purchase a Klein bottle from KleinBottle.com (*http://kleinbottle .com/*) at their earliest convenience. The confirmation email and packing slip materials are worth the price of admission by themselves.

Discussion

The html YQL table is useful for quick-and-dirty data gathering. Keep in mind that data published using web service APIs might have different copyright considerations than data published using HTML. Also, sites typically at least make some kind of announcement before making breaking changes to their web service APIs, while website markup is usually much more fluid.

YQL handles invalid HTML by tidying and transforming the contents into well-formed XML, running the XPath expression against the document, and returning the results to you as JSON. Extreme cases of pathological bad markup can defeat YQL, but in general the process is fairly robust.

In addition to the html table, YQL provides a number of generic data tables that work with different data formats found across the Web. These include an xml table for fetching XML, a csv table for CSV data, a microformats table that extracts microformat data from web pages, and a feed table for extracting data from RSS and Atom feeds. For example, the following code fetches a list of the most recently posted YUI Theater videos from the YUI project's YouTube channel.

```
var url   = 'http://gdata.youtube.com/feeds/base/users/yuilibrary/uploads?alt=rss',
    query = 'select * from feed where url="' + url + '"';

Y.YQL(query, function (response) {
   // ... display video links and titles here ...
});
```

See Also

Recipe 9.7; the XPath 1.0 specification (*http://www.w3.org/TR/xpath/*).

5.9 Querying Data Using DataSource

Problem

You want to supply an application with data using an abstraction layer, so that you can change the source of the data with minimal impact on the rest of your code.

Solution

Load the datasource rollup or one of its modules such as datasource-local, datasource-function, datasource-io, or datasource-get. Instantiate a new DataSource object of the appropriate type and set its source attribute to some local data, a JavaScript function that returns data, or a URL for making a web service request. Then call sendRe quest() to fetch the data. sendRequest() is asynchronous for DataSource.IO and Data Source.Get, and synchronous for DataSource.Function and DataSource.Local.

Example 5-13 uses DataSource to make a JSONP request to GitHub, fetching live data about issues filed against the JSLint project. The example instantiates a Y.Data Source.Get object and configures the source to be a web service URL. It then calls sendRequest(), providing a callback method for success that writes the returned data into the DOM.

Example 5-13. Using a remote JSON DataSource

```
<!DOCTYPE html>
<title>Using a remote JSON DataSource</title>

<h1>JSLint: Recently closed issues</h1>
<ol id="issues"></ol>

<script src="http://yui.yahooapis.com/3.5.0/build/yui/yui-min.js"></script>
<script>
YUI().use('datasource-get', 'node-base', function (Y) {
    var src = 'https://api.github.com/repos/douglascrockford/JSLint/issues?state=closed',
        dataSource = new Y.DataSource.Get({ source: src });

    function displayIssues(rsp) {
        var issues = rsp.response.results[0].data,
            template = '<li><a href="{html_url}">{id}</a> {title}</li>',
            ol = Y.one('#issues');
        Y.Array.each(issues, function (issue) {
            ol.append(Y.Lang.sub(template, issue));
        });
    }

    dataSource.sendRequest({
        on: {
            success: displayIssues
        }
    });
});
</script>
```

 Unlike Y.jsonp(), Y.DataSource.Get tacks the JSON callback function onto the URL automatically. The default name for the JSONP parameter is "callback". To change this assumption, set the scriptCallbackParam attribute before making the request:

```
dataSource.set('scriptCallbackParam', 'cbFunc');
```

Example 5-14 illustrates how to use a local DataSource. Instead of a URL, the src vari- able represents locally stored data about issues.

Example 5-14. Using a local DataSource

```
<!DOCTYPE html>
<title>Using a local DataSource</title>

<h1>JSLint: Recently closed issues</h1>
<ol id="issues"></ol>

<script src="http://yui.yahooapis.com/3.5.0/build/yui/yui-min.js"></script>
<script>
YUI().use('datasource-local', 'node-base', function (Y) {
    var src = [
        { 'id': 2318990, 'html_url':'#', 'title':'Bug? inconsistent whitespace flagging' },
        { 'id': 2092345, 'html_url':'#', 'title':'newcap has no effect on `this`' },
        { 'id': 1920535, 'html_url':'#', 'title':'Filtering the body of a "for in" loop' }
    ];
    var dataSource = new Y.DataSource.Local({ source: src });

    function displayIssues(rsp) {
        var issues = rsp.response.results,
            template = '<li><a href="{html_url}">{id}</a> {title}</li>',
            ol = Y.one('#issues');
        Y.Array.each(issues, function (issue) {
            ol.append(Y.Lang.sub(template, issue));
        });
    }

    dataSource.sendRequest({
        on: {
            success: displayIssues
        }
    });
});
</script>
```

Comparing Examples 5-13 and 5-14 side by side, notice that the `displayIssues()` function is *almost* identical. Example 5-13 has the line:

```
var issues = rsp.response.results[0].data,
```

while Example 5-14 has the line:

```
var issues = rsp.response.results
```

This is because the response object has a slightly different structure for `DataSource.Get` versus `DataSource.Local`. It would be really nice if the response objects had an identical structure, because then the `displayIssues()` function would be exactly the same in both cases. For a solution to this problem, refer to Recipe 5.10.

Discussion

`DataSource` is a universal adapter for retrieving data from disparate sources and normalizing it. `DataSource` offers:

Abstraction over multiple types of data providers

For example, a `DataTable` or `AutoComplete` widget can consume any `DataSource` and display its data, regardless of whether the data originally came from a local variable, a remote web service, or an arbitrary function.

There are four basic types of `DataSources`:

- `DataSource.Local`, for abstracting data stored in a local variable, as shown in Example 5-14.
- `DataSource.Get`, for abstracting data fetched using script loading, as shown in Example 5-13.
- `DataSource.IO`, for abstracting data fetched using XHR. Usage is almost identical to `DataSource.Get`:

  ```
  var dataSource = new Y.DataSource.IO({ source: '/io.php' });
  ```

- `DataSource.Function`, for abstracting data provided by an arbitrary function. This could be data from `localStorage`, data returned by a Web Worker, or any number of things:

  ```
  var dataSource = new Y.DataSource.Function({
      source: function (request) {
          // Lots of interesting work here
          return data;
      }
  });
  ```

To fully normalize data from disparate sources, you can plug the `DataSource` with a `DataSchema`. For more information, refer to Recipe 5.10.

Caching

If you load the module `datasource-cache` and plug `DataSource` with `Y.Plugin.Data SourceCache`, you can cache results from requests. For example:

```
dataSource.plug(Y.Plugin.DataSourceCache, { max: 10 });
```

caches the first 10 unique requests. This is particularly useful for `DataSource.Get` and `DataSource.IO`. If the browser has `localStorage` available, you can save `Data Source` data offline:

```
dataSource.plug(Y.Plugin.DataSourceCache, {
    max: 10,
    cache: Y.CacheOffline
});
```

Polling

Ordinarily, you make a single request by calling `dataSource.sendRequest(request Config)`, as shown in Example 5-13. However, if you also load the `datasource-pollable` module, `DataSource` gains additional API methods for polling. To start polling, call:

```
var transactionId = dataSource.setInterval(5000, requestConfig);
```

This makes the specified request every five seconds, until you call:

```
dataSource.clearInterval(transactionId);
```

Take care not to confuse `DataSource` with other YUI objects that are meant to "hold data" or to "represent a 'thing'," such as `Y.Model`. It is usually better to think of `Data Source` as an adapter for data, rather than a concrete representation of that data.

See Also

Recipe 5.10; Recipe 8.11; Recipe 8.17; the `DataSource` User Guide (*http://yuilibrary .com/yui/docs/datasource/*).

5.10 Normalizing DataSource Responses with a DataSchema

Problem

You want to normalize data provided in the `DataSource response` object, so that other components can use the `DataSource` without needing any special logic that depends on the original source of that data.

Solution

Load the appropriate `DataSource` schema plugin module, such as `datasource-json schema`. Before calling `sendRequest()`, plug the `DataSource` with a schema that defines a `resultListLocator` string (to define a path into the data) and a `resultFields` array (to select particular fields to use).

Example 5-15 solves the problem discussed in Recipe 5.9, namely that `DataSource .Get` and `DataSource.Local` have slightly different response objects. This slight difference means that a component calling `dataSource.sendRequest()` must provide a different success handler function depending on whether the `DataSource` is remote or local.

To normalize this difference away, you can plug the `DataSource` with a `Y.Plugin.Data SourceJSONSchema`, providing a `schema` object with two properties:

- `resultListLocator` indicates that the fields of interest reside one level down, on a `data` property on the root object.
- `resultFields` selects the fields of interest: `html_url`, `id`, and `title`. Any other fields get thrown away.

When the user invokes `sendRequest()`, the `DataSource.Get` instance applies the schema, which enforces this structure on the response data—it walks down one step to the `data` property, selects three fields, and attaches these fields directly to `rsp.response .results`. The response object now has the same structure as the response object in Example 5-14, which means Example 5-15 can reuse the exact same `displayIssues()` function.

This is important because other components in this application can now call `data Source.sendRequest()` blindly. Thanks to the schema, the difference between local and remote data sources has been abstracted away.

Example 5-15. Normalizing a remote JSON DataSource with a DataSchema

```
<!DOCTYPE html>
<title>Normalizing a remote JSON DataSource with a DataSchema</title>

<h1>JSLint: Recently closed issues</h1>
<ol id="issues"></ol>

<script src="http://yui.yahooapis.com/3.5.0/build/yui/yui-min.js"></script>
<script>
YUI().use('datasource-get', 'datasource-jsonschema', 'node-base', function (Y) {
    var src = 'https://api.github.com/repos/douglascrockford/JSLint/issues?state=closed',
        dataSource = new Y.DataSource.Get({ source: src });

    function displayIssues(rsp) {
        var issues = rsp.response.results,
            template = '<li><a href="{html_url}">{id}</a> {title}</li>',
            ol = Y.one('#issues');
        Y.Array.each(issues, function (issue) {
            ol.append(Y.Lang.sub(template, issue));
        });
    }

    dataSource.plug(Y.Plugin.DataSourceJSONSchema, {
        schema: {
            resultListLocator: 'data',
            resultFields: ['html_url', 'id', 'title']
        }
    });

    dataSource.sendRequest({
        on: {
            success: displayIssues
        }
    });
});
</script>
```

Discussion

In addition to the `datasource-jsonschema` plugin, YUI provides `datasource-array schema`, `datasource-textschema`, and `datasource-xmlschema` for manipulating Data Source response data. All `DataSchema` implementations support a `resultListLocator` string to provide a path to a list or array of data, and a `resultFields` array to select individual fields within that list. The exact nature of each depends on the type of data you are processing. For example, a `DataSource.IO` that fetches XML can plug itself with `Y.Plugin.DataSourceXMLSchema`, in which case `resultListLocator` and `resultFields` are XPath expressions:

```
dataSource.plug(Y.Plugin.DataSourceXMLSchema, {
    schema: {
        resultListLocator: '//issues',
        resultFields: ['html_url', 'id', 'title']
    }
});
```

resultFields can not only select fields, but also rename fields. For example, if you
didn't like the field name 'html_url' that the GitHub API returns, you could rename
it to 'url' with this schema:

```
dataSource.plug(Y.Plugin.DataSourceJSONSchema, {
    schema: {
        resultListLocator: 'data',
        resultFields: [{ key: 'url', locator: 'html_url' }, 'id', 'title']
    }
});
```

Renaming fields is useful if you are trying to work with disparate APIs that are describing
roughly the same thing (for example, if your application is designed to display issue
data from both GitHub and Bitbucket). If renaming the field with a key and locator
isn't enough, you can also supply a parser function to transform the field's data.

While DataSchema plugins are designed to work with DataSource, you can also use
DataSchema standalone, calling the apply() method to apply the schema to any object.
For example, you could load the dataschema-json module to apply a JSON schema
without involving DataSource at all:

```
var schema = {
    resultListLocator: 'foo[2].bar',
    resultFields: [
        'baz',
        { key: 'quux', locator: 'quux.content' },
        { key: 'numFlumphs', parser: function (n) { return n.toExponential(); } }
    ]
};

var normalizedData = Y.DataSchema.JSON.apply(schema, data);
```

For more information, refer to DataSchema's documentation.

See Also

Recipe 5.9; the DataSchema User Guide (*http://yuilibrary.com/yui/docs/dataschema/*); the
DataSchema class gallery module (*http://yuilibrary.com/gallery/show/dataschema-class*).

CSS

Although YUI is primarily a JavaScript framework, it also provides CSS resources. YUI's CSS support dates back to very early releases of YUI 2, and has now evolved to include:

- YUI CSS Reset, which nulls out default browser styles.
- YUI CSS Base, which together with YUI CSS Reset, sets all browsers to have a common baseline look and feel.
- YUI CSS Fonts, which provides a consistent set of font sizes across all browsers.
- YUI CSS Grids, which enables you to quickly create sophisticated layouts using very minimal CSS.

Although developed alongside the YUI 3 JavaScript APIs, the YUI stylesheets are not tied to YUI 3 JS in any way. They work just fine with legacy YUI 2 code, with other JavaScript libraries, or with no JavaScript at all.

Like YUI JavaScript, YUI CSS can be combo loaded, minified, gzipped, and served from the Yahoo! CDN. For example, the combo load URL for YUI CSS Reset and YUI CSS Fonts looks like:

```
http://yui.yahooapis.com/combo?3.5.0/build/cssreset/reset-min.css
&3.5.0/build/cssfonts/fonts-min.css
```

YUI CSS Reset, Base, and Fonts come in two flavors: global and contextual. By default, these stylesheets apply to every element in the page. To restrict them to a subsection of the page, you can load the contextual version of the stylesheet. For example:

```
http://yui.yahooapis.com/3.5.0/build/cssreset/reset-context-min.css
```

loads a version of CSS Reset scoped to act only on elements that descend from the class `yui3-cssreset`. Similarly, you can pull in `base-context-min.css` (scoped to act under `yui3-cssbase`), and `fonts-context-min.css` (scoped to act under `yui3-cssfonts`). To generate the exact combo load URL for your needs, use the YUI Dependency Configurator (*http://yuilibrary.com/yui/configurator/*).

It is also possible to load YUI CSS as CSS modules, using `YUI().use('css reset', ...)`. However, it is much more common to load the stylesheets using static `<link>` elements at the top of the document. YUI CSS is less about functionality and much more about design, which should be applied even if JavaScript is turned off.

Recipe 6.1 explains how to eliminate default browser styles using YUI CSS Reset, and why this is a good idea.

Recipe 6.2 explains how to restore a set of cross-browser defaults using YUI CSS Base.

Recipe 6.3 describes how to use YUI CSS Fonts to normalize fonts and font sizes without overriding user preferences.

Recipe 6.4 introduces YUI CSS Grids, a highly efficient and easy-to-use framework for implementing layouts.

Recipe 6.5 explains how to use YUI grid units and media queries to create a responsive design that adjusts from phones to tablets to desktop monitors.

Recipe 6.6 demonstrates how to use the CSS component of the `button-base` module to create attractive, consistent form buttons.

6.1 Normalizing Browser Style Inconsistencies

Problem

You want to tear down conflicting default browser styles so that it is easy to style your application consistently.

Solution

Use YUI's CSS Reset stylesheet to provide a clean foundation to build on, as shown in Example 6-1.

Example 6-1. YUI CSS Reset

```
<!DOCTYPE html>
<title>YUI CSS Reset</title>
<link rel="stylesheet"
    href="http://yui.yahooapis.com/3.5.0/build/cssreset/reset-min.css">

<h1>YUI CSS Reset</h1>
<p>I like YUI CSS Reset for these <em>three</em> reasons:</p>
<ol>
    <li>It is minified, gzipped, and served from a central CDN.</li>
    <li>It can easily be combo loaded and served with other YUI stylesheets.</li>
    <li>It does a great job normalizing away default browser styles.</li>
</ol>
```

Discussion

When an HTML page does not provide explicit CSS for a property, browsers fall back to their built-in CSS defaults. These defaults help display unstyled pages in some reasonable form, but they are wildly inconsistent between browsers. For example, one browser might indent ordered lists using `padding`, while another might use `margin`. If you just set a list's `padding`, your lists will look correct in the first browser, but badly distorted in the second.

A general solution to this problem is to reset all default styles to the same baseline. Reset stylesheets have been around since at least 2004, and come in many different flavors, ranging from just setting `margin` and `padding` to 0 on a few elements to more extensive resets like YUI CSS Reset.

YUI CSS Reset lies more on the aggressive end of the spectrum, even removing bold and italic styles from semantic inline elements like `<strong>`, `<em>`, and `<cite>` (though it does not affect elements such as `<b>` and `<i>`). The goal is a high degree of normalization and fine-grained control, at the cost of requiring more CSS to tear down styles and to build your page back into some kind of presentable form. This kind of tight control is useful for helping maintain cohesive layout and typography in any web page, but is arguably even more important for web applications, where being just a pixel or two off is often immediately noticeable.

YUI CSS Reset does not waste bytes resetting deprecated and invalid elements, so if your page includes an `<applet>`, you must reset that yourself. YUI CSS Reset also avoids common design errors found in other reset stylesheets, such as using the * universal selector (bad for performance) or clobbering `:focus` (bad for accessibility).

See Also

"The History of CSS Resets" (*http://sixrevisions.com/css/the-history-of-css-resets/*); "Should You Reset Your CSS?" (*http://sixrevisions.com/css/should-you-reset-your-css/*).

6.2 Rebuilding Uniform Base Styles

Problem

You want to make sure that your application has a consistent CSS foundation with YUI Reset, but you don't want to start with a completely unstyled page.

Solution

Add YUI CSS Base to the YUI combo load URL alongside YUI CSS Reset, as shown in Example 6-2. YUI CSS Base adds back commonly used styles such as indenting for list items, margins for block elements, italic for `<em>` and other logical inline elements, dotted underlines for `<abbr>`, and more.

Example 6-2. YUI CSS Base (with Reset)

```
<!DOCTYPE html>
<title>YUI CSS Base (with Reset)</title>
<link rel="stylesheet" href="http://yui.yahooapis.com/combo
?3.5.0/build/cssreset/cssreset-min.css&3.5.0/build/cssbase/cssbase-min.css">

<h1>YUI CSS Base (with CSS Reset)</h1>
<p>I like YUI CSS Base for these <em>three</em> reasons:</p>
<ol>
    <li>It is minified, gzipped, and served from a central CDN.</li>
    <li>It can easily be combo loaded and served with other YUI stylesheets.</li>
    <li>It speeds up development by adding back a sensible set of default styles.</li>
</ol>
```

Discussion

YUI CSS Base must be used alongside (and immediately after) YUI CSS Reset. If you prefer to rebuild your styles yourself, you can always use Reset alone.

In addition to using Base as a quick way to get back to a reasonable baseline look, you can also use it as a kind of scaffolding during development. Add in Base at the beginning of the development process to make the page readable, and then swap it out later for a hand-tailored stylesheet when you are getting closer to releasing to production.

6.3 Applying Consistent Fonts

Problem

You want to use the same font in all browsers and make sure that the font size scales up and down consistently.

Solution

Add YUI CSS Fonts to the YUI combo load URL alongside YUI CSS Reset (and optionally, YUI CSS Base, as shown in Example 6-3). By default, ordinary text appears in 13px Arial with a 16px `line-height`, while text in `<pre>` and `<code>` elements uses the `monospace` font family. You can make elements larger or smaller using the percent declarations listed shortly in Table 6-1.

Example 6-3. YUI CSS Fonts (with Reset and Base)

```
<!DOCTYPE html>
<title>YUI CSS Fonts (with Reset and Base)</title>
<link rel="stylesheet" href="http://yui.yahooapis.com/combo
?3.5.0/build/cssreset/reset-min.css&3.5.0/build/cssbase/base-min.css
&3.5.0/build/cssfonts/fonts-min.css">

<h1>YUI CSS Fonts (with CSS Reset and Base)</h1>
<p>I like YUI CSS Fonts for these <em>three</em> reasons:</p>
```

```
<ol>
    <li>It is minified, gzipped, and served from a central CDN.</li>
    <li>It can easily be combo loaded and served with other YUI stylesheets.</li>
    <li>It provides a consistent set of resizable fonts.</li>
</ol>
```

To avoid hearing your hip designer friends shriek in horror, you can override the Arial default with a single declaration:

```
body { font-family: some-better-font }
```

Discussion

Declaring font sizes in percentages rather than pixels enables users to resize their own fonts across more browsers. However, finding the boundaries is a tricky art; a percentage value that might round to 16 pixels in one browser could round to 17 pixels in another. Table 6-1 lists optimal cross-browser percentage values from 10px to 26px.

Table 6-1. Font pixels and percent values

Pixels	Percentage
10px	77%
11px	85%
12px	93%
13px	100%
14px	108%
15px	116%
16px	123.1%
17px	131%
18px	138.5%
19px	146.5%
20px	153.9%
21px	161.6%
22px	167%
23px	174%
24px	182%
25px	189%
26px	197%

For example, for 18px <h1> elements, set:

```
h1 { font-size: 138.5% }
```

YUI CSS Fonts is designed to address font size disparities in a wide variety of browsers, going all the way back to IE 6. IE 6 only has the concept of text resizing (x-small, small, medium, ...), with large jumps in size between each stage. YUI CSS Fonts provides for smaller jumps. Newer versions of IE and most other browsers support a separate concept called "page zoom" with more graceful scaling factors. Even newer versions of IE do not resize pixel font sizes, so YUI CSS Fonts declares its base font in pixels for all browsers except IE.

6.4 Laying Out Content with Grids

Problem

You want to create a multicolumn layout using CSS.

Solution

Use YUI CSS Grids (optionally combo loaded with YUI CSS Reset, Base, and Fonts), as shown in Example 6-4. YUI CSS Grids relies on a top-level *grid* class named yui3-g that directly contains one or more *unit* classes that start with yui3-u. The Grids "unit system" consists of classes of the form yui3-u-*x*-*y*, where *x/y* is some fraction that is a multiple of 1/24. Assigning a class of yui3-u-*x*-*y* sets that column to be a fraction *x/y* of the parent element's width.

Example 6-4. YUI CSS Grids: three-column layout

```
<!DOCTYPE html>
<title>YUI CSS Grids: three-column layout</title>
<link rel="stylesheet"
    href="http://yui.yahooapis.com/3.5.0/build/cssgrids/cssgrids-min.css">
<style>
body { margin: auto; width: 960px; }
p    { margin: 0px; border: 1px solid #000; }
</style>

<div class="yui3-g">
    <div class="yui3-u-1-3"><p>1/3 of the width</p></div>
    <div class="yui3-u-1-2"><p>1/2 of the width</p></div>
    <div class="yui3-u-1-6"><p>1/6 of the width</p></div>
</div>
```

Example 6-4 adds some cosmetic CSS to `<p>` to make the grid structure more visible, but otherwise it is very bare bones. The example also includes some CSS on the containing `<body>` to center the layout and set its overall width. This is entirely optional. You can align the grid however you like, and set it to whatever width you like (or not).

You may also freely stack grids on top of other grids and nest grids inside each other without side effects, as shown in Example 6-5.

Example 6-5. YUI CSS Grids: stacked and nested layout

```
<!DOCTYPE html>
<title>YUI CSS Grids: stacked and nested layout</title>
<link rel="stylesheet"
    href="http://yui.yahooapis.com/3.5.0/build/cssgrids/cssgrids-min.css">
<style>
body { margin: auto; width: 960px; }
p    { margin: 0px; border: 1px solid #000; }
</style>

<div class="yui3-g">
    <div class="yui3-u-1-4"><p>1/4</p></div>
    <div class="yui3-u-1-2">
        <div class="yui3-g">
            <div class="yui3-u-1-2"><p>1/2 (of my parent)</p></div>
            <div class="yui3-u-1-2"><p>1/2 (of my parent)</p></div>
        </div>
    </div>
    <div class="yui3-u-1-4"><p>1/4</p></div>
</div>
<div class="yui3-g">
    <div class="yui3-u-1-3"><p>1/3</p></div>
    <div class="yui3-u-1-2"><p>1/2</p></div>
    <div class="yui3-u-1-6"><p>1/6</p></div>
</div>
```

Any direct child of a yui3-g must be a container with a yui3-u* unit class of some kind. If you add a naked `<div>` as a child of yui3-g, your layout will break.

Avoid adding margins, padding, and borders directly to unit `<div>`s. If you want to create gutters and other effects, the recommended pattern is to create and style a child `<div class="content">` inside the unit.

Keep in mind that you do not necessarily need to use `<div>`s. If you prefer to think of grid units as list items, and you have a reset stylesheet in place, you can always do something like:

```
<ul class="yui3-g">
    <li class="yui3-u-1-3">...</li>
    <li class="yui3-u-2-3">...</li>
</ul>
```

Discussion

YUI CSS Grids is an extremely efficient CSS grids framework. At under 1.5K of CSS, it is two to three times smaller than nearly all other popular grid frameworks. As with all YUI assets, Grids is served combo loaded, minified, and gzipped from the CDN.

Grids also avoids the problem of "div-itis" and "class-itis," thanks to its minimal semantics: two levels of `<div>`s with no spacer elements or extra classes required. (If you want to apply internal padding or borders, a third `<div class="content">` is recommended.) YUI CSS Grids does not impose any canned layouts; you can use the provided 1/24 measurement units, or just set arbitrary pixel or percentage widths. Nesting is easy because each unit correctly determines its width based on the width of its container.

The main disadvantage of YUI CSS Grids is that it does not work in very old browsers. It actually does work in IE 6, but does not work in Firefox 2 and below.

When web designers started abandoning table-based layouts about a decade ago, they turned to CSS floats, the most feasible strategy at the time for placing columns next to each other. Over time, ad hoc techniques evolved into reusable frameworks, and today there are many mature float-based grid frameworks to choose from.

Unfortunately, floats have many side effects when used for layout, which in turn require hacks to work around. Lining up grids properly can cause rounding issues. Sizes can vary across browsers. Older browsers can have bad interactions with scrolling and float-based designs. It is hard to center floating `<div>`s with respect to each other. For bidirectional text, you cannot simply set `dir="rtl"`—you have to manually fix all your floats.

Instead of using `float`, YUI CSS Grids uses `display: inline-block`. The benefits of `inline-block` include:

- Greatly reducing size and complexity. Because YUI CSS Grids doesn't need layer upon layer of hacks to handle edge cases, it is considerably smaller and less buggy than traditional `float-based` grid frameworks.
- Alignment and centering is trivial. For example, `text-align: center` and even `vertical-align: middle` and `bottom` finally work as expected.
- For bidirectional text, you can freely set `dir="rtl"` to a section or to the whole page.

One area where both `float` and `inline-block` layouts currently still fall short is in equalizing column heights. The tried-and-true strategy is to use CSS colors and backgrounds to create the illusion that the columns are equal height. Alternatively, you can trigger table layout mode by setting the grid to be `display: table` and the units to `display: table-cell`. This won't work in IE 7 and below, but if necessary, you can always fix that up with JavaScript. Aren't you glad you didn't give up and use tables (*http://giveupandusetables.com/*)?

See Also

Nicole Sullivan's OOCSS (*http://oocss.org/*); "Give Floats the Flick in CSS Layouts" (*http://www.sitepoint.com/give-floats-the-flick-in-css-layouts/*); "Farewell Floats: The Future of CSS Layout" (*http://designshack.co.uk/articles/css/farewell-floats-the-future-of-css-layout/*).

6.5 Using Grids for Responsive Design

Problem

You want to design a layout that adapts itself to a wide variety of devices, ranging from small phones to tablets up to large desktop computers.

Solution

Create a grid using `yui3-u` units. While `yui3-u-x-y` units take up a fixed fraction of their parent container, by default `yui3-u` units collapse to the width of their inner content, making them an ideal building block for implementing fluid layouts and for creating fixed-size columns.

After setting up the grid, use *media queries* to define how the layout should respond to different screen sizes. Example 6-6 illustrates a relatively simple responsive layout that supports three broad classes of devices, plus a fallback for older browsers:

Phones
> If the viewport is 480px or smaller, the stylesheet overrides all `yui3-u` units to use `display: block` instead of `display: inline-block`. The navigation `<div>` appears on top of the content, rather than to the left side.

Tablets and small desktops
> If the viewport is between 481px and 960px, the stylesheet switches to a fixed column for the navigation and a fluid column for the content area. To create a fixed lefthand column, first make room by adding left padding to the parent container, then set the fixed column's width and use a negative left margin to drag it over to the correct location. Finally, set the fluid column's width to 100% so it can fill the remaining space.

Larger desktops
> If the viewport exceeds 960px, the stylesheet switches to a fixed size for both columns, centered with respect to the viewport.

Legacy browsers
> If the browser does not support media queries at all, it receives a fallback layout. In this case, the fallback layout is identical to the "larger desktop" layout, although in general, the fallback layout could be completely different.

The page also adds a `<meta name="viewport">` element to improve presentation in mobile browsers. Without this element, Safari on iOS and other mobile browsers typically fall back to displaying a zoomed-out version of the desktop layout, rather than the mobile layout.

To see the example in action without having to resort to multiple devices, simply resize your browser window and watch the layout transition as the browser matches different media queries.

Example 6-6. Using Grids for responsive design

```
<!DOCTYPE html>
<title>Using Grids for responsive design</title>
<meta name="viewport" content="width=device-width, initial-scale=1.0">
<link rel="stylesheet"
    href="http://yui.yahooapis.com/3.5.0/build/cssgrids/cssgrids-min.css">
<style>
/* Default layout for browsers that do not support media queries */
body     { margin: auto; width: 960px; }
.nav     { width: 240px; }
.main    { width: 720px; }

/* Phone: completely vertical layout */
@media screen and (max-width: 480px) {
    body    { margin: inherit; width: inherit; }
    .yui3-u { display: block; }
    .nav    { width: 100%; }
    .main   { width: 100%; }
}

/* Tablet to small desktop: side nav, fluid layout */
@media screen and (min-width: 481px) and (max-width: 960px) {
    body    { margin: inherit; width: inherit; }
    .layout { padding-left: 240px; }
    .nav    { margin-left: -240px; width: 240px; }
    .main   { width: 99%; }
}

/* Desktop: max out with a centered, 960px fixed width layout */
@media screen and (min-width: 961px) {
    body    { margin: auto; width: 960px; }
    .nav    { width: 240px; }
    .main   { width: 720px; }
}
</style>
<div class="yui3-g layout">
    <div class="yui3-u nav">
        <ul>
            <li><a href="#">Chapter 1</a></li>
            <li><a href="#">Chapter 2</a></li>
            <li><a href="#">Chapter 3</a></li>
        </ul>
    </div>
    <div class="yui3-u main">
        <p>The author of these Travels, Mr. Lemuel Gulliver, is my ancient and
        intimate friend; there is likewise some relation between us on the
        mother's side.  About three years ago, Mr. Gulliver growing weary of the
        concourse of curious people coming to him at his house in Redriff, made a
        small purchase of land, with a convenient house, near Newark, in
        Nottinghamshire, his native country; where he now lives retired, yet in
        good esteem among his neighbours.</p>

        <p>Although Mr. Gulliver was born in Nottinghamshire...</p>
    </div>
</div>
```

Discussion

Example 6-6 is just the skeleton of a responsive design—one that only attempts to handle layout, and in a relatively simple way. A more production-quality responsive design would likely have a more complex layout to worry about, plus additional media query styles for doing things like adjusting image sizes, showing and hiding different elements, and more.

For simplicity, the example uses only three media queries. You can always design and test your layout using a more fine-grained range of media queries, depending on your available time and budget.

See Also

Ethan Marcotte's original article on responsive design (*http://www.alistapart.com/articles/responsive-web-design/*); *Smashing Magazine*'s article "Responsive Web Design: What It Is and How To Use It" (*http://coding.smashingmagazine.com/2011/01/12/guidelines-for-responsive-web-design/*); Mozilla's article "Using the viewport meta tag to control layout on mobile browsers" (*https://developer.mozilla.org/en/Mobile/Viewport _meta_tag*).

6.6 Creating Consistent Buttons

Problem

You want to add buttons that have a consistent and modern look and feel across browsers.

Solution

Load YUI's CSS Button stylesheet and add the class `yui3-button` to any button that needs styling. The stylesheet sets consistent padding, corners, and backgrounds for buttons, in their normal state and in the `:hover` and `:active` state.

Example 6-7 demonstrates three buttons: a default grey active button, a button flagged as disabled with the `yui3-button-disabled` class, and a customized error button with a different background color and size. YUI CSS Button is designed to make it easy to override the background colors, foreground colors, and more.

Example 6-7. Creating consistent buttons

```
<!DOCTYPE html>
<title>Creating consistent buttons</title>
<link rel="stylesheet"
    href="http://yui.yahooapis.com/3.5.0/build/cssbutton/cssbutton-min.css">
<style>
.giant-error { background: #c44; font-size: 150%;}
</style>
```

```
<button class="yui3-button">active</button>
<button class="yui3-button yui3-button-disabled">disabled</button>
<button class="yui3-button giant-error">error</button>
```

Figure 6-1 illustrates the results of Example 6-7.

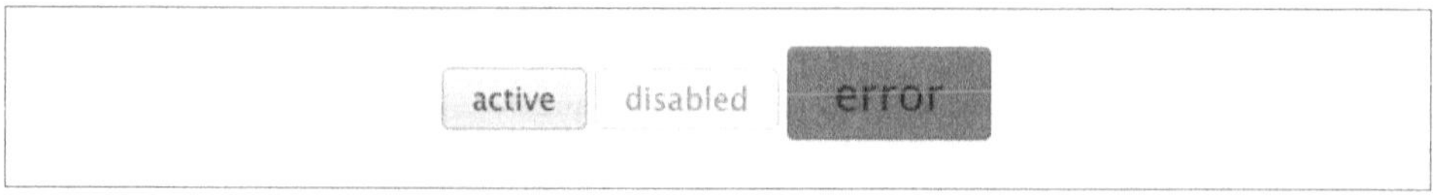

Figure 6-1. Three CSS buttons

Discussion

Like YUI CSS Grids, while on the surface YUI CSS Button might appear to be similar to other stylesheets, under the hood it is significantly ahead of the curve. In many button stylesheets, creating a button with a variant color means resorting to a CSS button tool to generate dozens of redundant lines of CSS code just for that new button type. By contrast, YUI CSS Button uses gradients intelligently, relying on highlights and shadows to serve as a generic masking layer. This makes it trivial to design different buttons simply by overriding the color and background color.

YUI also supports a wide range of browsers—legacy browsers display reasonably nice-looking buttons, while newer browsers display rounded corners and subtle gradients. Many popular button stylesheets degrade poorly on   Internet Explorer, even versions of Internet Explorer that do in fact support advanced CSS features.

YUI CSS Button is actually a subcomponent of the JavaScript modules `button-base` and `button-group`. The `button-base` module dynamically creates buttons with correct ARIA (Accessible Rich Internet Applications) roles and states for accessibility, and provides some event management. The `button-group` module adds the ability to define groups of buttons that act like radio buttons or checkboxes.

If you just want attractive buttons, YUI CSS Button is designed so that you can load and use it completely standalone. If you want the richer behavior provided by `button-base` and `button-group`, loading either of these modules will pull in the CSS automatically (much like a widget).

See Also

YUI Button User Guide (*http://yuilibrary.com/yui/docs/button/*).

Infrastructure

If you do some cursory searches about YUI, you might hear people say that it's "an Ajax library with widgets." Dig a little further, and you'll probably hear phrases like, "YUI supports rich web applications," or that it "helps provide structure," or that it "scales well with larger code bases."

Well, that's easy enough to say—but what is it *specifically* about YUI that makes it suitable for larger applications? Arguably, this boils down to a handful of key features.

The first is YUI's Loader and module system, which makes it possible to efficiently reassemble just the chunks of code you need, when you need them.

The second is YUI's highly configurable custom event system, which provides an obvious way to decouple components.

The third is YUI's ecosystem of tools for testing, deploying, and documenting your professional-grade code.

The fourth is YUI's `Base` infrastructure, discussed in this chapter.

The YUI `Base` object is *the* fundamental building block for major YUI components and apps. Casual users of YUI don't necessarily need to know much about `Base`, but if you're a component builder, you should understand that much of the library either powers `Base`, or is powered by it. `Base`'s descendants include:

- `Widget`, the foundation for `Overlay`, `Slider`, `Calendar`, and all other core widgets. This chapter explains how to create your own widgets from scratch. For example usage of the core widgets, refer to Chapter 8.

- Utility objects such as `Cache`, `DataSource`, `RecordSet`, and `Plugin.Base`.

- The App Framework, which was heavily inspired by the Backbone.js MVC library, but with YUI idioms. The App Framework supports full-fledged JavaScript applications on both the client and server sides. It is loose enough to be used piecemeal, but provides structure for managing larger apps. Like Backbone.js, the App Framework isn't strict MVC—for instance, a YUI `View` is more of a classical view with some controller functionality mixed in. The App Framework has also evolved to include progressive Ajax enhancement (`Pjax`) and general management for single-page apps (`App`).

 If Backbone.js is so nifty, why not just wrap it as a YUI module and call it a day? That approach would have a) dragged in unnecessary dependencies that YUI already provides, and b) failed to leverage YUI's powerful custom event system.

If you have a lot of free time on your hands, take a look at the source code for the oldest widgets in the YUI 2 source tree, such as `TreeView` or `DataTable`. Even as far back as YUI 0.10.x, you will see useful patterns around state management and message passing starting to emerge. YUI 2 started to standardize those patterns, and YUI 3 finally codified them in the `Base` and `Widget` objects. Understanding this `Base` infrastructure is what enables you to build your own widgets, rather than just exercising widgets designed by others.

Recipe 7.1 describes the `Attribute` API, which helps you manage an object's state. Along with `EventTarget` (discussed in Chapter 4), this API is a critical building block for understanding YUI infrastructure.

Recipe 7.2 builds on the previous recipe, introducing the `Base` object. `Base` includes attribute management, event handling, easy extension and augmentation, and a standard init/destroy lifecycle. Recipe 7.3 demonstrates an easier way to define `Base` objects, at the cost of loading another module.

Recipe 7.4 introduces `Widget`, the foundational object for visible, reusable components in YUI. `Widget` extends `Base`, adding strong conventions for rendering and extension.

Recipes 7.5 and 7.6 cover common use cases for widgets: how to create a widget that constructs itself from static HTML already on the page, and how to enable widgets to communicate with remote web services. See also Recipe 11.6 on how to internationalize a widget's user interface strings.

The `PluginHost` API makes it easy to add and remove bundles of functionality to `Base`-derived components. Recipe 7.7 explains how to create a simple plugin that adds methods to the host's prototype, while Recipe 7.8 illustrates a more complex plugin that alters the host's existing behavior.

Widgets and views almost always have associated CSS resources. Recipe 7.9 shows how to use the Loader to load a widget's CSS as a YUI module. Recipe 7.10 describes YUI skins, an alternative mechanism that (potentially) enables users to toggle the look and feel.

Recipe 7.11 introduces the App Framework with an example of `Model`, an object that represents data as attributes.

Recipe 7.12 provides an example implementation of `Model`'s `sync()` API, which enables you to read or persist a model's data in local or remote data stores.

Recipe 7.13 introduces ModelList and explains how to implement a sync layer that loads data from multiple Models at once.

Recipe 7.14 describes View, a distant cousin of Widget that renders HTML, but with lighter conventions and some handy syntax for handling user interactions through DOM events.

A key design pattern in the App Framework is to loosely couple models and views together, such that changes to model data get reflected in the page. Recipe 7.15 sets up this relationship between a single Model and View, while Recipe 7.16 sets up this relationship for an entire ModelList.

Recipe 7.17 shows how to use Router to save new URLs into browser history.

Finally, Recipe 7.18 introduces routes, which map URL paths within your application to JavaScript functions. Together with history management, this enables you to create full-page JavaScript applications with true URLs.

 Because Base, Widget, and the App Framework are substantial APIs, the examples in this chapter are a little different from the rest of the book. First, the code examples are longer, ranging from 30 lines and higher. Second, this chapter relies on YUI.add() to define reusable modules, so please review the relevant recipes in Chapter 1 if necessary. Third, despite their length, the code samples in this chapter are meant to clearly illustrate a small number of topics. A complete widget with professional-quality CSS or a grand finale full-page app would blow way past the size of recipe that makes sense for this cookbook. For more examples, refer to the Widget User Guide (*http://yuilibrary.com/yui/docs/widget/*) and the App Framework User Guide (*http://yuilibrary.com/yui/docs/app/*).

7.1 Managing State with Attributes

Problem

You want to manage an object's state through a central point of control, possibly adding special constraints and behaviors that go beyond what simple object properties provide.

Solution

Create an object to hold your state and augment it with Attribute. The Attribute API can configure how you can get and set an attribute, which values it can take, and more. Changing an attribute's value also causes the host instance to fire a custom event, which makes it easy to monitor state with event listeners. For example, attempting to change the foo attribute fires a fooChange custom event, which you can observe, prevent, react to, and so on.

Though it is fine to use `Attribute` by itself, experienced YUI developers use `Base`, which incorporates `Attribute` and adds some important functionality. For more information, refer to Recipe 7.2.

The concept of "a bag of attributes" is pretty generic, so let's pick a specific example from the world of physics. Example 7-1 defines `Electron` with two attributes, `charge` and `energy`, each with different constraints.

Example 7-1. Managing state with attributes

```
<!DOCTYPE html>
<title>Managing state with attributes</title>

<script src="http://yui.yahooapis.com/3.5.0/build/yui/yui-min.js"></script>
<script>
YUI.add('electron', function (Y) {
    var REST_ENERGY = 511.00;

    function Electron(config) {
        this.addAttrs({
            charge: {
                value: -1,
                readOnly: true
            },
            energy: {
                value: REST_ENERGY,
                validator: function (en) {
                    return (en >= REST_ENERGY);
                }
            }
        }, config);
    }

    Y.Electron = Y.augment(Electron, Y.Attribute);
}, '1.0', {requires: ['attribute']});

YUI().use('electron', function (Y) {
    var e1 = new Y.Electron({ energy: 708.72, charge: 2 });
    Y.log("e1's energy is " + e1.get('energy') + ' MeV.');
    Y.log("e1's charge is " + e1.get('charge'));

    var e2 = new Y.Electron();
    e2.on('energyChange', function (ev) {
        Y.log("Trying to change e2's energy to " + ev.newVal + ' ...');
    });
    e2.after('energyChange', function (ev) {
        Y.log("e2's energy changed from " + ev.prevVal + ' to ' + ev.newVal);
    });
    e2.set('energy', 400);
    e2.set('energy', 1200);
});
</script>
```

Within the `Electron()` constructor is a configuration object named `attrs` that defines the attributes' behavior:

- The `charge` attribute has a default value of −1, and cannot be changed. All electrons in the universe have the same charge.
- The `energy` attribute has a default value of 511.00 MeV (million electron-volts), and cannot drop below this value. A free electron at rest has an energy strictly determined by its mass, per E=mc². Any additional energy goes into the electron's motion.

The constructor then calls `addAttrs()` to actually define attributes on the object. `addAttrs()` takes the `attrs` object to define attributes, along with an optional config object that enables the user to set attributes to different values at construction time.

Finally, the `YUI.add()` callback augments `Electron`'s prototype with all of `Attribute`'s properties and methods. This includes `addAttrs()` for defining multiple attributes at once, `get()` and `set()` for reading and writing attribute values, and many others.

The `YUI().use()` callback creates two electron instances. The first instance attempts to set both the energy and the charge in the constructor. Setting the `energy` attribute works fine, but setting `charge` has no effect. Because the attribute is `readOnly`, the `Electron` instance obeys the laws of physics and rejects the user-provided value.

The second instance creates a free electron at rest and sets two listeners: an `on()` listener for when someone attempts to change the electron's energy, and an `after()` listener for when that change is successful.

Setting the energy to the illegal value of 400 MeV triggers the `on()` handler, but not the `after()` handler. When an attribute's `validator()` returns `false`, the `set()` method prevents the change attempt.

Setting the energy to 1,200 MeV passes validation, so both the `on()` and `after()` handlers execute. Every attribute change event includes a `prevVal` and `newVal` property, representing the old value and new value, respectively.

Discussion

The primary responsibility of the `Attribute` API is to manage state. The first critical feature is having centralized getters, setters, and validators, which manage how state can be set. The second critical feature is automatic firing of change events. You can set `on()` listeners to react to change *attempts*, at which point you can call `ev.preventDefault()` to prevent the change from happening, much like calling `ev.preventDefault()` on a `submit` event prevents a form from submitting. You can also set `after()` listeners to react to changes that actually do happen.

Individual attributes support a wide range of configurations, some of which include:

lazyAdd

> A Boolean property that, if `true`, defers initializing the attribute until the first `get()` or `set()` call. This can help improve performance if you have a large number of attributes or if an attribute requires a remote call to initialize itself.

valueFn

> A function that returns a default value for the attribute, overriding `value` (unless `valueFn()` returns `undefined`). `valueFn` is useful when you need to define the default value at class instantiation time, or if you need access to the `this` object in order to determine the default.

validator

> A function that receives the value to change the attribute to, returning `true` if this change should go through, and `false` otherwise. For simple validators, you can often just assign one of the `Y.Lang.*` type checking methods discussed in Recipe 9.1.

getter *and* setter

> Functions for normalizing the attribute, called by `get()` and `set()`, respectively. Getters and setters are meant to normalize data, not produce side effects. For example, a setter might take any falsy value and turn it into a real `false`, but it should not change some other value or directly refresh a widget or view's UI. For secondary effects, use an `after()` listener to react to the attribute's value successfully changing.

broadcast

> An integer that controls whether the attribute's `*Change` custom events get broadcast, as described in Recipe 4.7. By default, an attribute's custom events have a broadcast of `0`, but you can change this to `1` to broadcast to the top-level `Y`, or `2` to broadcast to `Y.Global`.

If you don't need advanced features like setting defaults, performing validation, and listening for changes, you can always just store state in lightweight object properties. There is also nothing wrong with using a mix of attributes and properties—attributes when you have complex state management requirements, properties when you don't.

Individual attributes don't have to be primitive types. If you set an attribute to be an object:

```
particle.set('vector', {
    position : {
        x : 0,
        y : 0,
        z : 0
    },
    time : 0
});
```

then you can get and set attribute properties using dot notation:

```
var t0 = particle.get('vector.time');
particle.set('vector.position.x', 10);
```

The `Attribute` API also pulls in the `EventTarget` API, enabling any object that hosts attributes to publish, fire, and handle events. In addition to `prevVal` and `newVal`, change events also include `attrName` and `subAttrName` properties, representing the name of the attribute that changed and the full dot notation path (if any). These two APIs together are powerful; attributes not only manage their own state, but also send and receive messages about state changes.

As mentioned earlier, while `Attribute` and `EventTarget` make a reasonable foundation for building event-driven applications, the preferred pattern is to go a little further and extend `Base` instead of directly augmenting an object with `Attribute`.

See Also

Recipe 4.10 for more about how `on()` and `after()` behave for custom events; Recipe 9.1 for information on `Y.Lang.*` type checking methods; Recipe 9.5 for background on `Y.augment()`; Luke Smith's YUIConf 2011 talk, "Class Inheritance and Composition Patterns in YUI" (*http://www.youtube.com/watch?v=_zhQIfT7g58*); the YUI `Attribute` User Guide (*http://yuilibrary.com/yui/docs/attribute/*); `Attribute` API documentation (*http://yuilibrary.com/yui/docs/api/classes/Attribute.html*); Wikipedia articles on the electron (*http://en.wikipedia.org/wiki/Electron*) and rest energy (*http://en.wikipedia.org/wiki/Invariant_mass*).

7.2 Creating Base Components with Y.extend()

Problem

You want to build a reusable object that can serve as a foundational component in your application.

Solution

Load the `base-base` module, extend `Base` (or an object derived from `Base` such as `Widget` or `Model`), and add custom behavior to the object's prototype. The `Base` object not only includes the highly useful `Attribute` and `EventTarget` APIs, but also enables the object to host plugins and provides a framework for object initialization and destruction.

Example 7-2 illustrates how to use `Y.extend()` to create a more sophisticated version of the `Electron` from Example 7-1.

Example 7-2. Creating a Base-derived object with Y.extend()

```
<!DOCTYPE html>
<title>Creating a Base-derived object with Y.extend()</title>

<script src="http://yui.yahooapis.com/3.5.0/build/yui/yui-min.js"></script>
```

```
<script>
YUI.add('electron', function (Y) {
    var REST_ENERGY = 511.00;

    function Electron() {
        Electron.superclass.constructor.apply(this, arguments);
    }

    Electron.NAME = 'electron';

    Electron.ATTRS = {
        charge: {
            value: -1,
            readOnly: true
        },
        energy: {
            value: REST_ENERGY,
            validator: function (en) {
                return (en >= REST_ENERGY);
            }
        }
    };

    Y.Electron = Y.extend(Electron, Y.Base, {
        initializer: function () {
            Y.log("SMASH! Here's your electron!");
        },
        getSpeed: function () {
            var e_ratio = REST_ENERGY / this.get('energy');
            return Math.sqrt(1 - e_ratio * e_ratio);
        }
    });
}, '1.0', {requires: ['base-base']});

YUI().use('electron', function (Y) {
    var e = new Y.Electron();
    Y.log('The electron is now moving at ' + e.getSpeed() + 'c.');
    e.set('energy', 850);
    Y.log('The electron is now moving at ' + e.getSpeed() + 'c.');
});
</script>
```

Let's break down this example step-by-step.

First, there's the Electron() constructor function, which includes a weird-looking Electron.superclass property—where did that come from? It turns out that superclass is a special property added by Y.extend() (which we haven't called *quite* yet, but never mind that). The full meaning of this line is, "Call my parent's constructor and pass in any arguments that I received."

Next, the Electron adds a NAME static property. Every Base-derived object must have a NAME, which, among other things, serves as the prefix for any custom events that the object fires. This enables other objects to distinguish between, say, a menu:select event and a treenode:select event. For another example of this, refer to Recipe 4.7.

Next is the ATTRS property, which defines the same attributes shown in Example 7-1: a hash of attribute names, each with its own hash of attribute configuration properties.

After that, you call Y.extend() on Electron with Base. This sets Base as the super class for Electron, lets Electron inherit Base's methods and properties, and adds a couple of new methods to the prototype:

initializer()

> Performs any initialization specifically required for this particular object. This is a standard method that many (but not all) Base-derived objects implement. The initializer() is a good place to publish() any specialized custom events that your object needs to fire, as shown in Example 4-9. There is also an equivalent destruc tor() method for doing teardown. For more information about the Base object lifecycle, refer to this recipe's Discussion.

getSpeed()

> Calculates the speed of the electron as a multiple of the speed of light, c. When the electron is at rest, the speed is 0. As the electron's energy increases, its speed asymptotically approaches c.

 Since the speed calculation is the same for any massive relativistic particle, it might make sense to implement getSpeed() in a separate object and augment Electron, rather than defining getSpeed() directly on Electron's prototype.

Discussion

Unlike DOM, events, and Ajax, the Base object doesn't have a strong analog in other frameworks. If you take a superficial tour through YUI, Base is easy to overlook. This is unfortunate, as Base represents years of refinement on what constitutes a generic, flexible building block for an application. Objects that derive from Base get:

- State management (from Attribute)
- Event handling (from EventTarget, via Attribute)
- Easy extension and augmentation of the prototype
- Class-level extensions (mixins)
- Instance-level plugins
- A standard init/destroy lifecycle

The one obvious feature Base does not provide out of the box is rendering—that is what Widget and View are for. For more information, refer to Recipes 7.4 and 7.14.

Because Base-derived objects can have long inheritance chains, Base supplies a particular model for creating and destroying instances properly. When you call Base's constructor, the constructor first fires an `init` custom event; then starting with `Base` itself, it steps down through each object in the inheritance chain. If the constructor received a `config` parameter, it inspects `config` for attributes and sets any it finds. It then executes the object's `initializer()` method (if any), passing in the `config` object (if any), and steps down the chain again.

If the constructor receives a configuration object `{foo: 'bar'}`, and `foo` is an attribute, `Base` sets the `foo` attribute to `'bar'` automatically. If `foo` is not an attribute, you can still handle that value as you see fit in your `initializer()` method. This behavior makes it easy for users to configure your objects at instantiation time.

Calling `Base`'s `destroy()` method fires a `destroy` custom event and then steps backward through the object hierarchy all the way up to `Base` itself, executing any `destructor()` methods it finds. Any given `initializer()` and `destructor()` methods should only set up or tear down resources for the object they are defined on, not any other objects up or down the chain. If your object does not need any special setup or teardown logic, it is safe to omit these methods.

If you need to modify individual instances rather than the object prototype, `Base` provides the `plug()` and `unplug()` methods for adding and removing functionality on the fly. For more information about how to create plugins, refer to Recipes 7.7 and 7.8. For some examples of plugins in action, refer to Recipes 3.7 and 3.9.

 When you're reading about a `Base`-derived component in the API documentation, it's sometimes helpful to uncheck the "Show inherited" checkbox. This filters the API documentation down to just what that specific component offers (new and overridden methods and properties).

See Also

Recipe 4.7 for an example of `Base`-derived objects interacting with each other; the YUI `Base` User Guide (*http://yuilibrary.com/yui/docs/base/*); `Base` API documentation (*http://yuilibrary.com/yui/docs/api/classes/Base.html*); `EventTarget` API documentation (*http://yuilibrary.com/yui/docs/api/classes/EventTarget.html*).

7.3 Creating Base Components with Y.Base.create()

Problem

You want to extend `Base` using a pattern that's easier to remember than the `Y.extend()` approach. Alternatively, you want to extend `Base` using a pattern that makes it easy to mix in extensions.

Solution

Load the `base-build` module and use the static `Y.Base.create()` method, as shown in Example 7-3.

Example 7-3. Creating a Base-derived component with Y.Base.create()

```
<!DOCTYPE html>
<title>Creating a Base-derived component with Y.Base.create()</title>

<script src="http://yui.yahooapis.com/3.5.0/build/yui/yui-min.js"></script>
<script>
YUI.add('electron', function (Y) {
    var REST_ENERGY = 511.00;

    Y.Electron = Y.Base.create('electron', Y.Base, [], {
        initializer: function () {
            Y.log("SMASH! Here's your electron!");
        },
        getSpeed: function () {
            var e_ratio = REST_ENERGY / this.get('energy');
            return Math.sqrt(1 - e_ratio * e_ratio);
        }
    }, {
        ATTRS: {
            charge: {
                value: -1,
                readOnly: true
            },
            energy: {
                value: REST_ENERGY,
                validator: function (en) {
                    return (en >= REST_ENERGY);
                }
            }
        }
    });
}, '1.0', { requires: ['base-build'] });

YUI().use('electron', function (Y) {
    var e = new Y.Electron();
    Y.log('The electron is now moving at ' + e.getSpeed() + 'c.');
    e.set('energy', 850);
    Y.log('The electron is now moving at ' + e.getSpeed() + 'c.');
});
</script>
```

Comparing Examples 7-2 and 7-3 side by side, the latter is slightly more succinct:

1. The first parameter sets the static `NAME` property.
2. The second parameter specifies the object to extend. When you are using `Y.Base.create()`, this must be `Base` or a descendant such as `Widget`.

3. The third parameter is an array of zero or more objects for `Y.Base.create()` to mix in to the object. The example just hacks around this parameter by passing in an empty array. However, if there were a `Relativistic` object with utility methods to borrow for `Electron`, you could do something like:

```
Y.Electron = Y.Base.create("electron", Y.Base, [Y.Relativistic], { ...
```

This is object composition, not object inheritance. In other words, `Y.Electron instanceof Base` is `true`, but `Y.Electron instanceof Y.Relativistic` would be `false`.

4. The fourth parameter is an object containing anything else you want to add to the object's prototype. This is the equivalent of `Y.extend()`'s third parameter.

5. The fifth parameter contains static properties and methods to add, such as `ATTRS`. `Y.Base.create()` already sets the name as the first parameter, so you don't need to define a `NAME` property here.

`Y.Base.create()` also creates a slightly different object than `Y.extend()`—the constructor generated by `Y.Base.create()` has some extra logic that improves runtime performance when the object is further extended. The cost is flexibility. Once you use `Y.Base.create()`, any further extensions require using `Y.Base.create()`.

Discussion

The main motivation for `Y.Base.create()` was to make it easy to add multiple mixins. Some core YUI objects make heavy use of mixins. For example, there are a number of standard `Widget` mixin objects that provide simple generic behaviors, such as `Widget Position`, `WidgetModality`, and `WidgetButtons`. It turns out that the `Overlay` and `Panel` widgets have no intrinsic behavior of their own—they just extend `Widget` and mix in a large list of `Widget*` extension objects. In other words, `Overlay` and `Panel` are defined as one-liners with `Y.Base.create()`.

However, many YUI developers don't care about this mixin feature. They prefer `Y.Base.create()` simply because it is more compact than the "standard" `Y.extend()` pattern.

The benefit of `Y.extend()` is that it comes with the `YUI` global object and thus avoids having to load the `base-build` module. If you don't plan to use mixins, and if the aesthetics don't bother you, use `Y.extend()`. But if the thought of typing out the boilerplate constructor function fills you with dread, use `Y.Base.create()`.

This book uses `Y.Base.create()` from here on out.

See Also

Recipe 8.2; Recipe 8.5.

7.4 Creating a Basic Widget

Problem

You want to build a reusable object that represents some visible component in your application.

Solution

Extend `Widget` and add custom behavior to the object's prototype. `Widget` extends `Base`, adding an API for rendering the object as HTML. The `Widget` API has five core lifecycle methods to implement: `initializer()`, `destructor()`, `renderUI()`, `bindUI()`, and `syncUI()`.

Example 7-4 illustrates how to further enhance the `Electron` example from Example 7-3, turning it into a visible widget that responds to user interactions. It might seem a little odd to have a visible electron widget, but let's roll with it.

Example 7-4. Creating a basic widget

```
<!DOCTYPE html>
<title>Creating a basic widget</title>
<style>
.yui3-electron          { width: 175px; }
.yui3-electron-content  { background: #ff0; border: 1px #000 solid; }
.yui3-electron-content p { margin: 5px; }
</style>

<p>Click the electron to increase its energy by 10%.</p>
<div id="demo"></div>

<script src="http://yui.yahooapis.com/3.5.0/build/yui/yui-min.js"></script>
<script>
YUI.add('electron', function (Y) {
    var REST_ENERGY = 511.00;

    Y.Electron = Y.Base.create('electron', Y.Widget, [], {
        destructor: function () {
            this.get('contentBox').all('p').remove(true);
        },
        getSpeed: function () {
            var e_ratio = REST_ENERGY / this.get('energy');
            return Math.sqrt(1 - e_ratio * e_ratio);
        },
        boostEnergy: function () {
            this.set('energy', 1.1 * this.get('energy'));
        },
        renderUI: function () {
            this.get('contentBox')
                .append('<p class="ch">Charge: ' + this.get('charge') + '</p>')
                .append('<p class="en">')
                .append('<p class="sp">');
```

```
        },
        bindUI: function () {
            this.get('contentBox').on('click', this.boostEnergy, this);
            this.after('energyChange', this.syncUI, this);
        },
        syncUI: function () {
            var energyStr = 'Energy: ' + this.get('energy').toPrecision(5) + ' MeV',
                speedStr  = 'Speed: ' + this.getSpeed().toPrecision(5) + ' c';
            this.get('contentBox').one('.en').setHTML(energyStr);
            this.get('contentBox').one('.sp').setHTML(speedStr);
        }
    }, {
        ATTRS: {
            charge: {
                value: -1,
                readOnly: true
            },
            energy: {
                value: REST_ENERGY,
                validator: function (en) {
                    return (en >= REST_ENERGY);
                }
            }
        }
    });
}, '1.1', {requires: ['base-build', 'widget']});

YUI().use('electron', function (Y) {
    var e = new Y.Electron();
    e.render('#demo');
});
</script>
```

Figure 7-1 illustrates the results of Example 7-4.

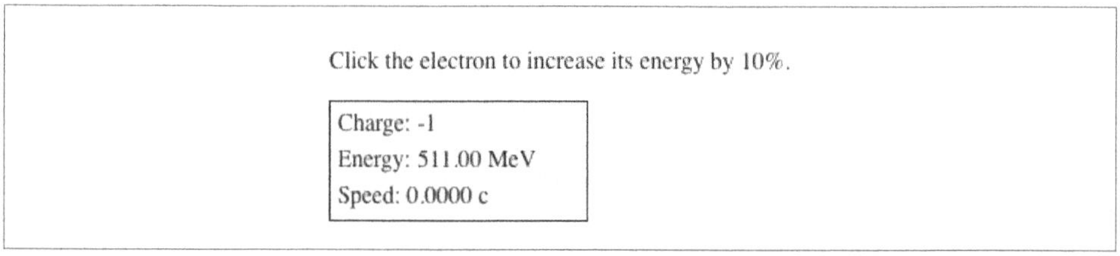

> Click the electron to increase its energy by 10%.
>
> Charge: -1
> Energy: 511.00 MeV
> Speed: 0.0000 c

Figure 7-1. A basic widget

The destructor() lifecycle method is from the Base API. The Electron widget does not require any special setup logic, but it includes some teardown logic to clean up the nodes it creates. For more information about widget destructors, refer to this recipe's Discussion.

The getSpeed() method is the same as it was in Example 7-2. The widget version also includes a boostEnergy() method, to be used as an event handler.

The widget's main render() method calls renderUI(), bindUI(), and syncUI() in that order. Widgets should implement these three methods instead of overriding render() itself:

1. renderUI() constructs or patches a DOM tree to define the widget's basic structure. Every widget has a boundingBox attribute, the node that determines the widget's size and position, and a contentBox attribute, the node that contains the widget's content and its look and feel. You do not have to create these boxes yourself; they are containers for adding more elements.

   In the example, renderUI() populates the contentBox with the initial structural elements that Electron needs to display the charge, energy, and speed. Since the charge is always –1, this is hardcoded into the display. For the energy and speed, renderUI() creates two paragraphs. The bindUI() and syncUI() methods will update the paragraphs as the widget's state changes.

2. bindUI() sets event listeners that update the widget's appearance according to widget state changes. Thanks to the Attribute API, you can just store the widget's state as attributes and listen for attribute change events.

   In the example, bindUI() sets two listeners:

   - A click listener on the entire widget calls boostEnergy(), which increases the energy attribute value by 10%, causing the widget to fire an energyChange event.

   - An energyChange listener catches each energy boost and calls syncUI() to resync the widget according to its current attribute state. The reason to use after() listeners rather than on() listeners is to ensure that the UI resyncs in response to *successful* state changes, rather than change *attempts*. A state change can be foiled if the state change fails validation, if the user calls preventDefault(), and so on.

3. syncUI() updates the widget's appearance according to its current state. This method gets called once when the user calls render(), and may be called again by the widget's own event listeners in response to state changes.

   In the example, syncUI() updates the contents of the paragraphs that display the electron's energy and speed. Here, syncUI() triggers multiple page reflows—a possible optimization point, should performance become an issue.

 Example 7-4 is a simple widget, so it is acceptable to refresh the entire UI at once in the after() listener. In more complex widgets, refreshing the entire UI on any single attribute change could lead to flickering and slowdowns when many attributes are set at once. Complex widgets should assign one after() listener for each attribute that affects the UI, each after() listener should change only the piece of the UI that reflects the attribute, and UI changes should always be done through the after() listener, never through the attribute setter.

The render() function also fires a render event as a notification.

In the YUI().use() callback, the user instantiates a new Electron and calls render(), passing in the demo <div> as the parentNode for the widget. This causes YUI to create the boundingBox and contentBox <div>s, appending them into the document as demo's first child.

When rendered, the Electron's boundingBox automatically has the classes yui3-widget and yui3-electron, and the child contentBox automatically has the class yui3-electron-content. These classes are hooks for setting the widget's size and its look and feel.

Discussion

YUI's two foundational objects for building visible page components are Widget and View. A widget is a *public component* that other developers can reuse on a wide variety of websites, while a view is an *internal component*, a "piece of a page" meant to be used on a specific website. For more information about views, refer to Recipe 7.14.

Beyond what the Base API provides, the Widget API derives most of its power from having well-established conventions around rendering. These conventions include:

- Breaking rendering into orderly phases described by the abstract methods ren derUI(), bindUI(), and syncUI(). Many widgets implement all three, although as Examples 7-5 and 7-6 illustrate, this is not strictly necessary.

- The boundingBox node, which specifies the widget's size and position. For each object in your Widget hierarchy, YUI stamps the bounding box with the class yui3-*name*, where *name* is the object's NAME property.

  The bounding box should carry only sizing and positioning properties such as width, height, top, left, display, and float; it should *not* carry padding, border, background, or any other look-and-feel properties. This separation of concerns makes it easier to maintain the widget's size and position across different browser box models. The bounding box can also contain any decorative HTML elements that your widget needs, as siblings to the content box.

- The contentBox node, a child of boundingBox that contains all of the widget's content elements. YUI stamps the content box with the class yui3-*name*-content, where *name* is the object's NAME property. You can use this hook to apply look-and-feel CSS properties such as borders, padding, and colors.

  By default, the content box and bounding box are <div>s. If your widget is a table, a list, or something else entirely, you can override the CONTENT_TEMPLATE and BOUNDING_TEMPLATE properties.

- A set of conventions for changing the widget's visual and functional state:
  — focus() toggles the focused attribute to true and adds a class on the bounding box, yui3-*name*-focused. blur() reverses this.

— hide() toggles the hidden attribute to true and adds a class on the bounding box, yui3-*name*-hidden. show() reverses this.

— disable() toggles the disabled attribute to true and adds a class on the bounding box, yui3-*name*-disabled. enable() reverses this.

For each of these methods, YUI leaves it up to you to decide what actual effect should happen. Should hide() set display:none or visibility:hidden on the entire widget? Should the widget fade away? Should the widget animate and collapse into some minimized state? To implement a particular effect, you can either use the yui3-*name*-state class hook or listen for the *state*Change event. Most core YUI widgets provide this behavior as part of their CSS skin.

• The HTML_PARSER property, which provides a standard way to implement progressive enhancement, constructing the widget from a chunk of markup in the page. For an example of this in action, refer to Recipe 7.5.

• The strings attribute, which, along with Y.Intl, enables you to change the widget's UI strings based on the user's locale. For more information, refer to Recipe 11.6.

When a widget renders, it automatically creates any boundingBox and contentBox elements it needs and sets classes on those elements. The example passed a parent node directly into render(), causing the widget to generate a bounding box and content box inside that node. Alternatively, you can first set the widget's boundingBox or content Box attribute to point to an existing node, and then call render() with no argument. For example, if you had invoked the widget like this:

```
var e = new Y.Electron({boundingBox: '#demo'});
e.render();
```

then the demo <div> would have become the bounding box, rather than the parent of the bounding box. If for some reason you fail to supply a boundingBox attribute, a contentBox, or a parentNode, then the widget renders as the first child of the <body>.

As mentioned earlier in Recipe 7.2, calling destroy() invokes all destructors in the inheritance chain. The Widget destructor removes the boundingBox and the contentBox from the DOM, and detaches all listeners bound to those nodes. If the user calls destroy(true), the widget recursively destroys and removes all child nodes of the contentBox as well.

When designing a destructor(), follow the general rule of, "clean up everything you explicitly add." For example, Electron adds three <p> nodes, so its destructor is responsible for calling remove(true) on each node to remove it from the DOM and detach any event listeners. If your widget sets listeners using Y.on() or Y.Global.on(), or sets listeners on elements that lie outside the boundingBox, you must clean these up in your destructor() method.

Custom event listeners typically don't need special cleanup logic; as long as they reside on the widget instances, they get cleaned up when the user calls destroy(). However, if your widget set up custom event listeners on some other object, you must detach them manually.

When a widget fires a custom event, the event name is automatically prefixed with the widget's name. If you set a listener on the widget instance itself, the prefix is optional:

```
var electron = new Y.Electron();
electron.on('someevent', callbackFoo);
```

But for subscribers on any other object, the prefix is required:

```
Y.on('electron:someevent', callbackBar);
```

For DOM events that fire within the bounding box, the widget fires a corresponding custom event, prefixed with the widget's name. For example, if the user clicks within the `Electron`'s bounding box, you can listen for an ordinary `click` event, or an `electron:click` custom event. You can use this feature to listen only for events that pertain to the widget. In an event handler for any widget custom event, YUI sets the default context to be the widget instance, not the node that fired the event. To customize the list of DOM events that get mirrored by custom events, update the widget's `UI_EVENTS` property.

There are three ways to build more features into a widget. The first is extension, which incorporates functionality into every new instance of the widget. You can use `Y.Base.create()` to extend any object derived from `Base`, not just vanilla `Base` or `Widget`. The second is mixing in extension objects, demonstrated in Recipe 8.8. The third way is to create plugins that can add functionality to specific widget instances. For more information, refer to Recipe 7.7.

See Also

The YUI `Widget` User Guide (*http://yuilibrary.com/yui/docs/widget/*); `Widget` API documentation (*http://yuilibrary.com/yui/docs/api/classes/Widget.html*); Ryan Grove's MSDN article, "Building Reusable Widgets with YUI 3" (*http://msdn.microsoft.com/en-us/scriptjunkie/gg576919.aspx*); Daniel Barreiro's YUIBlog article, "The 'MakeNode' Widget Extension" (*http://www.yuiblog.com/blog/2011/09/12/updated-the-makenode-widget-extension/*).

7.5 Creating a Widget That Uses Progressive Enhancement

Problem

You want to create a widget that livens up an existing block of HTML on the page, rather than constructing its nodes purely from data in JavaScript. Users with JavaScript turned off will at least get some sort of basic HTML and CSS experience instead of an empty `<div>`.

Solution

Use the widget's `HTML_PARSER` static property to extract data from HTML on the page, then render the widget into the box that contains the static markup. Example 7-5 alters the `Electron` example from Example 7-4 to progressively enhance an existing `<div>`.

Example 7-5. Creating a widget that uses progressive enhancement

```
<!DOCTYPE html>
<title>Creating a widget that uses progressive enhancement</title>
<style>
#demo, .yui3-electron          { width: 175px; }
#demo, .yui3-electron-content  { background: #ff0; border: 1px #000 solid; }
#demo p, .yui3-electron-content p { margin: 5px; }
</style>

<p>Click the electron to increase its energy by 10%.</p>
<div id="demo">
    <p class="ch">Charge: -1</p>
    <p class="en">Energy: <span class="value">611.50</span> MeV</p>
    <p class="sp">Speed: 0.54926 c</p>
</div>

<script src="http://yui.yahooapis.com/3.5.0/build/yui/yui-min.js"></script>
<script>
YUI.add('electron', function (Y) {
    var REST_ENERGY = 511.00;

    Y.Electron = Y.Base.create('electron', Y.Widget, [], {
        destructor: function () {
            this.get('contentBox').all('p').remove(true);
        },
        getSpeed: function () {
            var e_ratio = REST_ENERGY / this.get('energy');
            return Math.sqrt(1 - e_ratio * e_ratio);
        },
        boostEnergy: function () {
            this.set('energy', 1.1 * this.get('energy'));
        },
        bindUI: function () {
            this.get('contentBox').on('click', this.boostEnergy, this);
            this.after('energyChange', this.syncUI, this);
        },
        syncUI: function () {
            var energyStr = 'Energy: ' + this.get('energy').toPrecision(5) + ' MeV';
            var speedStr  = 'Speed: ' + this.getSpeed().toPrecision(5) + ' c';
            this.get('contentBox').one('.en').setHTML(energyStr);
            this.get('contentBox').one('.sp').setHTML(speedStr);
        }
    }, {
        ATTRS: {
            charge: {
                value: -1,
                readOnly: true
            },
```

```
                energy: {
                    value: REST_ENERGY,
                    validator: function (en) {
                        return (en >= REST_ENERGY);
                    }
                }
            },
            HTML_PARSER: {
                energy: function (srcNode) {
                    var enValue = srcNode.one('.en .value');
                    return enValue ? parseFloat(enValue.get('text')) : REST_ENERGY ;
                }
            }
        });
    }, '1.1', {requires: ['base-build', 'widget']});

    YUI().use('electron', function (Y) {
        new Y.Electron({ srcNode: '#demo' }).render();
    });
    </script>
```

The changes from the original `Electron` include:

- The demo `<div>` now contains static HTML markup representing the initial state of the widget. The CSS has also changed so that an `id` of `"demo"` is enough to style the widget's appearance.

- The `renderUI()` method is no longer needed, since the markup it created is already on the page. The `syncUI()` method now sets the widget's appearance, both on initial rendering and in response to state changes. If you wanted a widget that could render around existing markup *or* populate an empty `<div>`, you could add `renderUI()` back.

- The widget includes an `HTML_PARSER` static property. `HTML_PARSER` maps the initial state of one or more attributes to information that can be parsed out of the document. In this case, the widget extracts a float value for the electron's `energy` attribute out of the page's markup. To make this easier to do, the markup wraps the energy value in a `<span>`.

- The widget is configured with a `srcNode` set to be the demo `<div>`. In general, the `srcNode` is an existing node in the document used for progressive enhancement. By default, the widget treats `srcNode` as the content box. Calling `render()` automatically creates the bounding box around this node and stamps them both with widget classes and generated IDs.

This example behaves just like the original `Electron`, albeit with a different starting energy. To really see the difference between the two, turn JavaScript off. The original example is completely broken, while the progressively enhanced example displays static HTML, though it does not respond to clicks.

Discussion

Progressive enhancement isn't just for human users who have JavaScript turned off. For example, if you have a fancy menu widget that provides navigation for your site, progressive enhancement would help ensure that your site has a basic, friendly linking scheme for search engines to crawl. Progressive enhancement can also save you from the nightmare of a single JavaScript bug causing your entire site to implode. A simpler experience of text, links, and graphics is better than no experience at all.

One way to think about progressive enhancement is that it is simply another configuration option for a widget. You can set the `Electron`'s configuration by calling `new Y.Electron({ energy: 550 })`, or you can parse that `{ energy: 550 }` out of the markup. To help you extract configuration out of markup, `HTML_PARSER` is a hash of configuration property names mapped to one of three parsing methods:

- A CSS selector, as in `attribute: '#foo .bar'`. This sets the initial attribute value to a node on the page. This option is useful for selecting an individual node the widget needs, such as an informational pane or button.

- A CSS selector in an array, as in `attribute: ['#foo .bar']`. This sets the initial value to a `NodeList` on the page. This option is useful for selecting and updating multiple similar nodes, such as a group of list items or rows in a table.

- An arbitrary function, as in Example 7-5. This sets the initial value to a string, a number, or really any interesting data structure that you can extract from the page. The function receives the `srcNode` as an argument.

At initialization time, the widget automatically sets the values of any `HTML_PARSER` properties that correspond to attributes. If an `HTML_PARSER` property name does *not* correspond to an attribute, you can still handle that property with some custom logic in your `initializer()`.

In Example 7-5, the static markup is deliberately styled to look exactly like the widget will after rendering. This might not always be convenient to do, particularly if your widget loads its CSS as a module or as a skin. The goal of progressive enhancement is not full fidelity, but basic functionality.

Also note that the example takes a particular approach of just reusing the existing markup on the page, leaving out the `renderUI()` phase. An alternative approach is to use `renderUI()` to construct the widget in JavaScript, and then make the widget visible in the document only when the entire structure is ready. For more information about these strategies, refer to the YUI `Widget` User Guide.

See Also

Recipe 8.10; Recipe 11.1; the Progressive Enhancement section of the YUI `Widget` User Guide (*http://yuilibrary.com/yui/docs/widget/#progressive*); Nicholas Zakas's tech talk on progressive enhancement (*http://vimeo.com/25491048*).

7.6 Rendering Remote Data with a Widget

Problem

You want to display a Twitter status widget on your page, but you don't want the widget to break or slow the page down when Twitter is throwing fail whales.

Solution

Create a widget that uses the JSONP utility to request tweets asynchronously and display them in a list, as shown in Example 7-6. When a request times out or returns an error, the widget handles the problem gracefully and displays a friendly message.

Example 7-6. Resilient Twitter status widget

```
<!DOCTYPE html>
<title>Resilient Twitter status widget</title>

<div id="tweets"></div>

<script src="http://yui.yahooapis.com/3.5.0/build/yui/yui-min.js"></script>
<script>
YUI.add('twitter', function (Y) {

    Y.Twitter = Y.Base.create('twitter', Y.Widget, [], {
        TWITTER_URL: 'http://api.twitter.com/1/statuses/user_timeline.json?' +
            'screen_name={username}&count={maxTweets}&trim_user=1&callback={callback}',
        TWEET_TEMPLATE: '<li class="{classes}">{content}</li>',

        renderUI: function () {
            var tweetList = Y.Node.create('<ul/>').addClass(this.getClassName('list'));
            this._set('tweetList', tweetList);
            this.get('contentBox').append(tweetList);
        },
        syncUI: function () {
            this.renderTweets('Loading tweets...');
            this.refresh();
        },
        refresh: function () {
            var url = Y.Lang.sub(this.TWITTER_URL, this.getAttrs([
                'maxTweets', 'username'
            ]));

            Y.jsonp(url, {
                context: this,
                on: {
                    success: function (tweets) {
                        this.set('tweets', tweets);
                        this.renderTweets();
                    },
                    failure: function () { this.renderTweets('Error fetching tweets.'); },
                    timeout: function () { this.renderTweets('Request timed out.'); }
```

```
                },
                timeout: this.get('timeout')
            });
        },
        renderTweets: function (message) {
            var tweetList = this.get('tweetList'),
                tweets    = this.get('tweets');

            tweetList.empty();
            tweetList.setHTML((!message && tweets.length) ?
                this.buildTweets(tweets) : this.buildMessage(message)
            );
        },
        buildTweets: function (tweets) {
            return Y.Array.map(tweets, function (tweet) {
                return Y.Lang.sub(this.TWEET_TEMPLATE, {
                    content: tweet.text,
                    classes: this.getClassName('tweet')
                });
            }, this).join('');
        },
        buildMessage: function (message) {
            return Y.Lang.sub(this.TWEET_TEMPLATE, {
                content: message || 'No tweets to display.',
                classes: this.getClassName('msg')
            });
        }
    }, {
        ATTRS: {
            username:  { },
            maxTweets: { value: 5 },
            timeout:   { value: 3000 },
            tweetList: { readOnly: true },
            tweets:    { value: [] }
        }
    });
}, '1.0.0', {requires: ['base-build', 'widget', 'jsonp', 'array-extras']});

YUI().use('twitter', function (Y) {
    new Y.Twitter({ username: 'yuilibrary' }).render('#tweets');
});
</script>
```

As a template for making API requests, the widget stores TWITTER_URL and TWEET_
TEMPLATE as prototype properties, so that they can be overridden by instances or by
extending the widget further. The template strings are parameterized so that they can
be processed by Y.Lang.sub(). For more information about substitution, refer to
Recipe 9.7.

The renderUI() method creates an unordered list, stamps it with a generated class name
of yui3-twitter-list, and appends it to the content box. The node reference to the
tweet list is also stored in the tweetList attribute. Note that the tweetList attribute is
defined as read only, so renderUI() sets it by calling _set() rather than set() in order

to bypass the read-only check. This pattern creates a "protected" attribute—an attribute that your widget updates internally, but that users of your widget shouldn't normally be messing with.

The syncUI() method displays a "Loading" message and calls refresh() to fetch data from Twitter. The widget skips providing a bindUI() method because it does not respond to user interactions.

After substituting in the username and desired number of tweets to TWITTER_URL, refresh() uses the JSONP module to fetch data from Twitter. On success, the widget stores the results as an array in the tweets attribute and renders the results. Otherwise, it renders an error message. For more information about JSONP and YUI, refer to Recipe 5.6.

Finally, the workhorse renderTweets() method is responsible for clearing out the tweet List and generating new list items using either buildTweets() or buildMessage(). If all has gone well, the method iterates over the array of raw tweet data and renders the tweets as list items. Otherwise, the method displays a single list item containing a message. To see these messages in action, you can break the TWITTER_URL or change time out to some extremely small value.

Discussion

Example 7-6 is quick to render and doesn't completely fall down if a network failure occurs. The widget could refresh itself every few minutes, or it could provide users a button to manually refresh tweets, in which case you should add bindUI() to add the event listener. To make the widget even more robust, you could cache tweets in local Storage so that the widget has even better fallback behavior in the face of network failures.

As for styling, the rendered tweets aren't very fancy. The widget does provide a number of CSS hooks; in addition to the classes on the bounding box and content box, the widget decorates the list and list items with getClassName(), a utility method that generates a class name with a prefix based on the widget's name. This approach is better than hardcoding class names, because if you extend the widget further, the class names would update appropriately.

Naturally, you could always ignore the Widget API and just write a set of functions to fetch Twitter data and add some <ul>s and <li>s to the DOM. As a one-time solution, that's a fine approach. The goal of the Widget API is to make your code easier to use and extend. You can internationalize the loading and error messages, as shown in Recipe 11.6, or add progressive enhancement, as shown in Recipe 7.5. You can add skins that get automatically loaded, as shown in Recipe 7.10. You can add mixins and plugins that make your widget modal, or draggable, or any number of things.

See Also

Twitter API documentation (*https://dev.twitter.com/docs*).

7.7 Creating a Simple Plugin

Problem

You want to add a couple of methods or properties to individual instances of a widget, without having to create a full-fledged extension that affects every instance.

Solution

Create a plugin object and use the widget's `plug()` method to add the plugin to that instance. By convention, YUI plugins should reside in the `Plugin` namespace.

Example 7-7 defines a plugin for the `Chart` widget. The example chart helps visualize a set of data about a group of software engineers and their commits for the most recent sprint. The `Plugin.Stats` enhances the `Chart` instance with the ability to calculate statistics about the underlying data set.

Example 7-7. Creating a simple plugin

```
<!DOCTYPE html>
<title>Creating a simple plugin</title>
<style>
#demo { height: 300px; width: 300px;}
</style>

<div id="demo"></div>

<script src="http://yui.yahooapis.com/3.5.0/build/yui/yui-min.js"></script>
<script>
YUI.add('stats-plugin', function (Y) {
    Y.Plugin.Stats = function (config) {
        this.chart = config.host;
        this.values = this.chart.getAxisByKey('values').get('data');
    };

    Y.Plugin.Stats.NS = 'stats';

    Y.Plugin.Stats.prototype = {
        getMean: function () {
            var i, sum = 0;
            for (i = 0; i < this.values.length; i += 1) {
                sum += this.values[i];
            }
            return sum / this.values.length;
        }
    };
```

```
}, '1.0', { requires: ['charts'] });

YUI().use('stats-plugin', function (Y) {
    var data = [
        ['Alice', 'Bob', 'Carol', 'Donald', 'Edgar', 'Frieda'],
        [27, 9, 85, 40, 55, 48]
    ];

    var chart = new Y.Chart({
        dataProvider: data,
        type: 'column',
        render: '#demo'
    });

    chart.plug(Y.Plugin.Stats);
    Y.one('body').append('<p>Mean = ' + chart.stats.getMean() + ' commits</p>');
});
</script>
```

In its most basic form, a plugin is a generic object with:

- A constructor function. Plugging the instance invokes the plugin's constructor and passes in a configuration object that includes a host property. The host property points to the object instance hosting the plugin. Most plugins store this reference at this point so that they can access their host object's methods and properties later on.

- A static NS property. The entire plugin is stored as a property of the host object under that namespace. This means you must never use a name that could be a member of the host, and plugins that happen to have the same namespace cannot occupy the same host instance. If you forget to provide a namespace, host objects that derive from Base will silently ignore your plugin.

- One or more properties or methods on the prototype. This defines the API that the plugin provides to the host.

From the instance, you can access plugin methods and properties through the namespace: instance.namespace.method(). In the example, you can calculate the mean by calling charts.stats.mean(). Presumably a real stats plugin would provide a richer variety of statistical methods.

For more information about the Chart widget, refer to Recipe 8.14.

Discussion

The plug() method and the corresponding unplug() method are provided by the Plugin.Host API. YUI mixes Plugin.Host into Node and any object derived from Base, which means that a great variety of core YUI objects are pluggable. YUI includes plugins for making objects draggable, for animating widgets, and much more. Plugins make it easy to decompose a complex widget into a simpler base widget with a suite of plugins, which enables your widget's users to mix and match what they need.

Plugins are designed to modify individual object instances. Technically, the `Plugin`
`.Host` API does allow you to plug objects at the prototype level, but you should probably
use `Y.augment()`, `Y.extend()`, or `Y.Base.create()` for that.

The plugin approach described in this recipe is just a constructor and namespace, plus
one or more arbitrary methods and properties. If you need to design plugins with richer
behavior, refer to Recipe 7.8.

See Also

The YUI Plugin User Guide (*http://yuilibrary.com/yui/docs/plugin/*); `Plugin.Host` API
documentation (*http://yuilibrary.com/yui/docs/api/classes/Plugin.Host.html*); `Plugin`
`.Drag` (*http://yuilibrary.com/yui/docs/api/classes/Plugin.Drag.html*) and `Plugin.WidgetA`
`nim` (*http://yuilibrary.com/yui/docs/api/classes/Plugin.WidgetAnim.html*) for making a
widget draggable or animatable, respectively.

7.8 Creating a Plugin That Alters Host Behavior

Problem

You want to create a "title plugin" that adds a title to any widget by hijacking the
rendering phase of the host object.

Solution

Extend `Plugin.Base` and call the `afterHostMethod()` to inject code that will execute just
after the host widget's `renderUI()` method, as shown in Example 7-8.

Example 7-8. Creating a plugin that alters host behavior

```
<!DOCTYPE html>
<title>Creating a plugin that alters host behavior</title>

<div id="demo"></div>

<script src="http://yui.yahooapis.com/3.5.0/build/yui/yui-min.js"></script>
<script>
YUI.add('title-plugin', function (Y) {
    Y.Plugin.Title = Y.Base.create('titlePlugin', Y.Plugin.Base, [], {
        initializer: function () {
            if (this.get('rendered')) {
                this.addTitle();
            } else {
                this.afterHostMethod('renderUI', this.addTitle);
            }
        },
        destructor: function () {
            this.titleNode.remove(true);
        },
```

```
            addTitle: function () {
                var boundingBox = this.get('host').get('boundingBox');
                this.titleNode = Y.Node.create(this.get('titleElement'));
                this.titleNode.setHTML(this.get('title'));
                boundingBox.prepend(this.titleNode);
            },
            titleNode: null,
        }, {
            NS: 'title',
            ATTRS: {
                title: { value: '' },
                titleElement: { value: '<h3/>' }
            }
        });
    }, '1.0', { requires: ['base-build', 'plugin'] });

    YUI().use('title-plugin', 'calendar', function (Y) {
        var calendar = new Y.Calendar({ width: '300px'});
        Y.one('body').addClass('yui3-skin-sam');

        calendar.plug(Y.Plugin.Title, { title: 'Example Calendar' });
        calendar.render('#demo');
    });
    </script>
```

Example 7-8 implements an `initializer()` function to inject additional behavior into the host. If the widget is already rendered, the plugin adds the title as the first child of the widget's bounding box; otherwise, the plugin automatically adds the title when the widget is rendered. The corresponding `destructor()` function ensures that unplugging the widget also destroys the title node.

When `plug()` is called, the second argument is an object that gets passed to the plugin's constructor at initialization time, which in turn sets the plugin's `title` attribute. For more information about the init phase and attributes, refer to Recipe 7.2.

Unlike Example 7-7, there is no code in the constructor to store a reference to the plugin's host. Instead, the plugin just retrieves the `host` attribute as needed. The widget automatically sets this attribute when the plugin is instantiated.

For simplicity, the plugin leaves out the code for changing the title's appearance after the widget is plugged, by calling `widget.title.set()`. Since the plugin derives from `Base`, this is easy to fix—just add a listener on the plugin for `titleChange` and `title ElementChange` events, and update the title node accordingly.

Discussion

While the generic approach in Recipe 7.7 is often all you need, extending `Plugin .Base` adds all the familiar benefits of the `Base` API, such as attributes, the ability to publish and listen for events, and the init/destroy lifecycle. Interestingly, as `Base`-derived objects, advanced plugins can themselves host plugins. That's right: plugins themselves are pluggable. Theoretically, the plugins that plug the plugin could have plugins, but if you're thinking about going down that road, you should probably quit while you're ahead.

Beyond the `Base` API, advanced plugins offer a few extra methods for altering or responding to the behavior of the host. These include `onHostEvent()`, `afterHostEvent()`, `beforeHostMethod()`, and `afterHostMethod()`. The latter two methods are a variation of the AOP techniques discussed in Recipe 4.12. When you unplug the host, any event listeners and advice functions injected by these methods automatically detach themselves.

 A common mistake when you are writing advanced plugins is to make NS a static property of the ATTRS object. Always remember that NS should be a static property of the plugin itself, not ATTRS.

See Also

Recipe 8.15; the YUI Plugin User Guide (*http://yuilibrary.com/yui/docs/plugin/*); `Plugin.Base` API documentation (*http://yuilibrary.com/yui/docs/api/classes/Plugin.Base .html*); Pat Cavit's YUI 3 plugin tutorial (*http://patcavit.com/2010/07/01/simple-yui3 -plugin-tutorial/*).

7.9 Bundling CSS with a Widget as a CSS Module

Problem

You want YUI to automatically load CSS resources along with your widget's JavaScript.

Solution

Define a custom module group with two modules:

- A module containing your CSS, with `type: 'css'`. This instructs the Loader to fetch the file with a `<link>` element rather than a `<script>` element.
- A module containing your JavaScript, with the CSS module declared as a dependency. This ensures that if a user loads the JavaScript module, the CSS resources automatically load as well.

Then set `base` and `path` so that YUI loads the appropriate files for each module. For more information about how to configure module groups and why they are necessary here, refer to Recipe 1.11.

Example 7-9 illustrates how you might break up Example 7-4 into three parts: an HTML file that contains module metadata and renders the module, a JavaScript module that defines the widget's behavior, and a CSS module that defines the widget's presentation.

Example 7-9. Creating a widget with a CSS module

./widget_css_module.html: Defines the metadata for the electron module and its corresponding electron-css module. Also includes a use() call that instantiates and renders an Electron.

```
<!DOCTYPE html>
<title>Creating a widget with a CSS module</title>

<p>Click the electron to increase its energy by 10%.</p>
<div id="demo"></div>

<script src="http://yui.yahooapis.com/3.5.0/build/yui/yui-min.js"></script>
<script>
YUI({
    groups: {
        localModules: {
            base: './ex1/',
            modules: {
                'electron': {
                    path: 'electron/js/electron.js',
                    requires: ['base-build', 'widget', 'electron-css']
                },
                'electron-css': {
                    path: 'electron/css/electron.css',
                    type: 'css'
                }
            }
        }
    }
}).use('electron', function (Y) {
    var e = new Y.Electron();
    e.render('#demo');
});
</script>
```

./ex1/electron/js/electron.js: Provides the YUI.add() statement that contains the JavaScript code for Electron. See Example 7-4 for the complete contents of the YUI.add().

```
YUI.add('electron', function (Y) {
    var REST_ENERGY = 511.00;

    ...

}, '1.1', { requires: ['base', 'widget', 'electron-css'] });
```

./ex1/electron/css/electron.css: Provides the CSS to load.

```
.yui3-electron           { width: 175px; }
.yui3-electron-content   { background: #ff0; border: 1px #000 solid; }
.yui3-electron-content p { margin: 5px; }
```

Discussion

The YUI Loader not only can load CSS, but it can also be very fine-grained in its behavior, fetching only the assets required by the JS modules on a particular page. Even if you do something tricky like loading a widget conditionally, you can load the widget's CSS conditionally as well.

There are two basic strategies for fetching CSS with the Loader. The first is to create a CSS module, as shown in Example 7-9. The second is to flag a JavaScript module as skinnable, as discussed in Example 7-10.

See Also

Recipe 1.11; Recipe 7.10; Recipe 11.6; widget class names and CSS (*http://yuilibrary .com/yui/docs/widget/#CSS*).

7.10 Bundling CSS with a Widget as a Skin

Problem

You want YUI to automatically load a CSS skin along with your widget's JavaScript, possibly with an eye on supplying different themes for different situations.

Solution

Define a custom module group, setting `base` and `path` so that YUI loads your module's JavaScript from the correct filepath. Make sure that your CSS skin assets are in the correct location according to YUI's conventions for loading skin files and set `skinnable: true`. See Example 7-10.

> For more information about how to configure module groups and why they are necessary here, refer to Recipe 1.11.

Example 7-10. Creating a widget with a skin

./widget_css_skin.html: Defines the `electron` module's metadata: its name, its requirements, its paths, and the fact that it is skinnable. Also includes a `use()` call that instantiates and renders the `Electron`.

```
<!DOCTYPE html>
<title>Creating a widget with a skin</title>

<body class="yui3-skin-sam">

<p>Click the electron to increase its energy by 10%.</p>
<div id="demo"></div>
```

```
<script src="http://yui.yahooapis.com/3.5.0/build/yui/yui-min.js"></script>
<script>
YUI({
    groups: {
        localModules: {
            base: './ex2/',
            modules: {
                'electron': {
                    path: 'electron/js/electron.js',
                    requires: ['base-build', 'widget'],
                    skinnable: true
                }
            }
        }
    }
}).use('electron', function (Y) {
    var e = new Y.Electron();
    e.render('#demo');
});
</script>
</body>
```

./ex1/electron/js/electron.js: Provides the `YUI.add()` statement that contains the Java-Script code for `Electron`. See Example 7-4 for the complete contents of the `YUI.add()`.

```
YUI.add('electron', function (Y) {
    var REST_ENERGY = 511.00;

    ...

}, '1.1', { requires: ['base-build', 'widget'], skinnable: true });
```

./example1/electron/assets/skins/sam/electron.css: Provides the CSS file to load. The CSS file contains a mix of *core styles* that apply to all widgets, and *skin styles* that vary the widget's appearance. A skin should provide a cohesive set of decorative CSS styles, but not affect the widget's general layout.

Since this CSS file defines styles for the `'sam'` skin, all styles are scoped within the class `yui3-skin-sam`. Users must add this class to their markup for the skin to take effect.

```
/* Core styles */
.yui3-electron           { width: 175px; }
.yui3-electron-content   { background: #ff0; border: 1px #000 solid; }
.yui3-electron-content p { margin: 5px; }

/* Skin styles */
.yui3-skin-sam .yui3-electron-content { background: #0ff;}
```

Discussion

YUI's skinning system is, to put it kindly, rather baroque.

Per YUI convention, skin styles are scoped to work under a class of yui3-skin-*skin-name*. Users can then apply a skin by stamping that class on the <body> or on a <div>, as shown in Example 7-10.

The default YUI 3 skin is the sam skin, named after its designer, Sam Lind. If you create only one skin, you should always name it 'sam' unless you really know what you're doing.

As mentioned in Recipe 1.11, setting skinnable to true instructs the Loader to automatically create a <link> element and load a CSS file using a URL of:

```
base/module-name/assets/skins/skin-name/module-name.css
```

The complicated path to the CSS file is due to the Loader, which constructs a unique skin path just based on the module name and the current skin, without needing any extra metadata. The YUI Builder tool supports the Loader's behavior, taking CSS files with this layout:

```
srcpath/module-name/assets/module-name-core.css
srcpath/module-name/assets/skins/skin-name/module-name-skin.css
```

and minifying and concatenating the core CSS and skin CSS into a single file, one for each skin. In other words, if you have a build process that mimics what the core YUI team does to build YUI 3, this system makes a lot of sense. If not, then...probably not.

While all core widgets provide a sam skin, some core widgets also ship with a night skin—a darker skin designed to look nice on mobile devices. To apply an alternative skin across the board, users can change the default skin in the YUI configuration, as shown in Example 7-11.

Example 7-11. Configuring the "night" skin as the default

```
YUI({
    skin: {
        defaultSkin: 'night'
    }
    // more config here
}).use('example-widget', function (Y) {
    // exercise the widget here
});
```

It is also possible to load "override" skins just for particular widgets, or even mix different skins for different components on the same page—though this probably won't win you any awards for design or good taste. For more information, refer to the YUI Config object's API documentation.

See Also

Recipe 1.9; Recipe 1.11; Recipe 7.9; Recipe 11.6; the "Understanding Skinning" tutorial (*http://yuilibrary.com/yui/docs/tutorials/skins/*); Config API documentation (*http://yuilibrary.com/yui/docs/api/classes/config.html#property_skin*) for the skin property;

YUI Scaffolding (*https://github.com/evangoer/yui3-scaffolding*), which includes an example widget that pulls in a skin; Luke Smith's pattern for loading a local skin (*https://gist.github.com/1244430*).

7.11 Representing Data with a Model

Problem

You want to represent a bundle of related data as a model that you can perhaps reuse in an MVC-style (Model/View/Controller) application.

Solution

Extend Model and add an attribute for each data field you want to represent. Model extends Base, adding a few utility methods and a sync lifecycle (discussed in Recipe 7.12).

Example 7-12 is a simple representation of bookmark data that uses two attributes: a title and a url. On initialization, the bookmark sets a titleChange listener that logs the new value and the previous value.

The demo <div> displays the bookmark's current title in the markup. The bookmark instance adds the demo <div> as a target for any custom events it emits, and the <div> has an after() event listener that responds to any successful change to the bookmark's title by updating the <div>'s contents. The model uses the getAsHTML() utility method to escape any possibly dangerous HTML. For this reason, the <strong> in the example gets escaped to <strong>.

For good measure, the example includes a button that calls the bookmark's undo() method. If you view the browser console alongside the browser page and click the button, you can watch the bookmark and its <div> toggle back and forth between two states.

Example 7-12. Representing data with a model

```
<!DOCTYPE html>
<title>Representing data with a model</title>

<div id="demo"></div>
<button id="undo">Undo</button>

<script src="http://yui.yahooapis.com/3.5.0/build/yui/yui-min.js"></script>
<script>
YUI.add('bookmark', function (Y) {

    Y.Bookmark = Y.Base.create('bookmark', Y.Model, [], {
        initializer: function () {
            this.after('titleChange', function (ev) {
                Y.log('Was: ' + ev.prevVal + ', Now: ' + ev.newVal);
```

```
            });
        }
    }, {
        ATTRS: {
            title: {},
            url: {}
        }
    });
}, '1.0', { requires: ['model'] });

YUI().use('bookmark', 'node-base', function (Y) {
    var bookmark = new Y.Bookmark({
        title: 'YUI Library',
        url: 'http://yuilibrary.com'
    });
    bookmark.after('titleChange', function () {
        Y.one('#demo').setHTML(bookmark.getAsHTML('title'));
    });
    bookmark.set('title', 'YUI Library -- now with <strong>MVC</strong>!');

    Y.one('#undo').on('click', function () { bookmark.undo(); });
});
</script>
```

Discussion

Any object that carries the Attribute API serves as a pretty good model already. As mentioned in Recipe 7.1, attributes have a variety of rich behaviors that include custom getters and setters, custom validators, and perhaps most important of all, automatically fired change events. The Model API adds a few more capabilities:

- On any attribute change, Model fires a coalesced change event in addition to the individual attribute change events. This makes it convenient to re-render a view or widget whenever its underlying model changes, as you only need to set one listener.

- The utility methods getAsHTML() and getAsURL() help to safely display model data in an HTML or URL context.

- The toJSON() method converts a model into a chunk of easy-to-parse JSON data. You can also pass the model instance directly to Y.JSON.stringify().

- As demonstrated in Example 7-12, models support a single level of undo. The undo() method reverts the last change, and change events carry the previous value and the new value.

- Finally, models support a syncing layer that enables you to sync attribute values with some kind of persistence layer or remote data source. For more information, refer to Recipe 7.12.

Comparing Model to DataSource, you can think of Model as a tangible "thing" that holds data, while DataSource is more of an adapter for moving data from one place to another. Another key difference is that developers typically instantiate and use DataSource directly, while Model is meant to be extended.

All models have two built-in "infrastructure" attributes: id and clientId. The id attribute is a unique, persistent ID that you set yourself when implementing a syncing layer. The clientId attribute is automatically generated for you and is useful for retrieving Models from ModelLists, but it does not persist across page views.

Beyond id and clientId, any attributes you add to a model are "data" attributes. Attributes, Models, and ModelLists provide great flexibility in modeling your data. For example, if a bookmark had tags, you could design the tags attribute as a simple array of strings, an array of objects, or even a ModelList containing Models, each of which is a tag. With this in mind, it's usually best to design your data structures by starting small and building something simple that works, rather than committing upfront to some kind of grand architecture.

See Also

The YUI Model User Guide (*http://yuilibrary.com/yui/docs/model/*); Model API documentation (*http://yuilibrary.com/yui/docs/api/classes/Model.html*); the YUI DataSource User Guide (*http://yuilibrary.com/yui/docs/datasource/*).

7.12 Persisting Model Data with a Sync Layer

Problem

You want to represent a bundle of related data as a model that you can persist or sync to some storage layer.

Solution

Extend Model and implement the sync() method. The sync() method takes three parameters: an action string, an options object, and a callback method to execute when the operation is complete.

Example 7-13 uses localStorage as a sync layer. This example does not display changes in the HTML, just in the browser console. However, it does include a handy button to clear localStorage, making it easy to replay the example from the beginning.

The example first creates a new, empty Bookmark with a particular ID. The example then calls load() to fetch the bookmark's data from localStorage, with a callback function to execute on completion. Under the hood, load() calls sync() with an action of "read".

- If localStorage does not return anything for the given ID, the load() callback receives an error. The callback responds to that error by creating a new Y.Bookmark object and calling save(). (This error handling behavior is deliberately contrived: it is just meant to show how the API works.)

Because the bookmark does not yet have an ID, it is considered "new." Under the hood, calling save() on a "new" model calls sync() with an action of "create". The sync() implementation sets the bookmark's id attribute and adds the stringified version of the bookmark to localStorage. Subsequent page views will retrieve the saved bookmark, rather than creating a fresh one.

- If localStorage successfully retrieves data for the given ID, the empty bookmark's title and url are set with the stored data. Note that the sync() implementation just needs to fetch the data as a string and pass it into the callback function. Once that happens, Model automatically parses the string and sets the bookmark's data for you.

Example 7-13. Persisting model data with a sync layer

```
<!DOCTYPE html>
<title>Persisting model data with a sync layer</title>

<button id="clear">Clear localStorage</button>

<script src="http://yui.yahooapis.com/3.5.0/build/yui/yui-min.js"></script>
<script>
YUI.add('bookmark', function (Y) {

    Y.Bookmark = Y.Base.create('bookmark', Y.Model, [], {
        sync: function (action, options, callback) {
            var data, err = null;

            switch(action) {
                case 'create':
                    this.set('id', 'ID_' + this.get('url'));
                    data = this._update();
                    break;
                case 'update':
                    data = this._update();
                    break;
                case 'read':
                    data = localStorage.getItem(this.get('id'));
                    if (! data) {
                        err = '"' + this.get('id') + '" not found in localStorage.';
                    }
                    break;
                default:
                    err = 'Invalid action';
            }

            if (Y.Lang.isFunction(callback)) {
                callback(err, data);
            }
        },
        _update: function () {
            var data = this.toJSON();
            localStorage.setItem(data.id, Y.JSON.stringify(data));
            return data;
        }
```

```
    }, {
        ATTRS: {
            title: {},
            url: {}
        }
    });
}, '1.0', { requires: ['model', 'json-stringify'] });

YUI().use('bookmark', 'node-base', function (Y) {
    var bookmark;

    Y.one('#clear').on('click', function () {
        localStorage.clear();
        Y.log('Cleared localStorage. Please reload the page.');
    });

    bookmark = new Y.Bookmark({ id: 'ID_http://yuilibrary.com' });
    bookmark.load(function (err, data) {
        if (err) {
            var bmark = new Y.Bookmark({
                title: 'YUI Library',
                url: 'http://yuilibrary.com'
            });
            Y.log(err);
            bmark.save(function (err, data) {
                Y.log('Bookmark data persisted. Please reload the page.');
            });
        }
        else {
            Y.log('Retrieved: ' + bookmark.get('title') + ', ' + bookmark.get('url'));
        }
    });
});
</script>
```

Discussion

A "sync layer" is anything that persists data for your model: localStorage, a web service, even a cookie. If your model is designed to run on a server, it could sync directly with an RDBMS or with a NoSQL database. If your sync layer is read only, it could be a scraped web page.

Users should never call sync() directly. Instead, they should call load(), save(), and destroy(). These methods are somewhat analogous to SQL queries:

- load() is analogous to SELECT * FROM table WHERE ID = '...'. Here, load() calls sync() with an action of "read". Your read logic must fetch data from the sync layer and pass it into the sync() callback.

   The model's id attribute acts like a primary key. If you have a known, valid id already, you can create an empty Model instance and use the ID to load() the contents:

```
var bookmark = new Y.Bookmark({ id: 'some_unique_id' });
bookmark.load(myLoadCallback);
```

Users should not call load() on a new, empty Model instance and expect that to work—that would be like trying to fetch a single row from a table without knowing the row's primary key. To check whether a model has had its id set yet, call isNew(). As mentioned in Recipe 7.11, all models have an automatically generated clientId attribute, but the clientId is not suitable for use with a sync layer.

- save() on a model with an id is analogous to UPDATE table SET (column assignments) WHERE ID = '...'. Here, save() calls validate() to verify that the model is in a good state, and then calls sync() with an action of "update". Your update logic must update the existing object in the sync layer.

  Calling save() with a known id enables a user to manipulate an existing model's data and commit the changes back to the sync layer:

  ```
  bookmark.set('url', 'http://jsfiddle.net');
  bookmark.save(mySaveCallback); // action is 'update'
  ```

- save() on a model without an id is analogous to INSERT INTO table (columns) VALUES (values). Here, save() calls validate() to verify that the model is in a good state, and then calls sync() with an action of "create". Your create logic is responsible for assigning the model a unique ID and adding a new object to the sync layer.

Thus, a user who doesn't yet have the model's id can construct a new Model in memory and commit it to the sync layer. When mySaveCallback() returns, the bookmark has an id attribute, provided by the sync() method:

```
var bookmark = new Y.Bookmark({
    url: 'http://jsperf.com',
    title: 'My framework vs. your framework: FIGHT!'
});
bookmark.save(mySaveCallback); // action is 'create'
```

This is somewhat similar to how an RDBMS can autogenerate primary keys for newly inserted rows. The difference is that the responsibility for generating unique IDs falls to you, the sync() implementer.

Once the new bookmark is saved, its id attribute has been set, which means isNew() returns false and subsequent save() calls are invoked as an update, not a create.

 Sometimes, the only difference between the update handler and the create handler is that the latter needs to assign a new ID. However, if the semantics for create and update are not the same—for example, the sync layer requires an HTTP PUT for creates and an HTTP POST for updates—then you can account for that here as well.

- destroy() destroys the local object instance, as destroy() does for any Base-derived object. However, if a user calls delete(options, callback), and the options object has a delete property of true, destroy() also calls sync() with an action of "delete", as in:

      bookmark.destroy({ 'delete': true }, myDestroyCallback);

  Sync implementations can use this to allow the user to optionally delete data from the sync layer. The operation then becomes analogous to DELETE FROM table WHERE ID = '...'.

When implementing a model, do not override load(), save(), or destroy(). Your job is to implement a sync() method that handles one or more of the four actions, depending on your use case. For example, if a model scrapes its data from a web page, it only needs to implement the "read" action.

The one thing a sync() implementation *must* do is execute the callback function that it received. This callback wraps the user-provided callback function (if any) and provides some additional behavior:

- If you pass in a falsy err such as false, null, or undefined, this indicates that the sync operation succeeded. Model calls parse() to parse the data. If parsing succeeds, Model sets its attribute values accordingly and fires a load or save event. If not, Model fires an error event. Either way, Model then executes the user's callback.

  To work with parse(), the data parameter must be either a hash suitable for passing into setAttrs(), or a JSON string that can be parsed into said hash. If your sync layer returns XML or some other format, you should override the model's parse() method so that it returns an attribute hash. If massaging your data into an attribute hash requires heavy manipulation, that logic should reside in parse(), not sync().

- If you pass in a truthy err such as a nonempty string or object, this indicates that the sync operation failed. Model fires an error event and executes the user's callback. parse() does not get called, and the model's data does not change.

  It is up to you to determine what "failure" means and what to report. Ideally, err should be a string or an object containing meaningful error information for other components in your application to use. For example, if you call a REST API and receive a 400 Bad Request, err could include the HTTP response code, a string error explanation, and any relevant HTTP headers.

Besides parse(), another customization point is the validate() method, which Model calls asynchronously at the start of a save(). Your validate() function receives two parameters: an attrs parameter representing a hash of all the model's attributes, and a callback function. When you are done validating the contents of attrs, execute the callback function. If you pass anything other than null or undefined, Model aborts the save and fires an error.

By default, a model's ID is the `id` attribute. However, you can change this by overriding the model's `idAttribute` property on the prototype. For example, in Example 7-13, setting `idAttribute` to `'url'` would mean that the URL is the bookmark's unique identifier, that an unset `url` attribute represents a "new" bookmark, and so on. This would simplify Example 7-13 by eliminating the `'ID_'` prefix.

See Also

The YUI Model User Guide (*http://yuilibrary.com/yui/docs/model/*); Model API documentation (*http://yuilibrary.com/yui/docs/api/classes/Model.html*); the YQL Model Sync gallery module (*http://yuilibrary.com/gallery/show/model-sync-yql*); the REST Model Sync gallery module (*http://yuilibrary.com/gallery/show/model-sync-rest*).

7.13 Managing Models with a Syncing ModelList

Problem

You want to load a group of models from a storage layer and manage them as a list.

Solution

Extend `ModelList` and implement the `sync()` method. Unlike with `Model`, a `ModelList`'s `sync()` implementation only needs to handle the `read` action.

Example 7-14 defines a `Bookmark` object and a `BookmarkList` that can contain bookmark objects.

`Bookmark`'s `sync()` method can perform creates, reads, and updates. The implementation is somewhat similar to the `sync()` implementation in Example 7-13. The main difference is that here `sync()` stores all bookmarks in a stringified array in `localStorage`, under the key name `"bookmarks"`. This ends up creating some annoying extra work involving array and JSON manipulation.

`BookmarkList`'s `sync()` method performs only bulk reads. Thanks to the way that individual bookmarks are stored, retrieving the entire list is a snap; just retrieve the raw string data from `localStorage` and parse it into an array.

When the example runs, it calls `load()` on the `ModelList` to fetch all bookmark data from `localStorage`. If there are no bookmarks stored, it calls the `ModelList`'s `create()` method twice to create two new bookmarks. This convenience method creates a new `Model` instance, calls the `Model`'s `save()` method to persist the data, and calls `add()` to add the `Model` to the `ModelList`.

Example 7-14. Managing models with a syncing ModelList

```
<!DOCTYPE html>
<title>Managing models with a syncing ModelList</title>
```

```
<button id="clear">Clear localStorage</button>

<script src="http://yui.yahooapis.com/3.5.0/build/yui/yui-min.js"></script>
<script>
YUI.add('bookmark-list', function (Y) {

    Y.Bookmark = Y.Base.create('bookmark', Y.Model, [], {
        sync: function (action, options, callback) {
            var data,
                index,
                err = null,
                bookmarks = Y.JSON.parse(localStorage.getItem('bookmarks')) || [];

            function findIndex(id) {
                for (var ix = 0; ix < bookmarks.length; ix += 1) {
                    if (id === bookmarks[ix].id) {
                        return ix;
                    }
                }
                err = '"' + this.get('id') + '" not found in localStorage';
                return -1;
            }

            switch(action) {
                case 'create':
                    this.set('id', 'ID_' + this.get('url'));
                    data = this.toJSON();
                    bookmarks.push(data);
                    localStorage.setItem('bookmarks', Y.JSON.stringify(bookmarks));
                    break;
                case 'update':
                    index = findIndex(this.get('id'));
                    if (index != -1) {
                        data = this.toJSON();
                        bookmarks[index] = data;
                        localStorage.setItem('bookmarks', Y.JSON.stringify(bookmarks));
                    }
                    break;
                case 'read':
                    index = findIndex(this.get('id'));
                    if (index != -1) {
                        data = bookmarks[index];
                    }
                    break;
                default:
                    err = 'Invalid action';
            }

            if (Y.Lang.isFunction(callback)) {
                callback(err, data);
            }
        },
    }, {
```

```
        ATTRS: {
            title: {},
            url: {}
        }
    });

    Y.BookmarkList = Y.Base.create('bookmarkList', Y.ModelList, [], {
        model: Y.Bookmark,
        comparator: function (bookmark) {
            return bookmark.get('title');
        },
        sync: function (action, options, callback) {
            var data, err = null;

            if (action === 'read') {
                data = Y.JSON.parse(localStorage.getItem('bookmarks')) || [];
            }
            else {
                err = 'Invalid action';
            }

            if (Y.Lang.isFunction(callback)) {
                callback(err, data);
            }
        }
    });

}, '1.0', { requires: ['model', 'model-list', 'json'] });

YUI().use('bookmark-list', 'node-base', function (Y) {
    var list = new Y.BookmarkList();

    Y.one('#clear').on('click', function () {
        localStorage.clear();
        Y.log('Cleared localStorage. Please reload the page.');
    });

    list.load(function (err, data) {
        if (list.size() === 0) {
            Y.log("No bookmarks saved yet. Let's create some...");
            list.create({ url: 'http://yuilibrary.com', title: 'YUI Library' });
            list.create({ url: 'http://yuiblog.com', title: 'YUI Blog' });
            Y.log('Two bookmarks persisted. Please reload the page.')
        }
        else {
            list.each(function (bookmark) {
                Y.log('Retrieved: ' + bookmark.get('title') + ', ' + bookmark.get('url'));
            });
        }
    });
});
</script>
```

Discussion

At its core, ModelList is just an ArrayList of Models. You can iterate through models using each() or some(), append a model using add(), get an individual model using item(), filter out unwanted models using filter(), and much more. ModelLists are ideal for filtering and paging through a large group of Models.

Besides ArrayList methods, ModelList offers a few key features:

- The model property. If a ModelList is designed to always contain the same type of Model, set the model property to that class. This enables you to call add(), create(), and reset() using attribute hashes, as shown in Example 7-14.

- Model events automatically bubble up to all ModelLists that contain that Model. This feature makes ModelList an ideal "switchboard" for listening and responding to attribute change events. ModelLists themselves fire six events: add, error, remove, reset, load, and create.

- The load() method, which is analogous to SELECT * FROM table. As with Model, load() for ModelList calls sync() with an action of "read". Your read logic must fetch data from the sync layer and pass it into the sync() callback. Ideally, a ModelList's load() should do a single read request that returns all models in the data store, as shown in Example 7-14.

ModelList does not currently expose a save() method, although you can always implement one yourself. A naive ModelList save() might iterate through all Models, calling save() on each one. However, it is probably more efficient to write some logic that takes into account the capabilities of your sync layer.

 Keep in mind the difference between model.save(), modellist .add(model), and modellist.create(model). Calling save() persists an individual model. Calling add() appends a Model to a ModelList. Calling create() combines both operations.

See Also

The YUI ModelList User Guide (*http://yuilibrary.com/yui/docs/model-list/*); ModelList API documentation (*http://yuilibrary.com/yui/docs/api/classes/ModelList.html*); Array List API documentation (*http://yuilibrary.com/yui/docs/api/classes/ArrayList.html*).

7.14 Rendering HTML with a View

Problem

You want to represent a piece of a page as a simple, self-contained, renderable object with its own set of events.

Solution

Extend `View` and implement its `render()` method, as shown in Example 7-15. You can also use the `events` property as a shorthand for configuring the view's event listeners.

Example 7-15. Rendering HTML with a view

```
<!DOCTYPE html>
<title>Rendering HTML with a view</title>
<style>
.error { border: 1px #600 solid; padding: 2px; background: #faa; color: #400; }
</style>

<script src="http://yui.yahooapis.com/3.5.0/build/yui/yui-min.js"></script>
<script>
YUI().add('errorpane', function (Y) {
    Y.ErrorPane = Y.Base.create('errorpane', Y.View, [], {
        events: {
            'button': {'click': 'fadeOut'}
        },
        fadeOut: function () {
            this.get('container').hide(true, Y.bind(this.destroy, this));
        },
        render: function () {
            var container = this.get('container');
            container.setHTML('<button>Ignore</button> ' + this.get('msg'));
            Y.one('body').append(container);
            return this;
        }
    }, {
        ATTRS: {
            msg: {}
        }
    });
}, '1.0', { requires: ['view', 'transition'] });

YUI().use('errorpane', function (Y){
    var errorpane = new Y.ErrorPane({
        msg: 'kernel: 1p0 on fire',
        container: Y.Node.create('<div class="error"/>')
    });
    errorpane.render();
});
</script>
```

Discussion

Like `Widget`, `View` is a component that renders HTML. Both extend `Base` and inherit the powerful `Attribute`, `EventTarget`, and `PluginHost` APIs. However, widgets and views serve different purposes.

A widget is a generic visible component designed to be reused across different websites, such as a table, calendar, menu, or chart. For this reason, the `Widget` API has rich behavior and strong conventions that make it easy for other YUI developers to get up to speed quickly with any new widget they need to use.

A view is a convenient wrapper around a chunk of HTML. A view could represent your site's footer, a blog post, a set of controls, or even an entire page (which can in turn contain child views). Unlike widgets, which solve a common problem for everybody, views solve a particular problem with building *your* site. This means that views can get away with having a lighter, less structured API.

Another way to think about this is, a widget is something you might submit to the gallery; a view, probably not.

This is not to say that you can't use widgets and views in the same application. You could have a view sidebar that renders a widget calendar, or construct a widget using views as internal building blocks. For example, the `DataTable` widget now uses views to control the overall presentation of the table's head, foot, and body, along with models to hold individual rows of data.

Though `View` has few conventions, the one method you must implement is `render()`. This method is very loose, lacking the three-phase structure of `Widget`'s `render()` method. It is up to you to define how and where the view should render its markup. Likewise, `View` has no conventions around bounding boxes or content boxes, just an optional `container` attribute that represents the element that contains the view. By default, `container` is a `<div>`, but you can set this to be any CSS selector string, native DOM node, or YUI node. When a `View` instantiates, `container` automatically becomes a `Node` instance (if it isn't already).

The `events` property is a helper for attaching events. It is a hash of CSS selectors representing nodes to listen on, each of which contains a hash of event names and handler functions (or string method names). Any event handlers you specify here reside on the `container` node and use event delegation. This not only assigns event listeners to lots of child nodes efficiently, but also enables you to destroy and re-render the internal contents of the `container` node without losing event listeners.

 To set `after()` listeners, use the view's `initializer()` method.

To generate the view's HTML, you can use the optional `template` property to hold a template string, and then use `Y.Lang.sub()` or a more sophisticated templating scheme such as Handlebars.js to generate the HTML. Alternatively, you can build up a DOM structure using `Y.Node.create()` and similar methods.

Views lack a built-in convention around internationalization like the `Widget strings` attribute that will be discussed in Recipe 11.6. However, there is no reason you can't use `Y.Intl` or even follow the `Widget strings` convention to the hilt. Likewise, views lack `Widget`'s `HTML_PARSER`, so progressive enhancement is something you must implement yourself.

Ultimately, you should use `View` if its API makes your life easier. If you can solve most of a problem by calling `setHTML()` on a node, `View` is overkill.

See Also

The YUI `View` User Guide (*http://yuilibrary.com/yui/docs/view/*); `View` API documentation (*http://yuilibrary.com/yui/docs/api/classes/View.html*).

7.15 Rendering a Model with a View

Problem

You want to represent a model as a chunk of HTML that changes appearance in response to changes in the model's data.

Solution

Create a model and a view. Then, in the view's `initializer()` method:

1. Use `addTarget()` to configure the model to send its custom events to the view.
2. Assign `after()` event handlers that listen for attribute changes and re-render all or part of the view's HTML.

Example 7-16 returns to the example of the bookmark model. Not only are bookmarks finally visible in the page (hooray!), but they also now have a title, a URL, *and* an array of string tags. The model includes an `addTag()` utility method that adds new tags without creating duplicates and escapes the user's input data to prevent cross-site scripting exploits.

When instantiating a view, you can pass in a `model` attribute in the constructor, which creates a handy reference to a `Model` instance. `BookmarkView` relies on this feature to associate itself with an underlying `Bookmark` model. Data flows through this miniature application as follows:

1. The page loads. The view displays the underlying model data, along with a form for adding tags.
2. The user enters a new tag and clicks the Add button.
3. The click triggers the view's `addTag()` method, which updates the model's `tags` attribute. Note that `addTag()` does not need to create a local copy of the `tags` array—the `Attribute` API handles this for you.
4. The model responds by automatically firing a `bookmark:tagsChange` event.

5. Thanks to addTarget(), the view receives the model's events. The view responds to the bookmark:tagsChange event by re-rendering just the section of the view that displays the list of tags.

For extra robustness, BookmarkView's initializer() also sets a listener for the model Change event. If you decide to associate the view with a different model after instantiation time, the view will automatically call removeTarget() and addTarget() accordingly.

Example 7-16. Rendering a model with a view

```
<!DOCTYPE html>
<title>Rendering a model with a view</title>

<script src="http://yui.yahooapis.com/3.5.0/build/yui/yui-min.js"></script>
<script>
YUI.add('bookmark', function (Y) {

    Y.Bookmark = Y.Base.create('bookmark', Y.Model, [], {
        addTag: function (tag) {
            var tags = this.get('tags');
            if (! Y.Lang.isString(tag)) { return; }
            tag = Y.Escape.html(Y.Lang.trim(tag));
            if (Y.Array.indexOf(tags, tag) !== -1) { return; }

            tags.push(tag);
            this.set('tags', tags);
        }
    }, {
        ATTRS: {
            title: {},
            url: {},
            tags: { value: [] }
        }
    });

    Y.BookmarkView = Y.Base.create('bookmarkView', Y.View, [], {
        events: {
            '.add button': { click: 'addTag' }
        },
        template: '<dt><a href="{url}">{title}</a></dt>'
            + '<dd class="tags">Tags: {tags}</dd><dd class="add">'
            + '<form><input type="text"><button>Add Tag</button></form></dd>',
        initializer: function () {
            var model = this.get('model');

            this.after('bookmark:tagsChange', this.reRenderTags, this);
            this.after('modelChange', function (ev) {
                ev.prevVal && ev.prevVal.removeTarget(this);
                ev.newVal && ev.newVal.addTarget(this);
            });

            model && model.addTarget(this);
        },
```

```
            destructor: function () {
                var model = this.get('model');
                model && model.addTarget(this);
            },
            render: function () {
                var model = this.get('model'),
                    bookmarkData = {
                        url:   model.get('url'),
                        title: model.get('title'),
                        tags:  model.get('tags').join(', ')
                    },
                    content = Y.Lang.sub(this.template, bookmarkData),
                    container = this.get('container')

                container.setHTML(content);
                if (! container.inDoc()) {
                    Y.one('body').append(container);
                }
                return this;
            },
            addTag: function (ev) {
                var input = this.get('container').one('.add input');
                this.get('model').addTag(input.get('value'));
                input.set('value', '');
                ev.preventDefault();
            },
            reRenderTags: function () {
                var tags = this.get('container').one('dd.tags');
                tags.setHTML('Tags: ' + this.get('model').get('tags').join(', '));
            }
        }, {
            ATTRS: {
                container: { value: Y.Node.create('<dl/>') }
            }
        });
    }, '1.0', { requires: ['model', 'view'] });

    YUI().use('bookmark', 'node-base', function (Y) {
        var bookmark = new Y.Bookmark({
            title: 'YUI Library',
            url: 'http://yuilibrary.com',
            tags: ['javascript', 'yui']
        });
        var bookmarkView = new Y.BookmarkView({ model: bookmark });
        bookmarkView.render();
    });
    </script>
```

 If your render() method uses templates, you can often just use Model's toJSON() method to substitute in values, as in Y.Lang.sub(this.template, this.model.toJSON()). Example 7-16 does a little extra work to set up a bookmarkData object, because it's doing something a little more complicated with tags.

Discussion

`addTarget()` is your friend for working with the YUI App Framework. `addTarget()` and event listeners enable you to wire together an application that consists of loosely coupled models and views.

This architecture means you can refactor your rendering code without having to worry very much about how your data management code works, and vice versa. You can rewrite a view's `render()` method without having to touch the model, or change how an attribute's `validator` function works without affecting the view.

Breaking your application into models and views also makes it easy to represent the same data in multiple ways. For example, a single bookmark model could have a read-only "standard" view, an "editor" view for changing bookmark data, and a "tag summary" view that aggregates tag data for multiple bookmarks. If the user edits a bookmark's data, all views that are wired up to that model automatically reflect the changes.

 Setting `model` in the `View`'s constructor sets the `View`'s `model` attribute, but events from the `Model` do not bubble to the `View` unless you configure this relationship with `addTarget()`. Also note that from a `Model` instance you cannot tell which views are listening to the model's events, unless you set these references manually.

See Also

`Model` API documentation (*http://yuilibrary.com/yui/docs/api/classes/Model.html*); `View` API documentation (*http://yuilibrary.com/yui/docs/api/classes/View.html*); Nicholas Zakas's "YUI Theater: Scalable JavaScript Application Architecture" (*http://yuilibrary.com/theater/nicholas-zakas/zakas-architecture/*); Daniel Barreiro's YUIBlog article "A Recipe for a YUI 3 Application" (*http://www.yuiblog.com/blog/2011/04/01/a-recipe-for-a-yui-3-application/*). The last two links don't discuss the App Framework specifically, but do talk about how to organize larger JavaScript applications and prevent components from getting too tightly coupled.

7.16 Rendering a ModelList with a View

Problem

You want to represent multiple models as chunks of HTML that change appearance in response to changes to the list.

Solution

Create a model and two views: one view to render an individual model's data, and one view to render the entire list of models. In the second view, store a reference to a ModelList instance using the modelList attribute, and call addTarget() in the initializer() to ensure that the ModelList's coalesced change events bubble to the view.

Example 7-17 is a variation of the approach used in Recipe 7.15. Here, addTarget() creates a relationship between a single master view and a ModelList, rather than between individual views and models. Also note that instead of extending ModelList, the example just uses a vanilla ModelList instance. Unlike with Model, extending Model List is not required. This particular app only handles adding new bookmarks, but could be fleshed out to handle edits and deletes.

The BookmarkView defines its default container to be an <li> rather than a <div>. To override the default, you must use valueFn rather than value. By default, View already sets container with its own valueFn, which takes priority over value.

> The optional template property is helpful for holding template strings, but string concatenation gets ever more awkward as your templates get more complex. For sophisticated applications, consider using a basic helper function, as shown in Recipe 9.7, or even a full-fledged templating system such as Handlebars.js. You can also use the trick of storing template strings in a <script type="text/x-template> element, as discussed in Recipe 9.7.

Example 7-17. Rendering a ModelList with a view

```
<!DOCTYPE html>
<title>Rendering a ModelList with a view</title>

<script src='http://yui.yahooapis.com/3.5.0/build/yui/yui-min.js'></script>
<script>
YUI.add('bookmark', function (Y) {

    Y.Bookmark = Y.Base.create('bookmark', Y.Model, [], {
        initializer: function () { Y.log('Added: ' + this.get('url')) }
    }, {
        ATTRS: {
            title: {},
            url: {},
        }
    });

    Y.BookmarkView = Y.Base.create('bookmarkView', Y.View, [], {
        template: '<a href="{url}">{title}</a>',
        render: function (parentContainer) {
            var content  = Y.Lang.sub(this.template, this.get('model').toJSON()),
                container = this.get('container');
```

```
            container.setHTML(content);
            if (container.get('parent') !== parentContainer) {
                parentContainer.append(container);
            }
            return this;
        }
    }, {
        ATTRS: {
            container: {
                valueFn: function () { return Y.Node.create('<li/>'); }
            }
        }
    });

    Y.BookmarksView = Y.Base.create('bookmarksView', Y.View, [], {
        template: '<form action="#">' +
            '<label>Title: <input type="text" name="linkTitle"></label>' +
            '<label>URL: <input type="text" name="linkURL"></label>' +
            '<input type="submit" value="Add Bookmark">' +
            '</form> <ul></ul>',
        events: {
            'form': { 'submit': 'addBookmark' }
        },
        initializer: function () {
            var modelList = this.get('modelList');

            this.after('modelList:add', this.renderBookmark, this);
            this.after('modelListChange', function (ev) {
                ev.prevVal && ev.prevVal.removeTarget(this);
                ev.newVal && ev.newVal.addTarget(this);
            });

            modelList && modelList.addTarget(this);
        },
        destructor: function () {
            var modelList = this.get('modelList');
            modelList && modelList.addTarget(this);
        },
        render: function () {
            var container = this.get('container');
            if (! container.inDoc()) {
                container.append(this.template);
                Y.one('body').append(container);
            }
            return this;
        },
        addBookmark: function (ev) {
            this.get('modelList').add({
                title: ev.target.get('linkTitle').get('value'),
                url: ev.target.get('linkURL').get('value')
            });
            ev.preventDefault();
        },
```

```
        renderBookmark: function (ev) {
            var view = new Y.BookmarkView({ model: ev.model });
            view.render(this.get('container').one('ul'));
        }
    }, {
        ATTRS: {
            modelList: { value: new Y.ModelList({ model: Y.Bookmark }) }
        }
    });
}, '1.0', { requires: ['model', 'model-list', 'view'] });

YUI().use('bookmark', function (Y) {
    var bookmarks = new Y.BookmarksView();
    bookmarks.render();
});
</script>
```

Discussion

A View that represents a ModelList is particularly useful for displaying aggregated Model data. For example, individual views could display quantities and subtotals for each line item in a shopping cart, while a master view could render the container for the line items and display the total for the cart.

When juggling Models, ModelLists, and Views in the same application, avoid using a verbose naming scheme like, " BookmarkModel, BookmarkModelView, BookmarkModelList View." Let the base model be a Bookmark, rendered by a BookmarkView, and build from there. To indicate a ModelList, use the plural form of the model's name (Bookmarks) or append "List" (BookmarkList). Alternatively, if you prefer to think of the view as fundamental, let the base view be a Bookmark, backed by a BookmarkModel.

As with models, you can associate a ModelList with a view in the constructor:

```
var view = new ExampleView({ modelList: someModelList });
```

As with the model attribute, the modelList attribute is just a convention. You must still call addTarget() yourself and implement render() yourself.

See Also

Model API documentation (*http://yuilibrary.com/yui/docs/api/classes/Model.html*); ModelList API documentation (*http://yuilibrary.com/yui/docs/api/classes/ModelList.html*); View API documentation (*http://yuilibrary.com/yui/docs/api/classes/View.html*); the YUI TODO List (*http://yuilibrary.com/yui/docs/app/app-todo.html*) example app; Photos Near Me (*https://github.com/ericf/photosnear.me*), another example YUI app; GitHub Users (*http://jsfiddle.net/ericf/SzxJv/*), an extremely minimal app.

7.17 Saving State Changes in the URL

Problem

You want to use Node's load() method to dynamically replace sections of a page in response to user clicks, but you also want to store those state changes in browser history so that the Back button continues to work.

Solution

Use event delegation to wrap a click handler around every link on the page that serves as a "navigation link"—in this case, any link within the nav <ul>. In the event handler, use Node's load() method to fetch the content from the target page. Then use Router's save() method to set a new URL in the user's location bar and update the browser history.

Example 7-18 is similar to Example 5-4. Besides using event delegation, the main difference between the two is that Example 7-18 extracts the filepath of the loaded file and saves that path as a new state in the browser's history.

removeRoot() is a handy utility method for extracting the path component of a URL. The save() method is designed to work with paths such as */jack.html*, not full URLs such as *http://localhost:8000/jack.html*.

Like its predecessor, Example 7-18 is an example of progressive enhancement. If Java-Script is active, clicking a navigation link dynamically replaces the content pane with new markup and updates the URL as the user would expect. If JavaScript is inactive, navigation links still work, but they reload the entire page.

Example 7-18. Using Router to save state changes in the URL

```
<!DOCTYPE html>
<title>Using Router to save state changes in the URL</title>

<h1>Nursery Rhymes</h1>
<ul id="nav">
    <li><a href="jack.html">Jack Be Nimble</a></li>
    <li><a href="bopeep.html">Little Bo Peep</a></li>
    <li><a href="row.html">Row, Row, Row Your Boat</a></li>
</ul>
<div id="main"></div>

<script src="http://yui.yahooapis.com/3.5.0/build/yui/yui-min.js"></script>
<script>
YUI().use('router', 'node-event-delegate', 'node-load', function (Y) {
    var router = new Y.Router();

    Y.one('body').delegate('click', function (ev) {
        var url = ev.target.get('href'),
            path = router.removeRoot(url);
```

```
        ev.preventDefault();

        Y.one('#main').load(url, '#main');
        router.save(path);
    }, '#nav a');
});
</script>
```

 Because this example uses HTML `History`, it must be served from a web server, not the local filesystem.

The example relies on loading content from static HTML files that resemble Example 7-19.

Example 7-19. Sample static HTML page (jack.html)

```
<!DOCTYPE html>
<title>Jack Be Nimble</title>

<h1>Nursery Rhymes</h1>
<ul id="nav">
    <li><a href="jack.html">Jack Be Nimble</a></li>
    <li><a href="bopeep.html">Little Bo Peep</a></li>
    <li><a href="row.html">Row, Row, Row Your Boat</a></li>
</ul>
<div id="main">
<p>
    Jack be nimble,<br>
    Jack be quick,<br>
    Jack jump over<br>
    The candlestick.
</p>
</div>
```

While Example 7-18 creates and uses a `Router` instance, you can also extend `Router`, as shown in Recipe 7.18.

Discussion

`Router` is a machine that maps URLs to application state. Its two main features are:

- Recording application state changes using URLs, as shown in Example 7-18. The example calls `save()` in response to a link click, but the general idea is that you would call `save()` whenever you want to save some interesting moments in your application.

- Responding to URL path changes by executing one or more JavaScript functions; in other words, *URL-based routing*. For more information, refer to Recipe 7.18.

`save()` is the workhorse method for updating browser history. There is a similar `replace()` method; `save()` adds a new entry to history, while `replace()` overwrites the current history entry. `replace()` is useful when you need to update the URL and possibly dispatch to a new route, but you don't want to clutter browser history with yet another event. For both methods, `Router` also includes a good deal of defensive code to work around buggy native `pushState()` implementations.

By default, `Router` configures its history behavior according to the browser's capabilities. If the browser supports HTML `History`, `save()` and `replace()` update history using the browser's native `pushState()` method, which generates a real URL. If not, `save()` and `replace()` update history with a hash-based URL. For example, in a legacy browser, `save('/foo')` saves a URL of *http://example.com/#foo* rather than *http://example.com/foo*.

Providing good URLs for good browsers and bad URLs for bad browsers is usually the correct approach. However, if you need to override this behavior, you can explicitly set `Router`'s `html5` attribute:

- To force all browsers to use real URLs, call `router.set('html5', true)`. Browsers that do not support `pushState()` will make a request to the server that results in a full page load.

- To force all browsers to use legacy hash URLs, call `router.set('html5', false)`. This essentially declares that you have no server-side logic for handling inbound requests, so you are giving up any hope of having robust, reusable URLs.

 Do not set `html5` to `false` unless you fully understand the consequences for maintaining your application in the months and years to come.

Saving state changes as URLs is a powerful technique. Properly used, browser history management addresses a number of usability issues around web applications, such as supporting the Back button and allowing bookmarking and link sharing. However, handling inbound links requires at least some server-side logic, as discussed in "Discussion" on page 219.

You can use `Router` independently from or together with the other components in the App Framework. How you manage your application's state is orthogonal to how you choose to render your application's HTML or sync your application's data.

See Also

Recipe 9.12; the YUI `Router` User Guide (*http://yuilibrary.com/yui/docs/router/*); `Router` API documentation (*http://yuilibrary.com/yui/docs/api/classes/Router.html*); "Are hashbang URLs a recommended practice?" (*http://www.quora.com/Are-hashbang -URLs-a-recommended-practice*).

7.18 Defining and Executing Routes

Problem

You want to render different screens within your application, and possibly even different sections within each page, based on some kind of URL hierarchy.

Solution

Use Router to define a set of *routes* that map URL paths within your application to JavaScript functions that generate the appropriate HTML.

Example 7-20 represents a fake blog management application that illustrates how to configure routes. The application uses event delegation to trap clicks on navigation links and call the router's save() method. Calling save() not only updates the location bar and browser history, but also *dispatches* the URL path to the router, evaluating the path against its routes in order and executing the callback for the first route that matches.

Example 7-20. Defining and executing routes

```
<!DOCTYPE html>
<title>Defining and executing routes</title>

<div id="nav"><a href="/admin">Admin</a> | <a href="/posts">Blog Posts</a></div>
<div id="subnav"></div>
<div id="main"></div>

<script src="http://yui.yahooapis.com/3.5.0/build/yui/yui-min.js"></script>
<script>
YUI().add('blog', function (Y) {
    Y.Blog = Y.Base.create('blog', Y.Router, [], {
        initializer: function () {
            Y.one('body').delegate('click', function (ev) {
                var path = this.removeRoot(ev.target.get('href'));
                ev.preventDefault();
                this.save(path);
            }, 'a', this);
        },
        showAdminScreen: function (req, res, next) {
            Y.one('#subnav').setHTML('<p>(admin buttons)</p>');
            Y.one('#main').setHTML('<p>(general admin functions)</p>');
        },
        listPosts: function (req, res, next) {
            Y.one('#subnav').setHTML('<ul'
                + '<li><a href="/posts/3">Blogging is Hard</a></li>'
                + '<li><a href="/posts/2">What I Had For Lunch Today</a></li>'
                + '<li><a href="/posts/1">Hello World</a></li>'
                + '</ul>');
            Y.one('#main').setHTML('');
            next();
        },
```

```
            editPost: function (req, res, next) {
                Y.one('#main').setHTML('Editing post ' + req.params.id);
            }
        }, {
            ATTRS: {
                routes: {
                    value: [
                        { path: '/admin', callback: 'showAdminScreen' },
                        { path: /^\/posts/, callback: 'listPosts' },
                        { path: '/posts/:id', callback: 'editPost' }
                    ]
                }
            }
        });
    }, '1.0', { requires: ['router', 'node-event-delegate'] });

    YUI().use('blog', function (Y) {
        var blog = new Y.Blog();
    });
    </script>
```

 This example must be served from a web server, not the local filesystem.

Each route callback receives three parameters:

- A req parameter representing the request. It contains:
  - A path string representing the original URL path
  - A url string representing the full URL
  - A query object containing a hash of HTTP query parameter names and values
  - A params property that is either a hash of captured string parameters or an array of captured regex matches
  - A src string that is "popstate" when the user hits the Forward or Back button; "add" for other user actions such as link clicks

  In Example 7-20, the path of "/posts/:id" causes Router to capture the substring after /posts/ as a named parameter, passing it into editPost() as req.params.id. In a real blog application, this parameter could be used to fetch blog post data from a database.

- A res parameter. In YUI 3.5.0, route callbacks receive three parameters: req, res, and next—but to maintain backward compatibility with legacy code, res and next are actually identical. In future versions of YUI, res will carry information about the response, breaking compatibility with legacy code.

- A next parameter that is an executable function. By default, a router executes only the first route that matches, but calling next() causes it to continue evaluating routes. This technique is called *route chaining*.

  In Example 7-20, the listPosts() method is responsible only for painting a section of the page. Because listPosts() calls next(), a path such as /posts/2 not only triggers listPosts(), but continues on to editPost() as well.

Thus:

1. Navigating to the */admin* path displays a fake "admin screen."
2. Navigating to any URL underneath */posts* displays a hardcoded fake list of the most recent "blog posts." Executing next() causes Router to continue looking for possible matching routes.
3. Navigating to a particular post ID such as */posts/2* not only displays the list of current blog posts, but also displays a fake "edit screen" for the specified post beneath that.

It's worth emphasizing that the callbacks shown in Example 7-20 are fake and contain only throwaway code. Real routing callbacks might fetch data using Ajax, or use views to render some well-crafted HTML. Those views in turn could rely on models to supply data such as titles, body content, and categories. The models could sync to a storage layer, and so on.

Discussion

Router's client-side routing is inspired by the Express web serving framework for Node.js. Router does not currently work on the server and lacks some of Express's advanced server-side routing features. However, if you use Router on the client and Express on the server, you should be able to share some routing code.

When writing a single-page app, you will need to have at least *some* server-side backing. For example, if your Products page resides at the path */products*, and a user bookmarks a link to a particular product such as *http://example.com/products/hotdogs*, that link will 404 unless the server routes GET /products/hotdogs to the */products* page.

In Router, a *route* is defined as a mapping between a URL path and a callback function. Paths can be:

- Simple string matches, as in "/admin"
- Placeholders, as in "/posts/:id", where id matches everything up to the next / character
- "Splat" placeholders, as in "/posts/*path", where path matches everything including subsequent / characters
- Regular expression matches, as in /^\/posts/

You can specify a callback as a named function, as an anonymous function, or as the string name of a method on the Router object. For more information about route syntax and parameter capturing, refer to the Router API documentation.

Although route chaining is optional, it is a useful technique for dividing responsibility between different functions. For example, an application with hierarchical URLs of the form */mainnav/subnav/content* could use route chaining to designate one function to display the main navigation, which chains to a function that displays the subnavigation, which chains to a third function that displays the main content.

You can add routes by:

1. Extending Router and setting the routes attribute to an array of route definitions, as shown in Example 7-20.

2. Providing routes at construction time:

```
var router = new Y.Router({
    routes: [
        { path: "/foo", function: "fooHandler" },
        ...
    ]
});
```

3. Calling the route() method after instantiation to add an individual route:

```
router.route("/foo", function () { ... });
```

 If you have paths that chain from another path, their handlers must call next()! Route chaining does not occur by default.

Calling save() or replace() not only updates the URL, but also triggers a dispatch, causing the router to evaluate routes. In browsers that do not support HTML History, the router triggers a dispatch on initial page load, since this is necessary to support hash-based URLs. To manually trigger a dispatch at any time without changing the URL, call dispatch().

As an example of when to call dispatch(), consider a single-page application that physically resides under the URL */app*. You've also added some server-side logic to direct all requests to any path under */app* to this single page. A user copies a link within your application, *http://example.com/app/foo/bar/123*, and shares it with a friend. When the friend clicks the link, the server directs the request of GET /app/foo/bar/123 to your app. Without an initial dispatch, the friend will be directed to your application's home page, not the expected page. An initial router.dispatch() resolves this problem by evaluating routes and constructing the correct page for that URL.

The advantage of the "redirect and do an initial `dispatch()`" pattern is that almost all router code resides on the client. You need only a relatively small amount of server-side code to redirect requests to */app*.

The disadvantage of this pattern is that almost all router code resides on the client. If the user has JavaScript turned off, or if the "user" is actually a search engine spider crawling your site, your site will break.

It is also a good practice to call `upgrade()` on initial page load. In browsers that support HTML `History`, this checks whether the URL is a hash-based URL (possibly copied and pasted from a legacy browser) and automatically upgrades the URL to a real URL, triggering a dispatch. In browsers that do not support HTML `History`, calling `upgrade()` has no effect.

See Also

The YUI `Router` User Guide (*http://yuilibrary.com/yui/docs/router/*); `Router` API documentation (*http://yuilibrary.com/yui/docs/api/classes/Router.html*); Express JS (*http://expressjs.com/*).

Using Widgets

One of the most popular features YUI offers is its suite of prepackaged widgets. As discussed in previous chapters, in YUI parlance, a *widget* is a generic visible component designed to be reused across different websites, such as a table, calendar, menu, or chart. Conceptually, a YUI widget is similar to a Dojo widget or a jQuery UI plugin.

The YUI `Widget` API is unique in that it provides strong conventions. Despite being designed to address wildly different tasks, all YUI widgets share a huge number of common behaviors:

- All YUI widgets use the same conventions for rendering.
- All YUI widgets use the same approach for configuring the widget at construction time and for changing the configuration later on.
- All YUI widgets share a large group of common configuration settings and methods. The external API works the same way for hiding a widget, disabling a widget, controlling a widget's size, destroying a widget instance, and many other common functions.
- All YUI widgets follow the same basic structural conventions for their container elements and the CSS classes on those containers.
- All YUI widgets fire custom events when their configuration state changes and at other interesting moments.
- All YUI widgets can receive custom events and can be added to an event target chain.
- All YUI widgets can add plugins to augment a particular widget instance's behavior. Features such as being "draggable" or "resizable" are broken out into plugins, which means that you add and use those features in the same way for every widget.
- All YUI widgets use the same mechanisms for changing the widget at the prototype level, either by extending the widget or by mixing new methods into the widget's prototype. The core library provides a large number of mixins—in fact, some widgets are composed solely from mixins and don't have any unique methods or properties of their own.

In other words, if you've used one YUI widget, it's easy to learn how to use another. If you are designing new widgets, you get a rich set of behaviors for free, and other YUI developers can get up and running with your widget quickly.

This chapter explains how to exercise some of the core widgets. To learn how to create new widgets from scratch, refer to Chapter 7.

 Understanding the YUI infrastructure APIs is critical for getting the most out of YUI. Even if you aren't planning to build a new YUI widget right this second, it's a good idea to read through Chapter 7, or at least its first four recipes, to understand how the common `Base`, `Attribute`, and `Widget` APIs work.

Recipe 8.1 demonstrates how to instantiate, render, and configure widgets. If you don't have time to read Chapter 7, this recipe should at least get you started on basic widget usage.

Recipes 8.2, 8.3, and 8.4 explain how to use `Overlay`, the most generic core widget. `Overlay` is a simple, unskinned container object designed to hold and move around any markup you like.

Recipes 8.5 and 8.6 introduce `Panel`, a superset of `Overlay` with a skin. `Panel` is designed for creating message panels, dialogs, and small forms.

Recipe 8.7 shows how to use `Overlay` to implement a fancy reusable tooltip.

Recipe 8.8 goes much further than the previous recipe, using `Overlay` as the foundation for a lightbox/slideshow-style interaction. This recipe illustrates how to mix in additional widget extensions. It also demonstrates how to listen for state changes and update the UI in response, rather than the more brittle method of reacting directly to UI events.

Recipe 8.9 introduces `Slider`, a widget for selecting a range of numeric values.

Recipe 8.10 explains how to use `TabView` to provide tab navigation.

Recipes 8.11, 8.12, and 8.13 describe how to display tabular data with the `DataTable` widget, ranging from basic usage to fetching remote data using `DataSource`.

Recipe 8.14 explains how to display data in a graph using the `Chart` widget.

Recipe 8.15 discusses `Calendar`, which enables users to select dates. Recipe 8.16 explains how to create `Calendar` rules to disable date ranges and otherwise customize date cells.

Finally, Recipes 8.17 through 8.20 discuss `AutoComplete`, covering everything from fetching remote data to highlighting and formatting.

8.1 Instantiating, Rendering, and Configuring Widgets

Problem

You want to add a YUI widget to your page.

Solution

Load the module that provides the widget, instantiate a widget instance (optionally passing in any configuration attributes) and call the `render()` method to append the widget into the DOM. Example 8-1 illustrates basic widget usage, instantiating a 300-pixel-wide calendar and rendering it into the demo `<div>`.

Example 8-1. Instantiating and rendering a 300-pixel-wide calendar

```
<!DOCTYPE html>
<title>Instantiating and rendering a 300-pixel-wide calendar</title>

<body class="yui3-skin-sam">
<div id="demo"></div>

<script src="http://yui.yahooapis.com/3.5.0/build/yui/yui-min.js"></script>
<script>
YUI().use('calendar', function (Y) {
    var calendar = new Y.Calendar({
        width: 300
    });
    calendar.render('#demo');
});
</script>
</body>
```

Figure 8-1 illustrates the results of Example 8-1.

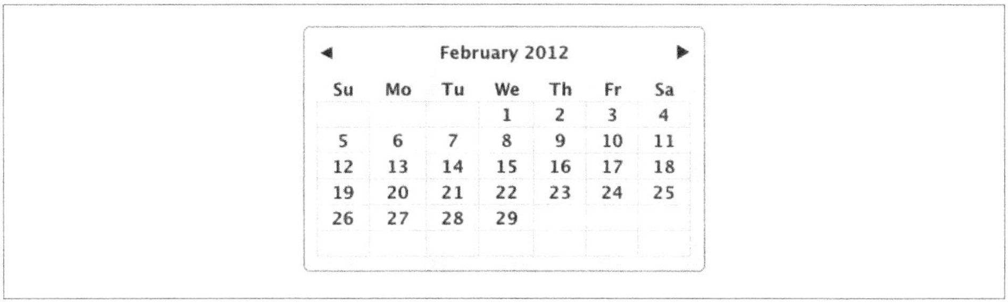

Figure 8-1. A 300-pixel-wide calendar

You can do this more compactly by chaining `render()` off the constructor. Many examples in this book use the chained pattern:

```
var calendar = new Y.Calendar({ width: 300 }).render('#demo');
```

This is the equivalent of:

```
var calendar = new Y.Calendar({ width: 300, render: '#demo' });
```

In other words, you can render the calendar into the demo `<div>` by setting the `render` configuration attribute, or by calling the `render()` method, either chained directly off the constructor, or sometime later on.

 Many YUI methods that you might otherwise think return nothing, such as `addClass()`, `append()`, and `render()`, actually return a reference to their own object instance so that you can use chaining. These methods are flagged as "chainable" in the API documentation.

Usually, it's a good idea to save a handle to the widget so that you can manipulate it later on. However, if you don't need the handle, you can leave it out:

```
new Y.Calendar({ width: 300 }).render('#demo');
```

The reason to set the calendar's `width` is that most widgets expand to fill their containing box. If you've already set the demo `<div>`'s size using CSS (or simply don't care), the JavaScript could be even more compact:

```
new Y.Calendar().render('#demo');
```

Where do a YUI widget's CSS resources come from? By default, when you load a YUI core widget module, the Loader also loads that widget's `sam` skin, a CSS file with that widget's styles, all scoped to the class `yui3-skin-sam`. Since the `sam` skin is the default for all core widgets and most third-party widgets, it is usually good practice to add `yui3-skin-sam` to the `<body>` in any page where you are loading widgets. However, there's also nothing wrong with adding `yui3-skin-sam` to any element that contains the widget. For an example of using an alternative skin for just one widget, refer to Example 8-12.

Discussion

The widget's constructor takes an optional configuration object that sets the widget's *attributes*. An attribute is like a "super property"—it can have special getters, setters, validators, and other behaviors. Perhaps most important of all, attributes fire events whenever they are changed.

Some attributes are present for all widgets, while others are specific to a particular type of widget. For example, `width` is a common widget attribute, while `maximumDate` only applies to `Calendar` widgets. In the YUI API documentation, a widget's attributes will have their own section alongside the widget's methods, properties, and events. For more information about the `Attribute` API, refer to Recipe 7.1.

Setting initial attribute values in the constructor is convenient, but you can also set them later on by calling set():

```
var calendar = new Y.Calendar();
calendar.set('width', 300);
calendar.render('#demo');
```

The render() method can take a CSS selector string or a YUI node.

As a technical point, every YUI widget creates a *bounding box* and a *content box*, which are usually (but not always) <div>s. If you call render('#demo'), the bounding box and content box <div>s render *inside* the demo <div>, creating a structure of:

```
demo div
    bounding box div
        content box div
            calendar elements ...
```

If you instead set the demo <div> as the contentBox attribute and just call render(), the content box *becomes* the demo <div>. Thus, instantiating a widget like this:

```
var calendar = new Y.Calendar({
    width: 300,
    contentBox: '#demo',
}).render();
```

yields a structure of:

```
bounding box div
    content box div (aka the demo div, same thing)
        calendar elements ...
```

Along with the contentBox, there is also a srcNode attribute for widgets that use progressive enhancement to construct themselves from existing HTML markup. For example, you can build a TabView widget from pure JavaScript, or from <ul>s and <div>s on the page. To see the difference, compare Example 8-13 to Example 8-14.

If you haven't specified where render() should append the widget, YUI defaults to appending the widget into the <body>. For absolutely positioned widgets such as Overlay and Panel, this is fine. Widgets without an absolute position should usually be rendered into a specific container.

See Also

Recipe 4.6; Recipe 7.1; Recipe 7.2; Recipe 7.4; Recipe 8.15; the Widget User Guide (*http://yuilibrary.com/yui/docs/widget/*).

8.2 Creating an Overlay

Problem

You want to create a generic, absolutely positioned container for markup.

Solution

Instantiate an `Overlay` widget, specifying its *xy* position and populating its header, body, and footer content in the constructor, as shown in Example 8-2.

Example 8-2. Creating an overlay from JavaScript

```
<!DOCTYPE html>
<title>Creating an overlay from JavaScript</title>
<style>
.yui3-overlay    { width: 200px; border: 1px #259 solid; border-radius: 5px; }
.yui3-widget-hd { background: #00cccc; padding: 2px; }
.yui3-widget-bd { background: #47a3ff; padding: 2px; }
.yui3-widget-ft { background: #0a85ff; padding: 2px; }
</style>

<button id="hide">Hide</button> <button id="show">Show</button>
<p>Dear Overlay: I'm feeling a bit smothered. Respectfully yours, P.</p>

<script src="http://yui.yahooapis.com/3.5.0/build/yui/yui-min.js"></script>
<script>
YUI().use('overlay', function (Y) {
    var overlay = new Y.Overlay({
        headerContent: 'Head',
        bodyContent: 'Body',
        footerContent: '<b>Foot</b>',
        xy: [20, 40]
    }).render();

    Y.one('#hide').on('click', function () { overlay.hide(); });
    Y.one('#show').on('click', function () { overlay.show(); });
});
</script>
```

Figure 8-2 illustrates the results of Example 8-2.

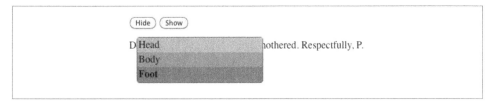

Figure 8-2. An overlay from JavaScript

As Example 8-2 demonstrates, an `Overlay` widget, well...*overlays*. The user can't select the obscured region of the paragraph until you hide the overlay again.

Alternatively, you can set the `srcNode` attribute to create an overlay from preexisting markup on the page. In this case, you can add some extra CSS to handle the case where JavaScript is not yet loaded. Example 8-3 creates an overlay from an existing `<div>`, but hides the markup it uses until the moment the overlay instantiates.

Example 8-3. Creating an overlay from markup

```
<!DOCTYPE html>
<title>Creating an overlay from markup</title>
<style>
#overlay { display: none; }
#overlay.yui3-overlay-content { display: block; }
.yui3-overlay    { width: 200px; border: 1px #259 solid; border-radius: 5px; }
.yui3-widget-hd { background: #00cccc; padding: 2px; }
.yui3-widget-bd { background: #47a3ff; padding: 2px; }
.yui3-widget-ft { background: #0a85ff; padding: 2px; }
</style>

<button id="hide">Hide</button> <button id="show">Show</button>
<p>Dear Overlay: I'm feeling a bit smothered. Respectfully, P.</p>

<div id="overlay">
    <div class="yui3-widget-hd">Head</div>
    <div class="yui3-widget-bd">Body</div>
    <div class="yui3-widget-ft"><b>Foot</b></div>
</div>

<script src="http://yui.yahooapis.com/3.5.0/build/yui/yui-min.js"></script>
<script>
YUI().use('overlay', function (Y) {
    var overlay = new Y.Overlay({ srcNode: '#overlay', xy: [20, 40] }).render();

    Y.one('#hide').on('click', function () { overlay.hide(); });
    Y.one('#show').on('click', function () { overlay.show(); });
});
</script>
```

While overlays support a header/body/footer structure, you don't have to follow this convention. Example 8-4 illustrates perhaps the simplest possible overlay. It is unstyled and positioned in the top-left corner, partially covering the Hide and Show buttons.

Example 8-4. Creating an extremely basic overlay

```
<!DOCTYPE html>
<title>Creating an extremely basic overlay</title>

<button id="hide">Hide</button> <button id="show">Show</button>

<div id="overlay">Generic Overlay</div>

<script src="http://yui.yahooapis.com/3.5.0/build/yui/yui-min.js"></script>
<script>
YUI().use('overlay', function (Y) {
    var overlay = new Y.Overlay({ srcNode: '#overlay' }).render();

    Y.one('#hide').on('click', function () { overlay.hide(); });
    Y.one('#show').on('click', function () { overlay.show(); });
});
</script>
```

Figure 8-3 illustrates the results of Example 8-4.

Figure 8-3. An extremely basic overlay

You can always set() the headerContent, bodyContent, or footerContent attributes later on by any means you like, perhaps even by making a remote I/O or YQL call.

Discussion

Interestingly, the Overlay object has *no* intrinsic properties or methods of its own. You build up Overlay by extending the fundamental Widget object and by mixing in small, general-purpose widget extensions that provide additional behaviors. These extensions include:

WidgetPosition
> Makes a widget positionable, adding x and y attributes and a move() method for moving the widget around

WidgetPositionAlign
> Enables a widget to be centered within or aligned with respect to a node or the viewport

WidgetPositionConstrain
> Enables a widget to be constrained within a node or the viewport

WidgetStack
> Manages a widget's z-index, including extra shim support that activates only for IE6

WidgetStdMod
> Adds header, body, and footer sections to a widget's contentBox

In other words, while you can move an overlay to a new position by setting its x or y attribute or by calling the move() method, you can easily add these features to *any* YUI widget you create or extend. The simplest way to mix attributes, methods, and properties into your own custom widgets is the Y.Base.create() method. For more information, refer to Recipe 7.3.

An overlay is a generic container. Its CSS provides only basic structural behavior such as setting visibility: hidden when the widget is in the hidden state. Since Overlay is one of the very few core widgets that does not ship with a look and feel, it is also one of the very few core widgets that doesn't need a yui3-skin-sam class added to the <body>. For a widget similar to Overlay that includes more features and comes with a skin, refer to Recipe 8.5.

See Also

The Overlay User Guide (*http://yuilibrary.com/yui/docs/overlay/*); Overlay API documentation (*http://yuilibrary.com/yui/docs/api/classes/Overlay.html*); Kevin Isom's "Getting to Know the YUI 3 Overlay" (*http://kevinisom.info/post/11056899037/getting -to-know-the-yui-3-overlay*).

8.3 Aligning and Centering an Overlay

Problem

You want to move an overlay to appear just below a form control.

Solution

Instantiate an Overlay and snap it to the desired location by calling the align() method. The align() method takes two parameters:

node
> A Node reference or CSS selector for a node to align the widget against.

points
> An array containing two points to align: a point on the widget, followed by a point on the target node. There are nine alignment points, defined as static properties on Y.WidgetPositionAlign. For example, Y.WidgetPositionAlign.TR is the top-right corner, while Y.WidgetPositionAlign.CC is the center of the object.

In Example 8-5, the overlay starts out visible and centered with respect to the viewport. Clicking the first button calls align(), moving the top-left corner of the widget to the bottom center of the target node. Clicking the second button calls the sugar method centered(), which returns the overlay to the current center of the viewport. (Calling centered(*node*) centers the overlay within a node.)

Example 8-5. Aligning and centering an overlay

```
<!DOCTYPE html>
<title>Aligning and centering an overlay</title>
<style>
.yui3-overlay   { width: 200px; border: 1px #c02727 solid; border-radius: 5px; }
.yui3-widget-hd { background: #3b5bdf; padding: 2px; }
.yui3-widget-bd { background: #fff64c; padding: 2px; }
.yui3-widget-ft { background: #c02727; padding: 2px; }
</style>

<button id="kneel">Come to ME, Overlay!</button>
<button id="flyaway">No, I defy you</button>

<script src="http://yui.yahooapis.com/3.5.0/build/yui/yui-min.js"></script>
<script>
```

```
YUI().use('overlay', function (Y) {
    var overlay = new Y.Overlay({
        headerContent: 'Head',
        bodyContent: 'Body',
        footerContent: 'Foot',
        centered: true
    }).render();

    Y.one('#kneel').on('click', function () {
        overlay.align('#kneel', [Y.WidgetPositionAlign.TL, Y.WidgetPositionAlign.BC]);
    });
    Y.one('#flyaway').on('click', function () { overlay.centered(); });
});
</script>
```

Figure 8-4 illustrates the results of Example 8-5 just after a user clicks the "Come to ME, Overlay!" button.

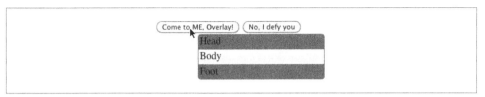

Figure 8-4. A centered and aligned overlay

Discussion

Aligning and centering rely on absolute positioning. If you center a widget within the viewport, and the user resizes the window, the widget stays where it is. If you call set('x', 350) to move the overlay to a new absolute *x* coordinate, the *y* coordinate stays the same.

Like all features in Overlay, alignment and centering are provided by a generic extension object, WidgetPositionAlign. You can mix in this functionality to any other widget by using Y.Base.create() or Y.Base.mix() to mix in WidgetPosition and WidgetPosition Align. For example, making Calendar widgets alignable is as easy as:

```
Y.Base.mix(Y.Calendar, [Y.WidgetPosition, Y.WidgetPositionAlign]);
new Y.Calendar({ width: 200, centered: true }).render('#demo');
```

Mixing and matching features like this is one of the more powerful aspects of YUI's infrastructure.

See Also

Recipe 7.3; WidgetPositionAlign API documentation (*http://yuilibrary.com/yui/docs/ api/classes/WidgetPositionAlign.html*).

8.4 Making an Overlay Draggable

Problem

You want to create a generic container for markup that the user can drag around.

Solution

Instantiate an `Overlay` and plug it with the `Y.Plugin.Drag` plugin.

Example 8-6 creates two overlapping overlays. It reuses the same CSS from Example 8-2, but visually distinguishes between the two by omitting the footer from the first overlay, and the header from the second. `overlayTop` also calls `plug(Y.Plugin.Drag)` to make the instance draggable. `overlayBottom` is a little bit more advanced, passing in a second config object to `plug()` that defines a drag handle, a variation of the technique shown in Example 3-11. Unlike `overlayTop`, you can drag `overlayBottom` only from its head `<div>`.

Example 8-6. Creating two draggable overlays

```
<!DOCTYPE html>
<title>Creating two draggable overlays</title>
<style>
.yui3-overlay    { width: 200px; border: 1px #259 solid; border-radius: 5px; }
.yui3-widget-hd { background: #00cccc; padding: 2px; }
.yui3-widget-bd { background: #47a3ff; padding: 2px; }
.yui3-widget-ft { background: #0a85ff; padding: 2px; }
</style>

<p>Dear Overlay: I'm feeling a bit smothered. Respectfully, P.</p>

<script src="http://yui.yahooapis.com/3.5.0/build/yui/yui-min.js"></script>
<script>
YUI().use('overlay', 'dd-plugin', function (Y) {
    var overlayBottom = new Y.Overlay({
        headerContent: 'Head [drag handle!]',
        bodyContent: 'Body'
    });

    var overlayTop = new Y.Overlay({
        bodyContent: 'Body',
        footerContent: 'Foot',
        xy: [30,30],
        zIndex: 1
    });

    overlayBottom.plug(Y.Plugin.Drag, { handles: ['.yui3-widget-hd'] });
    overlayTop.plug(Y.Plugin.Drag);
    overlayBottom.render();
    overlayTop.render();
});
</script>
```

Figure 8-5 illustrates the results of Example 8-6.

Figure 8-5. Two draggable overlays

Discussion

The key difference between extensions like `WidgetStack` and plugins like `Plugin.Drag` is that extensions add behavior to all instances of an object, while `plug()` and `unplug()` add and remove behavior from particular instances.

Note that along with setting a drag handle, `overlayTop` also sets a higher `zIndex` attribute. By default, both overlays would have a `zIndex` of 0, and so the first object to render would be the one on the top of the stack. `zIndex`, provided by the `WidgetStack` extension, provides control over the stack order.

See Also

Recipe 3.7; Recipe 7.7; `WidgetStack` API documentation (*http://yuilibrary.com/yui/docs/ api/classes/WidgetStack.html*).

8.5 Creating a Simple, Styled Information Panel

Problem

You want to provide the user an informational message in a styled pane, without having to resort to using a gross `alert()` box.

Solution

Instantiate a `Panel` widget, setting the `bodyContent` to whatever HTML message you need to display. Unlike the bare-bones `Overlay`, `Panel` ships with a skin that looks more like a panel an operating system might display, with colors, gradients, and controls.

Example 8-7 displays a centered `Panel` widget with a cautionary message. Unlike a native `alert()` box, a panel does not have to be modal; you can choose whether the user is blocked from interacting with other elements on the screen. Clicking the "x" button or pressing the Escape key dismisses the panel. As an alternative to setting `centered: true`, you can use `WidgetPosition` to set the panel at a particular *x,y* coordinate, or `WidgetPositionAlign` to snap the panel against some other element, just like you can with an overlay.

Example 8-7. Creating a simple, styled informational panel

```
<!DOCTYPE html>
<title>Creating a simple, styled informational panel</title>

<body class="yui3-skin-sam">

<script src="http://yui.yahooapis.com/3.5.0/build/yui/yui-min.js"></script>
<script>
YUI().use('panel', function (Y) {
    var panel = new Y.Panel({
        width: 300,
        centered: true,
        bodyContent: 'CAUTION: Watch out for random panels.'
    }).render();
});
</script>
</body>
```

Figure 8-6 illustrates the results of Example 8-7.

Figure 8-6. A simple, styled informational panel

Discussion

Panel is a superset of Overlay. Like Overlay, Panel has no intrinsic properties or methods of its own—it is a Widget, plus a long list of generic Widget extensions, plus a fancy skin. Panel includes the five extensions Overlay uses (described in Recipe 8.2), and adds:

WidgetAutohide
> Makes it easy to configure listeners for click events and keystrokes that hide the widget

WidgetButtons
> Makes it easy to add buttons to the widget's header and footer

WidgetModality
> Enables modal widgets that darken the screen and mask out interactions with other elements on the page

Panel's extra functionality derives from these three additional extensions and their default behavior. The WidgetAutohide extension uses its hideOn attribute to set a default hide listener for the Escape key. The WidgetButtons extension creates a default button in the header (if available) that closes the panel. The WidgetModality extension provides the `modal` attribute for flagging the panel as modal, along with a `focusOn` attribute that controls how to direct focus to the panel.

For an example that demonstrates a more complex modal panel with buttons, refer to Recipe 8.6. For an example that demonstrates modality with a custom `hideOn` attribute, refer to Recipe 8.8.

See Also

The `Panel` User Guide (*http://yuilibrary.com/yui/docs/panel/*); `Panel` API documentation (*http://yuilibrary.com/yui/docs/api/classes/Panel.html*).

8.6 Creating a Modal Dialog or Form

Problem

You want to force the user's attention onto a modal dialog or form.

Solution

Define buttons as simple objects, including an `action` field that specifies the dialog or form's behavior. Then instantiate a `Panel` with whatever HTML content you like, setting `modal` and `centered` to `true`, passing in the buttons as an array to the `buttons` attribute. See Example 8-8.

 If your form accepts and redisplays user input, be sure to pass that input through `Y.Escape.html()` so that the resulting string cannot be used in a cross-site scripting attack.

Example 8-8. Creating a modal dialog or form

```
<!DOCTYPE html>
<title>Creating a modal dialog or form</title>
<style>
#houndReleaseForm { display: none; }
.yui3-widget-bd #houndReleaseForm { display: block; }
</style>

<body class="yui3-skin-sam">
<form id="houndReleaseForm" action="#">
    <label for="hounds">Hounds to release:</label>
    <input type="text" name="hounds" id="hounds" value="all of them">
</form>

<script src="http://yui.yahooapis.com/3.5.0/build/yui/yui-min.js"></script>
<script>
YUI().use('panel', 'escape', function (Y) {
    var okButton = {
        value: 'ok',
```

```
                    section: Y.WidgetStdMod.FOOTER,
                    action: function (ev) {
                        var numHounds = Y.Escape.html(Y.one('#hounds').get('value'));
                        Y.one('body').append('<p>Hounds released: ' + numHounds + '</p>');
                        ev.preventDefault();
                        this.hide();
                    }
            };

            var cancelButton = {
                    value: 'cancel',
                    section: Y.WidgetStdMod.FOOTER,
                    action: function (ev) {
                        ev.preventDefault();
                        this.hide();
                    }
            };

            var panel = new Y.Panel({
                    width: 300,
                    centered: true,
                    modal: true,
                    headerContent: 'Release the hounds?',
                    bodyContent: Y.one('#houndReleaseForm'),
                    buttons: [ okButton, cancelButton ]
            }).render();
});
</script>
</body>
```

Figure 8-7 illustrates the results of Example 8-8 before the form is submitted.

Figure 8-7. A modal dialog or form

The rest of the screen behind the panel is dark grey and cannot be interacted with while the modal panel is active. The dotted border indicates that the panel currently has focus.

Discussion

Example 8-8 is pretty simple, but if you're just looking for a classic OK/Cancel dialog, you can strip it down further. Replace the form HTML with a message, and change the

OK button's `action` to whatever is appropriate. Ideally, you should come up with more informative labels than "OK" and "Cancel."

`WidgetButtons` includes one predefined button: an "x" button that closes the widget. You can create that button with:

```
var button = { type: 'close' };
```

This is the only predefined `type` available, although you can define more button types by adding them to the `WidgetButtons.DEFAULT_BUTTONS` hash. As shown in Example 8-8, a button object is just a simple object with these fields:

value
> Specifies the button's HTML or string label

section
> Selects whether the button appears in the `Y.WidgetStdMod.HEADER` or `Y.WidgetStdMod.FOOTER`

href
> Specifies a URL to navigate to when the button is invoked

action
> Provides a custom callback function to execute when the button is clicked

classNames
> Specifies a string class name or array of string class names to add to the button

In Example 8-8, the form markup is embedded on the page rather than generated purely in JavaScript. To avoid a flash of unstyled content, the example uses a trick similar to the one used in Example 8-3. CSS initially sets the form to `display:none`, then flips the form back to `display:block` once the widget renders.

See Also

`WidgetButtons` API documentation (*http://yuilibrary.com/yui/docs/api/classes/WidgetButtons.html*); `WidgetModality` API documentation (*http://yuilibrary.com/yui/docs/api/classes/WidgetModality.html*); `WidgetAutohide` API documentation (*http://yuilibrary.com/yui/docs/api/classes/WidgetAutohide.html*).

8.7 Creating a Tooltip from an Overlay

Problem

HTML already provides a `title` attribute that creates a generic but limited browser tooltip. You want to create a tooltip that can hover below any HTML element and that is easy to style however you like.

Solution

A naive solution would be to instantiate one `Overlay` widget for each element on the page that needs a tooltip, storing the tooltip information in a JavaScript array of strings.

However, there's a better approach lurking in plain sight. The plain old `title` attribute has two key virtues: it embeds tooltip information right next to the content it is describing, and it makes it easy for nonengineers to add tooltips.

To mimic this approach, you can use custom data attributes with the tooltip widget. A custom data attribute has a prefix of `data-` and can legally be added to any HTML element. You can use this HTML feature to store tooltip strings in a custom `data-tooltip` attribute. Also note that since only one tooltip is shown at a time, it's possible to create one instance and reuse it, rather than creating dozens of copies.

Example 8-9 starts by defining CSS for the tooltip, including advanced features such as `border-radius` and `box-shadow`. The traditional morass of vendor CSS prefixes has been omitted for clarity. Older browsers will still see a tooltip, but get a mildly degraded experience.

The example then instantiates the tooltip with the `visible` attribute set to `false`. When the tooltip renders, its markup will be on the page, ready to be shown.

The `enter()` and `leave()` callback functions handle the `mouseenter` and `mouseleave` events, respectively. The `enter()` function snaps the tooltip's top-left corner to the bottom center of the target node, sets the `bodyContent` to the value of the target node's tooltip, and shows the tooltip. The `leave()` function hides the tooltip, but does not bother to move it.

The example uses event delegation to listen for `mouseenter` and `mouseleave` events. Any `mouseenter` or `mouseleave` event on an element that has a `data-tooltip` attribute will trigger the corresponding callback function. Delegation is particularly useful in this example, where you don't know ahead of time how many elements to be listening on, and where the number could potentially be very large. For more information about how delegation works, refer to Recipe 4.5.

Example 8-9. Creating a tooltip from an overlay

```
<!DOCTYPE html>
<title>Creating a tooltip from an overlay</title>
<style>
.yui3-overlay {
    background: #ff5;
    padding: 3px;
    border: 1px #a92 solid;
    border-radius: 5px;
    box-shadow: 3px 3px 2px #a92;
}
p { width: 300px; padding: 5px; background: #d72; }
</style>
```

```
<p data-tooltip="Floss every day.">This is some text with a helpful tooltip.</p>
<p>Sorry, no tooltip here.</p>
<p data-tooltip="Only own identical socks.">More text with a helpful tooltip.</p>

<script src="http://yui.yahooapis.com/3.5.0/build/yui/yui-min.js"></script>
<script>
YUI().use('overlay', 'event-mouseenter', function (Y) {
    var tooltip = new Y.Overlay({ width: 200, visible: false });

    function enter(ev) {
        var node = ev.currentTarget;
        tooltip.align(node, [Y.WidgetPositionAlign.TL, Y.WidgetPositionAlign.BC]);
        tooltip.set('bodyContent', node.getAttribute('data-tooltip'));
        tooltip.show();
    }
    function leave(ev) {
        tooltip.hide();
    }
    Y.delegate('mouseenter', enter, 'body', '*[data-tooltip]');
    Y.delegate('mouseleave', leave, 'body', '*[data-tooltip]');

    tooltip.render();
});
</script>
```

Figure 8-8 illustrates the results of Example 8-9.

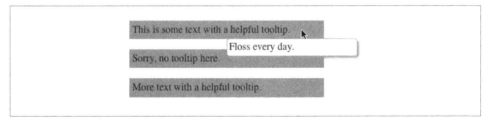

Figure 8-8. A tooltip created from an overlay

Discussion

The event-mouseenter module (included in the larger event rollup) provides the mouseenter and mouseleave YUI synthetic events. These two events are abstractions over the lower-level mouseover and mouseout events. The mouseover event is much more "chatty" than mouseenter; mouseover fires for every child element in the container of interest, while mouseenter fires only for the top-level container. This makes mouseenter more suitable for an interaction that involves hovering over a container.

The generic overlay is easy enough to tweak and turn into a tooltip with just a small amount of code. It could be enhanced further by:

- Making the location of the tooltip configurable (above, below, right, left), perhaps by using a second, optional `data-*` attribute.
- Adding more CSS to include some kind of graphical arrow or other pointer to the target node.
- Hiding the tooltip if the user's mouse hasn't moved after *n* seconds.
- Providing a fade transition rather than a simple hide and show, perhaps by using the `gallery-overlay-transition` module or the `WidgetAnim` plugin.

If the tooltip becomes very fancy, you could refactor it to use `Y.extend()` or `Y.Base.cre ate()` to create a full-fledged, self-contained `Tooltip` object. The `enter()` and `leave()` functions could be methods on the `Tooltip`'s prototype. You could set the delegation in the widget's `initializer()`, store the handles, and then detach them in the widget's `destructor()`. For an example of incorporating the tooltip code into a widget, complete with ARIA attributes for accessibility, refer to Recipe 11.3.

 If you create a `Y.Tooltip` by mixing in `Widget` extensions instead of extending `Overlay`, you will end up leaving out `Overlay`'s CSS. This is a fine way to go, but you will have to add a few basic structural CSS rules such as setting the visibility when the object is hidden.

See Also

Recipe 4.5; Recipe 4.11; Recipe 11.3; `Plugin.WidgetAnim` API documentation (*http:// yuilibrary.com/yui/docs/api/classes/Plugin.WidgetAnim.html*); basic CSS3 transition support in the `gallery-overlay-transition` module (*http://yuilibrary.com/gallery/ show/overlay-transition*); a nice-looking and fully featured tooltip in the `gallery-yui-tooltip` module (*http://yuilibrary.com/gallery/show/yui-tooltip*); custom data attributes described in the HTML5 elements specification (*http://dev.w3.org/html5/spec/elements .html*).

8.8 Creating a Lightbox from an Overlay

Problem

You want to display one or more images in a modal lightbox, similar to Lokesh Dhakar's Lightbox2 project.

Solution

Use `Y.Base.mix()` to mix the `WidgetModality` and `WidgetAutohide` extensions into `Over lay`. Then create a single, centered, modal overlay that indexes links to images and enables the user to page through the list.

Like Example 8-9, Example 8-10 acts as a form of progressive enhancement, using information in the markup to construct itself. And like the tooltip, the lightbox creates only one, reusable instance to handle all the images on the page. Here is how it works step-by-step:

1. For modal widgets, YUI creates a masking `<div>` behind the widget to prevent users from interacting with other elements on the page. The `<div>` has a class of `yui3-widget-mask`. Panel's skin styles this masking `<div>` by setting the background color and opacity. However, `Overlay`'s very minimal skin doesn't include this CSS, so the lightbox has to re-create this rule.

2. After mixing in extensions, the example creates a new modal, invisible widget. `hideOn` is a sugar attribute provided by `WidgetAutohide` that makes it easy to define events for hiding the widget. The lightbox assigns the Escape key and the `click outside` event as hide events.

3. The lightbox defines two methods. The `display()` method just recenters and shows the lightbox. The `setNewImage()` method is for regenerating the lightbox's internal `<img>` element, attaching a listener to the image's `load` event, and setting that image as the lightbox's new body content. Of course, images come in all sizes, but thanks to the event handler, the lightbox displays itself only *after* its image is done loading the `src`. This ensures that by the time the lightbox recenters itself, its dimensions are stable again.

4. After creating an empty image, the lightbox stores a list of all `<a>` elements that have a `rel="lightbox"` (thus following Lightbox2's convention). It then defines an `index` attribute to keep track of which image the lightbox is displaying. Since no images are currently selected, the lightbox sets the attribute to a default value of −1.

5. The lightbox then sets two attribute change listeners:
   - When the `visible` attribute changes to `false`, `Overlay`'s default CSS automatically hides the lightbox, but there is a little extra work to do. First, the index attribute must be reset to −1 (no image). Second, the lightbox's internal image needs to be destroyed and re-created.
   - When the `index` attribute changes to something other than −1, the lightbox fetches the corresponding `<a>` from its `anchors` property, gets the `href` value, and sets that to be the `<img>` element's `src` attribute. The `<img>` loads the image file, which fires a `load` event, which redisplays the lightbox.

6. The remainder of the code defines more event handlers for users. `Y.delegate()` listens for `click` events on all `<a rel="lightbox">` elements, indicating that the user has invoked the lightbox. A `Y.on()` `keydown` listener provides right- and left-arrow navigation through the list images, handling the edges by wrapping the index back to the beginning or end, as appropriate.

Example 8-10. Creating a lightbox from an overlay

```
<!DOCTYPE html>
<title>Creating a lightbox from an overlay</title>
<style>
.yui3-widget-mask    { background-color: #000; opacity: 0.8; }
.yui3-overlay        { background: #fff; padding: 10px; }
.yui3-overlay img    { max-width: 450px; max-height: 450px; }
.yui3-overlay:focus { outline: none; }
</style>

<a href="http://apod.nasa.gov/apod/image/9905/ngc4603_hst.jpg"
   rel="lightbox">NGC 4603</a>
<a href="http://apod.nasa.gov/apod/image/9906/trifidjet_hst.jpg"
   rel="lightbox">Trifid Jet</a>
<a href="http://apod.nasa.gov/apod/image/9907/jupiter_vg1.jpg"
   rel="lightbox">Jupiter</a>

<script src="http://yui.yahooapis.com/3.5.0/build/yui/yui-min.js"></script>
<script>
YUI().use('overlay', 'base', 'widget-modality', 'widget-autohide', function (Y) {
    Y.Base.mix(Y.Overlay, [Y.WidgetModality, Y.WidgetAutohide]);

    var lightbox = new Y.Overlay({
        modal: true,
        visible: false,
        hideOn: [
            { eventName: 'key', keyCode: 'esc', node: Y.one('document') },
            { eventName: 'clickoutside' }
        ]
    });
    lightbox.display = function () {
        this.centered();
        this.show();
    };
    lightbox.setNewImage = function (destroy) {
        var img = Y.Node.create('<img>');
        if (destroy) {
            this.get('bodyContent').destroy(true);
        }
        img.on('load', this.display, this);
        this.set('bodyContent', img);
    };

    lightbox.setNewImage();
    lightbox.anchors = Y.all('a[rel=lightbox]');
    lightbox.addAttr('index', { value: -1 });


    lightbox.after('visibleChange', function (ev) {
        if (ev.newVal === false) {
            this.setNewImage(true);
            this.set('index', -1);
        }
    });
```

```
lightbox.after('indexChange', function (ev) {
    var anchors, ix = ev.newVal;
    if (ix !== -1) {
        anchor = this.anchors.item(ix);
        this.get('bodyContent').set('src', anchor.get('href'));
    };
});

Y.delegate('click', function (ev) {
    var clickedIndex = lightbox.anchors.indexOf(ev.currentTarget);
    lightbox.set('index', clickedIndex);
    ev.preventDefault();
}, 'body', 'a[rel=lightbox]');

Y.on('keydown', function(ev) {
    var max = lightbox.anchors.size() - 1,
        index = lightbox.get('index');

    if (! lightbox.get('visible')) { return };

    switch(ev.keyCode) {
        case 37:  // left arrow
            index = (index === 0) ? max : index - 1;
            break;
        case 39:  // right arrow
            index = (index === max) ? 0 : index + 1;
            break;
    }
    lightbox.set('index', index);
});

    lightbox.render();
});
</script>
```

Figure 8-9 shows the results of Example 8-10 after a user selects one of the image links.

 Instead of destroying and re-creating the `<img>` element, why not reuse the element and just reset its `src` attribute? It turns out that in WebKit, changing `src` does not fire a `load` event if the actual value of `src` does not change. This leads to a subtle bug where if you dismiss the lightbox and then click on the same image you were just looking at, the lightbox does not reappear in Chrome or Safari.

Discussion

At only 70 lines of custom JS and CSS, Example 8-10 isn't as full featured and attractive as the real-deal Lightbox2. That said, Lightbox2 pulls in all of Prototype+Scriptaculous and adds many kilobytes of custom JS and images. If you're already building a Prototype +Scriptaculous page, that's probably not an issue, but if you're building a YUI page, it's worth thinking about reusing the code you already have.

Figure 8-9. A lightbox created from an overlay

The core of the lightbox's behavior is the `after('indexChange')` listener. When (and only when!) the `index` number changes, the lightbox responds by setting a new `<img>` with a new `src` value, but does *not* redisplay the lightbox. As mentioned earlier in the solution, the lightbox waits for the `load` event in order to ensure that its dimensions have reset.

The reason the lightbox is built this way is to make it easy to add more navigation methods. You can add Previous and Next buttons, a row of numbered links, navigation that jumps to the beginning or end, more keystrokes or gestures, whatever you like. They all work the same way: change the index number, and everything else handles itself. This technique also helps isolate the lightbox from unwanted DOM events. Even if the user generates a huge number of key events, only a tiny number of them really affect the lightbox.

This is a common pattern with YUI widgets, models, and views. Rather than reacting directly to a user's click, the click changes some underlying piece of data, which then causes the widget or view to refresh its appearance. For more examples of this pattern, refer to Recipes 7.15 and 7.16.

Of course, the example lightbox is bare bones, providing just enough code to illustrate the core slideshow mechanism and to supply enough controls to make the lightbox work. It could be enhanced by:

- Adding more visible UI controls, such as Previous and Next navigation, and an explicit close button.

- Adding touch and swipe support for tablet viewing.
- Adding captions, perhaps by fetching the string from the `title` attribute.
- Providing nice animations, such as a "loading" spinner, fades, or perhaps even a version of the "glide" transition that Lightbox2 uses.
- Improving runtime performance by caching previously used images and by prefetching the next few images in the list.

 On mobile devices, be careful about prefetching too aggressively, as this can severely impact users who have limited data plans.

- Using `Y.Base.create()` or `Y.extend()` to extend `Overlay` and create a full-fledged, self-contained `Lightbox` object. The example is halfway there already, with many of the relevant methods already attached to the lightbox instance. You would need to define these methods on the lightbox's prototype instead, and assign and detach event listeners in the `initializer()` and `destructor()`. Also note that mixing in `WidgetModality` and `WidgetAutohide` changes the behavior of *every* `Overlay` instance, so creating a self-contained lightbox would prevent that change from interfering with other overlays on the page.

See Also

`WidgetAutohide` API documentation (*http://yuilibrary.com/yui/docs/api/classes/WidgetAutohide.html*); `event-outside` API documentation (*http://yuilibrary.com/yui/docs/api/modules/event-outside.html*); Lokesh Dhakar's Lightbox2 project (*http://www.huddletogether.com/projects/lightbox2/*).

8.9 Creating a Slider

Problem

You want to enable the user to set a range of numeric values by dragging or sliding.

Solution

Instantiate a `Slider` widget and listen for the `slideStart`, `valueChange`, or `slideEnd` events. Unlike many widgets, `Slider` is a `<span>` rather than a `<div>`, so you can use it inline alongside form labels or other inline form elements.

Example 8-11 represents the simplest possible slider, plus an `after()` listener that dynamically writes the current value of the slider into the DOM. This slider's attributes are all at their defaults: a range of 0 to 100, a start value of 0, a horizontal orientation, and so on.

Example 8-11. Creating a default horizontal slider

```
<!DOCTYPE html>
<title>Creating a default horizontal slider</title>

<body class="yui3-skin-sam">
<p>Grade: <span id="slider"></span></p>
<p>I award you <span id="points">0</span> points.</p>

<script src="http://yui.yahooapis.com/3.5.0/build/yui/yui-min.js"></script>
<script>
YUI().use('slider', function (Y) {
    var slider = new Y.Slider().render('#slider'),
        points = Y.one('#points');

    slider.after('valueChange', function (ev) {
        points.setHTML(ev.newVal);
    });
});
</script>
</body>
```

Figure 8-10 illustrates the results of Example 8-11.

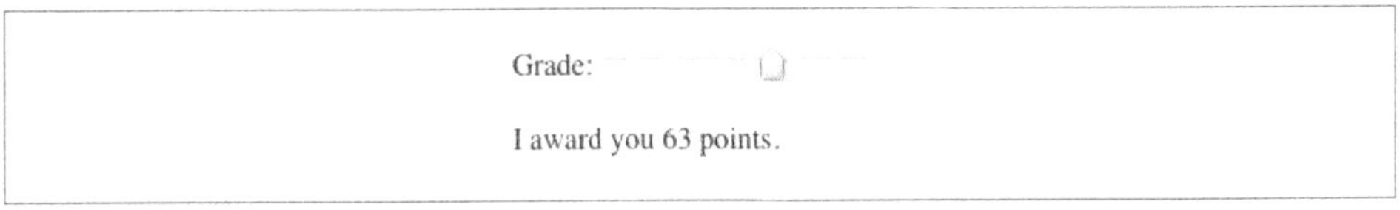

Grade:

I award you 63 points.

Figure 8-10. A default horizontal slider

Example 8-12 illustrates a slider with several attributes changed from the default. In addition to the axis changing to 'y' to create a vertical slider, the range and start values have changed, and min is intentionally set higher than max in order to flip the slider's orientation around. Even though the slider is vertical, it is still an inline element.

As a final touch, the example pulls in a different skin for the slider, named audio-light, by declaring an *override skin* for Slider in the YUI config. If an ordinary YUI widget gets loaded onto the page, YUI loads that module's sam skin. But if the slider-base module gets loaded, YUI loads the audio-light skin for Slider instead of the sam skin. The <body> applies the yui3-skin-sam class to handle widgets in general, while the slider is wrapped in a <div> with the yui3-skin-audio-light class that it needs.

Example 8-12. Creating a vertical slider with an audio-light skin

```
<!DOCTYPE html>
<title>Creating a vertical slider with an audio-light skin</title>
<style>
span.volume { vertical-align: top; }
</style>
```

```
<body class="yui3-skin-sam">
<div class="yui3-skin-audio-light">
    <span id="slider"></span>
    <span class="volume">Volume: <span id="value">4</span></span>
</div>

<script src="http://yui.yahooapis.com/3.5.0/build/yui/yui-min.js"></script>
<script>
YUI({
    skin: {
        overrides: {
            'slider-base': ['audio-light']
        }
    }
}).use('slider', function (Y) {
    var audioSlider = new Y.Slider({
        axis: 'y',
        min: 11,
        max: 0,
        value: 4
    }).render('#slider');

    var volume = Y.one('#value');
    audioSlider.after('valueChange', function (ev) {
        volume.setHTML(ev.newVal);
    });
});
</script>
</body>
```

Figure 8-11 illustrates the results of Example 8-12.

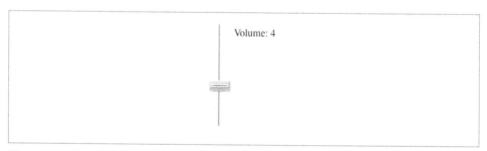

Figure 8-11. A vertical slider with an audio-light skin

Discussion

One option for making Example 8-12 simpler is to apply the `yui3-skin-audio-light` class to the `<body>`, get rid of the wrapper `<div>`, and pass in a YUI config like:

```
YUI({
    skin: 'audio-light'
}).use('slider', function (Y) {
```

Changing the default skin is easier, but it has the side effect of destroying the appearance of all widgets that lack an `audio-light` skin (read: most widgets). Use this approach only if you are sure that the page will not be loading any other components that require the `sam` skin, now or in the foreseeable future.

`Slider` is one of the few widgets that does have a wide variety of skins. It includes a base `sam` skin with an arrow button, a `round` skin with a round button, a `capsule` skin with a capsule-shaped button and tick marks along the slider, and an `audio` skin that looks like an audio control, plus "dark" versions of each. To compare all the `Slider` skins side-by-side, refer to Example: Alternate Skins (*http://yuilibrary.com/yui/docs/slider/slider-skin.html*).

See Also

Recipe 11.3; Recipe 11.4; the `Slider` User Guide (*http://yuilibrary.com/yui/docs/slider/*); `Slider` API documentation (*http://yuilibrary.com/yui/docs/api/classes/Slider.html*).

8.10 Creating a Tabview

Problem

You want to add tab navigation to your site.

Solution

Instantiate a `TabView` and create the `label` and `content` of each tab either dynamically through JavaScript, or by parsing HTML on the page.

Example 8-13 takes the dynamic approach, setting the tabview's `children` attribute to an array of objects and fixing the width at 500 pixels. After rendering the tabview, the example adds a third tab with the `add()` method. The `add()` method takes a tab object to add and an index number where the tab should be inserted. There is also a corresponding `remove()` method.

Example 8-13. Creating a tabview from JavaScript

```
<!DOCTYPE html>
<title>Creating a tabview from JavaScript</title>

<body class="yui3-skin-sam">
<div id="tabview"></div>

<script src="http://yui.yahooapis.com/3.5.0/build/yui/yui-min.js"></script>
<script>
YUI().use('tabview', function (Y) {
    var tabview = new Y.TabView({
        width: 400,
        children: [{
            label: 'A',
```

```
            content: '<p>This is Tab A.</p>'
        }, {
            label: 'B',
            content: '<p>This is Tab B.</p>'
        }]
    }).render('#tabview');

    tabview.add({
        label: 'C',
        content: '<p>This is Tab C. Surprised?</p>'
    }, tabview.size());
});
</script>
</body>
```

Figure 8-12 illustrates the results of Example 8-13.

Figure 8-12. A tabview created from JavaScript

Example 8-14 constructs itself by parsing markup on the page. This enables users with screen readers or browsers with JavaScript turned off to at least be able to use the plain navigation links to skip around the page. For more information about progressive enhancement and widgets, refer to Recipe 7.5.

Since all the data is defined in HTML, instantiating the tabview from markup is just a one-liner in JavaScript. To make things a little more interesting, Example 8-14 also sets a selectionChange listener on the tabs. Like many widgets, the default width for a tabview is 100%, so the second example runs across the viewport.

Example 8-14. Creating a tabview from markup

```
<!DOCTYPE html>
<title>Creating a tabview from markup</title>

<body class="yui3-skin-sam">
<div id="tabview">
    <ul>
        <li><a href="#a">A</a></li>
        <li><a href="#b">B</a></li>
        <li><a href="#c">C</a></li>
    </ul>
    <div>
        <div id="a">
            <p>This is Tab A.</p>
            <p>There have been <span id="num">0</span> tab switches so far.</p>
        </div>
```

```
            <div id="b"><p>This is Tab B.</p></div>
            <div id="c"><p>This is Tab C. Surprised?</p></div>
        </div>
</div>

<script src="http://yui.yahooapis.com/3.5.0/build/yui/yui-min.js"></script>
<script>
YUI().use('tabview', function (Y) {
    var tabview = new Y.TabView({ srcNode: '#tabview' }).render(),
        numSwitches = 0;

    tabview.after('selectionChange', function (ev) {
        numSwitches += 1;
        Y.one('#num').setHTML(numSwitches);
    });
});
</script>
</body>
```

Discussion

Similar to `Overlay` and `Panel`, much of `TabView`'s functionality comes from a generic mixin object named `WidgetParent`. `WidgetParent` provides the `children` attribute, the `add()` and `remove()` methods, and the `selectionChange` event. `WidgetParent` and `Widget Child` are useful for constructing tabs, menus, trees, and other widgets that contain other widgets.

Since `WidgetParent` has a `selection` attribute that tracks the currently selected `Widget Child`, Example 8-14 can just set a `selectionChange` listener to capture tab switches.

Alternatively, you could try to detect tab switches by listening for DOM `click` events:

```
Y.all('.yui3-tabview li').on('click', function (ev) {
    ...
}
```

However, this is a bad idea for three reasons.

First, repeated clicks on the same label do not indicate a tab switch.

Second, a tabview might supply additional ways to navigate to different tabs such as keystrokes or gestures, which a `click` listener would miss. This is the same reason why Example 8-10 relies on its own `indexChange` events to display a new image, rather than responding directly to DOM events.

Third, it is poor practice to depend on the internal structure of a widget's HTML. The HTML produced by a widget is a *reflection* of the data the widget represents, and the UI elements produced are a *consequence* of that data. Changes to the widget's data can trigger the widget to refresh its internal HTML, which in turn can destroy any DOM event listeners you might have set. If you need to react to widget state changes, listen directly for those state change events, not the DOM events that might have triggered the state change.

See Also

The `TabView` User Guide (*http://yuilibrary.com/yui/docs/tabview/*); `TabView` API documentation (*http://yuilibrary.com/yui/docs/api/classes/TabView.html*).

8.11 Creating a Basic DataTable

Problem

You want to display data in tabular form.

Solution

Instantiate a `DataTable` and provide it with a `columns` definition for its columns and a `data` definition for its rows, where the elements of the `columns` array match keys in the `data`. To hide certain columns, just leave the key out of the `columns` array.

Example 8-15. Creating a basic DataTable

```
<!DOCTYPE html>
<title>Creating a basic DataTable</title>

<body class="yui3-skin-sam">
<div id="datatable"></div>

<script src="http://yui.yahooapis.com/3.5.0/build/yui/yui-min.js"></script>
<script>
YUI().use('datatable', function (Y) {
    var data = [
        { id: 290, sev: 5, title: 'Sidebar misaligned in IE6' },
        { id: 819, sev: 1, title: 'Site is down' },
        { id: 100, sev: 3, title: 'Deployment is taking too long' },
        { id: 784, sev: 3, title: 'Marketing page has D YSlow grade' }
    ];

    var table = new Y.DataTable({
        columns: ['id', 'sev', 'title'],
        data: data
    });
    table.render('#datatable');
});
</script>
</body>
```

Figure 8-13 illustrates the results of Example 8-15.

In Example 8-15, the strings `'id'`, `'sev'`, and `'title'` are doing double duty—they are mapping directly to keys in the table's data, and they are also displayed directly as column labels. For a quick-and-dirty `DataTable`, this might be OK, but for friendly column labels, you should provide `columns` as an array of objects rather than a simple array of strings:

---

id	sev	title
290	5	Sidebar misaligned in IE6
819	1	Site is down
100	3	Deployment is taking too long
784	3	Marketing page has D YSlow grade

Figure 8-13. A basic DataTable

```
columns: [{ key: 'id', label: 'Ticket' }, { key: 'sev', label: 'Severity' } ...
```

Discussion

DataTable isn't just about generating HTML tables with a pretty skin. Using Data Table opens up a wide variety of features, including:

- Everything the standard Widget API has to offer, including the ability to mix in extensions, changing a table's behavior through plugins, and so on.
- Flexibility in formatting and filtering table data. For an example of a formatted DataTable, refer to Recipe 8.12.
- Integration with DataSource, a standard YUI adapter for a wide variety of data sources. For an example of fetching remote data and displaying it on the fly with DataTable, refer to Recipe 8.13.

Under the hood, DataTable represents its data as a ModelList, where each row is a Model. Each DataTable stores its ModelList under a data property, which means you can freely call table.data.indexOf() and other ModelList methods. Related properties include head, foot, and body, which grant you direct access to the View objects that control the table's general HTML structure.

See Also

Recipe 7.14, Recipe 7.11, and related recipes; the DataTable User Guide (*http://yuili brary.com/yui/docs/datatable/*); the DataTable 3.5.0+ Migration Guide (*http://yuilibrary .com/yui/docs/datatable/migration.html*); DataTable API documentation (*http://yuili brary.com/yui/docs/api/classes/DataTable.html*).

8.12 Formatting a DataTable's Appearance

Problem

You want to create a more complex table with a caption, column labels, nested table headings, and special formatting for table cell content.

Solution

Use the `caption` attribute to provide a caption. Change `columns` from a simple array of strings to an array of objects, including a `label` and a `formatter`.

Example 8-16 demonstrates how to create a table with more complex formatting. Columns now have a `key` and a `label`. The columns also now have a nested structure: the second "column" is actually just a `label` with an array of child columns. The third column has a simple `formatter` property that substitutes the value of the cell into a string template, while the fourth column has a `formatter` function—in this case, one that truncates the content.

For good measure, the table also flags three of the four columns with `sortable: true`. Alternatively, there is a `sortable` attribute for the overall table, where you can either supply an array of column keys to make individual columns sortable, or just set `sortable: true` to make all columns sortable.

Example 8-16. Creating a formatted DataTable

```
<!DOCTYPE html>
<title>Creating a formatted DataTable</title>

<body class="yui3-skin-sam">
<div id="datatable"></div>

<script src="http://yui.yahooapis.com/3.5.0/build/yui/yui-min.js"></script>
<script>
YUI().use('datatable', function (Y) {
    var truncate = function (o) {
        if (o.value.length > 30) {
            var trunc = o.value.slice(0, 27) + '...';
            return '<span title="' + o.value + '">' + trunc + '</span>';
        }
        return o.value;
    };
    var cols = [
        { key: 'id', label: 'Ticket' },
        { label: 'Ticket Overview', children: [
            { key: 'cat', label: 'Cat', sortable: true },
            { key: 'sev', label: 'Sev', sortable: true, formatter: 'S{value}' },
            { key: 'title', label: 'Description', formatter: truncate, allowHTML: true }
        ] }
    ];
    var data = [
        { id: 290, sev: 5, cat: 'UI', title: 'Sidebar misaligned in IE6' },
        { id: 819, sev: 1, cat: 'Ops', title: 'Site is down' },
        { id: 100, sev: 3, cat: 'Devel', title: 'Deployment is taking too long' },
        { id: 784, sev: 3, cat: 'UI', title: 'Marketing page has D YSlow grade' }
    ];

    var table = new Y.DataTable({
        columns: cols,
```

```
        data: data,
        caption: 'Open Tickets'
    });
    table.render('#datatable');
});
</script>
</body>
```

Figure 8-14 illustrates the results of Example 8-16 just after a user sorts the *Sev* column.

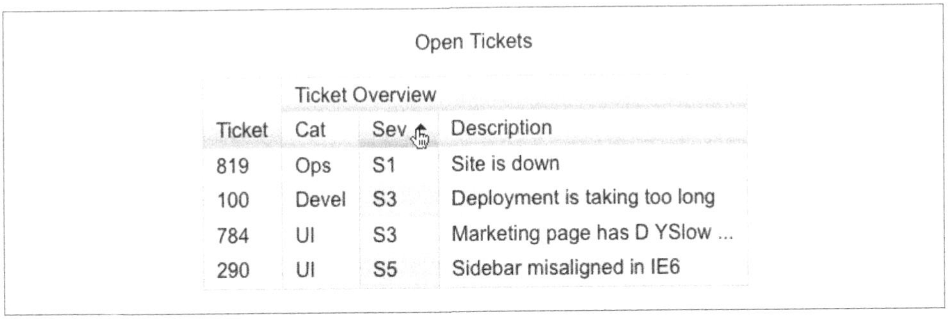

Figure 8-14. A formatted DataTable

Discussion

When creating a nested set of columns, keep in mind that any parent columns should have only the properties `label` and `children`, and should not have properties that control cell behavior such as `key`, `formatter`, or `sortable`. The columns that really matter are the lowest-level columns (i.e., the leaves of the tree).

Each column in the table has a `formatter` function that is responsible for returning the `innerHTML` for each cell in that column. The `formatter` function receives an "info" object containing various properties about the table cell, including the cell's `value`. The default `formatter` simply outputs the cell value. However, you can override `formatter` in any column with:

- A template string designed to be passed through `Y.Lang.sub()`. In Example 8-16, the Severity column generates cells of the form, "S1," "S2," ...

- An arbitrary function that generates whatever content you like. In Example 8-16, the Title column calls a custom `truncate()` function to truncate long values. If the value is truncated, the function wraps the value in a `<span>` so that the user can access it in full by hovering over the cell.

  A formatter function can either a) return a value, or b) just change `o.value` directly (and *not* have any return value). By default, `DataTable` HTML-escapes the cell's content. If you want to directly set the cell's `innerHTML`, then be sure to set `allowHTML: true`, as shown in Example 8-16.

If you want to get even more aggressive about changing cell markup, DataTable exposes a more advanced nodeFormatter function. However, this function has some performance implications. Consult the documentation for details.

See Also

The DataTable User Guide's "Formatting Cell Data" (*http://yuilibrary.com/yui/docs/datatable/#formatters*).

8.13 Displaying a Remote JSON DataSource in a DataTable

Problem

You want to display data from a remote web service API in tabular form.

Solution

Instantiate a DataSource.Get object and set the source to the API URL. Plug the DataSource instance with Plugin.DataSourceJSONSchema and apply a schema that locates the result data and selects the fields you are interested in displaying.

Then instantiate a DataTable, making sure that its columns values matches the result Field keys you specified in the schema. Plug the DataTable instance with Plugin.DataTableDataSource, and set the plugin's datasource attribute to the DataSource instance.

Finally, call the plugged DataSource's load() method, passing in any request parameters that the API call needs. See Example 8-17.

Example 8-17. Displaying a remote JSON DataSource in a DataTable

```
<!DOCTYPE html>
<title>Displaying a remote JSON DataSource in a DataTable</title>

<body class="yui3-skin-sam">
<div id="datatable"></div>

<script src="http://yui.yahooapis.com/3.5.0/build/yui/yui-min.js"></script>
<script>
YUI().use('datatable', 'datasource-get', 'datasource-jsonschema', function (Y) {
    var src, table;
    src = new Y.DataSource.Get({
        source: 'https://api.github.com/repos/isaacs/npm/issues'
    });
    src.plug(Y.Plugin.DataSourceJSONSchema, {
        schema: {
            resultListLocator: 'data',
            resultFields: [{ key:'number' }, { key:'title' }]
        }
    });
```

```
    table = new Y.DataTable({ columns: ['number', 'title'] });
    table.plug(Y.Plugin.DataTableDataSource, { datasource: src });
    table.render('#datatable');

    table.datasource.load({ request: '?per_page=10' });
});
</script>
</body>
```

Discussion

Assuming you already have some basic experience with DataSource and DataSchema, the trickiest part of this recipe is setting the correct resultListLocator in the schema. First, you must understand the structure of the data returned, which you can usually figure out by inspecting the returned object in your browser console. Once you understand the structure and have identified an array that you are interested in, set resultList Locator to a string that represents a JavaScript property lookup to that array. You can also use resultFields to select the fields of interest.

If you're making a call to a cross-domain web service that does not support JSONP, you can still use DataSource.Get by proxying through YQL instead of hitting the web service directly. In the case of YQL, the correct resultListLocator path should start with 'query.results.Result'.

See Also

Recipe 5.6; Recipe 5.7; Recipe 5.9; Recipe 5.10; "Example: DataTable + Data-Source.Get + JSON Data" (*http://yuilibrary.com/yui/docs/datatable/datatable-dsget .html*); "Example: DataTable + DataSource.IO + XML Data" (*http://yuilibrary.com/yui/ docs/datatable/datatable-dsio.html*).

8.14 Plotting Data in a Chart

Problem

You want to plot data in a chart, using the best vector graphics technology the user's browser has to offer.

Solution

Create an array of objects to represent your data. Then, as shown in Example 8-18, load the charts module and instantiate a Chart widget, specifying these attributes:

- The dataProvider containing the data to plot
- The categoryKey within the dataset to label the "category axis" of the chart (in this case, the x-axis)

- An explicit `height` and `width` (or alternatively, set these as CSS properties on the containing `<div>`)

Example 8-18. Creating a basic line chart

```
<!DOCTYPE html>
<title>Creating a basic line chart</title>

<div id="chart"></div>

<script src="http://yui.yahooapis.com/3.5.0/build/yui/yui-min.js"></script>
<script>
YUI().use('charts', function (Y) {
    var dataProvider = [
        { date: '1/15/2012', revenue: 45000, expenses: 22700 },
        { date: '2/15/2012', revenue: 38935, expenses: 23150 },
        { date: '3/15/2012', revenue: 36500, expenses: 23000 },
        { date: '4/15/2012', revenue: 43500, expenses: 23150 },
        { date: '5/15/2012', revenue: 57500, expenses: 24350 },
        { date: '6/15/2012', revenue: 79550, expenses: 23890 }
    ];

    var lineChart = new Y.Chart({
        dataProvider: dataProvider,
        categoryKey: 'date',
        width: 400,
        height: 300,
    }).render('#chart');
});
</script>
```

Figure 8-15 illustrates the results of Example 8-18.

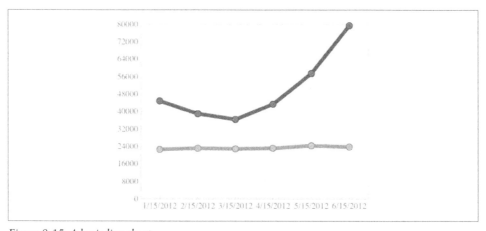

Figure 8-15. A basic line chart

Discussion

Chart is essentially a Graphic wrapped in a Widget. The Graphic utility is a vector graphics abstraction layer that draws images with SVG, Canvas, or VML, depending on what the browser supports. Graphic uses the capability-based loading technique described in Recipe 1.15 to load only the code it needs.

A chart contains one *category axis* and one or more *series* of data. Each series is plotted against the category axis. Charts can identify and parse these data structures:

- An array of key-indexed objects, as shown in Example 8-18.
- A multidimensional array. In this case, Chart selects the first array as the category axis, so you should omit the categoryKey.

```
var dataProvider2 = [
    ['1/15/2012', '2/15/2012', '3/15/2012', '4/15/2012', '5/15/2012'],
    [45000, 38935, 36500, 43500, 57500],
    [22700, 23150, 23000, 23150, 24350]
];
```

There is a dizzying variety of attributes for configuring a chart's appearance. To start with, there are 10 basic types of chart, controlled by the type attribute. You can specify a type of 'bar' for a horizontal bar chart, 'column' for a vertical bar chart, 'markerseries' for a disconnected scatter plot, 'area' to fill in the area under the points, and even 'pie' for a pie chart, along with several other options.

Beyond these basic types, each chart provides numerous attributes that control its appearance at a more granular level, some of which themselves are highly complex. The tooltip attribute sets highly configurable tooltips that appear as the user hovers the mouse over the data. The axes attribute can control the minimum, maximum, labeling, position, styling, and other features of the chart's axes, while the series attribute provides similar control over each of the chart's series. For more information, refer to the Chart User Guide (*http://yuilibrary.com/yui/docs/charts/*) and take a look at its examples.

See Also

Recipe 7.7; Chart API documentation (*http://yuilibrary.com/yui/docs/api/modules/charts.html*).

8.15 Choosing Dates with a Calendar

Problem

You want to enable users to select a date to be submitted in a form or to be consumed elsewhere in your application.

Solution

Instantiate a `Calendar` widget and listen for the `selectionChange` event. The event's `newSelection` property is an array of `Date` objects representing the dates the user currently has selected. Example 8-19 permits only one date to be selected at a time, but you can easily configure calendars that permit multiple dates to be selected (which is why `newSelection` is an array of `Date`s and not a single `Date`).

Example 8-19. Creating a basic calendar with selectionChange listener

```
<!DOCTYPE html>
<title>Creating a basic calendar with selectionChange listener</title>

<body class="yui3-skin-sam">
<div id="demo"></div>

<script src="http://yui.yahooapis.com/3.5.0/build/yui/yui-min.js"></script>
<script>
YUI().use('calendar', function (Y) {
    var calendar = new Y.Calendar({ width: 300 }).render('#demo');

    calendar.after('selectionChange', function (ev) {
        var date = ev.newSelection[0];
        date = Y.DataType.Date.format(date, { format: '%B %e, %Y' });
        Y.one('body').append('<p>You selected ' + date + '.</p>');
    });
});
</script>
</body>
```

Figure 8-16 illustrates the results of Example 8-19 after the user selects a date.

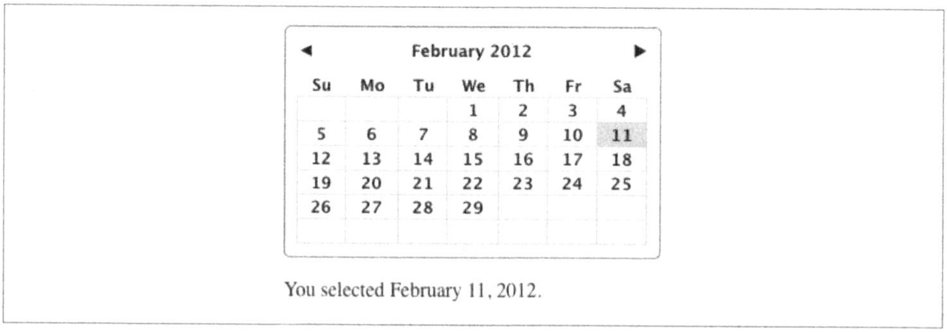

Figure 8-16. A basic calendar with selectionChange listener

Like most core widgets, `Calendar` has a variety of attributes that control its appearance and behavior. Example 8-20 illustrates some of these options in action:

- In the YUI configuration, `lang` is set to `'ru'`, which triggers the calendar's internationalization strings to display in Russian.

- `showPrevMonth` and `showNextMonth` are `true`, which means that the calendar shows trailing dates from the previous month and leading dates from the upcoming month, though these dates are not selectable.

- `selectionMode` is `'multiple-sticky'`, which enables users to select multiple dates with multiple clicks. The other `selectionMode` options are `'single'` (the default) and `'multiple'` (enables users to select multiple dates by Control-/Command-clicking and Shift-clicking).

- `date` is set to May 7, 2012, which sets the month the calendar opens to at render time to May 2012.

- `maximumDate` is set to December 21, 2012, which means that users cannot navigate to any months that occur after December 2012. There is also a corresponding `minimumDate` attribute, not set here.

- Finally, the calendar's `CONTENT_TEMPLATE` property is set to `CalendarBase.TWO_PANE_TEMPLATE`. When the calendar renders, May 2012 will be displayed on the left side and June 2012 will be displayed on the right.

Example 8-20. Creating a two-pane calendar with more options set

```
<!DOCTYPE html>
<title>Creating a two-pane calendar with more options set</title>

<body class="yui3-skin-sam">
<div id="demo"></div>

<script src="http://yui.yahooapis.com/3.5.0/build/yui/yui-min.js"></script>
<script>
YUI({ lang: 'ru' }).use('calendar', function (Y) {
    Y.CalendarBase.CONTENT_TEMPLATE = Y.CalendarBase.TWO_PANE_TEMPLATE;

    var calendar = new Y.Calendar({
        width: 400,
        showPrevMonth: true,
        showNextMonth: true,
        selectionMode: 'multiple-sticky',
        date: new Date(2012, 4, 7),
        maximumDate: new Date(2012, 11, 21),
    }).render('#demo');
});
</script>
</body>
```

Figure 8-17 illustrates the results of Example 8-20.

мая 2012													
Пн	Вт	Ср	Чт	Пт	Сб	Вс	Пн	Вт	Ср	Чт	Пт	Сб	Вс
30	1	2	3	4	5	6						1	2	3
7	8	9	10	11	12	13	4	5	6	7	8	9	10
14	15	16	17	18	19	20	11	12	13	14	15	16	17
21	22	23	24	25	26	27	18	19	20	21	22	23	24
28	29	30	31				25	26	27	28	29	30	1
							2	3	4	5	6	7	8

Figure 8-17. A two-pane calendar with more options set

Discussion

Although HTML standards now define new `<input>` types for selecting dates, these types have only very basic capabilities. `Calendar` is a dead-simple way to provide a much better user experience around date selection.

`Calendar` is entirely driven by string templates. As shown in Example 8-20, it is easy to create a two-pane calendar by overriding the `CONTENT_TEMPLATE`, and there is also a premade three-pane template available. With only a small amount of work, you can construct a full-year template.

Beyond that, it is possible to completely redo the rendering of `Calendar`. The default design is to help users select dates, but there is a reason the widget is named "Calendar" and not "DatePicker"—the engine that powers `Calendar` is flexible enough to be used in a wide variety of date-related applications, including a full-fledged calendar application.

If you do want to use `Calendar` to help users select dates in forms, it might be useful to align the widget with particular form fields. To do this, you can use `Y.Base.mix()` to mix in the `WidgetPosition` and `WidgetPositionAlign` extensions:

```
Y.Base.mix(Y.Calendar, [Y.WidgetPosition, Y.WidgetPositionAlign]);
```

This would grant all calendars access to the methods shown in Recipe 8.3.

 The `Calendar` widget also loads the `DataType.Date` object, which provides date formatting and other useful date-related utility methods.

See Also

The `Calendar` User Guide (*http://yuilibrary.com/yui/docs/calendar/*); `CalendarBase` API documentation (*http://yuilibrary.com/yui/docs/api/classes/CalendarBase.html*); `DataType.Date` API documentation (*http://yuilibrary.com/yui/docs/api/classes/DataType.Date.html*); YUI Theater: Allen Rabinovich's "YUI Calendar — A Case Study of Building Modules with Style" (*http://www.youtube.com/watch?v=dQfOuOUUYus*).

8.16 Defining Calendar Rules

Problem

You want to create a calendar with arbitrary sets of dates disabled or styled differently.

Solution

Define an object that contains a set of named *calendar rules*. Calendar rules are how `Calendar` provides convenient names for a range of dates, a set of repeating dates, or any combination thereof. Once you define a rule, you can use it to disable all dates that match the rule, disable all dates that *don't* match the rule, or apply custom rendering to every date that matches the rule.

To bind rules to your calendar, use `set()` to set the `customRenderer` attribute. The attribute value must be an object with a `rules` property that references your rules object. If all you are doing is enabling or disabling dates, this is enough. If you need to do custom cell rendering, add a `filterFunction` property that references a filtering function.

Example 8-21 defines two rules. The `end_of_days` rule matches December 31, 1999, plus all dates from 2000 to 9999. The calendar sets its `disabledDatesRule` attribute to `'end_of_days'`, disabling all dates that match this rule.

The `band_practice` rule matches all Tuesdays and Fridays in October, November, and December of any year. Whenever a calendar date matches at least one rule, this triggers the specified `filterFunction` and passes in the date, the node of the calendar cell, and the array of rule names that matched. In this case, the `filter()` implementation checks whether the match was for `'band_practice'`, and if so, adds a class to the table cell.

Example 8-21. Defining calendar rules

```
<!DOCTYPE html>
<title>Defining calendar rules</title>
<style>
.band-practice { color: #a00; }
</style>

<body class="yui3-skin-sam">
<div id="demo"></div>

<script src="http://yui.yahooapis.com/3.5.0/build/yui/yui-min.js"></script>
<script type="text/javascript">
YUI().use('calendar', 'datatype-date', 'datatype-date-math', function (Y) {
    var calendar = new Y.Calendar({
        width: 300,
        disabledDatesRule: 'end_of_days',
        date: new Date(1999, 11, 1),
    }).render('#demo');
```

```
    calendar.set('customRenderer', {
        rules: {
            '1999': {
                '11': {
                    '31': 'end_of_days'
                }
            },
            '2000-9999': {
                'all': 'end_of_days'
            },
            'all': {
                '9,10,11': {
                    'all': {
                        '2,5': 'band_practice'
                    }
                }
            }
        },
        filterFunction: function (date, node, rules) {
            if (rules.indexOf('band_practice') !== -1) {
                node.addClass('band-practice');
            }
        }
    });
});
</script>
</body>
```

Figure 8-18 illustrates the results of Example 8-21, with Tuesdays and Fridays marked red, and December 31 greyed out.

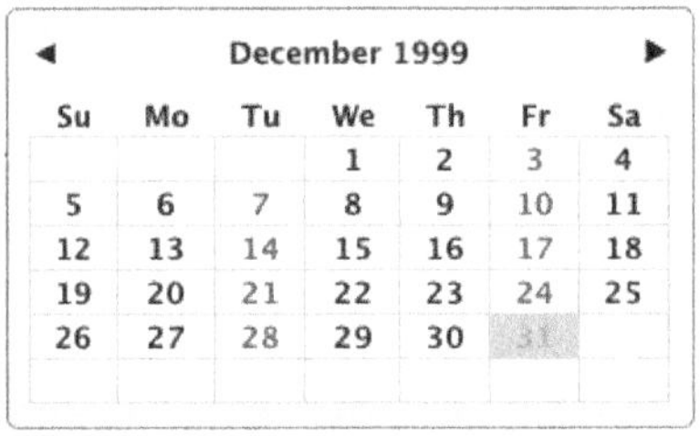

Figure 8-18. Calendar rules

Discussion

Calendar rules enable you to express large and complex groups of dates with very little syntax. Consider a more naive implementation where you disable dates by passing in an array of Date objects; the system would quickly break down if you needed to express very large numbers of dates or complicated repeating groups of dates.

A calendar rule is a nested object consisting of years, months, days, or weekdays. A weekday of 0 can refer to Sunday or Monday, depending on your locale. The syntax supports lists of comma-separated values ('2,3,4,7,23'), ranges separated by dashes ('2-4'), and combinations of the two, plus the keyword 'all'. As shown in Example 8-21, you can assign multiple nested structures to the same rule name: 'end_of_days' includes a single date in 1999, and then all dates for the years 2000–9999. (Eight thousand years should be a good enough apocalypse for anybody.)

8.17 Creating a Basic AutoComplete

Problem

You want to help users select from a long list of options using keyboard input.

Solution

Load the `autocomplete-plugin` module, then plug a text `<input>` node or `<textarea>` node with `Y.Plugin.AutoComplete` and configure the plugin's `source` to be an array of strings that will appear in the `AutoComplete` drop-down.

Example 8-22 creates a simple `AutoComplete` from a text `<input>` node and sets a `select` event listener on the `AutoComplete` instance. `AutoComplete` fires the `select` custom event whenever the user selects a result from the drop-down via keyboard, mouse, or touch. The event includes a `result` object with information about the user's selection.

Example 8-22. Plugging an input node with basic AutoComplete

```
<!DOCTYPE html>
<title>Plugging an input node with basic AutoComplete</title>

<form class="yui3-skin-sam">
    <label>Fruit: <input type="text" id="demo"></label>
</form>

<script src="http://yui.yahooapis.com/3.5.0/build/yui/yui-min.js"></script>
<script>
YUI().use('autocomplete-plugin', function (Y) {
    var input = Y.one("#demo").plug(Y.Plugin.AutoComplete, {
        source: ['apple', 'banana', 'cantaloupe', 'durian fruit']
    });

    input.ac.on('select', function (ev) {
        Y.one('body').append('<p>Yum, ' + ev.result.text + '!</p>');
    });
});
</script>
```

Figure 8-19 illustrates the results of Example 8-22.

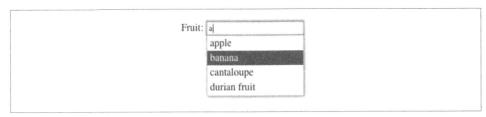

Figure 8-19. An input node with basic AutoComplete

As shown in Example 8-22, the `'ac'` namespace on the input node enables you to subsequently call `AutoComplete` methods. For example, to change the `AutoComplete`'s `source` after instantiation:

```
input.ac.set('source', ['blueberry', 'cherry', 'strawberry']);
```

If you prefer to use `AutoComplete` directly as a widget, you can load `autocomplete-list`, as shown in Example 8-23. To assign the widget to its input node, set the `input Node` attribute (*not* the `srcNode` attribute!). You must also explicitly render the widget, either by calling `render()` or by setting `render: true`.

Example 8-23. Using AutoComplete as a widget

```
YUI().use('autocomplete-list', function (Y) {
    var autocomplete = new Y.AutoComplete({
        inputNode: '#demo',
        source: ['apple', 'banana', 'cantaloupe', 'durian fruit']
    }).render();

    autocomplete.on('select', function (ev) {
        Y.one('body').append('<p>Yum, ' + ev.result.text + '!</p>');
    });
});
```

In this case, you would call methods on the widget instance directly:

```
autocomplete.set('source', ['blueberry', 'cherry', 'strawberry']);
```

Discussion

YUI `AutoComplete` was one of the first open source JavaScript autocomplete widgets, dating back to the first public release of YUI (0.10.0). It pioneered the APIs and interaction patterns that people take for granted today, and continues to be one of the most popular widgets that YUI offers. The latest version of `AutoComplete` is mobile-ready out of the box and fully accessible, with ARIA roles added for you automatically.

Within the basic concept of an "autocomplete widget," there are a number of different interaction patterns. You might expect "autocomplete" to be a simple text drop-down, possibly with highlighting or filtering. Or "autocomplete" could assist users in narrowing down their search query by providing images and other structured data in the result drop-down. "Autocomplete" could even mean abandoning the drop-down concept and instead rewriting large sections of the page as the user types.

The YUI 2 `AutoComplete` widget was monolithic. It included lots of code for the classic list-style interaction, even if you were building something very different. By contrast, YUI 3 `AutoComplete` is broken out into many different modules that let you choose the features you need. For example, `AutoComplete` provides a full array of keyboard functionality, but uses conditional module loading to avoid loading keyboard code that is not needed for iPhones and many Android phones. You can use this solid foundation and extension points to build all sorts of interesting autocomplete applications.

`AutoComplete` is extremely flexible about how it receives its source data. While the examples in this recipe all use a simple array, in general `AutoComplete` can use an array, an object, a function, a node representing an HTML `<select>`, a `DataSource`, an XHR URL, a JSONP URL, or a YQL query string. For more information, refer to Recipe 8.19.

See Also

Recipe 8.18; Recipe 8.19; Recipe 8.20; the `AutoComplete` User Guide (*http://yuilibrary .com/yui/docs/autocomplete/*); `AutoCompleteList` API documentation (*http://yuilibrary .com/yui/docs/api/classes/AutoCompleteList.html*).

8.18 Highlighting and Filtering AutoComplete Results

Problem

You want to alter the appearance of the autocomplete drop-down as the user types, either by highlighting results that match the query, or by filtering out results that don't.

Solution

Load the `autocomplete-plugin` module along with the `autocomplete-highlighters` module, the `autocomplete-filters` module, or both. When plugging the text `<input>` node or `<textarea>` node, specify the filtering behavior or highlighting behavior you want with the `resultFilters` or `resultHighlighter` attribute.

Example 8-24 augments a text input field with highlighting autocompletion. The example loads the `autocomplete-highlighters` module and sets the `resultHighlighter` attribute to `'phraseMatch'`. As the user types a query, the drop-down highlights any results containing that consecutive sequence of characters. For example, typing `'an'` highlights that sequence in `'banana'`, `'cantaloupe'`, and `'durian fruit'`.

Example 8-24. Plugging an input node with highlighting AutoComplete

```
<!DOCTYPE html>
<title>Plugging an input node with highlighting AutoComplete</title>

<form class="yui3-skin-sam">
    <label>Fruit: <input type="text" id="demo"></label>
</form>
```

```
<script src="http://yui.yahooapis.com/3.5.0/build/yui/yui-min.js"></script>
<script>
YUI().use('autocomplete-plugin', 'autocomplete-highlighters', function (Y) {
    var input = Y.one("#demo").plug(Y.Plugin.AutoComplete, {
        resultHighlighter: 'phraseMatch',
        source: ['apple', 'banana', 'cantaloupe', 'durian fruit']
    });
});
</script>
```

Figure 8-20 illustrates the results of Example 8-24.

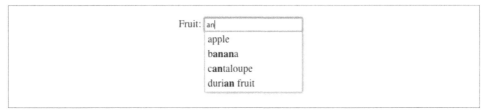

Figure 8-20. An input node with highlighting AutoComplete

While highlighting is a great way to draw the user's attention to results that match the query, you can also do the opposite, filtering out results that *don't* match the query. Filtering can be particularly useful if you have a fixed number of results, but the complete list is too long to scan comfortably.

The code in Example 8-25 is almost the same as in Example 8-24, except that it loads the `autocomplete-filters` module and sets the `resultFilters` attribute to `'phrase Match'`. As the user types a query, the drop-down filters out any results that lack that consecutive sequence of characters. For example, typing `'an'` filters out `'apple'` while preserving `'banana'`, `'cantaloupe'`, and `'durian fruit'`.

Example 8-25. Plugging an input node with filtering AutoComplete

```
YUI().use('autocomplete-plugin', 'autocomplete-filters', function (Y) {
    var input = Y.one("#demo").plug(Y.Plugin.AutoComplete, {
        resultFilters: 'phraseMatch',
        source: ['apple', 'banana', 'cantaloupe', 'durian fruit']
    });
});
```

Figure 8-21 illustrates the results of Example 8-25.

You can always combine filtering and highlighting by loading both `autocomplete-filters` and `autocomplete-highlighters` and setting both `resultHighlighter` and `resultFilters`.

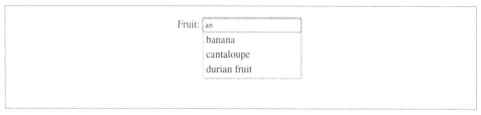

Figure 8-21. An input node with filtering AutoComplete

 There is an asymmetry here in that `resultFilters` is plural, which means you can supply a single filter or an array of filters. `resultHighlighter` is singular, which means you can supply only a single highlighter.

Discussion

To keep `AutoComplete` modular, all prepackaged highlighters and filters are broken out into `autocomplete-filters` and `autocomplete-highlighters`. These modules provide the following case-insensitive filters and highlighters:

charMatch

Matches individual characters anywhere in the result in any order, consecutive or not.

phraseMatch

Matches the complete query as a phrase anywhere in the result. If you're not sure which matching scheme to use, `phraseMatch` is a good default choice.

startsWith

Matches the complete query as a phrase at the start of the result.

subWordMatch

Matches individual words or subwords in the result, consecutive or not, ignoring nonword characters such as whitespace and punctuation.

wordMatch

Matches individual words in the result, consecutive or not, ignoring nonword characters such as whitespace and punctuation.

For each of these highlighters and filters, there is also a case-sensitive version (`phrase MatchCase`) and an *accent folding* version (`phraseMatchFold`). An accent folding highlighter or filter ignores diacritical marks, such as umlauts, circumflexes, and cedillas. In other words, a query string of "facade" would match "façade." This functionality is broken out into separate `autocomplete-filters-accentfold` and `autocomplete-highlighters-accentfold` modules. Accent folding can be handy if your user base belongs to a culture where it is acceptable to borrow foreign words without learning how to spell those words correctly.

YUI's client-side accent folding handles only a small subset of Unicode. If you need more extensive support, use a server-side accent folding library.

If you don't need any of these prepackaged highlighters and filters, you can easily define your own. A result filter is just a function that gets called each time the query value changes, taking the current query and an array of result objects as arguments, and returning a filtered array of result objects. As Example 8-26 demonstrates, you could write a custom "endsWith" result filter that returns only results that end with the current query.

Example 8-26. Writing a custom AutoComplete filter

```
<!DOCTYPE html>
<title>Writing a custom AutoComplete filter</title>

<form class="yui3-skin-sam">
    <label>Fruit: <input type="text" id="demo"></label>
</form>

<script src="http://yui.yahooapis.com/3.5.0/build/yui/yui-min.js"></script>
<script>
YUI().use('autocomplete-plugin', function (Y) {
    function endsWith(query, results) {
        query = query.toLowerCase();

        return Y.Array.filter(results, function(result) {
            var resultText = result.text.toLowerCase(),
                suffixIndex = resultText.length - query.length;

            return resultText.lastIndexOf(query) === suffixIndex;
        });
    }

    var input = Y.one("#demo").plug(Y.Plugin.AutoComplete, {
        resultFilters: endsWith,
        source: ['apple', 'banana', 'cantaloupe', 'durian fruit']
    });
});
</script>
```

Figure 8-22 illustrates the results of Example 8-26.

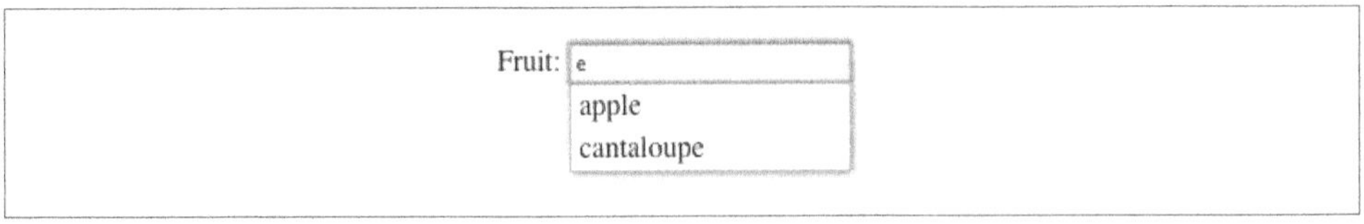

Fruit: e
apple
cantaloupe

Figure 8-22. A custom AutoComplete filter

Likewise, a result highlighter is a function that takes the current query and an array of result objects as arguments, and returns an array of HTML strings to be displayed to the user. As Example 8-27 shows, you can load the handy `highlight` module and call `Y.Highlight.all()` to automatically add HTML markup to the result string.

Example 8-27. Writing a custom AutoComplete highlighter

```
<!DOCTYPE html>
<title>Writing a custom AutoComplete highlighter</title>

<form class="yui3-skin-sam">
    <label>Fruit: <input type="text" id="demo"></label>
</form>

<script src="http://yui.yahooapis.com/3.5.0/build/yui/yui-min.js"></script>
<script>
YUI().use('autocomplete-plugin', 'highlight', function (Y) {
    function endsWith(query, results) {
        query = query.toLowerCase();

        return Y.Array.map(results, function(result) {
            var resultText = result.text.toLowerCase(),
                suffixIndex = resultText.length - query.length;

            if (resultText.lastIndexOf(query) === suffixIndex) {
                return Y.Highlight.all(result.text, query);
            }
            else {
                return result.text;
            }
        });
    }

    var input = Y.one("#demo").plug(Y.Plugin.AutoComplete, {
        resultHighlighter: endsWith,
        source: ['apple', 'banana', 'cantaloupe', 'durian fruit']
    });
});
</script>
```

Figure 8-23 illustrates the results of Example 8-27.

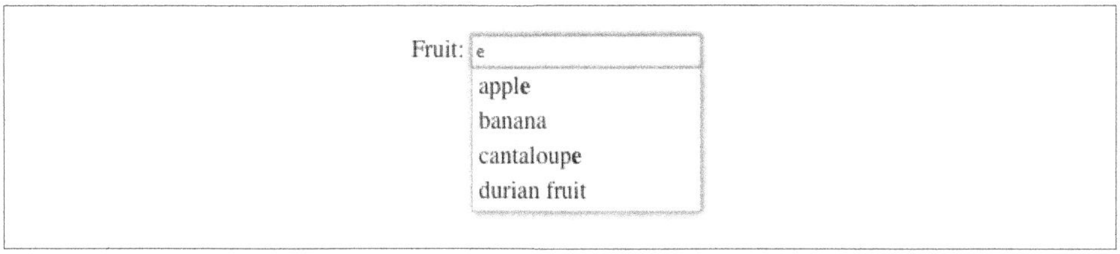

Figure 8-23. A custom AutoComplete highlighter

As written, Example 8-27 has an awkward edge-case bug where a query of `'na'` highlights the `'nana'` in `'banana'`. Unfortunately, the `Highlight` utility provides the methods all() for highlighting all substrings, word() for highlighting words within strings, and start() for highlighting at the beginning...but no end() for highlighting at the end of strings.

The Highlight methods all wrap the highlighted text in a <b> rather than a <strong>, since <b> is the closest thing semantically to HTML5's <mark> element. If you are willing to use an HTML5 shim or if you don't need to support older versions of Internet Explorer, you can change the markup by overriding Y.Highlight._TEMPLATE.

In addition to the highlight module, developing AutoComplete generated other useful standalone utilities:

- The text-accentfold module, which provides general accent folding capabilities through methods such as Y.Text.Accentfold.fold().
- The text-wordbreak module, which provides utility methods for splitting strings on word breaks and determining whether a character index represents a word boundary.
- The escape module, which provides HTML and regex escaping methods, discussed in Recipe 9.13.

See Also

Recipe 8.17; Recipe 8.19; Recipe 8.20; Recipe 9.13; Text.AccentFold API documentation (*http://yuilibrary.com/yui/docs/api/classes/Text.AccentFold.html*); Text.WordBreak API documentation (*http://yuilibrary.com/yui/docs/api/classes/Text.WordBreak.html*).

8.19 Using AutoComplete with Remote Data

Problem

You want to load AutoComplete's data from a remote search API, changing the displayed results as the user types the query.

Solution

Load the autocomplete-plugin and autocomplete-sources modules. When configuring the AutoComplete plugin, set the source attribute to a JSONP URL, including placeholders for the {query} and the {callback} parameters:

```
http://example.com/api/search.json?q={query}&callback={callback}
```

Test the results with a few example queries and make sure you understand the JSON response that the search service returns. If necessary, add a resultListLocator to drill down into the JSON to find the desired array of data, a resultTextLocator to identify a field within that array, or both. This concept is *extremely* similar to the resultList Locator and resultFields seen in Y.DataSchema.JSON. For more information, refer to Recipe 5.10.

Example 8-28 illustrates how to make a JSONP request to the Twitter Search API. This is a great API to experiment with, because it is one of the very few publicly available search APIs that does not require an API key. Within the JSON response, the `results` array holds the list of matching tweets, and within that array, the `text` property holds the actual tweet text. Setting `resultListLocator` and `resultTextLocator` to those values causes `AutoComplete` to display the correct array of strings in the drop-down.

To make things more interesting, the example also listens for the `select` event. Unlike the simpler `result` object in Example 8-22, in this example the `result` object carries structured information about the tweet, used to construct the tweet's permalink URL and navigate the user off the page.

Example 8-28. Fetching JSONP data for AutoComplete

```
<!DOCTYPE html>
<title>Fetching JSONP data for AutoComplete</title>

<form class="yui3-skin-sam">
    <label>Go to tweet: <input type="text" id="demo" style="width: 40em"></label>
</form>

<script src="http://yui.yahooapis.com/3.5.0/build/yui/yui-min.js"></script>
<script>
YUI().use('autocomplete-plugin', 'autocomplete-sources', function (Y) {
    var input = Y.one("#demo").plug(Y.Plugin.AutoComplete, {
        resultListLocator: 'results',
        resultTextLocator: 'text',
        source: 'http://search.twitter.com/search.json?q={query}&callback={callback}',
    });

    input.ac.on('select', function (ev) {
        var urlTemplate = 'http://twitter.com/{from_user}/status/{id_str}';
        window.location = Y.Lang.sub(urlTemplate, ev.result.raw);
    });
});
</script>
```

As an alternative to JSONP, you can use YQL. Example 8-29 searches through news articles belonging to the *Guardian*, a news site that, like Twitter, permits search API access without strictly requiring an API key.

The code turns out to be very similar to Example 8-28. Instead of setting a JSONP URL as the `source`, however, you provide a YQL query string. There is no need for a `{callback}` parameter, as YQL handles this detail for you. The `resultListLocator` and `resultTextLocator` are different (no surprise), and the `select` listener is actually a little simpler, because the *Guardian*'s API helpfully provides the full article URL directly in the response data. To test the example, try a query like `'football'`.

Example 8-29. Fetching YQL data for AutoComplete

```
<!DOCTYPE html>
<title>Fetching YQL data for AutoComplete</title>
```

```
<form class="yui3-skin-sam">
    <label>Read article: <input type="text" id="demo" style="width: 40em;"></label>
</form>

<script src="http://yui.yahooapis.com/3.5.0/build/yui/yui-min.js"></script>
<script>
YUI().use('autocomplete-plugin', 'autocomplete-sources', function (Y) {
    var input = Y.one('#demo').plug(Y.Plugin.AutoComplete, {
        resultListLocator: 'query.results.content',
        resultTextLocator: 'web-title',
        source: 'select * from guardian.content.search where q="{query}"',
    });

    input.ac.on('select', function (ev) {
        window.location = ev.result.raw['web-url'];
    });
});
</script>
```

Discussion

If you are considering calling a remote API to populate AutoComplete, there are two basic interaction types to think about.

In a "search assist"-like interaction, demonstrated in Examples 8-28 and 8-29, Auto Complete hits the API and returns new result sets as the user types.

In a "list select"-like interaction, demonstrated in Example 8-22, the result list data could be local or remote—but if it is remote, it is fetched only once. As the user types, AutoComplete helps the user sift through this static list of results.

AutoComplete's source attribute is very flexible, providing many different methods to support these interactions:

- If you pass source a simple array of strings, AutoComplete uses those strings in the drop-down:

      source: ['apple', 'banana', 'cherry']

- If you pass source an object with properties that are arrays of strings, AutoCom plete uses the user's query to match object properties, then displays that array in the drop-down:

      source: { small: ['micro', 'nano'], tiny: ['femto', 'atto'] }

- If you pass source a URL string, AutoComplete attempts to make a JSONP or XHR call on each query, depending on whether you provide a {callback} placeholder:

      source: 'http://xhrexample.com/search?q={query}'

  or:

      source: 'http://jsonpexample.com/search?q={query}&callback={callback}'

- If you pass source a YQL query string, AutoComplete attempts to make a YQL call on each query:

```
source: 'select * from some.table where q="{query}"'
```

- If you pass source a function, AutoComplete executes that function on each query, passing in a query and callback parameter. The function can return synchronously:

```
source: function (query) {
    // custom logic
    return ['This', 'is', 'synchronous', 'data'];
}
```

Or the function can return asynchronously, in which case it must execute the callback parameter when the array of results is ready:

```
source: function (query, callback) {
    someObject.on('someEvent', function (ev) {
        // custom logic, possibly involving the event object
        callback(['This', 'is', 'asynchronous', 'data']);
    });
}
```

- If you pass source any DataSource instance, AutoComplete loads data from the Data Source. This enables you to reuse data sources that you might have been using elsewhere in your code, apply schemas, and more. To handle the variable query part of the URL, set the requestTemplate attribute, which AutoComplete appends to the DataSource URL before each fetch:

```
requestTemplate: '?q={query}',
source: new Y.DataSource.Get({ source: 'http://example.com/search' });
```

See Also

Recipe 5.9; Recipe 8.17; Recipe 8.18; Recipe 8.20; "Example: Remote Data via Data-Source" (*http://yuilibrary.com/yui/docs/autocomplete/ac-datasource.html*).

8.20 Customizing the AutoComplete Result List

Problem

Instead of a boring list of strings, you want a result list that displays rich data using arbitrary HTML.

Solution

Set resultFormatter to a function that takes the current query and list of results as arguments, and returns an array of HTML strings that contain <div>s, images, links, or whatever markup you need. Then add CSS to make the results attractive.

Example 8-30 provides rich formatting for results from Yahoo! Local, pulled in using YQL. The `formatter` function defines a template string and then uses `Y.Array.map()` and `Y.Lang.sub()` to create a new array of HTML strings from the `result` object. For this particular example, substituting `result.raw` works perfectly as-is. More generally, you might need to fiddle with `result`'s data before executing `Y.Lang.sub()`.

Example 8-30. Returning local search results with a custom result formatter

```
<!DOCTYPE html>
<title>Returning local search results with a custom result formatter</title>
<style>
input#demo { width: 20em; }
.vcard { font-size: 11px; font-family: verdana; color: #555; }
.fn { font-size: 13px; background: #ddd; color: #000; padding: 2px; }
.yui3-aclist-item-active .vcard { color: #fff; }
.yui3-aclist-item-active .fn { background: #ddf; }
</style>

<form class="yui3-skin-sam">
    <label>In Palo Alto, find: <input type="text" id="demo"></label>
</form>

<script src="http://yui.yahooapis.com/3.5.0/build/yui/yui-min.js"></script>
<script>
YUI().use('autocomplete-plugin', 'autocomplete-sources', function (Y) {
    function formatter(query, results) {
        var template = '<div class="vcard">'
            + '<div class="adr">'
            + '<div class="org fn"><div class="organization-name">{Title}</div></div>'
            + '<span class="street-address">{Address}</span>, '
            + '<span class="locality">{City}</span>, '
            + '<span class="region">{State}</span> '
            + '</div>'
            + '<div class="tel"><span class="type">Tel</span>: {Phone}</div>';

        return Y.Array.map(results, function (result) {
            return Y.Lang.sub(template, result.raw);
        });
    };

    var input = Y.one("#demo").plug(Y.Plugin.AutoComplete, {
        resultListLocator: 'query.results.Result',
        resultTextLocator: 'Title',
        resultFormatter: formatter,
        source: 'select * from local.search where zip="94301" and query="{query}"'
    });
});
</script>
```

Figure 8-24 illustrates the results of Example 8-30.

Figure 8-24. Local search results with a custom result formatter

> For extra nerd points, the template string provides its markup using the hCard microformat (*http://microformats.org/wiki/hcard*).

Discussion

The custom formatter in Example 8-30 and the custom highlighter in Example 8-27 have some basic similarities. They both receive the `query` string and `results` array, they both return an array of HTML strings, and they both use `Y.Array.map()` for convenience. The difference is that highlighters generally use methods on `Y.Highlight`, while formatters typically use `Y.Lang.sub()` or some other templating system such as Handlebars. If you want to apply highlighting *and* formatting, you can use `Y.Highlight.all()` in your formatter along with your template logic (this is one of the reasons the formatter receives `query` as an argument).

Example 8-30 is, of course, a toy example. For one thing, there is no reason to hardcode Palo Alto, California, as the zip code. The example could also be improved with better CSS, by adding more information about the business, by showing the rating as graphical stars, and so on.

Using a formatter to display thumbnail images can be powerful, but take care to show images only if they are easy to recognize at a small size and visually distinct when shown alongside lots of other search results. Classic examples where thumbnail images are helpful include lists of photos, videos, and people (specifically, headshots or distinct avatars, not full-body photos).

See Also

Recipe 8.17; Recipe 8.18; Recipe 8.19; Recipe 9.7; "Example: Find Photos on Flickr" (*http://yuilibrary.com/yui/docs/autocomplete/ac-flickr.html*).

Utilities

Compared to other programming languages, JavaScript has historically included only a very small number of core utility methods. For years, if you wanted to trim whitespace from a string or enumerate an object's keys, you had to implement that functionality yourself.

Recently, JavaScript has been evolving to fill in some of these feature gaps. Newer JavaScript engines still provide very minimal core APIs, but the environment at least is starting to look a little more like what developers coming over from other languages might expect.

As a comprehensive JavaScript framework, YUI provides a large number of utility methods. Some YUI utility methods mirror a native ECMAScript method, enabling you to use native code when that is available, but falling back to YUI code in older browsers. Other YUI utility methods provide a nicer or more powerful wrapper around a lower-level native API. Finally, some YUI utility methods provide high-level features or solve common problems that aren't yet addressed by W3C or ECMAScript specifications.

This chapter provides a brief survey of some key YUI utilities, including language helpers (type checking, array and object manipulation) data converters, and formatters, application development (browser history), and form utilities (validation, keyboard and input change events).

As always, be sure to consult the YUI documentation in order to fully understand the API. Many recipes in this chapter show off only a small subset of what a particular utility can do. Also note that some of the utilities in this chapter come from the gallery. The gallery is a great place to look for high-quality components that were designed to scratch a particular itch.

Recipe 9.1 explains how to reliably determine a variable's type, a fundamental problem that has plagued JavaScript developers since the creation of the language.

Recipe 9.2 demonstrates how to iterate over arrays using YUI's built-in ECMAScript mirror methods provided by YUI's `Array` API.

Recipe 9.3 introduces the `collection` module, which fills out `Array` with additional ECMAScript mirror methods and adds extra power for filtering through arrays.

Recipe 9.4 explains how to merge multiple objects together.

Recipe 9.5 introduces the `oop` module, which fills out the YUI `Object` API with additional ECMAScript mirror methods and provides new ways to derive objects from other objects.

Recipe 9.6 describes function memoization and explains why this technique is useful.

Recipe 9.7 provides a simple substitution-based technique for templating.

Recipe 9.8 explains how to format numbers, which is useful for displaying currencies and other values that have units.

Recipe 9.9 introduces the `datatype-date` module, which provides `strftime` style date formatting and several other date manipulation methods.

Recipe 9.10 explains how to easily convert an XML string into an `XMLDocument` object.

Recipe 9.11 provides a handy utility for converting between keyword, hex, and RGB color representations.

Recipe 9.12 introduces the `history` module, which enables you to map complex JavaScript states back to real URLs and real browser history entries.

Recipe 9.13 shows how to sanitize user input with the `escape` module.

Recipe 9.14 explains how to use the `gallery-checkboxgroups` module as a helper for creating groups of checkboxes that share some specialized behavior.

Recipes 9.15 and 9.16 introduce two types of synthetic events that are useful when you are working with forms. The `gallery-event-nav-keys` module provides some nice sugar events for handling keyboard navigation, while the `event-valuechange` module solves the tricky problem of handling input changes in form fields—a use case that native DOM events like `change` and `input` fail to deal with properly.

Finally, Recipe 9.17 provides a brief overview of the `gallery-formmgr` module, which provides a great deal of control over most aspects of a form's lifecycle.

9.1 Determining a Variable's Type

Problem

You want to reliably determine the type of a variable, even if it was created in the context of another window or iframe.

Solution

Use `Y.Lang`'s type-detection utility methods. `Y.Lang` is part of the YUI seed file, so you don't need to load any extra modules in order to use it. Example 9-1 provides a whirlwind tour of YUI's type-detection features.

Example 9-1. Checking types

```html
<!DOCTYPE html>
<title>Checking types</title>

<script src="http://yui.yahooapis.com/3.5.0/build/yui/yui-min.js"></script>
<script>
YUI().use(function (Y) {
    var typeChecks = [
        Y.Lang.isArray([]),          // => true
        Y.Lang.isArray(arguments),   // => false
        Y.Lang.isArray('string'),    // => false

        Y.Lang.isBoolean(true),      // => true
        Y.Lang.isBoolean(0),         // => false

        Y.Lang.isDate(new Date()),   // => true
        Y.Lang.isDate(123),          // => false

        Y.Lang.isFunction(function () {}),   // => true
        Y.Lang.isFunction('test'),           // => false

        Y.Lang.isNull(null),         // => true
        Y.Lang.isNull(undefined),    // => false

        Y.Lang.isNumber(42),         // => true
        Y.Lang.isNumber('42'),       // => false
        Y.Lang.isNumber(NaN),        // => false

        Y.Lang.isObject({}),         // => true
        Y.Lang.isObject([]),         // => true (yep, arrays are objects!)
        Y.Lang.isObject('test'),     // => false
        Y.Lang.isObject(function () {}),        // => true
        Y.Lang.isObject(function () {}, true),  // => false ('failFn' flag)

        Y.Lang.isString('string'),   // => true
        Y.Lang.isString(42),         // => false

        Y.Lang.isUndefined(undefined),   // => true
        Y.Lang.isUndefined(null),        // => false

        Y.Lang.isValue(false),       // => true
        Y.Lang.isValue(0),           // => true
        Y.Lang.isValue(''),          // => true
        Y.Lang.isValue(null),        // => false
        Y.Lang.isValue(undefined),   // => false
```

```
        Y.Lang.type([]),           // => array
        Y.Lang.type(true),         // => boolean
        Y.Lang.type(new Date()),   // => date
        Y.Lang.type(new Error()),  // => error
        Y.Lang.type(function () {}), // => function
        Y.Lang.type(null),         // => null
        Y.Lang.type(42),           // => number
        Y.Lang.type({}),           // => object
        Y.Lang.type(/regexp/),     // => regexp
        Y.Lang.type('string'),     // => string
        Y.Lang.type(undefined)     // => undefined
    ];

    Y.Array.each(typeChecks, function (result) {
        Y.log(result);
    });
});
</script>
```

Example 9-1 also uses `Y.Array.each()` to iterate over the array. For more information, refer to Recipe 9.2.

Discussion

Type detection in JavaScript is tricky, since the native `typeof` operator doesn't always return what you might expect. For example, `typeof null` and `typeof []` both return the string `'object'`. The native `instanceof` operator also doesn't work as expected when used with values that were instantiated in another context, such as a different window or iframe. `Y.Lang` smooths out these and many other type-checking inconsistencies and provides a reliable set of utility functions to use.

Keep in mind that loose typing is one of the things that makes JavaScript flexible. It's often best to use type checking to determine how a function should operate on a given value rather than to enforce strict control over what kinds of values a function should accept.

See Also

Juriy Zaytsev's "Unnecessarily comprehensive look into a rather insignificant issue of global objects creation" (*http://perfectionkills.com/unnecessarily-comprehensive-look-in to-a-rather-insignificant-issue-of-global-objects-creation/*).

9.2 Iterating Over Arrays and Objects

Problem

You want to iterate over members of an array or members of an object and do some work on each item.

Solution

Beyond JavaScript's built-in `for` and `while` loop statements, YUI provides the static methods `Y.Array.each()`, `Y.Array.some()`, `Y.Object.each()`, and `Y.Object.some()`. As Example 9-2 shows, you can use these methods to cleanly iterate over an array or object, calling a function on each iteration.

Example 9-2. Iterating over arrays and objects

```
<!DOCTYPE html>
<title>Iterating over arrays and objects</title>

<script src="http://yui.yahooapis.com/3.5.0/build/yui/yui-min.js"></script>
<script>
YUI().use(function (Y) {
    var fruits = [ 'apple', 'mango', 'kiwi' ],
        veggies = { 'carrots': 0, 'radishes': 7, 'squash': 3 };

    Y.Array.each(fruits, function (fruit, index) {
        Y.log(index + ' = ' + fruit);
    });
    Y.Array.some(fruits, function (fruit, index) {
        Y.log('Hunting for mango... fruit was ' + fruit);
        return fruit === 'mango';
    });

    Y.Object.each(veggies, function (quantity, veggie) {
        Y.log('There are ' + quantity + ' ' + veggie);
    });
    Y.Object.some(veggies, function (quantity, veggie) {
        Y.log('Do we have any ' + veggie + '?');
        if (quantity > 0) {
            Y.log("Well, at least we're not out of " + veggie + '.');
            return true;
        }
    });
});
</script>
```

`Y.Array.each()` calls a function once for each item in an array, passing in as arguments the item, its index, and the array itself. `Y.Object.each()` calls a function once for each key in the object, passing in as arguments the key's value, the key, and the object itself.

`Y.Array.some()` and `Y.Object.some()` work like `each()`, but they stop iterating if the function returns `true`. This is similar to creating a `break` statement inside a native loop.

Discussion

When your needs are simple and can be accomplished with a small amount of inline code, the native `for` and `while` statements are usually fine, and are the fastest way to go. However, if each iteration involves a lot of work, or if each iteration will simply be calling another function anyway, then `each()` and `some()` can make your code more manageable. `Y.Array.each()` and `Y.Array.some()` are also convenient for working with `NodeLists`, discussed in Recipe 2.5.

Behind the scenes, `Y.Array.each()` and `Y.Array.some()` call the native `Array.proto type.forEach()` and `Array.prototype.some()` methods if those methods are available. These methods are part of ECMAScript 5, and have already gained wide support. Otherwise, YUI falls back to its own built-in implementations that work in older browsers. `Y.Object.each()` and `Y.Object.some()` both use a native `for...in` loop and both rely on `hasOwnProperty()` to avoid iterating over inherited properties like `Object.toString`.

`Y.Array` and `Y.Object` also provide a number of additional utility methods that mirror functions in ECMAScript 5. These include:

`Y.Array(object)`
> Returns a true JavaScript array representation of the specified "arraylike" object. Examples of arraylike objects include a function's `arguments` variable and native `HTMLElement` collections.

`Y.Array.hash(keyArray, valueArray)`
> Returns an object that uses the first array as keys and the second as values.

`Y.Array.indexOf(array, value)`
> Returns the first array index where the value was found, or −1 if the value is not in the array.

`Y.Object.hasValue(value)`
> Returns `true` if the object contains the specified value; `false` otherwise.

`Y.Object.keys(object)`
> Return an array containing the object's keys and values, respectively.

`Y.Object.owns(object, property)`
> Returns `true` if an object directly owns the property. `Y.Object.owns()` is safer than calling the object's native `hasOwnProperty()` directly, as it avoids errors caused by poorly written third-party code that clobbers `hasOwnProperty()`.

These methods and several others are part of the basic set of `Y.Array` and `Y.Object` methods included in the YUI seed file. As with `Y.Lang`, you don't need to load any extra modules in order to use them. For additional object and array methods, refer to Recipes 9.3 and 9.5.

See Also

Ryan Grove on why you shouldn't extend JavaScript natives (*http://wonko.com/post/ extending-javascript-natives*).

9.3 Filtering an Array

Problem

You want to filter out some unwanted contents from an array.

Solution

Load the `array-extras` module and call `Y.Array.filter()` to iterate through the array, executing a filter function on each array item (as shown in Example 9-3). The `filter()` method returns a new array that contains each item where the filter function returned a truthy value.

Example 9-3. Filtering an array

```
<!DOCTYPE html>
<title>Filtering an array</title>

<script src="http://yui.yahooapis.com/3.5.0/build/yui/yui-min.js"></script>
<script>
YUI().use('array-extras', function (Y) {
    var patrons = [ 'person', 'rope', 'frayed knot' ];

    var acceptablePatrons = Y.Array.filter(patrons, function (p) {
        return p !== 'rope';
    });

    Y.Array.each(acceptablePatrons, function (p) {
        Y.log(p);
    });
});
</script>
```

Discussion

If you need more power when working with arrays, the `array-extras` module augments `Y.Array` with extra array utility methods, many of which are also reflected in ECMA-Script 5. These extra methods help you filter or otherwise transform the array. They include:

`Y.Array.grep(`*array, pattern*`)`
> Returns a new array with members that matched the specified regular expression.

`Y.Array.map(`*array, mapFunction*`)`
> Applies `mapFunction` to every member of an array, returning another array that represents the return value of each `mapFunction` call. Differs from `Y.Array.each()` in that it returns an array.

`Y.Array.partition(`*array, filter*`)`
> Returns an object containing two arrays: the items that passed the filter and those that were rejected by the filter.

`Y.Array.reduce(`*`array, init, reduceFunction`*`)`

> Applies `reduceFunction` to every member of an array, building up a return value. Each `reduceFunction` call receives the return value of the previous call, the current element, the current array index, and the array itself. The `init` parameter provides an initial value to the first call of `reduceFunction`.

`Y.Array.unique(`*`array`*`)`

> Returns a new array with all duplicate items removed. For simple arrays of strings, you can use `Y.Array.dedupe()` for better performance.

For even more array methods, load the larger `collection` rollup, which includes modules such as `array-extras`, `array-invoke`, and `arraylist`. For example, `array-invoke` provides `Y.Array.invoke(`*`array, methodName, args*`*`)`, which iterates through the array and attempts to call the specified method on each member object, passing in zero or more specified arguments. If the object does not have the method, it is skipped. `Y.Array.invoke()` is a good way to initialize, plug, or destroy a large number of widgets at once.

9.4 Merging Objects

Problem

You want to merge multiple objects to create another object.

Solution

Use `Y.merge()` to combine one or more objects into a new merged object, as demonstrated in Example 9-4.

For primitive properties like numbers and strings, `Y.merge()` clones the value over to the merged object. Changing the property on the merged object does not affect the supplier object, and vice versa.

For properties that are objects, arrays, or functions, `Y.merge()` creates a reference to the value. Changing the property on the merged object changes the supplier object, and vice versa.

Example 9-4. Merging objects

```
<!DOCTYPE html>
<title>Merging objects</title>

<script src='http://yui.yahooapis.com/3.5.0/build/yui/yui-min.js'></script>
<script>
YUI().use(function (Y) {
    var reptileHouse = { reptiles: 47 },
        giraffeExhibit = { giraffes: 4 },
        aviary = {
            birds: 103,
```

```
            repairs: {
                reason: 'plumbing',
                completion: '21-Dec-2012'
            }
        },
        zoo = Y.merge(reptileHouse, giraffeExhibit, aviary);

    zoo.giraffes += 1;
    Y.log('increasing zoo.giraffes to ' + zoo.giraffes);
    Y.log('giraffeExhibit.giraffes remains at ' + giraffeExhibit.giraffes);

    zoo.repairs.reason = 'remodel';
    Y.log('changing zoo.repairs.reason to "' + zoo.repairs.reason + '"');
    Y.log('changes aviary.repairs.reason to "'  + aviary.repairs.reason + '"');
});
</script>
```

Discussion

If you merge multiple objects, later values override earlier values. In Example 9-4, if giraffeExhibit and aviary had a naming collision, aviary's value would win.

One helpful trick with Y.merge() is to call it on a single simple data object to create a shallow clone:

```
var reptileHouse2 = Y.merge(reptileHouse);
```

Another useful pattern for Y.merge() is if you have a simple configuration object, and you want to allow users to override your defaults:

```
function doSomething(userConfig) {
    var defaults = {
        hidden: true,
        width: 100
    };

    var config = Y.merge(defaults, userConfig);
}
```

Y.merge() can safely merge a userConfig that is null or undefined.

YUI also provides a method named Y.mix(). In its simplest form, Y.mix() acts almost exactly like Y.merge(). Calling Y.mix(foo, bar) mixes the properties of bar directly into foo, returning the object passed in as the first parameter.

9.5 Composing and Inheriting from Other Objects

Problem

You want to create objects that reuse code from other objects, by inheritance or by composition.

Solution

Load the oop module to bring in some additional tools for working with objects. Use Y.extend() to create a traditional inheritance hierarchy of objects, Y.augment() to augment an object instance or prototype with another object's capabilities, and Y.aggregate() to do deep merges of object instances.

Example 9-5 illustrates how you can use these methods:

1. A base Plant object has a climbs property on its prototype. Any new Plant() instance will have a climbs property of false.

2. A Vine object calls Plant's constructor and uses Y.extend() to extend Plant. Vine's prototype gains Plant's prototype properties, and then overrides climbs on the prototype to be true. Any new Vine() instance is an instance of a Vine, and also an instance of a Plant. In classical terms, Y.extend() creates an "is a" relationship: a Vine is a kind of Plant.

3. A Leaves object has a leafStatus() method. Calling Y.augment() supplies Vine with the capabilities of Leaves. As with Y.extend(), this copies Leaves's prototype properties over to Vine's prototype. The difference is that with Y.augment(), a Vine instance does not also become a Leaves instance. In classical terms, Y.augment() creates a "has a" or "uses a" relationship—a Vine has Leaves, but it isn't a kind of leaf.

4. The example creates a new Vine instance named vine, along with two ad hoc objects, lemon and lime. Y.aggregate() then adds in all properties and methods of lemon and lime into vine. Although lemon and lime each contain an object named pick, Y.aggregate() successfully merges pick.lemons() and pick.limes() into vine without clobbering anything.

Example 9-5. Extending, augmenting, and aggregating

```
<!DOCTYPE html>
<title>Extending, augmenting, and aggregating</title>

<script src="http://yui.yahooapis.com/3.5.0/build/yui/yui-min.js"></script>
<script>
YUI().use('oop', function (Y) {
    var vine, lemon, lime;

    function Plant(name) {
        this.name = name;
    }
    Plant.prototype.climbs = false;

    function Vine(name) {
        Vine.superclass.constructor.call(this, name);
    }
    Y.extend(Vine, Plant, {climbs: true});
```

```
    function Leaves() {
        Y.log('CONSTRUCTOR: I have leaves.');
    }
    Leaves.prototype.leafStatus = function () { return 'green' };

    Y.augment(Vine, Leaves);

    vine = new Vine('hybridvine');
    lemon = { pick: { lemons: function () { return 'Tangy!' } } };
    lime = { pick: { limes: function () { return 'Mojitos please!' } } };
    Y.aggregate(vine, lemon);
    Y.aggregate(vine, lime);

    Y.log(vine.name + ' can climb: ' + vine.climbs);
    Y.log(vine.name + " also has leaves. They're " + vine.leafStatus() + '.');
    Y.log('In fact, by default any Vine can climb: ' + Vine.prototype.climbs);
    Y.log(vine.name + ' produces lemons: ' + vine.pick.lemons());
    Y.log(vine.name + ' produces limes: ' + vine.pick.limes());
    Y.log('Is ' + vine.name + ' a Plant? ' + (vine instanceof Plant));
    Y.log('Is ' + vine.name + ' a Vine? ' + (vine instanceof Vine));
    Y.log('But is ' + vine.name + ' a Leaf? ' + (vine instanceof Leaves));
});
</script>
```

Believe it or not, in the real world you can graft together plants to create lemon/lime vines and even lemon/lime/orange vines.

Discussion

The official YUI documentation often refers to "classes." Strictly speaking, JavaScript doesn't yet have built-in classes—but this doesn't matter much, as you can use JavaScript prototypes to implement patterns that look an awful lot like classes in other languages. `Y.extend()` and `Y.augment()` are convenient tools for working with and thinking about JavaScript in a more classical way.

If you are working with the `Base` object or its descendants, you can use `Y.Base.create()` as an alternative to the generic `Y.extend()` and `Y.augment()`. For more information, refer to Recipe 7.3.

In Example 9-5, the console log reveals that the constructor for `Leaves` gets called just before `vine.leafStatus()` executes. This is a feature of `Y.augment()`, which has special logic for handling constructors. When `Y.augment()` copies methods from the supplier to the receiver, it sequesters all copied methods and delays calling the supplier's constructor until just before you first call one of the copied methods.

This ensures proper usage of the supplier object, but also enables you to augment the receiver multiple times without the performance hit of executing multiple supplier constructors at once. If you need to pass arguments to a supplier's constructor, use Y.augment()'s extended signature.

Y.aggregate() copies object properties rather than prototype properties. One of its key features is that it can do "deep merges" of the supplier's properties with properties already on the receiver. As shown in Example 9-5, for colliding properties that are objects, Y.aggregate() attempts to augment the receiver's object with the supplier's. For colliding properties that are arrays, Y.aggregate() appends the values in the supplier's array to the receiver's. If a true naming collision occurs, Y.aggregate()'s default behavior is to preserve the existing property on the receiver.

See Also

Luke Smith's YUIConf 2011 talk, "Class Inheritance and Composition Patterns in YUI" (*http://www.youtube.com/watch?v=_zhQIfT7g58*).

9.6 Automatically Caching Function Call Results

Problem

You have a function that, given the same input, always returns the same output value. Each time your function is called, you would like to cache the output and try to look up that value on subsequent calls (a technique called *memoization*).

Solution

Use Y.cached() to return a wrapped version of your function that automatically performs memoization. When you call the wrapper function with a certain parameter list, it first checks to see if it has a cached value stored for those input parameters, and if so, returns the results immediately. Otherwise, the wrapper function executes the original function, stores the results in the cache, and returns the results.

An example that benefits from caching is the classic recursive algorithm for calculating the *n*th number in the Fibonacci sequence:

```
function fib(n) {
    return (n === 1 || n === 2) ? 1 : fib(n - 1) + fib(n - 2);
}
```

The algorithm is correct, but the number of function calls grows exponentially with *n*. Depending on your browser and system, a value of *n* as low as 40 might cause a noticeable slowdown or a "hanging script" error.

Example 9-6 implements the same algorithm, but uses Y.cached() to return a wrapper function that stores previously calculated results.

Example 9-6. Efficiently calculating Fibonacci numbers

```
<!DOCTYPE html>
<title>Efficiently calculating Fibonacci numbers</title>

<div id="demo"></div>

<script src="http://yui.yahooapis.com/3.5.0/build/yui/yui-min.js"></script>
<script>
YUI().use('node-base', function (Y) {
    var fib = Y.cached(function (n) {
        return (n === 1 || n === 2) ? 1 : fib(n - 1) + fib(n - 2);
    });

    Y.one('#demo').append(fib(100));
});
</script>
```

The wrapper function makes it possible to calculate Fibonacci numbers that would choke the original function. When `fib(n)` calls `fib(n - 1)`, this looks up a previously calculated answer instead of recursively spawning thousands or even millions of other function calls.

Discussion

When it comes to scientific computing, JavaScript isn't exactly FORTRAN. However, if you do need to run expensive, repetitive calculations in JavaScript, memoization can help. Example 9-6 is a particularly dramatic example where memoization eliminates huge numbers of recursive function calls at a single stroke. More generally, `Y.cached()` can help address certain hot spots in your code, such as templating functions or string transformations that need to run frequently on a small set of values.

Take care to use `Y.cached()` only on functions that lack side effects.

> Do not confuse `Y.cached()` with `Y.Cache`. The former is a generic function memoization utility, included with the core YUI object. The latter is an API that abstracts techniques for storing data in the browser, included with the `cache` module.

9.7 Templating with Simple String Substitution

Problem

You want to generate chunks of HTML from data stored in an object. Instead of concatenating strings over and over, you want to use some sort of simple templating scheme.

Solution

Use `Y.Lang.sub()`, which scans a template string for tokens surrounded by curly braces. If a token in the string matches a property in a data object, `Y.Lang.sub()` replaces the token with the corresponding value from the object. Tokens that do not match any property in the object are left untouched. See Example 9-7.

Example 9-7. Templating with simple string substitution

```
<!DOCTYPE html>
<title>Templating with simple string substitution</title>

<div id="demo"></div>

<script src="http://yui.yahooapis.com/3.5.0/build/yui/yui-min.js"></script>
<script>
YUI().use('node-base', function (Y) {
    var template = '<p><b>{name}:</b> {job} of {loc}; In a relationship with {mate}</p>';
    var people = [
        { name: 'John Carter', job: 'Adventurer', loc: 'Virginia', mate: 'Dejah Thoris' },
        { name: 'Dejah Thoris', job: 'Princess', loc: 'Helium', mate: 'John Carter' },
        { name: 'Tars Tarkas', job: 'Jeddak', loc: 'Thark', mate: 'Gozava' }
    ];

    Y.Array.each(people, function (person) {
        var html = Y.Lang.sub(template, person);
        Y.one('#demo').append(html);
    });
});
</script>
```

Discussion

For small templates, defining a template string in JavaScript is usually fine. For larger template strings, you can use the `<script>` element to embed template markup inline within the HTML document:

```
<script id="template" type="text/x-template">
<p>
    <b>{name}:</b> {job} of {loc} |
    In a relationship with {mate}
</p>
</script>
```

and then retrieve the template string with `Y.one()`:

```
var template = Y.one('#template').getHTML();
```

This technique, dubbed "micro-templating" by jQuery creator John Resig, makes complex templates easier to visualize and manage. Be sure to set the `type` attribute to some non-JavaScript MIME-type such as `text/x-something` so that the browser does not attempt to execute the `<script>` block.

If you need more advanced string processing, you can load the substitute module to make Y.substitute() available. Y.substitute() does simple substitution like Y.Lang.sub(), but also lets you supply custom functions for processing tokens. If you prefer to use a real templating language with conditionals, loops, and partials, load the handlebars module, which is a YUI wrapper for the third-party Handlebars.js project. For server-side JavaScript, Jade is a template engine that works well with the popular Express framework.

See Also

Y.Lang.sub() API documentation (*http://yuilibrary.com/yui/docs/api/classes/Lang.html#method_sub*); Y.substitute() API documentation (*http://yuilibrary.com/yui/docs/api/classes/YUI~substitute.html*); Handlebars.js (*http://www.handlebarsjs.com/*); the Jade Node Template Engine (*http://jade-lang.com/*); John Resig's original article on JavaScript micro-templating (*http://ejohn.org/blog/javascript-micro-templating/*).

9.8 Formatting Numbers

Problem

You want to format a number into a string that displays some currency value.

Solution

Load the datatype-number module and call Y.DataType.Number.format(), passing in the number and a configuration object that specifies how to format the number.

Example 9-8 defines a US dollar format object, using the decimalPlaces property to zero-pad numbers out by two decimal places. You can use thousandsSeparator and decimalSeparator (not shown) to create different format objects for different locales.

Example 9-8. Formatting a number into a currency string

```
<!DOCTYPE html>
<title>Formatting a number into a currency string</title>

<div id="demo"></div>

<script src="http://yui.yahooapis.com/3.5.0/build/yui/yui-min.js"></script>
<script>
YUI().use('datatype-number', 'node-base', function (Y) {
    var usdFormat = {
        prefix: '$',
        suffix: ' (USD)',
        decimalPlaces: 2,
        thousandsSeparator: ','
    };
```

```
    function displayDollars(pennies) {
        return Y.DataType.Number.format(pennies/100, usdFormat);
    }
    Y.one('#demo').append(displayDollars(115380));
});
</script>
```

Discussion

Representing arbitrary decimal numbers in 64 bits as JavaScript does is inherently imperfect. To ensure precision in currency calculations, always store values and perform operations using integers, and show only decimal values at the very last moment, when displaying results to users. For example, if you are working with US dollars, you should operate in integers representing pennies and then divide by 100 at the very end of the calculation, as shown in Example 9-8.

See Also

The `DataType` User Guide (*http://yuilibrary.com/yui/docs/datatype/*).

9.9 Formatting Dates

Problem

You want to format standard JavaScript `Date` objects into a readable string.

Solution

Load the `datatype-date` module and call `Y.DataType.Date.format()`, passing in the `Date` object and an object with a `format` property, as shown in Example 9-9. The format string can contain any `strftime` format specifier, plus some extensions devised by the PHP project, plus some more extensions devised by YUI.

Example 9-9. Formatting dates

```
<!DOCTYPE html>
<title>Formatting dates</title>

<div id="demo"></div>

<script src="http://yui.yahooapis.com/3.5.0/build/yui/yui-min.js"></script>
<script>
YUI().use('datatype-date', 'node-base', function (Y) {
    var dateStr = Y.DataType.Date.format(new Date(), { format: '%A, %B %e, %Y' });
    Y.one('#demo').append('Today is ' + dateStr + '.');
});
</script>
```

Discussion

The `format()` method returns month and weekday names according to the current value of the YUI instance's `lang` property. For example, if the `lang` is `'fr'`, `format()` returns weekday strings like `'lundi'` and `'mardi'`. Strings such as `'am'` and `'pm'` and format specifiers such as `%x` and `%X` are also locale-specific. The `datatype-date` module currently defines over 80 sets of language strings.

Beyond `format()`, `DataType.Date` provides several other date utility methods that make it easy to compare dates and add months and years to dates.

See Also

The `gallery-toRelativeTime` module in Recipe 1.5; Recipe 8.15; the `DataType` User Guide (*http://yuilibrary.com/yui/docs/datatype/*); the complete list of format specifiers in the `DataType.Date.format()` API documentation (*http://yuilibrary.com/yui/docs/api/classes/DataType.Date.html#method_format*).

9.10 Parsing Arbitrary XML

Problem

You want to parse a string into an XML document.

Solution

Load the `datatype-xml` module and call `Y.DataType.XML.parse()`, passing in the string to parse (see Example 9-10). The method returns a native `XMLDocument` object representing the XML. If the string does not represent well-formed XML, the `XMLDocument` will contain errors rather than data you can walk through.

Example 9-10. Parsing arbitrary XML

```
<!DOCTYPE html>
<title>Parsing arbitrary XML</title>

<div id="book"></div>

<script src="http://yui.yahooapis.com/3.5.0/build/yui/yui-min.js"></script>
<script>
YUI().use('datatype-xml', 'node-base', function (Y) {
    var xmlString = '<book><title>The YUI 3 Cookbook</title>'
        + '<chapter id="loading"><title>Loading Modules</title>'
        + '<para>Consider the humble script element...</para></chapter></book>';

    var xml = Y.DataType.XML.parse(xmlString),
        ch1 = xml.firstChild.childNodes[1];
```

```
    Y.one('#book').append('<h1>Chapter 1: ' + ch1.childNodes[0].textContent + '</h1>');
    Y.one('#book').append('<p>' + ch1.childNodes[1].textContent + '</p>');
});
</script>
```

Discussion

There is also a `Y.DataType.XML.format()` method that can transform an `XMLDocument` object into a string of angle brackets. This method does not provide any pretty-printing or other fancy formatting options.

See Also

The `DataType` User Guide (*http://yuilibrary.com/yui/docs/datatype/*); DOM Core Document (*http://www.w3.org/TR/DOM-Level-2-Core/core.html#i-Document*).

9.11 Converting Color Values

Problem

You want to convert CSS color values between hex and RGB, or vice versa.

Solution

Load the `dom-style` module and call `Y.Color.toHex()` or `Y.Color.toRGB()`, as shown in Example 9-11.

Example 9-11. Converting color values

```
<!DOCTYPE html>
<title>Converting color values</title>

<div id="demo"></div>

<script src="http://yui.yahooapis.com/3.5.0/build/yui/yui-min.js"></script>
<script>
YUI().use('dom-style', 'node', function (Y) {
    var color = 'fuchsia',
        colorHex = Y.Color.toHex(color),
        colorRGB = Y.Color.toRGB(colorHex);

    Y.one('#demo').setStyle('color', colorRGB)
        .setHTML(color + ' === ' + colorHex + ' === ' + colorRGB);
});
</script>
```

Discussion

The `dom-style` module provides some of `Y.DOM`'s utility methods. `Y.Color` is buried inside `Y.DOM`—obscure, but simple and useful.

9.12 Managing History and the Back Button

Problem

You want to enable users to navigate your web application using the Back button.

Solution

Load the `history` module, which can add new entries to browser history that correspond to different states of your application. This module wraps the native `pushState` API. For browsers that don't support this API natively, the YUI `history` module falls back to a "hash"-based history technique.

Example 9-12 represents a control panel where the user can enable or disable an alarm of some kind. The example instantiates a `HistoryHash` object, which stores state using hash URLs. Hash URLs are brittle, but they work in old browsers and don't require any special support on the server side.

The example includes two event listeners. The first listener acts when the user selects a radio button, calling `addValue()` to create an entry in the browser history *and* store some metadata along with that history entry.

The second listener acts on the `history:change` event, which fires when the user selects a radio button (because `history.addValue()` was called) and when the user clicks the Back or Forward button, or otherwise changes the URL in the location bar. To avoid doing unnecessary DOM manipulation, the event listener checks whether a) the `history:change` event came from the user changing the URL in the location bar, and b) the `history:change` event represents a change to the alarm status.

The `addAlarm()` function is responsible for extracting the page's current state from the browser history and syncing the page's appearance accordingly. If the state is valid, `addAlarm()` sets the radio buttons; otherwise, it restores both radio buttons to their pristine, unchecked state. The page calls `addAlarm()` on page load to sync the page with the initial URL, and later on in response to (some) `history:change` events.

Example 9-12. Using hash history to store interstitial state

```
<!DOCTYPE html>
<title>Alarm Control</title>

<form id="demo">
    <p>Alarm:
        <label><input type="radio" name="alarm" value="enabled"> Enabled</label>
        <label><input type="radio" name="alarm" value="disabled"> Disabled</label>
    </p>
</form>

<script src="http://yui.yahooapis.com/3.5.0/build/yui/yui-min.js"></script>
```

```
<script>
YUI().use('history', 'node', function (Y) {
    var history = new Y.HistoryHash();

    function setAlarm() {
        var alarm = history.get('alarm');
        if (alarm === 'enabled' || alarm === 'disabled') {
            Y.one('input[value=' + alarm + ']').set('checked', true);
        }
        else {
            Y.all('input[type=radio]').set('checked', false);
        }
    }

    Y.one('#demo').on('change', function (ev) {
        history.addValue('alarm', ev.target.get('value'));
    });

    Y.on('history:change', function (ev) {
        if (ev.src === Y.HistoryHash.SRC_HASH && ev.changed.alarm) {
            setAlarm();
        }
    });

    setAlarm();
});
</script>
```

Example 9-13 is a variation that attempts to simulate real URLs instead of storing state in hash parameters. The differences include:

- The example instantiates a History instance, rather than a HistoryHash instance. History is a superset of HistoryHash—it causes YUI to use the advanced HTML History API in browsers that support this API, and fall back to using hash URLs otherwise.

- The history:change listener checks whether the event came from an HTML History popstate event.

- addValue() supplies a third parameter, a configuration object that contains a url property. If the browser supports the HTML History API, this sets the URL in the browser's location bar, creating the illusion that this particular application state is backed by a physical file. In less capable browsers, YUI ignores the url parameter and generates a hash-based URL.

Thus, in browsers that support HTML History, Example 9-13 generates "pages" of the form *http://localhost/enabled.html* and *http://localhost/disabled.html*. These "pages" are actually just states in a JavaScript application, not physical files. However, they behave a lot like physical files: Back/Forward navigation works, and in browsers that support HTML History, the location bar even displays a "pretty" URL for each state.

This example should be served from a real web server, not the local filesystem.

Example 9-13. Using HTML History to simulate real URLs

```
YUI().use('history', 'node', function (Y) {
    var history = new Y.History();

    function setAlarm() {
        var alarm = history.get('alarm');
        if (alarm === 'enabled' || alarm === 'disabled') {
            Y.one('input[value=' + alarm + ']').set('checked', true);
        }
        else {
            Y.all('input[type=radio]').set('checked', false);
        }
    }

    Y.one('#demo').on('change', function (ev) {
        var alarm = ev.target.get('value')
        history.addValue('alarm', alarm, { url: alarm + '.html' });
    });

    Y.on('history:change', function (ev) {
        if (ev.src === Y.HistoryHTML5.SRC_POPSTATE && ev.changed.alarm) {
            setAlarm();
        }
    });

    setAlarm();
});
```

Discussion

The simplest model of a web server is that each URL corresponds to a single physical file in a directory. Server-side logic breaks this model; a single endpoint can handle many types of requests, and might be distributed across many different physical or virtual servers. Nevertheless, well-designed server-side applications go to great lengths to hide this internal complexity and present clean, bookmarkable URLs.

Any sufficiently complex client-side application faces a similar problem. In a web application, a link click or other user action might represent some internal client-side state in a JavaScript application. So how do you map JavaScript application states to user-friendly URLs?

This is the problem that the HTML History API attempts to solve. The basic idea is:

1. A user clicks a link or takes some other action that results in a nontrivial state change.

2. Your application responds with an API call to create a new browser history entry, with a unique URL and title.

3. That same API call enables you to store metadata with that browser history entry.

4. When history changes for any reason, such as a user clicking a link or the Back button, you retrieve that history entry's stored metadata and use it to reconstruct the state of the application.

   This last step is critical. Both Examples 9-12 and 9-13 are careful to update the application's appearance *in response to* history:change events. A common pitfall when working with HTML History is to do this backward, changing the application's appearance and *then* adding a history entry. This leads to horrible state inconsistencies. Reacting to history change events helps ensure consistency regardless of the origin of the change.

HTML History enables you to write responsive web applications without losing the benefits of having clean URLs. You can fetch and repaint just the part of the page that needs to change, and still provide users with the URL behavior that they expect.

While the preceding examples store only a single string key/value pair, HTML History enables you to store arbitrary objects with each history entry. Generally, it is best to store just the data you need to reconstruct the application's state, not the entire state itself. If you need to store a lot of state information, consider caching this information in localStorage and using the History metadata as a pointer into that cache.

Setting the URL is nifty, but has some limitations. For security reasons, you can set only URLs that have the same origin as your web server. Also, generating URLs on the client is a lot less useful unless you have at least *some* server-side logic to support these URLs. Without routing support from the server, sharing the link *http://example.com/ enabled.html* with someone else would result in a 404.

For browsers that lack true HTML History support, History resorts to a hash-based technique. Each time you create a history entry and set some metadata, YUI stores that metadata in the URL as simple string key/value pairs, as in #alarm=enabled. Keep in mind that since browsers never pass hash parameters to the web server, hash-based URLs are extremely difficult to handle with server-side logic, which in turn leads to many other problems. To force YUI to always use one technique or the other, instantiate a HistoryHTML5 object or a HistoryHash object (as shown in Example 9-12) instead of a History object.

Alongside the url parameter, HTML History also supports setting a title parameter. Unfortunately, this parameter is a bit troubled. The HTML History specification distinguishes between a *history entry title* (a string that appears in the browser's History menu) and a *document title* (a string that appears in the browser title bar, derived from the familiar <title> element). In theory, setting the title parameter means setting the former, but not necessarily the latter. In reality, all browsers silently ignore the title parameter. If you want to set the document title, you should probably do it manually by calling Y.one('title').set('text', *text*).

See Also

Recipe 7.17; Recipe 7.18; the YUI History User Guide (*http://yuilibrary.com/yui/docs/history/*); Best Practices for History and Hash-based URLs (*http://yuilibrary.com/yui/docs/router/index.html#best-practices*); the HTML History specification (*http://www.whatwg.org/specs/web-apps/current-work/multipage/history.html*).

9.13 Escaping User Input

Problem

You want to allow users to enter strings that will be reflected on your pages, but you don't want to allow them to hijack your site by inserting arbitrary markup.

Solution

Load the escape module and call Y.Escape.html() to escape dangerous characters, as shown in Example 9-14. Y.Escape.html() escapes HTML characters, replacing them with harmless character entities. (This is conceptually a bit different from a sanitizer, which would remove unsafe HTML completely.)

Example 9-14. Sanitizing user input

```
<!DOCTYPE html>
<title>Sanitizing user input</title>

<form id="demo">
    <label for="text">Type something:</label>
    <input type="text" id="text" value="<marquee>OH NO!</marquee>">
    <input type="submit">
</form>

<script src="http://yui.yahooapis.com/3.5.0/build/yui/yui-min.js"></script>
<script>
YUI().use('escape', 'node-base', function (Y) {

    Y.one('#demo').on('submit', function (ev) {
        var raw = Y.one('#text').get('value'),
            sanitized = Y.Escape.html(raw);

        Y.one('body').append(sanitized);
        ev.preventDefault();
    });
});
</script>
```

Discussion

Without escaping, it is possible to do much more horrific things to your site than inserting a `<marquee>` (as hard as that might be to believe). An attacker that succeeds in inserting a `<script>` element can control the appearance and behavior of the page, steal credentials and other secrets, and much more. This form of attack is called *cross-site scripting* (XSS).

While many developers are aware of the dangers of XSS attacks, it is easy to underestimate the dangers of *self-XSS*—a transient JavaScript injection that affects only the user who performed the injection. Some developers dismiss self-XSS as a nonissue because there's no harm in a user executing JavaScript on his own machine, but this overlooks the possibility of phishing attacks. If a phisher can convince a user to paste something into a web page, or click something, or navigate to a URL, or do something else that executes local JavaScript in his browser, then the phisher can exploit the user's personal information or carry out actions on his behalf. This means you must not only escape user input that you plan to store and redisplay later, but also any input that will only be redisplayed locally to the same user who entered it.

`Y.Escape.html()` escapes strings according to the recommendations of the Open Web Application Security Project (OWASP). There is also a `Y.Escape.regex()` method for escaping strings intended for use in a regular expression.

See Also

Escape API documentation (*http://yuilibrary.com/yui/docs/api/classes/Escape.html*); OWASP's XSS Prevention Cheat Sheet (*https://www.owasp.org/index.php/XSS_%28Cross_Site_Scripting%29_Prevention_Cheat_Sheet*).

9.14 Assigning Special Behavior to a Checkbox Group

Problem

You want to create a "select all" checkbox that toggles the state of a group of other checkboxes.

Solution

Load the `gallery-checkboxgroups` module from the gallery. This module enables you to define a group of checkboxes and apply a function to control the state of the group. It includes several predefined classes, including `SelectAllCheckboxGroup`. See Example 9-15.

Example 9-15. Implementing a "select all" checkbox group

```
<!DOCTYPE html>
<title>Implementing a "select all" checkbox group</title>

<p>Yes! Please send me valuable and informative marketing information by:</p>
<form>
    <p><label><input type="checkbox" class="mkting" name="em"> Email</label></p>
    <p><label><input type="checkbox" class="mkting" name="sm"> Snail Mail</label></p>
    <p><label><input type="checkbox" class="mkting" name="tw"> Tweet</label></p>
    <p><label><input type="checkbox" class="mkting" name="cp"> Carrier Pigeon</label></p>
    <p><label><input type="checkbox" id="all" name="all"> I want it all, baby!</label></p>
</form>

<script src="http://yui.yahooapis.com/3.5.0/build/yui/yui-min.js"></script>
<script>
YUI().use('gallery-checkboxgroups', function (Y) {
    new Y.SelectAllCheckboxGroup('#all', '.mkting');
});
</script>
```

In Example 9-15, just instantiating a new `SelectAllCheckboxGroup` is enough to define the checkbox group. The constructor takes two parameters: a CSS selector for a single checkbox to act as the "select all" checkbox, and a CSS selector for the group of checkboxes that is under control. Deselecting the "select all" checkbox deselects all other checkboxes, and selecting or deselecting other checkboxes updates the "select all" checkbox, as you might expect.

Three other predefined constraints exist. For example, to apply the constraint that at least one checkbox must be selected, use `AtLeastOneCheckboxGroup`:

```
YUI().use('gallery-checkboxgroups', function (Y) {
    new Y.AtLeastOneCheckboxGroup('.mkting');
});
```

The module also includes `EnableIfAnyCheckboxGroup`, which enables some other group of form fields in response to the user selecting one of the checkboxes, and `AtMostOne CheckboxGroup`, which allows zero or one checkboxes to be selected (in contrast to a radio button group, which requires exactly one option to be selected).

Discussion

Checkbox groups are just a user interface nicety. They cannot stop a truly determined user from submitting the form with an "illegal" set of checkboxes checked, so be sure to validate all user input on the server side.

To create a custom checkbox group, extend the base `CheckboxGroup` class and implement the `enforceConstraints()` function. YUI calls this function every time the user selects or deselects a checkbox, passing in two parameters: an array of YUI `Nodes` representing all checkboxes in the group, and the integer index of the checkbox that changed state.

For example, the `AnnoyingCheckboxGroup` class in Example 9-16 implements an `enforceConstraints()` function that responds to state changes by randomly changing the state of all checkboxes in the group.

Example 9-16. Implementing a custom checkbox group

```
<!DOCTYPE html>
<title>Implementing a custom checkbox group</title>

<p>Yes! Please send me valuable and informative marketing information by:</p>
<form>
    <p><label><input type="checkbox" class="mkting" name="em"> Email</label></p>
    <p><label><input type="checkbox" class="mkting" name="sm"> Snail Mail</label></p>
    <p><label><input type="checkbox" class="mkting" name="tw"> Tweet</label></p>
    <p><label><input type="checkbox" class="mkting" name="cp"> Carrier Pigeon</label></p>
</form>

<script src="http://yui.yahooapis.com/3.5.0/build/yui/yui-min.js"></script>
<script>
YUI().use('gallery-checkboxgroups', function (Y) {
    function AnnoyingCheckboxGroup(checkboxes) {
        AnnoyingCheckboxGroup.superclass.constructor.call(this, checkboxes);
    }

    Y.extend(AnnoyingCheckboxGroup, Y.CheckboxGroup, {
        enforceConstraints: function (checkboxes, index) {
            Y.each(checkboxes, function (checkbox) {
                var state = Math.random() > 0.5;
                checkbox.set('checked', state);
            });
        }
    });

    new AnnoyingCheckboxGroup('.mkting');
});
</script>
```

 As an experienced JavaScript developer, you are responsible for always using your powers for good, not evil.

See Also

John Lindal's `gallery-checkboxgroups` module (*http://yuilibrary.com/gallery/show/ checkboxgroups*); "In the YUI 3 Gallery: Checkbox Group Behaviors" (*http://www.yui blog.com/blog/2010/03/01/gallery-checkbox-group/*); YUI 3 Checkbox Groups Examples (*http://jafl.github.com/yui3-gallery/checkboxgroups/*); Checkbox Groups API documentation (*http://jafl.github.com/yui3-gallery/yuidoc/module_gallery-checkboxgroups .html*).

9.15 Implementing Easy Keyboard Actions and Navigation

Problem

You want to enable the user to dismiss an overlay by pressing Escape.

Solution

Load the `gallery-event-nav-keys` module and listen for a synthetic DOM event named `esc`. If the user presses Escape, hide the overlay. See Example 9-17.

Example 9-17. Dismissing an overlay with Escape

```
<!DOCTYPE html>
<title>Dismissing an overlay with Escape</title>

<style>
.yui3-overlay {
    position: absolute; width: 200px; padding: 5px;
    color: #ddd; background: #a00; box-shadow: 3px 3px 2px #600;
}
</style>

<script src="http://yui.yahooapis.com/3.5.0/build/yui/yui-min.js"></script>
<script>
YUI().use('gallery-event-nav-keys', 'overlay', function (Y) {
    var overlay = new Y.Overlay({
        bodyContent: 'Press ESC to dismiss me',
        xy: [30, 30]
    });

    Y.on('esc', function (ev) {
        overlay.hide();
    });

    overlay.render();
});
</script>
```

The complete list of supported key events is: `backspace`, `down`, `enter`, `esc`, `left`, `page Down`, `pageUp`, `tab`, `right`, and `up`.

Discussion

The `gallery-event-nav-keys` module is tiny, but provides useful semantics for keyboard navigation support. It is nicer to work with keystrokes as events with names like `esc` and `pageDown` than it is to capture `keydown` events and inspect the `keyCode`.

For the particular use case of dismissing widgets using Escape, an alternative approach would be to mix in the `WidgetAutohide` extension, discussed in Recipe 8.5. It depends on your purpose; `WidgetAutohide` is focused on hiding widgets, while `gallery-event-nav-keys` is a simple and lightweight way to support navigation keys in general.

See Also

Recipe 4.11; Luke Smith's `gallery-event-nav-keys` (*http://yuilibrary.com/gallery/show/event-nav-keys*), `gallery-event-arrow` (*http://yuilibrary.com/gallery/show/event-arrow*), and `gallery-event-konami` (*http://yuilibrary.com/gallery/show/event-konami*) modules.

9.16 Reliably Detecting Input Field Changes

Problem

You want to be notified immediately when the user types or pastes anything in a text input field or textarea, even if she is still typing and the DOM `change` event hasn't fired yet.

Alternatively, you want a more reliable way to detect special multistroke characters generated by an *input method editor* (IME), which DOM events handle poorly.

Solution

Load the `event-valuechange` module, then subscribe to the synthetic `valueChange` event on the node you want to monitor for changes:

```
<!DOCTYPE html>
<title>Reliably Detecting Input Field Changes</title>

<form><input type="text" id="demo"></form>

<script src="http://yui.yahooapis.com/3.5.0/build/yui/yui-min.js"></script>
<script>
YUI().use('event-valuechange', function (Y) {
    Y.one('#demo').on('valueChange', function (ev) {
        Y.log('previously: ' + ev.prevVal + '; now: ' + ev.newVal);
    });
});
</script>
```

Discussion

Browsers provide a variety of events to capture changes to input fields, but each event has serious flaws:

- The `change` event fires only after the input field loses focus, making it unsuitable for capturing changes as the user types.

- Keyboard events like `keydown`, `keyup`, and `keypress` do fire for keyboard input, but they fail to capture changes made by other means, such as a mouse-initiated paste. Keyboard events are also inconsistent around IMEs and languages that require multiple keystrokes to create a single character.
- Recent versions of Firefox, Safari, Chrome, and Opera support an `input` event that handles both keyboard-triggered input and input via other means like pasting. However, `input` still behaves inconsistently with IMEs and multistroke characters, and it lacks support in Internet Explorer.

YUI's synthetic `valueChange` event solves all of these problems by polling for changes when a user is actively typing or pasting into an input field or textarea, and by using smart sliding timeouts to provide full support for IME input. This event was originally developed to support the `AutoComplete` widget, but is a useful generic component in its own right.

 `valueChange` polls only while the element is focused. It does not catch value changes at other times.

See Also

Recipe 4.11; Recipe 8.17; background on input method editors (*http://en.wikipedia.org/wiki/Input_method*).

9.17 Managing and Validating Forms

Problem

You want a general approach for validating form data on the client side and informing the user about errors.

Solution

Load the `gallery-formmgr` module and create a `FormManager` object. Form Manager can help manage almost all aspects of a form's lifecycle, such as manipulating field states, displaying error messages, and validation.

Example 9-18 assigns two form fields the CSS classes `yiv-required` and `yiv-integer: [0,130]`. These classes flag the fields for validation by Form Manager. On form submission, the event handler validates each field's value and automatically displays any error messages next to each field. If any errors occur, the event handler prevents the form's default action, enabling the user to correct the errors before trying again.

Example 9-18. Validating forms

```
<!DOCTYPE html>
<title>Validating forms</title>
<style>
.formmgr-status-failure { font-weight: bold; color: #f00; }
.formmgr-haserror .formmgr-message-text { color: #f00; }
</style>

<p id="form-status"></p>
<form method="get" action="http://yuilibrary.com" name="example_form">
    <p>
        <label for="username">Username</label>
        <input type="text" id="username" class="yiv-required">
    </p>
    <p>
        <label for="age">Age</label>
        <input type="text" id="age" class="yiv-required yiv-integer:[0,130]">
    </p>
    <p><input type="submit" value="Submit Form"></p>
</form>

<script src="http://yui.yahooapis.com/3.5.0/build/yui/yui-min.js"></script>
<script>
YUI().use('gallery-formmgr', function (Y) {
    var form = new Y.FormManager('example_form', {
        status_node: '#form-status'
    });

    Y.all('form p').addClass('formmgr-row')
    Y.all('input').insert('<span class="formmgr-message-text"/>', 'after');

    form.prepareForm();

    Y.one('form').on('submit', function (ev){
        form.validateForm();
        if (form.hasErrors()) {
            ev.preventDefault();
        };
    });
});
</script>
```

Discussion

Much of Form Manager's functionality relies on strong conventions around CSS class names. Each field (or closely related group of fields) must reside in a container with the class formmgr-row, and each field should have a corresponding element with a formmgr-message-text class to hold error messages and other notifications. Form Manager does not attempt to "guess" at the structure of your form, so you must create this markup yourself to help Form Manager out. You can embed this information in the static markup, but since these classes are just hooks for JavaScript anyway, you should feel free to add them with Y.all() if that seems like a cleaner option.

Form Manager uses CSS classes to stamp a field for validation. The prebuilt validators provide canned logic and default error message strings for when validation fails. There are four CSS-based validators: `yiv-required` for required fields, and `yiv-length:[x,y]`, `yiv-integer:[x,y]`, and `yiv-decimal:[x,y]` to require a range of string lengths, integer values, and decimal values, respectively.

For other validation types, you must drop down into JavaScript. Form Manager provides a compact `setRegex()` method for assigning a regular expression validator to a field. Beyond that, the `setFunction()` method enables you to set arbitrary validator logic on a field. There is also a `postValidateForm()` hook that gets called at the end of `validateForm()`, which enables you to run validation logic across multiple fields (such as requiring the user to at least provide an email address *or* a phone number).

 It should go without saying that client-side JavaScript validation is strictly a user interface enhancement, something that the user can easily disable or subvert. Always validate data on the server side.

This recipe only scratches the surface of what Form Manager can do. You can use it to inject arbitrary messages all over the form, enable and disable fields, and control form defaults. For more information, refer to Form Manager's documentation.

See Also

John Lindal's `gallery-formmgr` module (*http://yuilibrary.com/gallery/show/formmgr*); "In the YUI 3 Gallery: John Lindal's Form Manager" (*http://www.yuiblog.com/blog/2010/03/23/gallery-form-manager/*); Form Manager API documentation (*http://jafl.github.com/yui3-gallery/yuidoc/module_gallery-formmgr.html*); Greg Hinch's `gallery-form` module (*http://yuilibrary.com/gallery/show/form*), which sets validators and can generate form fields from simple data objects; Greg Hinch's blog post, "The YUI 3 Form Module—Forms and Validation Made Simple" (*http://www.yuiblog.com/blog/2009/12/03/yui-3-gallery-form-module/*); Murray Macchio's `gallery-formvalidator` module (*http://yuilibrary.com/gallery/show/formvalidator*), which is designed to support dynamic inline form validation (*http://www.alistapart.com/articles/inline-validation-in-web-forms/*).

Server-Side YUI

For many frontend engineers, running JavaScript on the server is an attractive notion. Wouldn't it be nice if you didn't have to write reams of code in JavaScript on the client, and then have to write much of that logic *again* in some other language for the server?

The good news for those engineers is that in recent years, the practice of writing server-side JavaScript has started to cross over into the mainstream. Clearly it hasn't become mainstream yet, as we still have to constantly say "server-side JavaScript" instead of just "JavaScript." Nevertheless, the server offers us the opportunity to write some really interesting JavaScript applications. And as a framework designed to tame JavaScript applications, it should be no surprise that YUI has focused on the server as one of its primary environments.

The specific server-side environment YUI targets is the popular Node.js framework. In a nutshell, Node.js is a JavaScript platform built on top of the V8 JavaScript runtime, with libraries for HTTP and other types of I/O. Just like a browser, Node.js runs in an event loop. And just like the browser, the primary way to pass messages and perform other I/O interactions in Node.js is to set listeners and respond asynchronously with callback functions. For many longtime backend engineers, writing asynchronous code in an event loop feels deeply weird. But for frontend engineers, this model is strikingly familiar.

The main advantage of the event loop is that it provides a straightforward way for ordinary mortals to write code that can handle a massive number of I/O operations. This is not to say that event loops are necessarily *the* one true way to write high-throughput apps, but they do the job and are relatively easy to reason about. That is, if you're a JavaScript programmer. Which you are. Yay!

Of course, event loops also bring many of the disadvantages of programming in the browser. If you make the mistake of performing an expensive computation in the browser, you can freeze the browser's UI thread. If you make the mistake of performing an expensive computation in Node.js, you can freeze your entire website. Like any technology, Node.js involves tradeoffs.

Besides I/O performance, another nice thing about Node.js is that you don't need to support an entire landscape of JavaScript engines with all their myriad inconsistencies and bugs. There's just one engine to target, and you control what that engine is and possibly even the hardware that the engine runs on. What a breath of fresh air! But that raises the question: if your favorite library was originally designed to correct for DOM, event, and Ajax bugs in browsers, what good is it going to do for you on the server?

Fortunately, YUI offers a lot more than simple page effects and browser corrections. For server-side applications, YUI provides all sorts of goodies, including:

- The powerful `Base` API and YUI custom event system for building decoupled components
- The App Framework for further structuring complex applications
- Object, array, and language utilities that go well beyond what ECMAScript standards provide
- A flexible module system that works perfectly well on the server, enabling you to select exactly what you need from an enormous library of existing code
- A suite of tools for building, deploying, testing, and documenting professional-quality programs

This chapter provides everything you need to get up and running with YUI in a Node.js environment.

Recipe 10.1 explains how to install and run YUI on Node.js using the familiar `YUI().use()` sandbox pattern.

Recipe 10.2 introduces the `useSync()` method, which enables you to load YUI modules synchronously alongside regular Node.js modules.

Recipe 10.3 demonstrates building a simple command-line tool, reusing a YUI `Base` object from Chapter 7. The example also shows how to load a custom YUI module from a separate file.

Recipe 10.4 shows how to make YQL calls on the server side.

Recipe 10.5 introduces the YUI REPL, a command-line tool for exploring JavaScript libraries, poking at web APIs, and doing rapid prototyping.

Finally, Recipe 10.6 demonstrates how to use YQL and Handlebars.js to build up a page with YUI and then send the results out over HTTP.

10.1 Installing and Running YUI on the Server

Problem

You want to use YUI to build a server-side component or a command-line tool.

Solution

Install the Node.js/npm/YUI 3 stack and test your work by running a simple script on the command line:

1. Install Node.js as a package according to the instructions on the Node.js wiki (*https://github.com/joyent/node/wiki/Installing-Node.js-via-package-manager*). If a suitable package is not available for your system, you can download a prepackaged binary for your platform (*http://nodejs.org/#download*) or install and build Node.js from source (*https://github.com/joyent/node/wiki/Installation*).

2. If necessary, install npm using the same package management system you used in the previous step. By default, Node.js 0.6.3 and above includes npm. However, some package maintainers prefer to maintain Node.js and npm as separate packages.

3. Enter a working directory and use npm to install the yui package:

   ```
   $ npm install yui
   ```

4. In the same directory, write the YUI script shown in Example 10-1 and save it as *nodejs_yui.js*.

   Example 10-1. A trivial server-side YUI script

   ```
   var YUI = require('yui').YUI;

   YUI().use('substitute', function (Y) {
       Y.log(Y.substitute('Hi! You are using YUI {version}.', YUI));
   });
   ```

5. Verify that the script is working:

   ```
   $ node nodejs_yui.js
   info: Hi! You are using YUI 3.5.0.
   ```

Discussion

The remarkable thing about Example 10-1 is that aside from the first line, it is identical to code you would run in the browser. The YUI module system runs unchanged: the same sandbox pattern and the same YUI().use() semantics all work on the server side.

Of course, on the server side, there's no such thing as the <script> element. Instead, you load libraries with a call to require(), a method defined in the CommonJS 1.1 module standard, Node.js's native module format. Since YUI modules predate CommonJS modules, the two formats have different semantics. However, it is still possible to load YUI modules in a way that looks a little more "Node-ish," as illustrated in Recipe 10.2.

YUI actually offers several npm packages. The main package to install is yui, which includes all of core YUI. Note that to activate YUI's DOM capabilities, you must install a server-side DOM implementation. For more information, refer to the Discussion in Recipe 10.6.

See Also

The `nodejs-yui3` project (*https://github.com/yui/nodejs-yui3*); the `yui3` npm package (*http://search.npmjs.org/#/yui3*); the `yui3-gallery` npm package (*http://search.npmjs.org/#/yui3-gallery*).

10.2 Loading Modules Synchronously on the Server

Problem

You want to attach YUI modules to the Y object synchronously at the top of your script, in much the same way that CommonJS modules work.

Solution

Set Y equal to the return value of `require('yui/module-name')` and then run your code directly without bothering to set up a `YUI().use()` sandbox.

Example 10-2 requires the `os` Node.js core module and the `substitute` YUI module, then uses them together to display information about your system's hardware.

Example 10-2. Loading a server-side YUI module with require()

```
var os = require('os'),
    Y  = require('yui/substitute');

Y.Array.each(os.cpus(), function (cpu) {
    Y.log(Y.substitute('CPU: {model} @ {speed} MHz', cpu));
});
```

To use more than one YUI module, you have two options. The first option is to simply call `require()` multiple times for the same Y instance. The results are cumulative (in other words, the final Y has all modules and their dependencies attached):

```
var Y = require('yui/substitute');
Y = require('yui/array-extras');
Y = require('yui/base-build');
```

Alternatively, you can load multiple modules as a batch by calling `require('yui').use()`:

```
var Y = require('yui').use('substitute', 'array-extras', 'base-build');
```

Discussion

As shown in Recipe 10.1, on Node.js you can continue to use the standard YUI pattern of loading modules asynchronously into a sandbox. However, server-side YUI also supports the more common server-side pattern of loading modules synchronously at the top of the script using `require()`.

If you need to pass a YUI configuration into YUI(), you can break loading into two steps. First, get a reference to the main YUI object by calling require('yui').YUI. Then call YUI().use() and pass in a useSync: true parameter. This parameter instructs YUI to load modules synchronously so that you can exercise the returned Y instance directly. Example 10-3 illustrates this pattern.

Example 10-3. Breaking loading into two steps with useSync

```
var os  = require('os'),
    YUI = require('yui').YUI,
    Y   = YUI({ useSync: true }).use('substitute');

Y.Array.each(os.cpus(), function (cpu) {
    Y.log(Y.substitute('CPU: {model} @ {speed} MHz', cpu));
});
```

Lines 2 and 3 in Example 10-3 are functionally equivalent to calling:

```
    var Y = require('yui').use('substitute');
```

The advantage of the useSync: true pattern is that it enables you to pass in additional YUI configuration. For example, this would enable you to squash Y.log() output by setting debug: false. The most important reason to use this pattern is of course providing YUI with metadata for custom YUI modules. For an example, refer to Recipe 10.3.

See Also

YUI on Node.js (*http://yuilibrary.com/yui/docs/yui/nodejs.html*); Node.js module documentation (*http://nodejs.org/docs/latest/api/modules.html*); Node.js os module API documentation (*http://nodejs.org/docs/latest/api/os.html*).

10.3 Using YUI on the Command Line

Problem

You want to write a command-line tool using YUI.

Solution

Load whichever modules you need from YUI, Node.js core, and elsewhere using require(). The useSync: true pattern discussed in Recipe 10.2 will enable you to supply your own metadata for custom YUI modules. Use process.argv to handle command-line arguments.

Example 10-4 illustrates a command-line tool named *cyclotron.js* that loads a custom electron module from a separate file, instantiates an Electron object, and prints its values. The electron module is an exact copy of the module shown in Recipe 7.3, saved to a file, *electron.js*.

When the user runs the command, he may pass in an optional -e or --energy option to supply a different energy value for the electron. Argument parsing is simplistic, slicing off the first two arguments ('node' and 'cyclotron.js') and then looping over any remaining parameters, using a switch statement to handle different cases. If any unknown options are detected, the tool prints a help statement and exits.

Example 10-4. Command-line tool that uses YUI Base

cyclotron.js: A command-line tool for generating electrons at different energies. Notice that for fullpath, Example 10-4 uses the Node.js variable __dirname to specify the base path to the module. In Node.js, the path is relative to the *node_modules* directory where the yui package is installed, so a naive path of './electron.js' would fail.

```
#!/usr/bin/env node

var YUI  = require('yui').YUI,
    Y = YUI({
        useSync: true,
        modules: {
            'electron': {
                fullpath: __dirname + '/electron.js',
                requires: ['base']
            }
        }
    }).use('electron');

var argv = process.argv.slice(2),
    arg,
    help = 'cyclotron.js -- Because outside CERN, we make our own fun.\n'
        + '  Usage: cyclotron.js [--energy <energy in MeV>]\n\n',
    electron,
    opts = {};

while(arg = argv.shift()) {
    switch(arg) {
        case '--energy':
        case '-e':
            opts.energy = argv.shift();
            break;

        default:
            Y.log('Unrecognized parameter: ' + arg, 'error');
            process.stdout.write(help);
            process.exit(1);
    }
}

electron = new Y.Electron(opts);
Y.log('Charge: ' + electron.get('charge'));
Y.log('Energy: ' + electron.get('energy') + ' MeV');
Y.log(' Speed: ' + electron.getSpeed().toPrecision(5) + ' c');
```

electron.js: The core of the `Electron` object, also seen in Recipe 7.3 and several other recipes.

```
YUI.add('electron', function (Y) {
    var REST_ENERGY = 511.00;

    Y.Electron = Y.Base.create('electron', Y.Base, [], {
        initializer: function () {
            Y.log("SMASH! Here's your electron!");
        },
        getSpeed: function () {
            var e_ratio = REST_ENERGY / this.get('energy');
            return Math.sqrt(1 - e_ratio * e_ratio);
        }
    }, {
        ATTRS: {
            charge: {
                value: -1,
                readOnly: true
            },
            energy: {
                value: REST_ENERGY,
                validator: function (en) {
                    return (en >= REST_ENERGY);
                }
            }
        }
    });
}, '1.0', { requires: ['base-build'] });
```

Executing the command using `node` yields output like:

```
$ node cyclotron.js --energy 792.13
info: SMASH! Here's your electron!
info: Charge: -1
info: Energy: 792.13 MeV
info:   Speed: 0.76410 c
```

If you don't like the `"info:"` prefix and the color coding provided by `Y.log()`, you could substitute in `console.log()` instead.

 Obviously this collision violates conservation of momentum. Presumably this is the fault of a bad detector, a feckless grad student, or (as is so very often the case) both.

Discussion

As Example 10-4 demonstrates, `Base` works beautifully on the server. Getters, setters, validators, and other YUI-isms all operate correctly, without any need for a DOM or a browser. Likewise, you can pull in custom YUI modules by defining your module's metadata for the YUI instances, just as you would in the browser.

While the `Base` API is a fine way to structure your code, for more complex tools, the App Framework might be appropriate. If you have already written an app that has a web GUI, you could potentially reuse the same models and just swap in new views that `render()` strings out to the command line.

If you choose to package a command-line tool as an `npm` module, users might want to install it with the `-g` option. This makes the command generally available on the system, which is presumably what users want when installing a command-line tool.

However, when developing against a library, many engineers prefer to install that library in their working directory (no `-g` option) so that they can build against that local isolated copy of the library. However, you can also use `-g` to install a single global copy of the library, and then use `npm link` to create symlinks from your working directory to the global library. For an explanation of how `npm` installs files on your system, run `npm help folders`.

 The line at the top of the script is a UNIX convenience that, along with running `chmod +x` (or similar), helps make the script directly executable. If you do this, the aforementioned approach of "blindly slicing off the first two args" won't work anymore. Either tweak the logic appropriately, or use a real arguments parser instead of the hokey one shown here.

See Also

Pretty terminal colors with Marak Squires's and Alexis Sellier's `colors.js` module (*https://github.com/Marak/colors.js*); better argument parsing with Isaac Z. Schlueter's `nopt` module (*https://github.com/isaacs/nopt*) or TJ Holowaychuk's `commander.js` module (*https://github.com/visionmedia/commander.js*).

10.4 Calling YQL on the Server

Problem

You want to fetch some data from the Web and manipulate it with YUI.

Solution

Create a `Y` instance with the `yql` module and fetch away. Example 10-5 searches the public Arxiv repository for scientific journals, but you can use any YQL table you like, including the popular HTML and RSS tables for scraping data from arbitrary web pages and feeds.

Example 10-5. Using YQL to search the Arxiv repository

```
var Y = require('yui/yql');

Y.YQL('select * from arxiv.search where search_query="all:electron"', function (r) {
    Y.each(r.query.results.entry, function (article, ix) {
        console.log((ix + 1) + '. ' + article.title);
    });
});
```

Discussion

Node.js provides some strong low-level utilities for working with HTTP and other network protocols. However, if you're looking for a higher-level abstraction for making web requests, YUI's YQL API offers all of the benefits described in Recipe 5.7:

- A standard syntax that helps normalize API calls across diverse systems
- A proxy and caching layer
- The ability to push the work of filtering and other preprocessing out into the YQL cloud

Most important of all, YUI's YQL API is asynchronous. As Node.js evangelists have repeated ad nauseam over the last few years, Node.js is designed as a "fast, nonblocking I/O system." The consequence of this design is that calls to remote data sources must be asynchronous in order to avoid stalling the main Node.js process. If you're looking for a feature-rich web service layer that already fits right into the Node.js I/O paradigm, look no further than YQL.

 Yahoo's server-side framework for Node.js, "Cocktails," uses YQL as *the* unified interface for making all web service calls within the system.

10.5 Using the YUI REPL

Problem

You are a technical recruiter. You want an efficient and practical method for determining whether an engineer is looking to be contacted, so as not to waste your time or the prospective candidate's.

Solution

Install the npm module yui-repl. Then run the yui3 command to enter the YUI 3 REPL (Read-Eval-Print Loop; pronounced "repple"), followed by the .io command to ping the GitHub User API.

Example 10-6 answers the question: is Isaac Z. Schlueter—former YUI core team member, now Node.js core team member, creator of `npm` and many other excellent tools—hireable?

Example 10-6. Hitting the GitHub User API with the YUI REPL

```
$ npm install -g yui-repl
...(snip)...
$ yui3
YUI@3.4.0> .io https://api.github.com/users/isaacs
Making IO Request: https://api.github.com/users/isaacs [done]
 (200 OK): Content-Type: "application/json; charset=utf-8"

{ type: 'User',
  email: '...(snip)...',
  bio: 'I do JavaScript. All the way. I\'m really happy at Joyent. Not gonna leave. Thanks.',
  url: 'https://api.github.com/users/isaacs',
  html_url: 'https://github.com/isaacs',
  created_at: '2008-05-04T19:43:46Z',
  gravatar_id: '73a2b24daecb976af81e010b7a3ce3c6',
  public_gists: 338,
  public_repos: 173,
  login: 'isaacs',
  blog: 'http://blog.izs.me',
  location: 'Oakland CA',
  name: 'Isaac Z. Schlueter',
  company: 'Joyent (and happy here, not looking for jobs, recruiters please do not email me)',
  hireable: false,
  avatar_url: '...(snip)...',
  id: 9287,
  followers: 704,
  following: 11 }

YUI@3.4.0> .exit
$
```

 The JSON output in this example is slightly cleaned up for readability.

Discussion

Many languages and frameworks provide a REPL. REPLs enable you to do simple interactive programming: type an expression, get the results of that expression. They are a great way to:

- Learn how a language or library works
- Inspect an API that you don't quite have memorized yet
- Quickly test and iterate on tiny snippets of code

The default Node.js installation includes a REPL that enables you to evaluate JavaScript expressions and exercise the Node.js API. The REPL also provides a handful of special commands: `.help`, `.break` for breaking out of a process, `.clear` for clearing the local context, and `.exit` for exiting the REPL (as demonstrated in Example 10-7).

Example 10-7. Basic Node.js REPL usage

```
$ node
> status = 'thirsty'
'thirsty'
> 'These pretzels are making me ' + status
'These pretzels are making me thirsty'
> resolve = require('path').resolve
[Function]
> resolve('.')
'/Users/goer/Documents/yui/current'
> .exit
$
```

The YUI REPL has the same functionality as the Node.js REPL, but provides access to the YUI library and adds several new commands that fetch and manipulate remote resources.

Example 10-6 illustrates the `.io` command, which makes an XDR I/O request to the specified URL. If you need the full HTTP headers for a URL, use the `.headers` command.

Example 10-8. Retrieving HTTP headers with the YUI REPL

```
YUI@3.4.0> .headers https://api.github.com/users/isaacs
Making IO Request: https://api.github.com/users/isaacs [done]
 (200 OK): Content-Type: "application/json; charset=utf-8"

{ server: 'nginx/1.0.4',
  date: 'Mon, 07 Nov 2011 17:13:24 GMT',
  'content-type': 'application/json; charset=utf-8',
  connection: 'keep-alive',
  status: '200 OK',
  'x-ratelimit-limit': '5000',
  etag: '"e50d74e5568a0ea1dd775281d02b6e58"',
  'x-ratelimit-remaining': '4973',
  'content-length': '764' }
```

Naturally, there is also a handy shortcut command for YQL calls, `.yql`, as shown in Example 10-9.

Example 10-9. Making a YQL request with the YUI REPL

```
YUI@3.4.0> .yql select astronomy from weather.forecast where location=94086
Making YQL Request: select astronomy from weather.forecast where location=94086 [done]
{ channel: { astronomy: { sunrise: '6:39 am', sunset: '5:04 pm' } } }
```

For inspecting HTML pages, the handy `.import` command fetches a remote document, creates a server-side DOM instance of the document, and loads the object into your REPL's context, all in one step. You can then traverse the document's structure with `Y.one()` and `Y.all()`, or call any other DOM-related method you like, as demonstrated in Example 10-10.

Example 10-10. Inspecting an HTML page with the YUI REPL

```
YUI@3.4.0> .import http://yuilibrary.com/yui/docs/api/classes/Base.html
Resetting Y to the default state [done]
Fetching URL: http://yuilibrary.com/yui/docs/api/classes/Base.html [done]
YUI@3.4.0> Y.all('div.method').size()
51
YUI@3.4.0> Y.all('div.method.inherited').size()
32
YUI@3.4.0> Y.all('#method_addAttr .arg code').getContent()
[ 'name', 'config', 'lazy' ]
```

Finally, as Example 10-11 illustrates, the `.use` command loads a YUI module into the context, enabling you to explore that module's API. You can even instantiate widgets on the server side.

Example 10-11. Instantiating a widget with the YUI REPL

```
YUI@3.4.0> .use calendar
Using modules: calendar [done]
YUI@3.4.0> calendar = new Y.Calendar()
{ _strs: {},
  _cssPrefix: 'yui3-calendar',
  _yuid: 'yui_3_4_0_1_1320681801000_162',
... (snip) ...
_tCfgs: null,
_tVals: null,
_handles: [ [Object] ] } }
YUI@3.4.0> calendar.get('date')
Tue, 01 Nov 2011 19:00:00 GMT
```

If you are unsure how a particular YUI module works, or if you are prototyping code that calls a remote web service, making live calls in the YUI REPL can be a fast and efficient way to feel out what you are trying to do.

10.6 Constructing and Serving a Page with YUI, YQL, and Handlebars

Problem

You want to use YUI to construct an HTML page on the server and serve it up over HTTP.

Solution

Load the Node.js `http` module along with any YUI modules you need to construct the response. Use `http.createServer()` to create an HTTP server to receive HTTP requests and write HTML output back to the client.

Example 10-12 makes a YQL call to fetch weather data and then uses Handlebars.js templating to construct and serve a simple dynamic HTML page on *http://localhost: 8001*. The user can pass in an optional `location` parameter in the query string.

Example 10-12. Constructing and serving a page with YUI, YQL, and Handlebars

```
var Y    = require('yui').use('handlebars', 'yql'),
    http = require('http'),
    parse = require('url').parse;

var templateSrc = '<!doctype html>'
    + '<title>Today\'s Sunrise/Sunset for {{loc.city}}, {{loc.region}}</title>'
    + '<h1>Today\'s Sunrise/Sunset for {{loc.city}}, {{loc.region}}</h1>'
    + '<ul><li>Sunrise: {{astro.sunrise}}</li><li>Sunset: {{astro.sunset}}</li></ul>';

var template = Y.Handlebars.compile(templateSrc);

http.createServer(function (req, res) {
    var query = parse(req.url, true).query,
        location = (query && query.location) || '94086';

    Y.YQL('select * from weather.forecast where location=' + location, function (r) {
        var channel = r.query.results.channel;
        res.writeHead(200, { 'Content-Type': 'text/html' });
        res.write(template({ loc: channel.location, astro: channel.astronomy }));
        res.end();
    });
}).listen(8001);
```

Discussion

Although the `http` module is fun to use, its API is pretty low-level. Unless you are creating a highly tailored server from scratch, it's usually better to use an established web-serving framework built on top of Node.js, such as Express.

For best performance, you should construct strings on the server using string concatenation, `Y.Lang.sub()` templating, or Handlebars.js templating, as shown in the example. Technically speaking, it is possible to use YUI's DOM APIs to construct pages on the server. This is an interesting feature because it not only provides some powerful and familiar methods for manipulating HTML, but it also means you can construct complete widgets and views on the server and serialize them over the wire.

However, to support this functionality, you must provide a server-side DOM implementation for YUI to use. The reason server-side YUI does not ship with a default DOM implementation is because constructing pages with a pure JavaScript DOM is relatively expensive. For an example of how to wire up server-side YUI with Elijah Insua's jsdom project, refer to YUI, Node.js, and the DOM (*http://yuilibrary.com/yui/docs/yui/nodejs-dom.html*).

See Also

The Handlebars.js project (*http://handlebarsjs.com/*); Node.js `http` module API documentation (*http://nodejs.org/docs/latest/api/http.html*); Elijah Insua's `jsdom` project (*https://github.com/tmpvar/jsdom*); Dav Glass's YUIConf talk on using Node.js and YUI 3 (*http://www.youtube.com/watch?v=L3gnGxtjiIY*); Express JS (*http://expressjs.com/*).

Universal Access

The main reason to build a web application in the first place is to make it widely available.

In one sense, "widely available" can mean "cross-platform support." Here, YUI breaks from current fashion—rather than creating a variant "Server Edition" or "Mobile Edition" of the library, YUI leverages its façade APIs and the YUI Loader to abstract away the differences between very different platforms. Whether in an old or new browser, whether in a mobile phone, a tablet, a laptop, or on Node.js, YUI uses the same basic strategies to present a uniform interface:

- Where there are bugs and missing features, YUI silently fills in the gaps and presents the same interface.
- Where necessary, YUI uses conditional loading to deliver exactly the right code to the right device.
- Where there are fundamental platform differences (such as gestures versus mouse actions, or using YUI Loader on the server), YUI provides abstractions that enable you to write cross-platform code.

However, "widely available" means more than just running in different environments. Web applications should be accessible to users who rely on assistive technology such as screenreaders. Web applications should also serve users around the world, reflecting the user's native language, locale, and other preferences.

Unfortunately, YUI can't abstract away differences between English and French the way it can abstract away differences between Firefox on Windows and Safari on iOS. What YUI *can* do is offer some library methods and design patterns that make it easier for your web applications to serve a wider audience.

To aid with internationalization, YUI offers the `lang` configuration variable and the `Y.Intl` object for managing languages and registering translated strings. Using `Y.Intl`, you can bundle translated UI strings with a widget and display those strings according to the `lang` configuration of the YUI instance. Some core YUI widgets ship with translated strings already, so presenting a `Calendar` to a Japanese or Russian audience is as simple as setting `lang` to `jp` or `ru`. Changing `lang` has other effects, such as altering the presentation of date format strings.

In the field of web accessibility, screenreaders are growing ever more powerful. The Accessible Rich Internet Application (ARIA) standard provides new tools to help you build accessible pages and applications. Some of YUI's widgets use ARIA attributes out of the box, and YUI's DOM APIs make it easy to add ARIA attributes to dynamic content.

ARIA attributes augment HTML elements with additional information so that a screenreader can interpret the meaning of that element. If a sighted user looks at a `Slider` widget, she can immediately grasp what the purpose of the widget is and can determine the slider position just by looking. But to a user operating a screenreader, the slider is just a `<span>`. ARIA enables screenreaders to provide a nonvisual interface for complex widgets, to correctly represent the current state of the widget, to ignore markup that is purely for visual display, and more.

Recipe 11.1 explains how to use YUI class hooks to avoid the Flash of Unstyled Content (FOUC), an irritating side effect of using progressive enhancement.

Recipe 11.2 shows how to augment an existing widget with ARIA attributes so that it can be used with a screenreader.

Recipe 11.3 takes the code from Recipe 11.2 and demonstrates how to wrap it up as a reusable plugin.

Recipe 11.4 demonstrates how to use YUI and ARIA to make an accessible form, including handling dynamic error message panes.

Recipe 11.5 introduces the `Y.Intl` utility.

Recipe 11.6 shows how to use `Y.Intl` to internationalize a widget's user interface strings.

11.1 Preventing the Flash of Unstyled Content

Problem

You want to provide better accessibility by using progressive enhancement to construct your widget from markup already on the page, but you want to avoid the dreaded Flash of Unstyled Content (FOUC). The FOUC can occur when a page adds some elements to the DOM, but the CSS meant to style those elements is not present for some reason.

Depending on timing, the browser might briefly display those elements unstyled, then display correctly.

Solution

YUI provides two CSS hooks for avoiding the FOUC:

- As soon as possible, YUI stamps the root `<html>` element with the class `yui3-js-enabled`.
- As a widget `render()` finishes, it removes any classes from the `boundingBox` or `srcNode` that have the name `yui3-widget-loading` or `yui3-`*widgetname*`-loading`.

To use these hooks, first add a class such as `yui3-tabview-loading` to the `srcNode` in the *static* HTML markup, and add a CSS rule like this:

```
.yui3-js-enabled .yui3-tabview-loading { display: none; }
```

If JavaScript is disabled, the root node never gets stamped with `yui3-js-enabled`, so the static source markup is visible. However, if JavaScript is enabled, then YUI quickly stamps the root, making the widget's source markup invisible. At the end of rendering, YUI removes `yui3-tabview-loading`, revealing the fully armed and operational battlesta—er, widget.

Example 11-1 demonstrates using these classes to hide a tabview's source markup until the moment it is ready to be displayed.

Example 11-1. Avoiding the Flash of Unstyled Content

```
<!DOCTYPE html>
<title>Avoiding the Flash of Unstyled Content</title>
<style>
.yui3-js-enabled .yui3-tabview-loading { display: none; }
</style>

<body class="yui3-skin-sam">
<div>header</div>
<div id="demo" class="yui3-tabview-loading">
    <ul>
        <li><a href="#a">A</a></li>
        <li><a href="#b">B</a></li>
    </ul>
    <div>
        <div id="a"><p>This is Tab A.</p></div>
        <div id="b"><p>This is Tab B.</p></div>
    </div>
</div>
<div>footer</div>

<script src="http://yui.yahooapis.com/3.5.0/build/yui/yui-min.js"></script>
<script>
YUI().use('tabview', function (Y) {
    new Y.TabView({ srcNode: '#demo' }).render();
});
```

```
</script>
</body>
```

Discussion

In Example 11-1, placing the YUI seed file at the bottom of the page does mean there is a short period of time when the markup might be visible, just before the YUI seed file loads. If this window of time turns out to be a problem, you don't have to wait for YUI to stamp the root—you can be more aggressive and do it manually by adding a tiny script to the `<head>`, as shown in Example 11-2.

Example 11-2. Really, really avoiding the Flash of Unstyled Content

```
<!DOCTYPE html>
<title>Really, really avoiding the Flash of Unstyled Content</title>
<script>document.documentElement.className = 'yui3-js-enabled';</script>
<style>
.yui3-js-enabled .yui3-tabview-loading { display: none; }
</style>

<body class="yui3-skin-sam">
....
```

As Example 11-2 demonstrates, `yui3-js-enabled` does *not* mean, "no JavaScript is available until this class appears," as any number of other scripts can run before the root gets stamped.

Using `display: none` is a simple option for dealing with the FOUC, but there are a number of variations. These include changing the visibility:

```
.yui3-js-enabled .yui3-tabview-loading { visibility: hidden; }
```

or moving the widget out of the viewport:

```
.yui3-js-enabled .yui3-tabview-loading { top: -10000px; left: -10000px; }
```

or more advanced techniques such as blocking out the region with a grey box or displaying a spinner.

As a general rule, try to avoid addressing the FOUC with additional classes such as `needs-js` or browser-specific hacks. The behavior YUI provides should be enough to solve the problem without watering down semantics further.

Yet another option for avoiding the FOUC is to manually construct the URL for the widget's CSS and pull those resources in using a static `<link>` element in the `<head>` of the document. This technique is fiddly and rather inflexible, but it does guarantee that the widget CSS will be present as early as possible. If you do this, you should configure the Loader with `fetchCSS: false`, so that YUI doesn't fetch the same stylesheets again dynamically.

See Also

A detailed technical explanation of the FOUC concept (*http://www.webkit.org/blog/66/the-fouc-problem/*).

11.2 Adding ARIA to Form Error Messages

Problem

You want to dynamically display error messages when a form field fails validation, but in a way that enables screenreaders to associate the error with the right field.

Solution

When you display the error message, add the following two ARIA attributes to the `<input>` field that failed:

- `aria-invalid="true"`, indicating that the result is invalid
- `aria-describedby="errorId"`, where *errorId* is the `id` of the element containing the error message

When the user clears the error and you remove or hide the error message, be sure to also remove the ARIA attributes you added previously.

Example 11-3 shows how to manage accessible error messages for a single form input. Notice that the example applies CSS to the `aria-invalid` state. ARIA attributes have semantic meaning, and there's no reason not to reuse them for sighted users as well.

Example 11-3. Adding ARIA-enabled form error messages

```
<!DOCTYPE html>
<title>Adding ARIA-enabled form error messages</title>
<style>
input[aria-invalid="true"] { border: 1px solid red; }
form p { padding: 5px; max-width: 500px; font-weight: bold; }
p.success { background: #cec; color: green; border: 1px solid green; }
p.error   { background: #ecc; color: red;   border: 1px solid red; }
</style>

<form id="quiz">
<label for="capital">What is the capital of California?</label>
<input type="text" name="capital" id="capital" required aria-required="true">
<input type="submit" value="Submit Answer">
</form>

<script src="http://yui.yahooapis.com/3.5.0/build/yui/yui-min.js"></script>
<script>
YUI().use('node-base', function (Y) {
    var quiz  = Y.one('#quiz'),
        input = Y.one('#capital');
```

```
    quiz.on('submit', function (ev) {
        var answer = ev.target.get('capital').get('value');
        ev.preventDefault();
        if (isValid(answer)) {
            showSuccess();
        }
        else {
            showErrorMessage();
        }
    });

    function isValid(answer) {
        return Y.Lang.trim(answer).toLowerCase() === 'sacramento';
    }

    function showErrorMessage() {
        var error = 'Wrong! Maybe you should just look it up on Wikipedia.';

        if (! input.hasAttribute('aria-invalid')) {
            input.setAttribute('aria-invalid', 'true');
            input.setAttribute('aria-describedby', 'err-capital');
            quiz.append('<p id="err-capital" class="error">' + error + '</p>');
        }
    }

    function showSuccess() {
        if (input.hasAttribute('aria-invalid')) {
            input.removeAttribute('aria-invalid');
            input.removeAttribute('aria-describedby');
            Y.one('#err-capital').remove();
        }
        quiz.append('<p class="success">Good job!</p>');
    }
});
</script>
</body>
```

Discussion

Example 11-3 illustrates how you can combine having ARIA attributes in the initial static HTML, and then add or modify ARIA attributes to reflect state changes. Initially, the <input> field has an **aria-required** attribute to indicate that the field is required. When the form is in an error state, the code adds more ARIA attributes; when the form returns to a non-error state, the code removes the error attributes.

In this case, the <input> field does not take an **aria-labelledby** attribute, since it has a <label> attribute already. However, the **aria-describedby** attribute is still useful, as its purpose is not to label the field, but to point to a relevant error message or instruction. In fact, **aria-describedby** can take a list of multiple space-delimited IDs, so it can point to an error message *and* an instruction. For example, the form could start out in this state:

```
<label for="capital">What is the capital of California?</label>
<input type="text" name="capital" id="capital" required aria-required="true"
    aria-describedby="hint-capital">
<p id="hint-capital" class="hint">Hint: Not Los Angeles.</p>
```

If the user makes a mistake, your code would add the error message and additional ARIA attributes:

```
<label for="capital">What is the capital of California?</label>
<input type="text" name="capital" id="capital" required aria-required="true"
    aria-invalid="true" aria-describedby="err-capital hint-capital">
<p id="err-capital" class="error">Wrong! Maybe you should look it up on Wikipedia.</p>
<p id="hint-capital" class="hint">Hint: Not Los Angeles.</p>
```

In this case, the code would need to change the value of the `aria-describedby` attribute, not blow it away.

See Also

Recipe 9.17; Karl Groves's discussion of `<label>` versus `aria-labelledby` versus `aria-describedby` in "Accessible Form Labeling & Instructions" (*http://www.karlgroves.com/2011/10/10/accessible-form-labeling-instructions/*); Ted Drake's recipe for creating dynamic form labels with ARIA (*http://yaccessibilityblog.com/library/dynamic-form-labels-aria.html*); Todd Kloot's "Easy Fixes to Common Accessibility Problems" (*http://yaccessibilityblog.com/library/easy-fixes-to-common-accessibility-problems.html*).

11.3 Building a Widget with ARIA

Problem

You want to build a sophisticated widget that provides ARIA attributes for better accessibility.

Solution

After creating the basic widget, add code to manage ARIA attributes throughout the widget's lifecycle:

1. In the widget's `initializer()`, use `setAttrs()` or `setAttribute()` to add a `role` and any additional `aria-*` attributes the widget requires to describe its initial state. Many ARIA attributes should reside on the widget's bounding box, although certain attributes belong either somewhere inside the widget or on some other element entirely.

2. In the widget's `initializer()`, use `after()` listeners to update ARIA state attributes in response to widget state changes.

3. In the widget's `destructor()`, update or clean up any ARIA attributes that do not reside on or inside the widget itself.

Example 11-4 is an advanced variation of the tooltip example from Example 8-9. The code from Recipe 11.2 is now more formally encapsulated into a YUI widget, and the tooltip now supports keyboard focus and blur events as well as mouseenter and mouse leave. The widget implements two ARIA attributes:

- role="tooltip", which resides on the bounding box and never changes
- aria-describedby="*id*", where *id* is the id of the tooltip, and the attribute itself resides on the element the tooltip is pointing to

To support aria-describedby, the widget defines a describes attribute to point to the node it is currently describing, and sets an after() listener for describesChange events. When the user's mouse enters or leaves an element, or if the user navigates to an element using the keyboard, this updates describes, which in turn updates aria-describedby. If you decide to destroy the tooltip instance, the destructor() uses describes to properly remove aria-describedby from the tooltip's target.

Example 11-4. Creating a tooltip widget with ARIA attributes

```
<!DOCTYPE html>
<title>Creating a tooltip widget with ARIA attributes</title>
<link rel="stylesheet"
    href="http://yui.yahooapis.com/3.5.0/build/cssbutton/cssbutton-min.css">
<style>
.yui3-tooltip {
    background: #ff5; padding: 3px; border: 1px #a92 solid;
    border-radius: 5px; box-shadow: 3px 3px 2px #a92;
    font: 13px lucida grande, verdana, sans-serif;
    position: absolute;
}
.yui3-tooltip-hidden { visibility: hidden; }
</style>

<button class="yui3-button"
    data-tooltip="Send your message. [CTRL+Enter]">Send</button>
<button class="yui3-button"
    data-tooltip="Cancel your message without saving. [CTRL+DEL]">Cancel</button>
<button class="yui3-button"
    data-tooltip="Save your message as a draft. [CTRL+S]">Save</button>

<script src="http://yui.yahooapis.com/3.5.0/build/yui/yui-min.js"></script>
<script>
YUI.add('tooltip', function (Y) {
    Y.Tooltip = Y.Base.create('tooltip', Y.Widget,
        [Y.WidgetPosition, Y.WidgetPositionAlign, Y.WidgetStack], {

        initializer: function () {
            this.get('boundingBox').setAttribute('role', 'tooltip');

            this.handles.enter = Y.delegate('mouseenter', this.associate,
                'body', '*[data-tooltip]', this);
            this.handles.leave = Y.delegate('mouseleave', this.disassociate,
                'body', '*[data-tooltip]', this);
```

```
                 this.handles.focus = Y.delegate('focus', this.associate,
                     'body', '*[data-tooltip]', this);
                 this.handles.blur  = Y.delegate('blur', this.disassociate,
                     'body', '*[data-tooltip]', this);

                 this.after('describesChange', this.toggleTooltip, this);
             },
             associate: function (ev) {
                 this.set('describes', ev.currentTarget);
             },
             disassociate: function () {
                 this.set('describes', null);
             },
             toggleTooltip: function (ev) {
                 var ALIGN = Y.WidgetPositionAlign,
                     cBox = this.get('contentBox'),
                     bBox = this.get('boundingBox');

                 if (ev.newVal) {
                     this.align(ev.newVal, [ALIGN.TL, ALIGN.BC]);
                     cBox.setHTML(ev.newVal.getAttribute('data-tooltip'));
                     ev.newVal.setAttribute('aria-describedby', bBox.get('id'));
                     this.show();
                 } else {
                     ev.prevVal.removeAttribute('aria-describedby');
                     this.hide();
                 }
             },
             destructor: function () {
                 Y.each(this.handles, function (handle) {
                     handle.detach();
                 });
                 if (this.get('describes')) {
                     this.get('describes').removeAttribute('aria-describedby');
                 }
             },
             handles: {}
         }, {
             ATTRS: {
                 visible:   { value: false },
                 describes: { value: null }
             }
         });
}, '1.0', { requires: ['widget-position-align', 'widget-stack', 'event'] });

YUI().use('tooltip', function (Y) {
    var tooltip = new Y.Tooltip({ width: '200px' });
    tooltip.render();
});
</script>
```

Discussion

YUI is invaluable for implementing ARIA in dynamic content such as error panes, widgets, and views. You can think of ARIA attributes much like CSS classes. An HTML page arrives with some classes that represent its initial visual state, and later on, YUI is responsible for updating those classes in response to state changes. Likewise, an HTML page should arrive with the ARIA attributes that represent its initial state, and YUI should then be responsible for updating ARIA to reflect state changes for screenreaders.

 Even if you correctly add ARIA attributes and test the results in a variety of environments, that still doesn't mean your code is accessible. Another major aspect for accessibility is adding full keyboard support. Review Chapter 4, and see also Recipe 9.15.

See Also

Example 8-9; ARIA on the Mozilla Developer Network (*https://developer.mozilla.org/en/ARIA*); WAI-ARIA roles (*http://www.w3.org/TR/wai-aria/roles*); WAI-ARIA states and properties (*http://www.w3.org/TR/wai-aria/states_and_properties*); Accessible Culture's article, "HTML5, ARIA Roles, and Screen Readers in March 2011" (*http://www.accessibleculture.org/articles/2011/04/html5-aria-2011/*).

11.4 Retrofitting a Widget with an ARIA Plugin

Problem

You have found a useful off-the-shelf widget, but it lacks ARIA attributes that would make it accessible.

Solution

Create a plugin to alter the widget's structure and behavior. In the plugin's `initial izer()`, use `setAttrs()` to add ARIA attributes to the host widget's bounding box, and add any `after()` listeners to update ARIA state attributes in response to widget state changes, saving a reference to the subscription handle. In the plugin's `destructor()`, remove all ARIA attributes and detach all listeners.

Most of the core YUI widgets and components ship with ARIA markup, but many widgets in the gallery do not. Example 11-5 retrofits the current `ProgressBar` gallery widget with a reusable plugin. The plugin defines an `addStaticARIA()` method to decorate the bounding box with the initial set of attributes, and an `addDynamicARIA()` method to add change event listeners.

If the progress bar is already in the rendered state (because the user set the `render` attribute in the constructor), the plugin adds the ARIA attributes immediately. Otherwise, the plugin uses `afterHostMethod()` to safely inject its behavior directly after the progress bar's rendering cycle.

To verify that the code is working, you can open the example in a screenreader that supports these ARIA roles and states, or open your browser's developer console and observe the effect on the DOM as you click the Increment button.

Example 11-5. Retrofitting a widget with an ARIA plugin

```
<!DOCTYPE html>
<title>Retrofitting a widget with an ARIA plugin</title>
<style>
.yui3-progressbar {
    border: 1px #888 solid;
    background: #ddd;
    border-radius: 3px;
    height: 25px;
}
.yui3-progressbar-slider {
    background: #55f;
    height: 25px;
}
.yui3-progressbar-label {
    float: left; padding: 3px;
    font: 14px verdana;
}
</style>

<div id="demo"></div>
<p><button id="increment">Increment</button></p>

<script src="http://yui.yahooapis.com/3.5.0/build/yui/yui-min.js"></script>
<script>
YUI.add('progressbar-aria-plugin', function (Y) {
    Y.Plugin.ProgressBarARIA = Y.Base.create('pbARIA', Y.Plugin.Base, [], {
        initializer: function () {
            var host = this.get('host'),
                box  = host.get('boundingBox');

            if (host.get('rendered')) {
                this.addStaticARIA();
            } else {
                this.afterHostMethod('render', this.addStaticARIA);
            }

            this.addDynamicARIA();
        },
        addStaticARIA: function () {
            var host   = this.get('host'),
                box    = host.get('boundingBox'),
                descBy = box.one('.yui3-progressbar-label').get('id')

            if (box.getAttribute('role') !== 'progressbar' ) {
                box.setAttrs({
                    'role': 'progressbar',
                    'aria-valuemin': 0,
                    'aria-valuemax': 100,
```

```
                    'aria-valuenow': host.get('progress'),
                    'aria-describedby': descBy
                });
            }
        },
        addDynamicARIA: function () {
            var box = this.get('host').get('boundingBox');

            this.afterHostEvent('progressChange', function (ev) {
                box.setAttribute('aria-valuenow', ev.newVal);
            });
        },
        destructor: function () {
            this.get('host').get('boundingBox')
                .removeAttribute('role')
                .removeAttribute('aria-valuemin')
                .removeAttribute('aria-valuemax')
                .removeAttribute('aria-valuenow')
                .removeAttribute('aria-describedby');
        }
    }, {
        NS: 'aria',
    });
}, '1.0', { requires: ['base-build', 'plugin'] });

YUI().use('gallery-progress-bar', 'progressbar-aria-plugin', function (Y) {
    var progressBar = new Y.ProgressBar({
        width: '300px',
        layout: '<div class="{labelClass}" id="' + Y.guid() + '">'
            + '</div><div class="{sliderClass}"></div>'
    });
    progressBar.plug(Y.Plugin.ProgressBarARIA);
    progressBar.render('#demo');

    Y.one('#increment').on('click', function (ev) {
        progressBar.increment(25);
    });
});
</script>
```

Discussion

YUI's DOM APIs offer some interesting possibilities for quickly retrofitting a page that has accessibility issues. For example, some sites use `<a>` as a clickable JavaScript button instead of `<button>`, which creates some problems. First, the screenreader will identify the link as an anchor element rather than a button. Second, if the button has an href="#", the screenreader will read that URL, but if the `<a>` lacks an href, then it will have no tab index and so will lie out of the default tab flow. However, Y.all() can easily fix both of these problems. Assuming the links have a class of "button", you could sweep through the page and fix this problem with:

```
Y.all('a.button').each(function (node) {
    node.setAttribute('role', 'button');
    if (! node.hasAttribute('href')) {
        node.setAttribute('tabindex', '0');
    }
});
```

Of course, a purist would frown on this kind of quick-fix approach. The ideal solution is to go back and correct the markup in your server-side HTML templates.

For completeness, Example 11-5 also supplies a `destructor()` that tears down all the attributes and listeners that it adds. It might seem a little odd to go to all this effort to remove ARIA attributes from a widget, but well-designed plugins should fulfill the contract of `unplug()`.

To help future-proof the plugin, the `initializer()` checks the bounding box for a `role` of `"progressbar"`, just in case future versions of `ProgressBar` happen to include ARIA attributes natively.

See Also

Recipe 7.7; Recipe 7.8; Anthony Pipkin's `gallery-progress-bar` module (*http://yuili brary.com/gallery/show/progress-bar*).

11.5 Defining Translated Strings

Problem

You want to be able to define translations for various strings in your user interface.

Solution

Each YUI module has a currently active language, which you can set by calling `Y.Intl.setLang()`.

For each module that needs translation, use `Y.Intl.add()` to register a set of translated strings, one for each language that your module supports. Then call `Y.Intl.get()` to retrieve an object containing the specified module's translated strings, and update or generate the relevant HTML.

Example 11-6 is a toy example that shows `Y.Intl.add()`, `Y.Intl.get()`, and `Y.Intl.set Lang()` working together. The example defines a `my-form` module with a method for updating the form's labels, plus three sets of translated strings for English, French, and Spanish. The example then loads the module, sets the module's active language to French, and refreshes the user interface.

For a more realistic example that shows how to lay out a widget with separate resource files, refer to Recipe 11.6.

Example 11-6. Defining translated strings

```
<!DOCTYPE html>
<meta charset="utf-8">
<title>Defining translated strings</title>

<form id="ui">
    <p><label for="name">name</label></p>
    <p><input id="name" name="name" type="text"></p>
    <p><label for="address">address</label></p>
    <p><input id="address" name="address" type="text"></p>
</form>

<script src="http://yui.yahooapis.com/3.5.0/build/yui/yui-min.js"></script>
<script>
YUI.add('my-form', function (Y) {
    Y.MyForm = {};
    Y.MyForm.updateLabels = function() {
        var strings = Y.Intl.get('my-form');
        Y.one('label[for=name]').setHTML(strings.name);
        Y.one('label[for=address]').setHTML(strings.address);
    }

    Y.Intl.add('my-form', 'en', {
        name: 'name',
        address: 'address'
    });
    Y.Intl.add('my-form', 'fr', {
        name: 'nom',
        address: 'adresse',
    });
    Y.Intl.add('my-form', 'es', {
        name: 'nombre',
        address: 'dirección',
    });
}, '1.0', {requires: ['node', 'intl']});

YUI().use('my-form', function (Y) {
    Y.Intl.setLang('my-form', 'fr');
    Y.MyForm.updateLabels();
});
</script>
```

Discussion

Example 11-6 works, but is actually somewhat overengineered. Why bother using Y.Intl.add()—why not just define strings in a simple JavaScript object and then pick out the strings you need at runtime?

If that's all you are doing, there's not much reason to use Y.Intl. The goal of Y.Intl is to make it easier to manage resource string definitions that have been broken out into separate files. In YUI, you define sets of language strings for each module. As shown in Recipe 11.6, YUI has conventions for structuring modules that enable you to define a module's language resources as separate asset files, much like a module's CSS resources.

If a module has resource strings, you can retrieve them by calling Y.Intl.get(). The bundle of strings you receive depends on the module's currently set *active language*:

- If a module has an active language, Y.Intl.get() fetches the module's strings for that language.

- If a module does not have an active language, Y.Intl.get() falls back to using the YUI instance's lang property, which represents that instance's list of *preferred languages*. This is a comma-separated string of language tags to try in order from left to right. For example, a string of 'pt-BR,pt,en' would mean try Brazilian Portuguese first, then Portuguese, and then, if all else fails, English.

The intl module relies on BCP 47 language tags, a combination of RFC 5646 and RFC 4647, as keys for individual language resources. BCP 47 tags range from fairly general (fr for French) to more specific (pt-BR for Brazilian Portuguese).

See Also

Recipe 11.6; the YUI Internationalization User Guide (*http://yuilibrary.com/yui/docs/ intl/*); "Example: Language Resource Bundles" (*http://yuilibrary.com/yui/docs/intl/intl -basic.html*); Y.Intl API documentation (*http://yuilibrary.com/yui/docs/api/classes/Intl .html*); RFC 5646 (*http://tools.ietf.org/html/rfc5646*); RFC 4647 (*http://tools.ietf.org/ html/rfc4647*).

11.6 Internationalizing a Widget

Problem

You would like to properly parameterize your widget's UI strings according to the user's preferred language, so that people in France can use your widget.

Solution

For each language that you need to support, define some resource strings using Y.Intl.add(). Then define the widget's strings attribute to access the resource strings, and make sure that any strings the widget displays in the UI are parameterized.

Example 11-7 enhances the Y.Electron example from Example 7-4 so that it supports the French language. In the original example, the same HTML file both defined and used the widget. By contrast, this internationalized example is a little more realistic— it breaks out the Electron widget code into its own JS file, provides two separate English and French resource bundle files, and provides YUI with the metadata it needs to stitch the module together.

Before walking through this example, be sure you understand how to define custom module groups, as discussed in Recipe 1.11.

 Example 11-7 is configured to run from a real web server. If you prefer to open *widget_intl.html* as a local file, change the base configuration field to be a relative filepath such as *./js/particles/*.

Example 11-7. Internationalizing a widget

The directory structure for the custom module group is:

```
js/
    particles/
        electron
            electron.css
            electron.js
            lang/
                electron_en.js
                electron_fr.js
widget_intl.html
```

Naturally, you could always add more modules alongside electron, such as proton, neutrino, higgs-boson, and so on.

js/particles/electron/electron.css: The Electron widget's CSS styles, to be loaded as a separate module. Alternatively, you could organize the electron module to load its CSS as a skin, which would eliminate the need to define a separate electron-css module, and open up the possibility of multiple skins. For more information, refer to Recipes 7.9 and 7.10.

```
.yui3-electron         { width: 175px; }
.yui3-electron-content { background: #ff0; border: 1px #000 solid; }
.yui3-electron-content p { margin: 5px; }
```

js/particles/electron/electron.js: The core Electron widget JS code. This file is similar to the YUI.add() statement in Example 7-4, with these changes:

- Instead of hardcoding UI strings like "Charge" and "Energy", renderUI() and syncUI() now rely on parameters stored in the strings attribute.
- The widget has a strings attribute that sets its default value with a valueFn. The valueFn uses Y.Intl to fetch the electron module's localized resources for the YUI instance's currently active language.
- The module declares dependencies on the intl module and the electron-css module.

```
YUI.add('electron', function (Y) {
    var REST_ENERGY = 511.00;

    Y.Electron = Y.Base.create('electron', Y.Widget, [], {
        destructor: function () {
```

```
                this.get('contentBox').all('p').remove(true);
            },
            getSpeed: function () {
                var e_ratio = REST_ENERGY / this.get('energy');
                return Math.sqrt(1 - e_ratio * e_ratio);
            },
            boostEnergy: function () {
                this.set('energy', 1.1 * this.get('energy'));
            },
            renderUI: function () {
                var charge = this.get('strings').charge;
                this.get('contentBox')
                    .append('<p class="ch">' + charge + ': ' + this.get('charge') + '</p>')
                    .append('<p class="en">')
                    .append('<p class="sp">');
            },
            bindUI: function () {
                this.get('contentBox').on('click', this.boostEnergy, this);
                this.after('energyChange', this.syncUI, this);
            },
            syncUI: function () {
                var s = this.get('strings');
                var energyStr = s.energy + ': ' + this.get('energy').toPrecision(5) + ' MeV';
                var speedStr  = s.speed + ': ' + this.getSpeed().toPrecision(5) + ' c';
                this.get('contentBox').one('.en').setHTML(energyStr);
                this.get('contentBox').one('.sp').setHTML(speedStr);
            }
        }, {
            ATTRS: {
                charge: {
                    value: -1,
                    readOnly: true
                },
                energy: {
                    value: REST_ENERGY,
                    validator: function (en) {
                        return (en >= REST_ENERGY);
                    }
                },
                strings: {
                    valueFn: function () {
                        return Y.Intl.get('electron');
                    }
                }
            }
        });
}, '1.1_intl', {requires: ['base-build', 'widget', 'intl', 'electron-css']});
```

js/particles/electron/electron_en.js: Registers a resource bundle of English language strings:

```
YUI.add('lang/electron_en', function (Y) {
    Y.Intl.add('electron', 'en', {
        charge: 'Charge',
        energy: 'Energy',
        speed: 'Speed'
```

```
        });
}, '1.1_intl');
```

js/particles/electron/electron_fr.js: Registers a resource bundle of French language strings:

```
YUI.add('lang/electron_fr', function (Y) {
    Y.Intl.add('electron', 'fr', {
        charge: 'Charge',
        energy: 'Énergie',
        speed: 'Vitesse'
    });
}, '1.1_intl');
```

widget_intl.html: Provides the HTML page that loads and uses the electron module. The page is similar to the HTML page in Example 7-4, but with these changes:

- The page includes a `<meta>` element to declare a character encoding of UTF-8. This ensures that the "É" in "Énergie" displays correctly, in case your web server is not already providing an HTTP header of Content-Type: text/html; charset=utf-8. Alternatively, you can design your language packs to use UTF-8 escape sequences for non-ASCII characters.

- Instead of embedding the Y.Electron's code and CSS directly in the HTML page, the page defines the metadata required to load the electron and electron-css modules. This includes the base path and filepath to *electron.js*, an array of module requirements, and an array of supported languages.

  Under electron, declaring lang: ['en', 'fr'] instructs the Loader to load the resources *lang/electron_en.js* and *lang/electron_fr.js*. The order of this array does not affect which language actually gets used; that is determined by the YUI instance's lang property.

- The YUI instance is configured with a lang property of 'fr, en', which instructs the instance to try using French strings first, and if that fails, English. In this case, when the widget calls Y.Intl.get('electron') to populate the strings attribute, the attribute will contain French string resources.

```
<!DOCTYPE html>
<meta charset="utf-8">
<title>Internationalizing a Widget</title>

<p>Click the Y.Electron to increase its energy by 10%.</p>
<div id="demo"></div>

<script src="http://yui.yahooapis.com/3.5.0/build/yui/yui-min.js"></script>
<script>
YUI({
    lang: 'fr, en',
    groups: {
        'particles': {
            base: '/js/particles/',
            modules: {
```

```
                'electron': {
                    path: 'electron/electron.js',
                    requires: ['base-build', 'widget', 'intl', 'electron-css'],
                    lang: ['en', 'fr']
                },
                'electron-css': {
                    path: 'electron/electron.css',
                    type: 'css'
                }
            }
        }
    }
}).use('electron', function (Y) {
    var e = new Y.Electron();
    e.render('#demo');
});
</script>
```

Discussion

The **strings** attribute is just a convention for storing resource strings. You can parameterize your UI strings any way you like, but setting **strings** by calling Y.Intl.get() is a standard YUI pattern.

Example 11-7 sets its language resources one time only. If you change lang to be 'en, fr', 'en', or just remove lang entirely, the strings for all widgets will be locked to English, not French. To change languages dynamically, you can call Y.Intl's set Lang() method:

```
    Y.Intl.setLang('electron', 'en');
```

This method fires an `intl:langChange` event, which you can listen for and respond to with:

```
    this.set('strings', Y.Intl.get('electron'));
    this.syncUI();
```

See Also

Recipe 1.11; Recipe 7.4; Recipe 7.9; Recipe 7.10; Recipe 11.5; the YUI Internationalization User Guide (*http://yuilibrary.com/yui/docs/intl/*); Y.Intl API documentation (*http://yuilibrary.com/yui/docs/api/classes/Intl.html*).

Professional Tools

With the rise of JavaScript has come a corresponding increase in the availability of tools for developing complex JavaScript applications. Only a few years ago, these kinds of tools were few and far between. For instance, it is a sobering thought to realize that the Firebug plugin didn't even exist until as late as 2006! At the time, it was something of a revelation to be able to inspect the inner workings of your code without resorting to `alert()` dialogs. Nowadays, every major browser ships with a highly capable native console. Developers of JavaScript now expect the same kind of toolset that developers of C, Java, Python, PHP, Perl, and other languages have enjoyed for years.

Since YUI focuses on developing sophisticated applications, it should be no surprise that it provides additional tools designed to help you develop JavaScript professionally. When you hear someone say "YUI," he is usually referring to the library APIs. However, YUI is actually a family of projects. YUI 3 is the most prominent example, but YUI also includes utility projects such as YUI Test, YUI Compressor, and YUI Doc. These are the same tools that the YUI team uses to build, test, maintain, and document YUI itself.

YUI tools are not coupled tightly to YUI 3 itself. You can use YUI Compressor to compress *any* JavaScript code, or YUI Test to test *any* JavaScript code. Even if you prefer some other JavaScript library, the standalone YUI toolset can still help you produce high-quality applications.

The bulk of this chapter focuses on testing JavaScript code. A healthy suite of high-quality tests is vital for giving you the confidence that you can fix bugs, add features, and refactor code without breaking things. JavaScript has historically been difficult to test for a variety of reasons. Early JavaScript testing frameworks were clumsy. JavaScript requires testing in multiple browsers, and browsers are tricky to automate. JavaScript applications interact with components across slow, unreliable networks.

Fortunately, better testing tools are now available. These include YUI Test, a test library and framework, and Yeti, a command-line test launcher that works with YUI Test, enabling you to run large unit test suites quickly in parallel on a (potentially) very large number of browsers.

At its core, YUI Test enables you to create and organize test cases using simple, sensible syntax. If you have used test frameworks in other languages, YUI Test supports familiar conventions: the concepts of building test suites, calling `setUp()` and `tearDown()` methods, and mocking out slow and unreliable dependencies. But YUI Test also provides features specific for JavaScript testing: DOM event simulation, asynchronous test support, and a full array of test events that you can subscribe to. YUI Test even provides command-line tools for performing code coverage analysis and for incorporating your tests into a continuous integration framework.

Recipes 12.1 and 12.2 explain how to use the YUI logging framework and how to display log output in a YUI `Console` widget. If you first learned JavaScript by playing around with `alert()` dialogs, you'll be pleased to know that `Y.log()` is a far better option, or at least as good as the `print()` and `echo()` statements found in other programming languages.

Recipes 12.3 through 12.7 cover unit testing with YUI Test. Recipes 12.3 and 12.4 describe the basics of writing test cases and organizing them into test suites. Recipes 12.5, 12.6, and 12.7 cover advanced topics in JavaScript unit testing: how to simulate clicks and other user-initiated events, how to mock out slow or unpredictable components, and how to use asynchronous testing to wait for events to complete.

While you can view test data in a console, it's often necessary to collect and store test result data for later analysis. Recipe 12.8 explains how to collect YUI Test result data at the source and POST it somewhere else for further analysis.

Recipe 12.9 introduces Yeti, a Node.js application that enables you to quickly launch your YUI Test test suite from the command line on a wide variety of browsers. One of the motivations behind Yeti was to make mobile testing easier.

Recipe 12.10 explains how to use Yeti with the third-party *localtunnel* utility to test your code on nearly any device, including your mobile phone.

Ordinarily, you run YUI tests in a browser, either by refreshing pages yourself or by driving browsers using Selenium, Yeti, or some other automation tool. Recipe 12.11 demonstrates how to use the *yuitest* command-line tool to test JavaScript specifically designed for the server side.

Recipe 12.12 leaves the world of testing behind to take a look at compressing JavaScript to maximize performance over the wire. YUI Compressor parses your JavaScript source code in order to maximize the number of characters that can be safely removed from your source file.

Rounding out our tour of YUI's professional tools is YUI Doc. Software libraries live and die by the quality of their documentation. Recipe 12.13 explains how to use YUI Doc to generate complete API reference documentation from comments in source code, similar to tools like Javadoc and Doxygen.

12.1 Enabling Debug Logging

Problem

You want to capture log output from your code in a flexible manner, instead of resorting to embarrassing old-school `alert()` dialogs.

Solution

Use `Y.log()` to log messages, warnings, and errors to your browser console. By default, `Y.log()` is included in the core YUI object. To enable logging to the browser console, create a YUI instance and call the `log()` method, as shown in Example 12-1.

Example 12-1. Basic debug logging

```
<!DOCTYPE html>
<title>Basic debug logging</title>

<script src="http://yui.yahooapis.com/3.5.0/build/yui/yui-min.js"></script>
<script>
YUI().use(function (Y) {
    Y.log('This is an informational debug message.', 'info', 'example_app');
    Y.log('This is a warning message.', 'warn', 'example_app');
    Y.log('This is a critical error message.', 'error', 'example_app');
});
</script>
```

Loading Example 12-1 into a browser displays a blank page, but the page is generating log messages. By default, your browser's error console captures YUI log output. Figure 12-1 displays an example   Firefox error console with Firebug installed.

Figure 12-1. Sending log output to the browser console

 For older browsers that lack an error console, you can instantiate a YUI `Console`, a widget designed to display log messages. For more information, refer to Recipe 12.2.

Discussion

Calling the log() method itself is straightforward. The method has the signature Y.log(msg, cat, src, silent), where:

msg
> Specifies the message to log.

cat *(optional)*
> Specifies a message category. Some browser consoles provide a special display mode for the categories info, warn, and error, as does the Console widget. However, you can provide any category name that makes sense for the object consuming the event.

src *(optional)*
> The source of the message. This is useful if you have multiple components that are firing log events and you need some way to distinguish the source.

silent *(optional)*
> If true, prevents the yui:log event from firing. This enables you to decide on the fly whether JavaScript components such as the Console widget are able to catch and display that particular message. Interestingly, the silent parameter does not affect whether the browser console displays the log message—this is controlled by the YUI instance's useBrowserConsole configuration setting, as described shortly.

When Y.log() executes, it broadcasts a custom yui:log event to Y.Global, which is available in every YUI instance.

The YUI object provides several configuration settings that affect Y.log()'s behavior:

debug
> When set to false, disables Y.log() entirely. The default is true. Logging statements can slow an application down, so YUI makes it easy to disable logging in production. YUI also provides a number of filtering capabilities that enable you to do things like turning on only error log messages, for a single module. If you need to leave logging enabled, you can be very fine-grained about how you do it.
>
> If you really want to disable all logging in production, the best approach is to use your build process to strip debug statements out of production code entirely, which reduces code paths and minimizes bytes over the wire. In fact, the YUI Builder tool that the YUI team uses does exactly this. For more information about how you can use YUI Builder with your own code, refer to *http://yuilibrary.com/projects/builder*.

filter
> Sets the default form for YUI modules to load: min, raw, or debug. The default is min. All native YUI modules ship in three forms:

module-min.js

> The minified version, with variable names minimized and comments and whitespace stripped. This is the version suitable for production use. For more information about how to generate your own minified JavaScript, refer to Recipe 12.12.

module.js

> The raw version, which includes full variable names, comments, and white-space. This is the version to use if you want to track down syntax and usage errors. For example, if you misspell a method name while using a minified YUI module, the browser will throw an unreadable error message. The `raw` filter enables you to track down exceptions and errors using the full human-readable YUI source code. Just don't forget to remove the filter when you're ready to ship.

module-debug.js

> The debug version, which includes all `log()` statements that the YUI team included for its own debugging purposes. This is the version to use if you want to learn about how YUI works by loading YUI components and watching log messages fly by. If you are trying to track down an error, stepping down from raw to debug might give you the extra information you need to figure out where the problem lies. (Or it might just be confusing.)

> The following minimal example demonstrates what the debug version has to offer. Open this HTML file and view the results in the browser console. (The reference to `NOT_A_MODULE` is an intentional error.)

```
<!DOCTYPE html>
<title>Using -debug files</title>
<script src="http://yui.yahooapis.com/3.5.0/build/yui/yui-debug.js"></script>
<script>YUI().use('node', 'NOT_A_MODULE', function (Y) {});</script>
```

filters

Specifies the form to load for specific modules, overriding the overall `filter` setting for those specific modules. For example:

```
YUI({
    filter: 'raw',
    filters: {
        autocomplete: 'debug',
        io: 'min'
    }
}).use(...);
```

retrieves the debug version of `autocomplete`, the minified version of `io`, and the raw version of all other modules.

logExclude

Disables logging for any log messages with a `src` that matches one of the disallowed values. For example, if you set:

```
YUI({
    filter: 'debug',
    logExclude: {
        'myfirstapp': true,
        node: true
    }
}).use(...);
```

then YUI suppresses any log message with a `src` of `myfirstapp` or `node`.

By convention, most YUI modules emit log messages with a `src` that matches the module name. However, some modules can emit log messages with alternative `src` values.

logInclude

Enables logging for any log messages with a `src` that matches one of the permitted values. For example, if you set:

```
YUI({
    filter: 'debug',
    logInclude: {
        'myfirstapp': true,
        node: true
    }
}).use(...);
```

then YUI permits only log messages with a `src` of `myfirstapp` or `node`.

useBrowserConsole

When set to `true`, enables `Y.log()` to write to the browser console. By default, this value is `true`, but instantiating a `Console` widget on the page sets this value to `false`. For more information, refer to Recipe 12.2.

`Y.log()` also works with Node.js, as an alternative to Node.js's built-in `console.log`. On the server side, `Y.log()` supports all the familiar configuration and event behaviors just described, plus its terminal output comes in a variety of attractive colors.

12.2 Rendering Debug Log Output in the Page

Problem

The browser console is taking up valuable screen space. You would rather test your application in full-screen mode, displaying any log output directly in the page.

Solution

Instantiate a Console widget. The presence of a console causes YUI to automatically redirect log output to the Console widget instead of the browser console.

Example 12-2 demonstrates logging with Y.log()'s extended signature. In addition to a string log message, the calls to Y.log() include a category (such as warn) and a source for the log message, all of which is displayed in the console instance.

Example 12-2. Rendering debug log output in the page

```
<!DOCTYPE html>
<title>Rendering debug log output in the page</title>

<div class="yui3-skin-sam" id="demo"></div>

<script src="http://yui.yahooapis.com/3.5.0/build/yui/yui-min.js"></script>
<script>
YUI().use('console', function (Y) {
    new Y.Console().render('#demo');

    Y.log('This is an informational debug message.', 'info', 'example_app');
    Y.log('This is a warning message.', 'warn', 'example_app');
    Y.log('This is a critical error message.', 'error', 'example_app');
});
</script>
```

The results are shown in Figure 12-2.

Figure 12-2. The Console widget

Each Console widget actually has its own local useBrowserConsole attribute, defaulted to false, that passes through to the YUI sandbox where it is instantiated. To preserve browser console logging, just set the Console's useBrowserConsole attribute back to true.

Discussion

`Console` is actually a generic widget for displaying messages, not just messages from `Y.log()`. By default, a `Console` widget is wired to listen for `yui:log` events, but you can easily reconfigure and extend it for different purposes. Key customization points for the `Y.log()`/`Y.Console` system include:

- Changing the `logSource` that the console is listening to
- Filtering the messages the console displays
- Hooking into the console's internal `entry` event, which fires whenever the console transfers a message to the print loop buffer
- Manipulating the console and changing its display behavior
- Changing the event type that the console listens for from `yui:log` to a custom event

Some of the interesting things you can do with `Console` include:

- *Creating a universal console.* By default, a console receives log events only from the YUI instance it belongs to. However, YUI broadcasts all `yui:log` events to `Y.Global`, so you can capture all log events in any YUI instance in the page by setting the console's `logSource` attribute to `Y.Global` as follows:

    ```
    new Y.Console({ logSource: Y.Global }).render();
    ```

- *Enabling highly specific log filtering.* While you can control `Y.log()`'s behavior by setting configurables in the YUI object, you can also filter messages within the `Console` widget. The simplest filtering option is the `logLevel`. For example, to include `warn` and `error` messages, but exclude info messages:

    ```
    new Y.Console({ logLevel: 'warn' }).render();
    ```

You can also apply a `logLevel` to the YUI object itself, which affects all consoles (including the browser console). Log-level filtering has no effect on custom categories, which lie outside the hierarchy.

Taking filtering one step further, you can suppress messages with custom event logic. Example 12-3 is a console designed to display error messages specifically related to uploads. It uses the previous `logLevel` technique to filter out `info` and `warn` messages, then hooks into the `entry` event to filter on the message content itself. Thus, the console displays only the third log message.

Example 12-3. Filtering log messages on console entry

```
<!DOCTYPE html>
<title>Filtering log messages on console entry</title>

<div class="yui3-skin-sam" id="demo"></div>

<script src="http://yui.yahooapis.com/3.5.0/build/yui/yui-min.js"></script>
<script>
YUI().use('console', function (Y) {
```

```
        var demo = new Y.Console({ logLevel: 'error' }).render('#demo');
        demo.on('entry', function (ev) {
            if (! /upload/.test(ev.message.message)) {
                ev.preventDefault();
            }
        });

        Y.log('This is a critical error message.', 'error', 'example_app');
        Y.log('File upload successful', 'info', 'example_app');
        Y.log('File upload failed: server refused connection.', 'error', 'example_app');
    });
</script>
```

You can also use the entry event to perform some custom work or relay the message to some other listener. However, be careful not to do too much work in an entry handler—if you have large message volumes, executing code here can get rather expensive.

- *Changing Console's appearance and functionality.* A common way to change a console is to augment it with the ConsoleFilters plugin:

```
new Y.Console().plug(Y.Plugin.ConsoleFilters).render();
```

This plugin gives the user more control over the console's output, creating a control pane with checkboxes that toggle messages on and off by category and source type.

To customize the console's appearance at a deeper level, you can change the HTML used to display messages by overriding the entryTemplate attribute.

- *Listening for a different custom event.* You can monitor a specific component by changing the logEvent. For example, if you use Y.fire() to fire foo:bar events:

```
Y.fire('foo:bar', {'msg': 'An important message', 'cat': 'info', 'src': 'meh'});
```

you can configure the console to listen for those events with:

```
new Y.Console({ logEvent: 'foo:bar' }).render();
```

To listen to a widget's attribute change events, you would also set logSource to point to the widget instance:

```
new Y.Console({
    logEvent: 'tabView:selectionChange',
    logSource: myTabView
}).render('#demo');
```

Keep in mind that Console widgets are designed to operate on objects with properties msg, cat, and src. In the preceding tabView:selectionChange example, the console will display log messages as you change tabs, but the message will be undefined.

Related to the Console widget is the Test.Console widget, a specialized console designed for use with the YUI Test unit testing framework. Console can display YUI Test results, but it is usually better to use Console for debugging and Test.Console for visualizing test results.

See Also

YUI Console User Guide (*http://yuilibrary.com/yui/docs/console/*); the `ConsoleFilters` plugin (*http://yuilibrary.com/yui/docs/console-filters/console-filters-intro.html*).

12.3 Writing Unit Tests

Problem

You want to create some assurance that a function works the way it was intended and will continue to work properly even if you change its internal implementation.

Solution

Load the `test-console` module and create unit tests for your function using the YUI Test unit testing framework. The `test-console` module contains the code for the `Test.Console` widget and pulls in the `test` module, which contains the core YUI Test libraries. `Test.Console` is a cousin to the `Console` widget, specifically designed for displaying YUI Test data. If for some reason you want to display test data through some other means, you can load the `test` module by itself.

Example 12-4 sets up a single test case by:

1. Providing a `trim()` function to test. This function could have been pulled in as a module, but in this case it's just defined locally.

2. Creating a test case and configuring it with an object literal containing tests. The tests evaluate a range of possible outcomes: leading whitespace, trailing whitespace, and trailing *and* leading whitespace.

   Each test case uses an *assert method* to validate results, using the convention of "expected value first." For example, the `Y.Assert.areEqual()` assert method compares the first parameter (the expected value) to the second parameter (the result of what you are testing) and fails the test if the two are not equal.

3. Creating a `Test.Console` widget to capture and display the test results. By default, `Test.Console` summarizes test results and displays failed test results in red, although you can customize this behavior.

4. Adding the test case to a test runner and invoking `run()` to execute the tests.

Example 12-4. Writing unit tests for a trim() function

```
<!DOCTYPE html>
<title>Writing unit tests for a trim() function</title>

<div class="yui3-skin-sam" id="demo"></div>

<script src="http://yui.yahooapis.com/3.5.0/build/yui/yui-min.js"></script>
```

```
<script>
YUI().use('test-console', function (Y) {
    // Implementation is not quite right; regex is missing a /g
    function trim(text){
        return text.replace(/^\s+|\s+$/, '');
    }

    var testCase = new Y.Test.Case({
        name: 'trim() Tests',

        'Leading whitespace should be removed': function () {
            var result = trim('    Hello world!');
            Y.Assert.areEqual('Hello world!', result);
        },

        'Trailing white space should be removed': function () {
            var result = trim('Hello world!    ');
            Y.Assert.areEqual('Hello world!', result);
        },

        'Leading and trailing white space should be removed': function () {
            var result = trim('    Hello world!    ');
            Y.Assert.areEqual('Hello world!', result);
        }
    });

    new Y.Test.Console().render('#demo');

    Y.Test.Runner.add(testCase);
    Y.Test.Runner.run();
});
</script>
```

Because the `trim()` function's regex is (intentionally) written incorrectly, the third test fails. This is actually great news—the tests have uncovered a poorly implemented feature! To fix the broken test, change the regex to /^\s+|\s+$/g and reload the page.

Discussion

In testing terms, a *unit* is an isolated chunk of code that you can test independently. In YUI Test, a unit corresponds to a method or function.

To create effective JavaScript unit tests, your code should keep method bodies small, and avoid blocking for user input (in other words, don't use `alert()` and the like). Each method should have a single purpose or correspond to a single operation, which makes it easier for unit tests to exercise the API and compare state before and after.

The idea behind traditional unit testing is that you are testing the implementation of a public interface. Your tests describe a set of input and output conditions that the method must satisfy, but the actual implementation of the method is irrelevant. This is called *black-box testing*. Black-box testing enables you to formally describe your input sets ahead of time, which not only helps you plan, but also serves as a form of technical specification. Black-box testing also gives you confidence that you can freely fix a method's bugs or even completely change its internals without accidentally breaking other code that depends on that method. For more information about developing enough high-quality tests to gain that assurance, refer to Recipe 12.4.

When YUI Test first debuted in 2008, the JavaScript testing landscape looked very different than it does today. Few developers paid much attention to JavaScript testing. The testing tools that did exist were faithful ports of frameworks designed for other languages, so were poorly adapted to JavaScript. YUI Test evolved quickly into a more natural JavaScript testing framework, complete with advanced features such as cross-browser event simulation and support for asynchronous testing.

If you are working with YUI library code, it is convenient to load the test framework as a YUI module, as in Example 12-4. However, you are also free to download and use YUI Test separately to test any JavaScript code you like, without any dependencies on the YUI libraries. The standalone package is referred to as "YUI Test Standalone." It includes a JavaScript library for testing, as well as self-contained documentation, examples, and some command-line utilities. You can install YUI Test Standalone by downloading the files and installing them manually, or as a Node.js `npm` package (`npm install -g yuitest`).

YUI Test also provides friendly test names, similar to "behavior-driven development" test frameworks such as Vows. Traditional xUnit-style frameworks require test function names to have a prefix of `test`, resulting in functions like `testLeadingWhitespaceRemoved()`.

The YUI Test Runner supports the xUnit convention, along with a second, more flexible convention:

```
'Leading white space should be removed': function () {
    ...
}
```

If you bind a function to a string property that contains a space and the word "should," the YUI Test Runner identifies this as a test function as well. These friendly test names are useful because they encourage you to think of your tests as behaviors that need to be satisfied. Just imagine—test results so easy to read, even a product manager can understand them! (Maybe this isn't such a great feature after all.)

In addition to following a naming convention, a test function must contain one or more *assert methods* to run during testing. An assert method tests whether a condition is valid. For example, the `areEqual()` assert method compares two values for equality, with an optional failure message as the third argument:

```
var name = 'Pat';
Y.Assert.areEqual('Pat', name, 'The name should be Pat');
```

If all of the conditions within a test function are satisfied, the test passes. If any condition is invalid, the assert method throws an error, which skips all remaining assertions and causes the test to fail.

YUI provides a full spectrum of assert methods, including:

- Equality and sameness assertions. In addition to `areEqual()` and `areNotEqual()`, YUI provides `areSame()` and `areNotSame()`, which test equality without doing any type coercion by using the `===` and `!==` operators. For example, in:

```
Y.Assert.areSame(2, '2');
Y.Assert.areEqual(2, '2');
```

the `areSame()` assertion would fail, since a number is not a string, but the `areEqual()` assertion would succeed thanks to type coercion.

- Data type assertions, including `isArray()`, `isBoolean()`, `isFunction()`, `isNumber()`, `isObject()`, and `isString()`. There are also two generic type assertions, `isTypeOf()` and `isInstanceOf()`, which rely on the `typeof` and `instanceof` operators, respectively. These last two operators in JavaScript are quirky, so be careful how you use them.

- Special value assertions, including `isTrue()`, `isNaN()`, `isNull()`, `isUndefined()`, and their opposites. These assertions do not perform any type coercion.

- Specialized assertion classes such as `DateAssert` and `ArrayAssert`, which provide methods such as `DateAssert.isTimeEqual()` and `ArrayAssert.containsItems()`.

For a complete list of available assert methods, refer to the API documentation.

There is no hard rule about the number of assertions that constitute a good test function. The goal is to verify a method's contract, to test each expected output for each given input. That said, some guidelines for using assertions and writing test functions include:

- Decouple unrelated assertions into different test functions. For instance, Example 12-4 could have had a test function that evaluated both leading whitespace and trailing whitespace, but this approach would have tested two unrelated input-output sets in the same function. If the first assertion fails, the second assertion is masked and never gets tested. It is better to test both input-output sets separately so that they don't interfere with each other.

- Provide well-written failure messages with each assertion. In YUI Test, every assert method takes an optional failure message as the last argument. Avoid writing failure messages that tell you *what happened*:

```
Y.Assert.areEqual('Hello world!', result, 'The result was not "Hello world!"');
```

This is a bad failure message, because you already know that the test failed. A good failure message tells you *what was expected*:

```
Y.Assert.areEqual('Hello world!', result, 'Must strip leading whitespace.');
```

With this approach, a list of failures becomes a list of unfulfilled requirements for you to evaluate. This way of thinking about test failures dovetails nicely with YUI Test's friendly test names feature.

- Make sure that individual test functions run quickly. Most test functions should simply contain one or more assert methods with just enough machinery to run those assertions. In particular, test functions should avoid dragging in real dependencies or performing expensive operations.

  The reason for this is that testing is effective only when it's done on a regular basis, so you must be able to run your tests early and often. Ideally, you should run tests after making any substantial change, and you should definitely run them before committing changes to source control. If your tests are slow, you won't run them, which leads to tests that become less and less relevant, which eventually leads to the total decay of the test suite.

- When necessary, create mock or fake dependencies. Unit testing is about testing small units of code in isolation. This means that you must have total control over the inputs to your functions under test. Using mock objects rather than real dependencies also has the side effect of speeding up your unit tests. For more information about mocking objects, refer to Recipe 12.6. There is a place for using real dependencies—this is called *integration testing*, and is discussed to some degree in Recipe 12.5.

See Also

YUI Test User Guide (*http://yuilibrary.com/yui/docs/test/*); YUI Test API documentation (*http://yuilibrary.com/yui/docs/api/modules/test.html*).

12.4 Organizing Unit Tests into Suites

Problem

You want to group your tests into suites to help organize your test code and create more meaningful test reports.

Solution

Create test cases to represent individual methods, and then group your test cases into a test suite to represent an entire object. Example 12-5 creates a test suite by:

1. Loading the json module as the code to test, along with the test-console module.
2. Creating two test cases and configuring them with object literals containing tests. The tests evaluate a range of possible outcomes: parsing a JSON string into a JavaScript object, parsing a JSON string into a JavaScript array, and the reverse operations (serializing JavaScript to JSON). Each test case uses assert methods to validate results.
3. Creating a Test.Console widget to capture and display the test results.

4. Creating a test suite with a suitable name and adding the test cases to the test suite.

5. Adding the test suite to a test runner and invoking run() to execute the tests.

Example 12-5. Grouping test cases into a test suite

```html
<!DOCTYPE html>
<title>Grouping test cases into a test suite</title>

<div class="yui3-skin-sam" id="demo"></div>

<script src="http://yui.yahooapis.com/3.5.0/build/yui/yui-min.js"></script>
<script>
YUI().use('json', 'test-console', function (Y) {
    var parseTests = new Y.Test.Case({
        name: 'parse() Tests',

        'JSON string should be parsed to JS object' : function () {
            var result = Y.JSON.parse('{"value":"YUI3"}');
            Y.Assert.isObject(result);
            Y.Assert.areEqual('YUI3', result.value);
        },

        'JSON string should be parsed to JS array' : function () {
            var result = Y.JSON.parse('[1, 2, 3, 4, 5]');
            Y.ArrayAssert.itemsAreSame([1, 2, 3, 4, 5], result);
        }
    });

    var stringifyTests = new Y.Test.Case({
        name: 'stringify() Tests',

        'JS object should be serialized to JSON string': function () {
            var result = Y.JSON.stringify({ value: 'YUI3' });
            Y.Assert.isString(result);
            Y.Assert.areEqual('{"value":"YUI3"}', result);
        },

        'JS array should be serialized to JSON string': function () {
            var result = Y.JSON.stringify([1, 2, 3, 4, 5]);
            Y.Assert.isString(result);
            Y.Assert.areEqual('[1,2,3,4,5]', result);
        }
    });

    var testSuite = new Y.Test.Suite('Y.JSON Tests');
    testSuite.add(parseTests);
    testSuite.add(stringifyTests);

    new Y.Test.Console().render('#demo');

    Y.Test.Runner.add(testSuite);
    Y.Test.Runner.run();
});
</script>
```

Discussion

Like other test frameworks, YUI Test supports a hierarchy of test cases and test suites. Each test suite can contain test cases and other test suites. However, only test cases can contain actual tests (method names that contain a space or begin with the word test).

So how many tests should you write, and how should you organize them? Here is a straightforward pattern to follow:

1. For each object you need to test, create one test suite.
2. For each method in the object to test, create one test case and add it to the object's test suite.
3. For each test case, create one test function for each input-output set in the method under test.

In this way, your test hierarchy mirrors the code you're testing. You can look at your code and figure out where you are missing test suites, and within those suites, where you are missing test cases.

The tricky part is the third step. How do you know how many test functions are enough? Too few tests means you're not actually verifying that your method works the way you think it does. But you also can't *exhaustively* test every possible combination of inputs. For most objects, that would lead to a test suite so mindbogglingly large that you probably would need to learn special mathematical notation just to write down the number of tests. More practically, each line of test code you write is code that could itself be incorrect, code that you have to support. So somewhere between the number 0 and the unfathomably large, there is some number of tests that is "good enough." Perhaps there is a way to reason intelligently about the number of tests that would illuminate something useful about a piece of code?

One way to look at the problem is to think about your function's inputs and outputs. Given an input value *x*, what should the output *y* be? What happens if you pass in an invalid value? Does your function have any interesting boundary values to consider? Note that some functions might take input but have no return value, instead making changes to an object or firing an event. In these cases, the "output" is somewhat less clear because the reaction to input can be affected by the current state of other objects.

For a slightly more formal approach to finding the minimum number of tests, you can use *structured basis testing*. In his book *Code Complete* (Microsoft Press), Steve McConnell describes structured basis testing as the idea that you must test each statement in a program at least once. Thus, to determine the minimum number of test cases for a function:

1. Start with the number 1. This represents the straight path through the function.
2. For each of the following tokens, increment by 1: `if`, `while`, `for`, `&&`, and `||`.
3. Add 1 for each `case` in a `switch` statement.

For example, if you have a function that contains a `for` loop and an `if` statement, structured basis testing indicates that you need a minimum of three tests:

- One test for the straight path through the function (all Boolean conditions are `true`).
- One test for the case where the initial `for` condition is `false` (the `for` loop is never executed).
- One test for the case where the `if` statement is `false`.

While you might very well need to add more tests, this analysis at least provides a starting point. Also note that you should continue to add tests each time a new bug is reported, to ensure that the bug stays fixed. Determining how and why a bug slipped by the test suite can help point to better strategies for improving the test suite as a whole.

Taking a closer look at Example 12-4, we see that `trim()` is just a one-line regex with no flow control statements to be found. This requires a *minimum* of one test. In reality, you almost certainly need more than that, as the regular expression is a mini-language all by itself. The three tests for the example seem reasonable. If the `trim()` function contained more branches and loops, structured basis testing would indicate which additional tests would need to be written.

If we turn our attention to Example 12-5, even before doing any analysis, it is obvious that more tests are required. The code tests only arrays and objects, and JSON obviously supports far more syntax than that! Looking at the `json` module source code and tallying paths in the main `_stringify()` method alone, it is clear that the current test suite is off by over an order of magnitude. If you really want to create a real-world, robust test suite for the `json` module, there is a lot of work to do.

See Also

The YUI `json-stringify` module source code (*https://github.com/yui/yui3/blob/master/src/json/js/stringify.js*); Scott Aaronson's essay on extremely large numbers (*http://www.scottaaronson.com/writings/bignumbers.html*).

12.5 Testing Event Handlers by Simulating Events

Problem

You've written a click handler function that needs testing. Despite your lightning-quick reflexes, it is impractical to test this code by manually clicking the button yourself.

Solution

Use YUI's event simulation utility to test event handlers by automatically exercising the DOM. Example 12-6 does this by:

1. Loading the `node-event-simulate` module, along with the `test-console` module.
2. Providing a controller with a click handler to test. This controller could have been pulled in as a module, but in this case it's just defined locally.
3. Creating a test case and configuring it with an object literal containing a setup function, a test, and a teardown function. The test simulates clicking the "button" (actually an invisible `<div>`) and then evaluates the results. The setup and teardown functions attach and detach the click handler.
4. Creating a `Test.Console` widget to capture and display the test results.
5. Adding the test case to a test runner and invoking `run()` to execute the tests.

Example 12-6. Testing a click handler with event simulation

```
<!DOCTYPE html>
<title>Testing a click handler with event simulation</title>

<div id="button"></div>
<div class="yui3-skin-sam" id="demo"></div>

<script src="http://yui.yahooapis.com/3.5.0/build/yui/yui-min.js"></script>
<script>
YUI().use('node-event-simulate', 'test-console', function (Y) {
    var controller = {
        handleClick: function (event) {
            event.target.addClass('clicked');
        }
    };

    var testCase = new Y.Test.Case({
        name: 'Test Click Handler',
        setUp: function () {
            Y.one('#button').on('click', controller.handleClick, controller);
        },
        tearDown: function (){
            Y.one('#button').detachAll();
        },
        'handleClick() should add the class "clicked" to the button': function () {
            var button = Y.one('#button');
            button.simulate('click');

            Y.Assert.isTrue(button.hasClass('clicked'),
                'Button should have a class of "clicked"');
        }
    });

    new Y.Test.Console().render('#demo');


    Y.Test.Runner.add(testCase);
    Y.Test.Runner.run();
});
</script>
```

Discussion

Methods that interact with the DOM are difficult to unit-test outside a real browser. For this reason, YUI enables you to unit-test DOM event handlers using event simulation.

Event simulation is a best-effort feature. Gesture events are not simulatable at all, and even the events that are simple enough to simulate don't always result in the exact same behavior as a real user-initiated DOM event. Before creating tests with simulated events, think about whether your application logic and user interface logic is too tightly coupled. Ideally, you should be able to exercise most of your application by firing custom events or setting attribute values rather than simulating user interactions.

 Use event simulation only for testing, never for operating your application in production. There is always a better way to do it.

At a certain point, event testing crosses over from unit testing into *functional testing*. Unlike unit testing, functional testing has real dependencies that are not mocked or faked. Functional testing tests the user's experience with the product rather than input-output sets for code. If you need to test that the user interface responds in a specific way to user interaction, then you really want to write some functional tests rather than unit tests.

Another "larger" kind of test is *integration testing*, where you are testing how well your code works with other modules, possibly written by other people. As with functional testing, in integration testing, you are admitting that you have real dependencies. If you are writing JavaScript code for the browser, it often makes sense to treat integration testing and functional testing as essentially the same thing, since it is hard to simulate the user experience (functional testing) without depending on large chunks of other people's code (integration testing).

If you are unsure whether something should be a unit test or a functional test, consider whether it is possible to write the test before the code in question actually exists. Unit tests can be written ahead of time; functional tests often cannot, because they are so closely tied to the particulars of the user interface.

While you can use YUI Test with YUI event simulation to write some basic functional tests, at some point you should consider driving your application with a dedicated functional testing tool. YUI Test includes command-line utilities designed to integrate with Selenium (*http://seleniumhq.org/*), a popular open source functional testing tool. For more information about how to drive Selenium with YUI Test, refer to the YUI Test documentation.

Returning to Example 12-6, you might be wondering, "Hey, where's the button?" All the browser displays is a white page with a Test.Console instance displaying test results, similar to previous examples. The "button" is just an empty `<div>`, and yet the test passes just fine. The test code "clicks" the button, the click handler adds a class to the button, and the assert method verifies that the class appeared as expected.

Of course, when you design your test pages, there's nothing stopping you from creating visible buttons. Your test buttons could even have attractive gradients and rounded corners. But as far as an automated test system is concerned, adding that extra markup and CSS is irrelevant. The event simulation code directly simulates a click in the DOM without regard to the button's aesthetics.

Example 12-6 uses both a `setUp()` and a `tearDown()` method. `setUp()` and `tearDown()` are conventions borrowed from JUnit and other xUnit-style test frameworks. For each test function in a test case, the YUI Test Runner runs the `setUp()` method before each test and runs the `tearDown()` method after each test, regardless of whether the test passed or failed. These methods are ideal for creating and destroying necessary data objects or attaching and detaching event listeners.

You can also configure `setUp()` and `tearDown()` methods for test suites. The YUI Test Runner calls the test suite's `setUp()` method before executing the `setUp()` method of the first test in the first test case. Likewise, the YUI Test Runner calls the test suite's `tearDown()` method after all tests in all child test cases and test suites have executed, including the last test's `tearDown()` method. Test suite `setUp()` and `tearDown()` methods are useful for creating global resources that are meant to be shared by all tests in a suite.

Finally, you can define an `init()` and `destroy()` method for each test case. The YUI Test Runner calls `init()` once, before calling any `setUp()` functions, and `destroy()` once, after calling any `tearDown()` methods. `init()` and `destroy()` enable you to set up and remove data that an *individual* test case needs. This is in contrast to defining suite-level `setUp()` and `tearDown()`, which run for all test cases in the test suite.

When the YUI Test Runner starts, it creates an empty `data` object and passes it into every `init()`, `setUp()`, `destroy()`, `tearDown()`, and test method. You can use this object to easily share data among methods and `TestCase` objects.

12.6 Mocking Objects

Problem

You have an application that has several components that are expensive to load and render. To provide a smoother user experience, you have cleverly taken advantage of an asynchronous function queuing mechanism to render your UI in chunks. Unfortunately, this makes your master `renderUI()` function hard to unit-test, because `renderUI()`'s job is to execute a queue of other rendering functions that inherently take a long time to run.

Solution

Use YUI Test's mock object facilities to create a fake asynchronous queue. In your unit test, you don't actually care that the "queue" renderUI() doesn't contain any real rendering functions. You just care about walking through renderUI()'s code paths.

Example 12-7 demonstrates how to use mock objects by:

1. Providing a renderUI() function to test. This function could have been pulled in as a module, but in this case it's just defined locally.

2. Creating a test case and configuring it with an object literal containing a test function.

3. Populating the test function with a mock object that represents the asynchronous queue of functions.

4. Defining the methods on the mock object that the test is expected to call, and the arguments each method should receive.

5. Calling renderUI() and verifying that the methods on the mock object that you expected to be called actually did get called.

6. Creating a Test.Console widget to capture and display the test results.

7. Adding the test case to a test runner and invoking run() to execute the tests.

Example 12-7. Testing with a mock object

```
<!DOCTYPE html>
<title>Testing with a mock object</title>

<div class="yui3-skin-sam" id="demo"></div>

<script src="http://yui.yahooapis.com/3.5.0/build/yui/yui-min.js"></script>
<script>
YUI().use('test-console', function (Y) {
    function renderUI(renderQueue, renderFnToSkip) {
        if (typeof renderFnToSkip === 'function' ) {
            renderQueue.remove(renderFnToSkip);
        }
        renderQueue.run();
    }

    var testCase = new Y.Test.Case({
        name: 'UI Rendering Tests',

        'App should start rendering, but with no Twitter widget' : function () {
            var mockQueue = Y.Mock(),
                renderTweetWidget = function () {};

            Y.Mock.expect(mockQueue, {
                method: 'remove',
                args: [renderTweetWidget]
            });
```

```
            Y.Mock.expect(mockQueue, {
                method: 'run',
                args: []
            });

            renderUI(mockQueue, renderTweetWidget);

            Y.Mock.verify(mockQueue);
        }
    });

    new Y.Test.Console().render('#demo');

    Y.Test.Runner.add(testCase);
    Y.Test.Runner.run();
});
</script>
```

Discussion

Mock objects eliminate test dependencies on other objects. If your code depends on an object that is simple and fast, it is acceptable to create that object directly, or perhaps in the setUp() method of your test case or test suite, perhaps in the test function itself. However, if your code depends on an object that:

- Relies on a network connection
- Performs some sort of expensive operation
- Returns unpredictable results

then you should use a mock object. Mock objects ensure that despite complex, unpredictable, or slow dependencies, you maintain rigorous control over all test inputs, and your tests continue to be reproducible and run quickly.

The classic case for a JavaScript mock object is for simulating XHR or some other network call. Network operations are a great thing to remove by mocking, since networks can be slow *and* unpredictable. Example 12-7 takes a slightly different tack, using a mock object to simulate an expensive series of rendering operations. To make the test code a little more interesting, the renderUI() function has an additional feature—it allows the caller to pass in a second, optional argument representing a component that should be removed from the queue.

So how does mocking work? If your code really depends on making an expensive call over the network, don't you actually need to make that call? When you are unit testing, the answer is no. Keep in mind that in a unit test, all you're really trying to do is exercise code paths through the function under test. Fake input data and fake responses are fine, as long as your function responds to the fake data the way you expected.

Thus, when you use a mock object, you don't care about its internals. What you *do* care about are the methods that get called on the mock object, including inputs and possibly any return values. You can think of Y.Mock.expect() as a kind of assertion about how you expect your code to exercise the object. Instead of asserting, "This variable should have the value 3," or "This variable should be a number," you are asserting, "This object should have this method called, with this argument list, and return this value."

To verify these expectations, you pass the mock object as input into the function you want to test, then call Y.Mock.verify() on the mock object. If your code calls a method on the mock object with the wrong arguments, the test fails immediately. Calling verify() further verifies that the method was called the correct number of times. The upshot is that if your test failed to call a method the expected number of times, passed in an incorrect value, or generated an incorrect return value, the test fails.

The example calls renderUI() with two arguments: the mock queue object to "run," and a (fake) function to "remove" from the queue. Looking at the implementation of renderUI(), the test should end up calling two methods on the mock object: remove (renderFnToSkip) and run(). This yields two expectations:

- The remove() method will be called with a single function argument named renderTweetWidget.
- The run() method will be called with an empty argument list.

Since the code doesn't use any return values, there is no reason to check for them in the expectation. In general, an expectation object may include:

name
> The string name of the method you expect to be called. (**Required.**)

args
> An array representing the list of arguments you expect to be supplied to the method. (**Required.**) If you pass incorrect arguments, the test fails even before you call verify().
>
> If you care only about the type of the argument and not its value, you can provide a special Y.Mock.Value in place of an actual value. Supported types include Y.Mock.Value.String, Y.Mock.Value.Number, Y.Mock.Value.Boolean, Y.Mock.Value .Object, Y.Mock.Value.Function, and even Y.Mock.Value.Any (if you don't care about the specific type of the value). Example 12-7 doesn't actually depend on the value of the argument passed into remove(), just the type, so you could rewrite the expectation as:

```
Y.Mock.expect(mockQueue, {
    method: 'remove',
    args: [Y.Mock.Value.Function]
});
```

> The reason the test uses a function specifically named renderTweetWidget is simply to make the example a little more concrete.

returns
> The value you expect the method to return.

error
>An error you expect the method to throw.

callCount
>The number of times you expect the method to be called with the given arguments.

If any of these defined expectations is not satisfied, the test fails. You are, of course, free to use ordinary assert methods right alongside expect() and verify().

Note that in Example 12-7, there is only a single test. An obvious second test is missing: the case where you *don't* pass in a function to skip. In that case, only the run() method should get called. What would testing that second code path look like? See Example 12-8.

Example 12-8. Adding a second mock object test

```
'The entire app should start rendering' : function () {
    var mockQueue = Y.Mock();

    Y.Mock.expect(mockQueue, {
        method: 'run',
        args: []
    });

    renderUI(mockQueue, null);

    Y.Mock.verify(mockQueue);
}
```

Passing null in as renderUI()'s second argument should cause renderUI() to only call run() with no arguments on the queue object. The test in Example 12-8 verifies that this is exactly what happens.

See Also

The AsyncQueue User Guide (*http://yuilibrary.com/yui/docs/async-queue/*).

12.7 Testing Asynchronously Using wait()

Problem

You need to pause your tests and resume them later in order to evaluate some state that will be present in the future.

Solution

Use YUI Test Case's ability to pause and resume a running test with wait() and resume(). Example 12-9 illustrates this by:

1. Providing a changeToRed() function to test. This function could have been pulled in as a module, but in this case it's just defined locally.

2. Creating a test case and configuring it with an object literal containing a test function. This test case is special in that it is designed to suspend until after the change ToRed() function completes its work.

3. Setting an event handler that listens for the example:red event. When the event handler triggers, it resumes the suspended test case and checks an assertion about the <body>'s current background color.

4. Calling changeToRed(), immediately followed by wait(). The wait() method immediately suspends the test case until something calls resume().

5. Creating a Test.Console widget to capture and display the test results.

6. Adding the test case to a test runner and invoking run() to execute the tests.

Example 12-9. Testing asynchronously with wait()

```
<!DOCTYPE html>
<title>Testing asynchronously with wait()</title>
<style>
.foo { background: #955; }
</style>

<div class="yui3-skin-sam" id="demo">

<script src="http://yui.yahooapis.com/3.5.0/build/yui/yui-min.js"></script>
<script>
YUI().use('test-console', function (Y) {
    function changeToRed(timeout) {
        setTimeout(function () {
            Y.one('body').addClass('foo');
            Y.fire('example:red');
        }, timeout)
    }

    var asyncTest = new Y.Test.Case({
        name: 'Asynchronous Transition Test with Events',

        'After 2 seconds, body should have class foo' : function () {
            var self = this;

            Y.on('example:red', function () {
                self.resume(function () {
                    Y.Assert.isTrue(Y.one('body').hasClass('foo'));
                });
            });

            changeToRed(2000);
            this.wait();
        }
    });

    new Y.Test.Console().render('#demo');
```

```
    Y.Test.Runner.add(asyncTest);
    Y.Test.Runner.run();
});
</script>
```

Discussion

Because changeToRed() doesn't complete its work until some timeout has occurred, we can't verify its results immediately. However, you can suspend the test case until conditions are right. There are two basic approaches:

- Suspend the test case until some event occurs, then resume the test case and run some assertions.
- Suspend the test case for some fixed period of time, then resume the test case and run some assertions, as illustrated in Example 12-10.

Since changeToRed() conveniently fires an event as soon as its work is complete, the first option seems like the way to go. To break down the listener step-by-step:

1. Y.on() sets a listener for the example:red event.
2. When the listener detects an example:red event, it triggers the event handler. The event handler does one thing: calls the test case's resume() method.
3. The resume() method accepts a single argument, and does two things:
   - Wakes up the test case from its suspended state.
   - Executes the function that was passed into resume(). This function should be responsible for running any assertions.

 Within the event handler function, the test case's this.resume() is no longer in scope. However, saving this to a variable self causes the event handler to close over the self variable, which enables the event handler to reference the test case and its methods.

After setting the listener, Example 12-9 calls the changeToRed() function, followed immediately by this.wait(), which suspends the test case. The test case remains suspended until the example:red event fires 2,000 milliseconds later, which triggers the event handler, which calls resume() to resume the test case.

You can see this in action if you load Example 12-9 in a browser and check the "status" checkbox to display additional status messages. The test console runs some test startup log messages, halting at the message:

```
Test case "Asynchronous Transition Test with Events" started
```

There, the test console waits until 2,000 milliseconds pass, the background changes to red, and the test case resumes from suspension.

Example 12-9 called wait() with no arguments, which caused the test to suspend until some other function calls resume(). However, similar to setTimeout(), the wait() method can take two arguments: a time period for which to suspend the test case, and a function to execute when the time period elapses. In this case, you do not need a resume() callback, and instead the wait() callback should contain assertions to run.

 Calling wait() with a fixed time period means you are basing a test on a race condition. This technique can fail unpredictably for various reasons, such as the browser event loop being bogged down. Use this technique only if there really is no event to listen to, or perhaps if you are trying to verify that something *didn't* happen as a result of the tested method call.

Example 12-10 is a variation where changeToRed() does *not* happen to fire an event on completion. In this case, you could rewrite your asynchronous test case to look like this.

Example 12-10. Testing asynchronously with no event to listen for

```
YUI().use('test-console', function (Y) {
    function changeToRed(timeout) {
        setTimeout(function () {
            Y.one('body').addClass('foo');
        }, timeout)
    }

    var asyncTest = new Y.Test.Case({
        name: 'Asynchronous Transition Test with No Event',

        'After 2 seconds, body should have class foo' : function () {
            changeToRed(2000);

            this.wait(function () {
                Y.Assert.isTrue(Y.one('body').hasClass('foo'));
            }, 2100);
        }
    });

    new Y.Test.Console().render('#demo');

    Y.Test.Runner.add(asyncTest);
    Y.Test.Runner.run();
});
```

Now, instead of waiting for an event, the test simply waits a fixed period of time for the body to change to red. After 2,100 milliseconds, the test case resumes and executes a function that contains an assertion. This assertion executes in the context of the test case object, so it still has access to all of the same data as the test that called wait(), including any properties and methods on the test case object itself.

For example, you could have your setUp() function add some data to the test case object as this.data.someval, and the wait callback function could access that data. You can even call this.wait() again from within the wait callback function.

Keep in mind that if you had guessed wrong and waited only 1,800 milliseconds, or if some external factor had interfered with the browser's timing, the background color would not yet be red, so the test would fail.

12.8 Collecting and Posting Test Results

Problem

You want to collect raw test data and store it somewhere for later analysis.

Solution

Use the YUI Test's Test Reporter to post test results to a remote server. Example 12-11 reuses most of the code from Example 12-5, but instead of simply running tests, the example now listens for the event that signals the end of testing. The event handler collects the results in JSON format and posts the data to a URI endpoint.

Example 12-11. Collecting and posting test results

```
<!DOCTYPE html>
<title>Collecting and posting test results</title>

<div class="yui3-skin-sam" id="demo"></div>

<script src='http://yui.yahooapis.com/3.5.0/build/yui/yui-min.js'></script>
<script>
YUI().use('json', 'test-console', function (Y) {
    var parseTests = new Y.Test.Case({
        name: 'parse() Tests',

        'JSON string should be parsed to JS object' : function () {
            var result = Y.JSON.parse('{"value":"YUI3"}');
            Y.Assert.isObject(result);
            Y.Assert.areEqual('YUI3', result.value);
        },

        'JSON string should be parsed to JS array' : function () {
            var result = Y.JSON.parse('[1, 2, 3, 4, 5]');
            Y.ArrayAssert.itemsAreSame([1, 2, 3, 4, 5], result);
        }
    });

    var stringifyTests = new Y.Test.Case({
        name: 'stringify() Tests',
```

```
'JS object should be serialized to JSON string': function () {
    var result = Y.JSON.stringify({ value: 'YUI3' });
    Y.Assert.isString(result);
    Y.Assert.areEqual('{"value":"YUI3"}', result);
},

'JS array should be serialized to JSON string': function () {
    var result = Y.JSON.stringify([1, 2, 3, 4, 5]);
    Y.Assert.isString(result);
    Y.Assert.areEqual('[1,2,3,4,5]', result);
}
});

var testSuite = new Y.Test.Suite('Y.JSON Tests');
testSuite.add(parseTests);
testSuite.add(stringifyTests);

new Y.Test.Console().render('#demo');

var testRunner = Y.Test.Runner.add(testSuite);

testRunner.subscribe(Y.Test.Runner.COMPLETE_EVENT, function() {
    var results = testRunner.getResults(),
        reporter = new Y.Test.Reporter('http://localhost/report.php');
    reporter.report(results);
});

testRunner.run();
});
</script>
```

Discussion

In previous examples, the test console displayed test results. As soon as you close the browser window, those test results disappear. This is OK for one-off testing, but if you are running tests on a regular basis, you will likely want to store the result data somewhere for later analysis.

Since the test data is trapped on the web page, what's the best way to get at it? The good news is that you don't have to roll your own XHR solution, or worse, scrape the data off the test page. YUI Test provides a handy utility in the YUI Test Reporter. You just need to get a results object from the Test Runner, invoke a Test Reporter instance, and call the report() method. When you call report(), Test Reporter creates a form and POSTs the data to the endpoint you specified with these fields:

results
    The results object serialized to a string.

useragent
    Your browser's user agent string.

timestamp
    The date and time the report was sent.

custom_field

    An extra custom field you added by previously calling addField(*custom_field,* *value*) on the Test Reporter instance. You can add multiple additional fields, but you cannot override the three built-in fields.

The form submission does not cause your test page to navigate away. Note that Test Reporter does not receive a response back from the endpoint, so there isn't a simple way to ensure that your POST succeeded.

You obtain a raw test results object by calling getResults() on the Test Runner. When you instantiate the Test Reporter, you can specify the test data format by passing in one of these constants as the second constructor argument:

Y.Test.Format.XML

    A YUI-specific representation of the test results in XML. This is the default.

Y.Test.Format.JSON

    A YUI-specific representation of the test results in JSON.

Y.Test.Format.JUnitXML

    A representation of the test results in JUnit XML (*http://www.junit.org*), a format that many testing tools heroically manage to support despite the fact that nobody is quite sure what the specification is.

Y.Test.Format.TAP

    A representation of the test results in TAP (Test Anything Protocol) format (*http://testanything.org/wiki/index.php/Main_Page*).

If you call getResults() before tests have finished running, the method returns null. In other words, you can't do this:

```
testRunner.run();
var results = testRunner.getResults();
```

because when getResults() executes, there is no chance that the Test Runner has completed its work yet. That's why Example 12-11 subscribes to the Y.Test.Runner. COMPLETE_EVENT event, which indicates that testing is over, and it is safe to extract and post test results.

So where exactly should you post the report data? If you are running some kind of third-party test harness or continuous integration tool, it might already support the JUnit XML or TAP formats. You can use YUI Test Reporter to POST data directly to some endpoint in the tool; or, if your tool's API doesn't support POSTing report data directly, you can always write a small proxy script that accepts POST data and then turns around and feeds the tool properly.

Alternatively, you can write a custom report display screen. This is more work, but it enables you to slice and dice the data any way you please. It also affords you the opportunity to flex your server-side JavaScript skills—or you can just bludgeon the problem into submission with PHP, as Example 12-12 demonstrates.

Example 12-12. Quick-and-dirty PHP test report script

```php
<?php
function escapeHTML($str) {
    return htmlentities($str, ENT_QUOTES | ENT_HTML5 | ENT_SUBSTITUTE, 'UTF-8');
}

if ($_SERVER['REQUEST_METHOD'] == "POST") {
    file_put_contents('/tmp/test_results.xml', $_POST['results']);
}
else {
    $results = simplexml_load_file('/tmp/test_results.xml');
    $tests = $results->xpath('//test');
?>

<!DOCTYPE html>
<title>Test Report for <?php echo escapeHTML($results['name']); ?></title>
<style>
    td { border: 1px #000 solid; padding: 2px }
    td.fail { background: #f33; }
</style>
<h1>
    Test Report for <?php echo escapeHTML($results['name']); ?>:
    <?php echo escapeHTML($results['total']); ?> total,
    <?php echo escapeHTML($results['failed']); ?> failed
</h1>
<table>
<tr>
    <th>Test</th>
    <th>Result</th>
    <th>Message</th>
</tr>
<?php
    foreach ($tests as $test) {
        $class = $test['result'] == 'fail' ? 'class="fail"' : '';
?>
<tr>
    <td><?php echo escapeHTML($test['name']); ?></td>
    <td <?php echo $class; ?>><?php echo escapeHTML($test['result']); ?></td>
    <td><?php echo escapeHTML($test['message']); ?></td>
</tr>
<?php } ?>
</table>
<?php } ?>
```

You can drop Example 12-12 into almost any web server running PHP 5. If the script does not run properly, check your server's INI settings: magic_quotes_gpc must be off, and open_basedirs must permit scripts to write to */tmp* (or wherever you want to write the test result data). To see the report script in action, modify Example 12-11 so that Y.Test.Reporter points to your PHP report script, open the HTML page in a browser to run the tests and post the data, and then open the PHP script in a browser to view the results.

This minimal, self-contained report script lacks certain desirable features such as reproducibility of results, robustness, and aesthetics. These flaws aside, the script does illustrate some basic principles:

- You need a component that handles incoming POST requests.
- That component must store the data persistently somewhere.
- On a GET request, the app must fetch the requested report.
- Finally, you must format the raw data for display.

The report script ignores the nested test suite/test case structure in the data and just lists the tests. If you have a large collection of test suites, you will almost certainly want a more sophisticated visual representation. Be sure to escape or sanitize data before displaying it to users in a browser.

See Also

JUnit (*http://www.junit.org*); TAP (*http://testanything.org/wiki/index.php/Main_Page*).

12.9 Precommit Testing in Multiple Browsers

Problem

You want to quickly run a series of automated tests to verify that your recent changes work in multiple browsers—before committing changes to version control.

Solution

Use the Yeti test launcher to asynchronously run tests at the command line in multiple browsers:

1. Install Node.js and npm if you haven't already. Then install the yeti package using npm. Since Yeti is a tool designed to be used all over your system, consider using the -g flag.

    ```
    $ npm install -g yeti
    ```

2. Invoke Yeti as a server on port 8000:

    ```
    $ yeti --server
    Yeti will only serve files inside /Users/goer/Documents/yui/current/examples
    Visit http://localhost:8000, then run:
        yeti <test document>
    to run and report the results.
    ```

3. Open *http://localhost:8000* in each browser you want to test. Each browser displays a web page that says, "Waiting for tests."

4. In a *separate* terminal window, run the yeti command-line utility on the HTML files containing your tests. Example 12-13 uses the trim() tests from Example 12-4.

Invoking Yeti on *test_case.html* causes each browser to run the tests embedded in *test_case.html* in parallel. When each browser finishes, it reports the YUI Test results back to the server. As soon as each result set arrives, Yeti prints the outcome, including any failures, to the command line. Until you stop the server with a Ctrl-C, Yeti continues to run any additional tests you invoke for all browsers attached to the server.

Example 12-13. Running multiple browsers with the Yeti server

```
$ yeti test_case.html
Waiting for results. When you're done, hit Ctrl-C to exit.
✖ yuitests1300945685398 on Safari (5.0.3) / MacOS
  2 passed,  1 failed
  in trim() Tests
    Leading and trailing white space should be removed Values should be equal.
      Expected: Hello world! (string)
      Actual: Hello world!     (string)

✖ yuitests1300945686048 on Firefox (3.6.15) / MacOS
  2 passed,  1 failed
  in trim() Tests
    Leading and trailing white space should be removed Values should be equal.
      Expected: Hello world! (string)
      Actual: Hello world!     (string)

✖ yuitests1300945686364 on Chrome (10.0.648.151) / MacOS
  2 passed,  1 failed
  in trim() Tests
    Leading and trailing white space should be removed Values should be equal.
      Expected: Hello world! (string)
      Actual: Hello world!     (string)
```

 Yeti caches assets while running tests, but when you run Yeti again, it busts the cache.

Discussion

In earlier sections, such as Recipe 12.3, running tests is a manual process—you have to load the test page in a browser and click Refresh. This isn't too bad with a single browser, but the more browsers you add, the clumsier this becomes. At the very least, this experience is far less pleasant than the code/test/debug cycle for any other language.

What you need is the ability to quickly run your tests in multiple browsers, so you can iterate on small changes before committing changes to version control. Selenium and its cousin TestSwarm do a fine job of automating browsers, but both are heavyweight tools that are designed for central infrastructure. While it is technically possible to drive precommit unit tests through Selenium or TestSwarm, they require you to set up your entire software stack, and they do not necessarily run tests quickly or provide immediate feedback. Therefore, these tools are more appropriate for system integration testing as part of a continuous integration process.

By contrast, Yeti is designed for fast precommit testing. It provides you with output on the command line as quickly as possible, advances to the next test immediately, and runs in parallel on multiple browsers. Yeti is sometimes described as a "highly personal" test tool because it is meant to run on your personal developer machine, and to test *your* local changes as opposed to your team's. Yeti's server mode is ideal for working offline. You can test any browsers running on your machine or in local virtual machines without needing a network connection to a central test server.

Yeti does not replace tools like Selenium and TestSwarm; rather, it complements them. A precommit test tool is designed to quickly run your tests immediately after changing your code, so that the changes are still fresh in your mind. The goal of a post-commit test tool is to exercise a large, integrated code base, ensuring that different components written by different people all work together properly.

Yeti is not the first precommit JavaScript test launcher. The older JSTestDriver project is a mature test launcher that has far more features than Yeti, and supports both precommit testing and continuous integration. However, you cannot use JSTestDriver with tests written with YUI Test. JSTestDriver requires test cases to be written with the JSTestDriver Test Framework, and focuses on testing pure JavaScript files, as opposed to JavaScript embedded in HTML. For this reason, Yeti was built to be a simple, fast test launcher for running existing HTML YUI Test pages unmodified.

 While Yeti requires test cases to be written with YUI Test, you can of course use YUI Test and Yeti to test any JavaScript code you like, not just YUI code.

Besides speed, Yeti's main feature is simplicity. It runs with no configuration or setup. Example 12-13 invokes Yeti as a server in order to attach multiple browsers to the test page. However, if you care only about quickly verifying your changes in a single browser, there is an even simpler method for using Yeti. You can skip steps 2 and 3 and just invoke yeti directly on the test files.

Example 12-14. Running a single browser with Yeti

```
$ yeti test_case.html
✖ yuitests1300893214487 on Safari (5.0.3) / MacOS
   2 passed,  1 failed
   in trim() Tests
     Leading and trailing white space should be removed Values should be equal.
       Expected: Hello world! (string)
       Actual: Hello world!     (string)

Failures: 1 of 3 tests failed. (1612ms)
```

If Yeti is not running as a server, it launches your system's default browser, runs the specified test pages, and exits. This simple mode still keeps you out of the browser and as close as possible to your code.

Yeti is fault tolerant. If it encounters a syntax error, an uncaught exception, or a file without tests, it reports the problem to you and continues running. To ensure that DOM-related tests behave properly, Yeti also requires HTML tests to load in Standards mode, not Quirks mode. If an HTML page lacks a doctype, Yeti reports this as an error. For security reasons, the Yeti server refuses to serve up pages that reside outside the directory where you started the server.

Beyond `--server`, Yeti also includes `--port` to run a Yeti server on an alternative port. You can also incorporate the Yeti server into scripts with the `--solo 1` option, which causes the server to exit with a summary after running all tests once, rather than waiting for an explicit interrupt. If any failures occur, Yeti exits with a nonzero status code.

12.10 Testing on Mobile Devices

Problem

You want to test your code in mobile browsers, but you can't figure out how to get Node.js and Yeti to run on your iPhone—at least, not without voiding your warranty.

Solution

Use `localtunnel` (*https://github.com/progrium/localtunnel/*) to expose your Yeti server to the outside world, then connect to the server using your mobile device.

 Using `localtunnel` exposes your machine to public web traffic, which introduces serious security ramifications. This goes double if you are tunneling from inside a VPN or corporate network to the outside world.

1. Start the Yeti server on port 8000:

        $ yeti --server

2. In a separate terminal window, use gem to install `localtunnel`:

        $ sudo gem install localtunnel

    If you have not already done so, you must install Ruby and the gem package manager first.

3. If you do not already have a public SSH key, create one by running `ssh-keygen`. Then upload your key and make port 8000 public on localtunnel.com with:

        $ localtunnel -k ~/.ssh/id_rsa.pub 8000
            This localtunnel service is brought to you by Twilio.
            Port 8000 is now publicly accessible from http://5832.localtunnel.com ...

The -k option is a one-time requirement that uploads your public SSH key to localtunnel.com. Subsequently, you can create new local tunnels simply by running `localtunnel` *portnumber*.

4. Open *http://yourid.localtunnel.com* in a mobile browser (or any browser). You should see the familiar Yeti "Waiting for tests" page.

5. In yet another terminal window, run the `yeti` command-line utility on the HTML files containing your tests. Example 12-15 uses the `trim()` tests from Example 12-4.

Example 12-15. Testing mobile devices using the Yeti server and localtunnel

```
$ yeti test_case.html
Waiting for results. When you're done, hit Ctrl-C to exit.
✘ yuitests1301164407717 on Safari (5.0.2) / iOS 4.2.1
  2 passed,  1 failed
  in trim() Tests
    Leading and trailing white space should be removed Values should be equal.
      Expected: Hello world! (string)
      Actual: Hello world!    (string)
```

Once you have a Yeti server running and addressable on the Web, it is easy to create a fairly large test cluster. Figure 12-3 is a photograph of a Yeti test cluster executing the YUI 3.5.0 test suite, running approximately 25 browsers on 18 physical devices (not all devices visible).

Discussion

As shown in Recipe 12.9, it is easy to test browsers running on your personal machine using Yeti in server mode. Mobile browsers are a little trickier, but `localtunnel` makes it trivial to serve up a test page over the public Web, which means you can point as many devices as you like to your Yeti instance. You are limited only by your imagination and your budget for purchasing mobile hardware.

In fact, Yeti was designed with the mobile world in mind. Instead of attempting to install software on many different machines and automate individual browsers, Yeti just serves up self-running test pages and collects test results. This model doesn't allow for sophisticated system integration testing à la Selenium, but it does enable you to quickly test an enormous variety of browsers, OS platforms, and devices. At the time of writing, YUI considers iOS 3, iOS 4, and Android 2 to be in the Browser Test Baseline, which means that these platforms are all tested and targeted for full support.

See Also

Ruby (*http://www.ruby-lang.org*); the gem package manager (*http://rubygems.org*); `localtunnel` (*https://github.com/progrium/localtunnel/*); Maximiliano Firtman's list of mobile emulators (*http://www.mobilexweb.com/emulators*).

Figure 12-3. Yeti test cluster (image courtesy Dav Glass)

12.11 Testing Server-Side JavaScript

Problem

You want to test your server-side code in Node.js.

Solution

Use YUI Test to run tests at the command line, purely within Node.js.

1. If you haven't already, install Node.js and the npm package manager. Then install the stable version of yuitest using npm:

   ```
   $ npm install -g yuitest
   ```

2. Run the yuitest command-line utility on JavaScript files and directories containing JavaScript files to test:

   ```
   $ yuitest test_case.js
   ```

Example 12-16 reuses the `trim()` function and tests from Example 12-4. Key differences include:

- Instead of using `YUI().use()` to load YUI Test as a YUI module, the script uses YUI Test Standalone. Since there is no `Y` object, the script calls test methods using the `YUITest` object instead of `Y.Test`.
- To ensure that this script could potentially run in both environments, the script first checks whether `YUITest` is attached to the `this` object (browser context), and if that fails, attempts to require `yuitest` as a Node.js module.
- Because this code might not be running in the browser, the `Test.Console` widget is removed. Output will appear in the log.
- The `run()` method is removed; otherwise, server-side YUI Test will run tests twice.

Example 12-16. Running YUI Test on the server side

```
// Implementation is not quite right; regex is missing a /g
function trim(text){
    return text.replace(/^\s+|\s+$/,  '');
}

var YUITest = this.YUITest || require('yuitest');

YUITest.Assert.areEqual(28, 28);

var testCase = new YUITest.TestCase({
    name: 'trim() Tests',

    'Leading white space should be removed': function () {
        var result = trim('    Hello world!');
        YUITest.Assert.areEqual('Hello world!', result);
    },

    'Trailing white space should be removed': function () {
        var result = trim('Hello world!    ');
        YUITest.Assert.areEqual('Hello world!', result);
    },

    'Leading and trailing white space should be removed': function () {
        var result = trim('    Hello world!    ');
        YUITest.Assert.areEqual('Hello world!', result);
    }
});

YUITest.TestRunner.add(testCase);
```

Discussion

The main difference between the `yeti` utility and the `yuitest` utility is:

- `yeti` is a specialized test runner designed to efficiently run YUI Test tests within one or more browser environments.

- `yuitest` is a command-line utility for running YUI Test tests on Node.js.

`yuitest` is great for testing command-line JavaScript utilities and JavaScript libraries that run within Node.js. However, this command-line utility cannot test JavaScript that manipulates the DOM or does anything else browser-specific. To use YUI Test in the browser, use one of the techniques discussed earlier in this chapter: open a test page manually, use Yeti to attach and automate multiple browsers, or use a full-fledged automation framework such as Selenium or Test Swarm.

12.12 Minifying Your Code

Problem

You want to make your code as small as possible so that it loads quickly over the network. You already plan to GZIP your code, but perhaps there's some way to actually shrink the code that GZIP is acting upon?

Solution

Use the YUI Compressor tool to safely remove comments, remove whitespace, and minimize local symbols where possible. A quick-and-dirty way to do this is to use the online YUI Compressor (*http://refresh-sf.com/yui/*):

1. Paste your code into the text box or upload your JavaScript as a file.

2. Click Compress. YUI Compressor converts your code into equivalent but smaller JavaScript. For example, the function:

```
// Returns strings like, "Merhaba, <name>!"
function randomGreeting(name, intlStrings){
    var langs = intlStrings.getLanguages();
    var randomLang = Math.floor(Math.random() * (langs.length - 1));
    var hello = intlStrings.getGreeting(randomLang);

    return hello + ", " + name + "!";
}
```

compresses to:

```
function randomGreeting(a,e){var d=e.getLanguages();
var c=Math.floor(Math.random()*(d.length-1));
var b=e.getGreeting(c);return b+", "+a+"!"};
```

which is 48% the size of the original. (There are two extra newlines here so that the line doesn't run off the page.)

3. GZIP the minified results.

The online version of YUI Compressor is easy to use, but is really only good for one-off conversions. To integrate YUI Compressor into your build process, you can download YUI Compressor and run it on the command line:

1. Install Java and Ant on your system if you have not already done so. Then download the latest release of YUI Compressor (*http://yuilibrary.com/download/yuicompressor/*).

2. Unzip the file in a working directory. From the top-level *yuicompressor-x.y.z/* directory, run the ant command to build YUI Compressor:

```
$ ~/Documents/yui/utils/yuicompressor-2.4.7 $ ant
Buildfile: /Users/goer/Documents/yui/utils/yuicompressor-2.4.7/build.xml

-load.properties:

-init:

build.classes:
    [mkdir] Created dir: ...

... (SNIP) ...

BUILD SUCCESSFUL
Total time: 6 seconds
```

This generates a usable JAR file in the *build/* directory.

3. Run `yuicompressor-x.y.z.jar` on a CSS or JavaScript file. The `-o` option writes the minified output to a file rather than `stdout`:

```
$ wc /tmp/electron.js
    51    161   1913 /tmp/electron.js
$ java -jar build/yuicompressor-2.4.7.jar -o /tmp/electron-min.js /tmp/electron.js
$ wc /tmp/electron-min.js
     0     17   1079 /tmp/electron-min.js
```

4. GZIP the minified results.

Discussion

When people speak of "compression" on the Web, they're often referring to HTTP compression. In HTTP compression, the server compresses source files with a scheme such as GZIP, and clients retrieve these files using HTTP, uncompress them, and use them. HTTP compression is an important part of your toolkit, and performance scoring utilities such as YSlow and Page Speed take this into account.

 Although GZIP works well on text files such as HTML, CSS, and JavaScript, it has little effect on binary images such as GIFs, JPEGs, and PNGs, as these files are already compressed. However, it is still possible to reduce compressed image file sizes further using other techniques. For example, try the YSlow Smush.it utility (*http://developer.yahoo.com/yslow/smushit/*).

However, there is a second approach for reducing file sizes that complements HTTP compression. This approach is called *minification*. A hand-authored JavaScript file contains all sorts of extra characters that are useful for humans responsible for *authoring* the code, but that aren't necessary for JavaScript engines responsible for *executing* the code.

For example, you might imagine writing a post-processor that strips extra whitespace and comments, resulting in a smaller file that still has the same behavior in the browser. This technique is straightforward and does in fact save a substantial number of bytes on top of what HTTP compression saves. Success! But can you do better?

With a more sophisticated approach, you can minify more aggressively. JavaScript engines do not require functions, variables, and other symbols to have long human-readable names. Converting those symbols to single letters would provide even more savings. However, blindly converting every variable name is dangerous. The algorithm has to differentiate between variables that are hidden safely in a local scope and variables that are accessible outside the program. At this point, the algorithm has to operate on JavaScript as a stream of tokens, not as a giant string.

The YUI Compressor is a Java command-line tool that relies on Mozilla's Rhino JavaScript engine to tokenize the source JavaScript file. This enables YUI Compressor to analyze the source and determine which symbol names are in a local scope and therefore safe to minify. By itself, variable renaming saves more bytes on average than simple whitespace stripping. Beyond that, parsing JavaScript enables YUI Compressor to run a battery of additional techniques, such as:

- Concatenating large strings by safely removing the + operator (which might have the side effect of slightly speeding up your code execution)
- Removing comments and whitespace
- Safely replacing bracket notation with dot notation where safe (`foo["bar"]` becomes `foo.bar`)
- Safely replacing quoted literal property names (for instance, `{"foo":"bar"}` becomes `{foo:"bar"}`)
- Removing semicolons in places where JavaScript's automatic semicolon insertion would terminate the statement anyway

Some of these techniques are actually bad practice for authoring code, precisely because they make the code hard for humans to read and maintain. But here, this is OK—minified code is for JavaScript engines, not humans.

In addition to JavaScript minification, YUI Compressor can also use regular expressions to minify CSS files. The result is minification that is efficient, but conservative and safe, typically shrinking file sizes 50% for JavaScript and 35% for CSS. Combining HTTP compression and minification, you can expect JavaScript files to be 85% smaller, and CSS to be about 80% smaller.

Unlike HTTP compression, minification is too slow to try to do on the fly. Minification should be part of your build process. In the YUI build process, all core library files are passed through both YUI Compressor and JSLint.

Certain coding practices can either help or hinder YUI Compressor's ability to do its job. Running YUI Compressor with the -v option displays advice on how to improve minification. In general, these practices include:

- Using every variable you define. If you're trying to make your program smaller, an excellent place to start is removing all dead code.

- Defining every variable you use. Failing to define a variable creates it in the global scope, which means it cannot be safely renamed.

- Defining a variable only once in a given scope.

- Avoiding the eval() function. The code executed in an eval() gains access to local variables in the scope where eval() is called. Since there is no way to know if the eval() will actually use any of these local variables, YUI Compressor cannot safely rename any variables in this scope.

- Avoiding the with statement. Like eval(), with interferes with code minification. Since with confuses the distinction between variables and object properties, YUI Compressor cannot safely rename any variables in the scope where with is called. Also note that with is no longer allowed when running in ECMAScript 5 strict mode.

- Minimizing the use of global variables. YUI Compressor cannot rename global variables for the obvious reason that other code on the page might be using those variables.

- Using constants to represent repeated literal values. Storing a common message string in a variable makes it easier to update and reuse that value later on. But as a bonus, this practice helps out YUI Compressor. YUI Compressor does not replace literal values, so defining common literal values as constants enables YUI to rename values that it couldn't rename before.

- Storing local references to objects and values. YUI Compressor can't rename global variables or multilevel object references, but storing these references in local variables enables YUI Compressor to rename them. In Example 12-17, YUI Compressor cannot minify MyApp.MyModule.MyClass.

Example 12-17. Failing to minify multilevel object reference

```
function frobozz(){
    if (MyApp.MyModule.MyClass.hasSword()) {
        MyApp.MyModule.MyClass.killTrollWithSword();
    }
    else {
        MyApp.MyModule.MyClass.death();
    }
}
```

However, if you store this object reference in a local variable, `MyApp.MyModule` `.MyClass` need only appear once at the top of this function, and YUI Compressor can then compress all the instances of the variable `myClass`. See Example 12-18.

Example 12-18. Successfully minifying local variable of multilevel object reference

```
function frobozz(){
    var myClass = MyApp.MyModule.MyClass;
    if (myClass.hasSword()) {
        myclass.killTrollWithSword();
    }
    else {
        myClass.death();
    }
}
```

Finally, YUI Compressor supports special syntax that provides fine-grained control over how minification works.

First, there are situations where you are required to preserve comments even in minified production code, such as copyright or license statements. To preserve a multiline comment, include an exclamation point as the first character:

```
/*! Copyright 2012, Great Underground Empire Inc. This is a very
 *  important license statement. If you fail to include this license,
 *  you might be eaten by a grue.
 */
```

Second, you can prevent individual local variables, function names, or function arguments from being renamed by using a *hint*. A hint is a string at the very beginning of the function definition that contains a comma-separated list of *variable*:nomunge tokens, as in:

```
function zorkmid(frobozz, xyzzy) {
    "xyzzy:nomunge, grue:nomunge, plugh:nomunge";

    var grue = true;
    function plugh() {...}
    ...
}
```

This would permit YUI Compressor to rename `frobozz`, but preserve `xyzzy`, `grue`, and `plugh`.

See Also

YUI Compressor (*http://yuilibrary.com/projects/yuicompressor/*); HTTP compression (*http://en.wikipedia.org/wiki/HTTP_compression*); YSlow (*http://developer.yahoo.com/ yslow*); YSlow Smush.it (*http://developer.yahoo.com/yslow/smushit/*); Page Speed (*http: //code.google.com/speed/page-speed/*); Rhino JavaScript engine (*http://www.mozilla.org/ rhino/*); Stoyan Stefanov's analysis of minification on JavaScript and CSS file sizes (*http: //www.phpied.com/reducing-tpayload/*).

12.13 Documenting Your Code

Problem

You want to make sure that people can figure out how to use your JavaScript API. ("People" can include your teammates, customers, and even yourself six months from now.)

Solution

Use YUI Doc to create documentation from comments in source code. Like YUI Test, YUI Doc is a standalone project. YUI Doc can generate documentation for non-YUI code or even languages other than JavaScript.

Example 12-19 takes the method from Recipe 12.7 and enhances it with some comments to generate API documentation. To show off the capabilities of YUI Doc a little better, changeToRed() is no longer a standalone function—it is now a method that belongs to a class, ColorChange, which in turn belongs to an Example module.

Example 12-19. Documenting a method

```
/**
 * Provides toy classes and methods used to show how unit testing
 * works in YUI Test.
 * @module example
 * @submodule example-async
 * @for ColorChange
 */

/**
 * Provides simple timed style changes that you can use to learn how
 * to write asynchronous tests.
 * @class ColorChange
 */
Example.ColorChange = {

    /**
     * After the specified timeout, changes the body of the document
     * to "rgb(255,0,0)" and fires an "example:red" event. This is a toy
     * function used to illustrate asynchronous testing.
     * @method changeToRed
     * @param {Number} timeout The number of ms to wait before changing
     *                         the body to red.
     */
    changeToRed: function (timeout) {
        setTimeout(function () {
            Y.one('body').addClass('foo');

            /**
             * Indicates that the background has changed to red. This is
             * the event to listen for when running an asynchronous test
             * with wait() and resume().
```

```
            * @event example:red
            * @type Event:Custom
            */
           Y.fire('example:red');
       }, timeout)
   }
};
```

To convert this into documentation:

1. Install Node.js and npm if you haven't already. Then install the yuidocjs package using npm. Since YUI Doc is a tool designed to be used all over your system, consider using the -g flag:

   ```
   $ npm install -g yuidocjs
   ```

    The yuidocjs npm package is, at the time of writing, alpha software. **The package name is subject to change.** Until the JavaScript version of YUI Doc stabilizes, you can always use the legacy Python version of YUI Doc (*http://developer.yahoo.com/yui/yuidoc/*).

2. Run yuidoc on the directory where your source code resides:

   ```
   $ yuidoc /path/to/src
   ```

   yuidoc recurses through the directory and generates a raw JSON representation of your documentation in *./out/*, along with finished HTML documentation files and assets. The HTML output has the same look and feel as the API documentation on yuilibrary.com. The look and feel is driven by Handlebars.js templates, and so is completely customizable.

Discussion

YUI Doc is a *documentation generator*, a tool that creates API documentation from specially formatted doc comments. The most famous tool of this type is probably Javadoc, but there are many others, including Doxygen, phpDocumentor, and JsDoc Toolkit.

Most documentation generators parse source code for a particular language or set of languages. YUI Doc is different in that it just parses YUI doc comments, which means you must explicitly declare every entity you are documenting. However, the advantage of this approach is that YUI Doc is language-neutral; you can use it to document an API in nearly any language, not just JavaScript.

Similar to Javadoc, YUI Doc's syntax relies on multiline comment blocks that contain YUI Doc *tags* that start with an @, such as @param or @returns. A YUI Doc comment block:

- Must contain one and only one of these primary tags: @module, @class, @method, @property, @event, or @attribute

- May contain a plain-text description
- May contain one or more secondary tags, such as @param, @type, and @returns

For more information about the available tags and how to use them, refer to the YUI Doc documentation.

YUI Doc represents a JavaScript library as an organized structure of modules and classes. A *module* in YUI Doc is an overarching piece of a larger library, vaguely analogous to a package in Python or Java. JavaScript does not (yet) have native modules, but modules are an important way to organize your library, and in fact YUI Doc requires you to define at least one module in your documentation. This focus on modules is another key differentiator between YUI Doc and other documentation generators. YUI Doc assumes that each module resides in its own top-level directory. Any code in a child directory automatically belongs to that module. It is also possible to break modules into submodules. For example, node is a module, and node-base and node-event-simulate are submodules.

Each module contains one or more *classes*. Although JavaScript is a prototypal language, if you have some object that you use in a classlike way, YUI Doc provides explicit support for this. Within classes, you can also define properties, events, and attributes (object configuration values).

The core feature of all documentation generators is that they ensure the documentation's source exists right next to the source code. This treats API documentation more like source code, which in turn helps keep the documentation accurate. If you add a parameter to a method, you are more likely to remember to update the documentation if that documentation source sits just a line or two above the method signature.

Although documentation generators are the right tool for writing API documentation, crafting effective doc comments is tricky. The problem is that you are serving two audiences: people who read the generated API documentation, and people who read the source code. Take care not to clutter your source with lots of "line noise" comments that make it hard to read your code. Doc comments should be informative but terse.

Perhaps the most common mistake is writing doc comments that simply restate the name of the method—for example, documentation like:

```
getColor(): Gets the color.
```

There is almost always *something* more useful to say than this. Focus on the "how" and the "why" rather than the "what." Is there an important pattern (or antipattern) to look out for? Edge cases to consider? Your doc comments should highlight things that would be hard to figure out simply by knowing the method signature or by reading the source code. If all else fails, keep in mind that poor doc comments are worse than empty doc comments.

On the other extreme, avoid writing very verbose doc comments, sprinkled with lots of special tags and metadata. As with any type of comment, don't let doc comments overrun your source code and become clutter. One nice thing about YUI Doc is that its syntax is relatively small, limited to a useful set of tags that describe components of the API and how they relate to each other. Other documentation generators offer dozens of additional tags that control the formatting or that duplicate metadata that is already in your version control system. These tags seem like nifty features, but lead to worse documentation.

Because YUI Doc does not actually parse JavaScript, it enables you to write doc comments far away from the method, class, or other component being documented. Don't do this. The key feature of documentation generators is making maintenance easier by keeping documentation close to the source. The only reason to break this pattern is for modules, which might not map directly to a particular continuous chunk of source code.

Don't abuse YUI Doc to write tutorials, conceptual guides, or other long form documentation. This kind of material belongs in a user manual or developer guide, not an API reference. Instead of using a documentation generator here, use a general documentation system such as DocBook or Sphinx. The good news is that raw YUI Doc output is just JSON, which you can transform and incorporate into a larger developer guide.

See Also

YUI Doc (*http://yuilibrary.com/projects/yuidoc/*); DocBook XML (*http://docbook.org*); Sphinx (*http://sphinx.pocoo.org*).

Index

We'd like to hear your suggestions for improving our indexes. Send email to *index@oreilly.com*.

About the Author

Evan Goer is a senior technical writer at Yahoo! in Sunnyvale, California, where he works for an engineering team that develops Yahoo!'s internal deployment infrastructure. He also works closely with the YUI core engineering team. Before that, Evan worked for startups and corporate behemoths alike, documenting everything from how to speed up applications on big-iron Sun hardware to how to treat cancer patients with electron beam radiation therapy.

Evan is a Sunnyvale native and holds a bachelor's of science in physics from Harvey Mudd College. He is on an eternal quest for the perfect documentation format and build system.

Colophon

The animal on the cover of *YUI 3 Cookbook* is a spotted cuscus (*Spilocuscus maculatus*), a reclusive, tree-dwelling marsupial. It is one of the largest members of the possum family. When the cuscus was first discovered, it was thought to be a monkey because of the way it moved through the trees and gripped branches with its prehensile tail.

Most spotted cuscuses can be found in New Guinea, but a small population also lives on the northern tip of Cape York in Australia. Their habitat consists of rainforest or dense forested areas of mangrove, eucalyptus, or other hardwood trees. These animals are primarily arboreal and nocturnal. During the day, they rest in tree hollows or nests they make of vegetation on tree branches. At night, they go out to feed—the cuscus's diet is largely made up of fruit, flowers, and leaves, but they are omnivorous and occasionally eat eggs and small birds or reptiles.

Spotted cuscuses are about the size of a large domesticated cat, averaging 3–13 pounds in weight and about 26 inches long (not counting the tail). Their tails are partially hairless to better grip branches, and are 13–24 inches long. Their paws also help in climbing trees: four toes have large claws, while the innermost is opposable—rather like a human thumb. The fur of the cuscus is thick and woolly, and the color varies between regions and gender (grey and white, or brown and white). Despite the name of the animal, only males have spots, though these are more like large splotches.

Cuscuses are very solitary animals, and only come together to mate. However, they do not have a specific breeding season, so can reproduce throughout the year (nor do they mate for life). As with other marsupials, a female cuscus shelters her young within a pouch on her stomach. The gestation period is around 13 days; after birth, the babies (initially weighing no more than 1 gram) spend 6–7 months in the pouch. Though there may be as many as three offspring in a litter, only one usually survives.

The cover image is from Wood's *Animate Creatures*. The cover font is Adobe ITC Garamond. The text font is Linotype Birka; the heading font is Adobe Myriad Condensed; and the code font is LucasFont's TheSansMonoCondensed.

Have it your way.

Get even more for your money.

Join the O'Reilly Community, and register the O'Reilly books you own. It's free, and you'll get:

- $4.99 ebook upgrade offer
- 40% upgrade offer on O'Reilly print books
- Membership discounts on books and events
- Free lifetime updates to ebooks and videos
- Multiple ebook formats, DRM FREE
- Participation in the O'Reilly community
- Newsletters
- Account management
- 100% Satisfaction Guarantee

Signing up is easy:

1. **Go to: oreilly.com/go/register**
2. **Create an O'Reilly login.**
3. **Provide your address.**
4. **Register your books.**

Note: English-language books only

To order books online:
oreilly.com/store

For questions about products or an order:
orders@oreilly.com

To sign up to get topic-specific email announcements and/or news about upcoming books, conferences, special offers, and new technologies:
elists@oreilly.com

For technical questions about book content:
booktech@oreilly.com

To submit new book proposals to our editors:
proposals@oreilly.com

O'Reilly books are available in multiple DRM-free ebook formats. For more information:
oreilly.com/ebooks

O'REILLY®

Spreading the knowledge of innovators   oreilly.com

Lightning Source UK Ltd.
Milton Keynes UK
UKOW06f0609240814

237396UK00002B/11/P